D1253422

Ezra Pound
AND
Dorothy Shakespear

Sketch of Ezra Pound by Gaudier-Brzeska (*ca.* 1913).

Ezra Pound

AND

Dorothy Shakespear,

Their Letters: 1909-1914)

EDITED BY OMAR POUND AND A. WALTON LITZ

A NEW DIRECTIONS BOOK

WILLIAM MADISON RANDALL LIBRARY UNC AT WILMINGTON

Copyright © 1926, 1934, 1935, 1948, 1950, 1956, 1958, 1959, 1962, 1967, 1968 by Ezra
    Pound
Copyright © 1973 by the Estate of Ezra Pound
Copyright © 1976, 1984 by The Trustees of the Ezra Pound Literary Property Trust
Copyright © 1979 by New Directions Publishing Corporation
Copyright © 1984 by Omar S. Pound
Copyright © 1984 by A. Walton Litz and Omar S. Pound
Copyright © 1984 by Michael B. Yeats

All rights reserved. Except for brief passages quoted in a newspaper, magazine, radio,
or television review, no part of this book may be reproduced in any form or by any
means, electronic or mechanical, including photocopying and recording, or by any in-
formation storage or retrieval system, without permission in writing from the Publisher.

Lines from "All Souls' Night" by W.B. Yeats, Copyright 1928 by Macmillan Publishing
Co., Inc., renewed 1956 by Georgie Yeats. Reprinted with permission of Macmillan.

Excerpts from W. B. Yeats' "All Soul's Night" and "Her Race" (Part V of "Upon
a Dying Lady") are reprinted by the permission of Michael B. Yeats and Macmillan,
London, Ltd.

Manufactured in the United States of America
First published clothbound by New Directions in 1984
Published simultaneously in Canada by George J. McLeod, Ltd., Toronto

Library of Congress Cataloging in Publication Data

Pound, Ezra, 1885–1972.
    Ezra Pound and Dorothy Shakespear, their letters, 1910–1914.
    (A New Directions Book)
    Includes index.
    1. Pound, Ezra, 1885–1972—Correspondence.   2. Pound,
Dorothy.   3. Poets, American—19th century—Correspondence.
I. Pound, Dorothy.   II. Pound, Omar S.   III. Litz, A. Walton.
IV. Title.
PS3531.082Z4895   1984   811'.52   84-11545
ISBN 0-8112-0900-8

New Directions Books are published for James Laughlin
by New Directions Publishing Corporation,
80 Eighth Avenue, New York 10011

PS3531
.082
.24895
1984

Contents

282380

In Memoriam
Walter Pilkington
Librarian, Hamilton College
1952–1976

Of great suavity and gentleness of deportment . . .

Canto 89

Preface

The correspondence between Ezra Pound and Dorothy Shakespear extends over more than six decades from 1910 until 1972, the year of the poet's death.[1] All the letters are of unusual literary interest, but those from the years before their marriage in April 1914 have a special importance, since very few letters from this period have been published. The standard edition of *The Letters of Ezra Pound,* edited by D. D. Paige, includes none from 1910–11 and only a handful from 1912–13, yet these were the crucial years in Pound's literary development and in the making of early modernist literature. The letters in this volume provide a detailed record of Pound's search for a new and personal style, and of his role in the avant-garde movements of 1912–14. At the same time they give a general portrait of late Edwardian and early Georgian society, with its characteristic tensions between the old and the new. Written before the events of the First World War had driven Pound toward his political and economic theories, and before anti-Semitism clouded his works, these letters portray a very different Ezra Pound from that of the received tradition—a young expatriate poet who was simultaneously involved in two literary generations, the companion of Yeats and Ford Madox Hueffer as well as of Wyndham Lewis and Gaudier-Brzeska.

The letters tell us in quite specific terms a great deal about Pound's early poetry. Ezra Pound was always an occasional poet, and these letters uncover many of the people, places, events, and books that are the hidden subjects of his early poems. When read in conjunction with this correspondence, for instance, *Canzoni* (1911) becomes very much "Dorothy's book," based on shared reading and the details of their personal relationship. The correspondence also shows that Pound had developed in his

---

[1] For a detailed description of the correspondence see Appendix III.

letters, long before he achieved it in his poetry, the nervous pastiche of public and private references which is characteristic of his major poetry from *Ripostes* (1912) onward. His first letter to Dorothy of 8 January 1910, written while he was still enmeshed in the imitative styles of his early verse, has the energy and crisp, elliptical form that one associates with the poetry of several years later.

The early letters of Ezra Pound and Dorothy Shakespear have all the appeal of any private correspondence between two intelligent people who have not yet entered what Henry James called "the country of the general lost freshness." But there is also a bittersweet quality which comes from our knowledge of what was to follow: the Great War that ended forever the world out of which these letters were written, the war in which so many of the actors in the letters—T. E. Hulme and Gaudier-Brzeska among them—were to die. We also know what the future held for Ezra and Dorothy: the increasing isolation and obsessions of the 1920s and 1930s, the wartime broadcasts, arrest and imprisonment, the years in St. Elizabeths, the final penitential silence. As in classical Greek drama, all this foreknowledge makes the reading of these letters a complex emotional experience.

In reading this correspondence one enters a world where the manners and social forms sometimes seem as remote as those of ancient Rome, but where the pressing interests—feminism, the occult, anti-imperialism— remind one of the recent past. Often in editing these letters we had the feeling that a half-century had dropped away, and that we were dealing with a time just before our own. It was, perhaps, one of the few periods in English social and literary history when an alien figure such as Ezra Pound could have made his way so quickly to the center of things. The revolutionary spirit, both literary and political, was quickening year by year. At the same time, the late-Victorian structure of clubs, societies, literary hostesses, country houses, bookshops, and serious journals was still in place, offering many opportunities to an ambitious young writer from the provinces. The destruction of this world in 1914–18 was clearly the determining force behind many of Ezra Pound's later obsessions and aberrations. In the *Pisan Cantos* he recalls again and again the events and people described in these letters, as if the memory of 1909–14 was the only stable point left in a disintegrating personal universe.

Ezra Loomis Pound was born on 30 October 1885 in the frontier town of Hailey, Idaho, where his father, Homer Loomis Pound, was Register of the U.S. Land Office. Homer Pound was the son of Thaddeus Coleman Pound, a prominent Wisconsin businessman who once served as Lieuten-

ant-Governor of the state; shortly before moving to Hailey in 1883 Homer
had married Isabel Weston of New York City (see the Biographical Ap-
pendix and Family Charts). When Ezra was two years old the family
moved to the East Coast, and in 1889 Homer was appointed Assistant As-
sayer at the U.S. Mint in Philadelphia. The Pounds soon settled in Wyn-
cote, a middle-class suburb of Philadelphia, where Ezra attended local
schools and the Cheltenham Military Academy. In 1901 he entered the
University of Pennsylvania, and a year later met William Carlos Williams,
a fellow-student who was to become his closest "poet friend." In 1903 he
transferred to Hamilton College, near Utica, New York, where he studied
Romance languages and medieval literature, receiving a Ph.B. degree in
1905. At Hamilton he began work on some of the poems that were later
published in his first volume of verse, *A Lume Spento* (1908). In 1905
he returned to the University of Pennsylvania and began work toward a
Masters degree, specializing in Latin, Old French, Provençal, Spanish, and
Italian. It was at this time that he met Hilda Doolittle, whose father was
Professor of Astronomy and director of the Flower Observatory. Later
Ezra collected some of his poems of 1905–07 into *Hilda's Book,* a hand-
bound, vellum-covered volume that he presented to her (see Appendix II).

After receiving an M.A. in Romance languages in 1906 Ezra spent the
summer in Europe on a university fellowship, pursuing his research on
the Spanish playwright Lope de Vega. (He had visited Europe twice be-
fore, in 1898 with his "Aunt Frank," Frances Weston, and in 1902 with
his father.) Returning to the University of Pennsylvania for further gradu-
ate work toward a doctorate, he found himself more and more at odds
with the narrow tastes and philological interests of his teachers. In the
summer of 1907 he decided to abandon graduate work, and began look-
ing for a teaching position; it was at this time that he met Mary Moore of
Trenton (see Biographical Appendix), to whom he later dedicated *Per-
sonae* (1909). In the autumn of 1907 he took up the post of lecturer in
Romance languages at Wabash College, a Presbyterian institution in Craw-
fordsville, Indiana, where he soon began to think of himself as an "exile."
The opening lines of his poem "In Durance," written at this time, sum up
his feelings:

> I am homesick after mine own kind,
> Oh I know that there are folk about me,
>   friendly faces,
> But I am homesick after mine own kind.

After four months Ezra's "Latin Quarter" behavior (which included be-
friending a stranded actress) led to his dismissal, and in February 1908 he

sailed for Europe, landing at Gibraltar and traveling to Venice, where *A Lume Spento* was published in July. By the end of September he had settled in London, where a second volume, *A Quinzaine for This Yule* ("Being selected from a Venetian sketch-book"), was published in December. In the same month there appeared an announcement that a "Short Introductory Course on the Development of the Literature of Southern Europe" by Ezra Pound, M.A., would be given at the Polytechnic in Regent Street in January-February 1909. At last Ezra felt that he had found a congenial place to live and write. "Am by way of falling into the crowd that does things here," he wrote to his friend William Carlos Williams on 3 February 1909. "London, deah old Lundon, is the place for poesy."

In contrast to Ezra Pound, Dorothy Shakespear grew up in a literary household frequented by the talented and the great. She was born in London on 14 September 1886. Her father, Henry Hope Shakespear, was a typical nineteenth-century family solicitor; her mother, Olivia, who was an intimate friend of William Butler Yeats, later became a minor Edwardian novelist (see the Biographical Appendix). Lionel Johnson, the nineties poet and member of the Rhymers' Club, was Olivia's first and favorite cousin. He wrote a poem to celebrate Dorothy's third birthday, and at the age of five she painted a small watercolor for him.

In the seventeenth century the Shakespear family were rope-makers in the east end of London; it is possible, but not probable, that they were related to William Shakespeare. In the late eighteenth century, with the expansion of trade and shipping, many of the Shakespears went to India, where they became a modest but well-known Indian army family, with close ties through two marriages to the Thackeray family (see the Family Charts in the Biographical Appendix). Dorothy was reared among relatives born in India who enchanted her with tales of the Indian Mutiny, massacres, merciful rescues, and stoic heroism.

Dorothy attended St. James's School at Southbourne in Hampshire, then moved with it to Crowborough in Sussex, and completed her schooling in West Malvern, Worcestershire, where St. James's is still located. She apparently had two especially good teachers—one in Latin and the other in painting. While at school she wrote two short plays and contributed to the school magazine.

As part of her education she spent a year in Geneva, where she became fluent in French, although with a slight Swiss accent. On her return the editors of the school newspaper asked her to write about her stay there. Dorothy's reply reveals her painterly gift for precise observation, and a characteristic distaste for sentimentality and the pathetic fallacy.

Switzerland!——If you had seen as much of it as I have just lately . . .
you would not have very poetical ideas on the subject. Snow, mountains,
brown rushing mountain torrents, the marvellous blue-green waters of the
Rhone, wooden chalets, blue lakes as clear as crystal, wonderful, weird,
winding mountain paths and passes——all these I have seen, and if they
seem to you fit subjects for a poem, take them and use them to the best of
your ability, and I'm sure you are very welcome!

I am quite safely home again, in London fogs and slush, with my books,
and I am quite contented! I looked vaguely at some pressed flowers from
the Gemi pass, and various long trudges we had been, but no sentimental
idea seems to come with them: There they are, dated and named, blue
gentians, forget-me-nots, lilies-of-the-valley that we found wild in a wood
near Ferney, where the great Voltaire lived; Soldanellas, little mauve things
coming up through the great patches of snow some six thousand feet up;
large white anemones . . . some little wild rhododendrons, a beautiful pale
pink colour; and a little piece of heath, that was growing between two
huge boulders just off the path, I secured. There isn't even any Edelweiss
to gloat over!

No, I am afraid these dried flowers won't inspire me; nothing will in-
spire me. . . . (*St. James's Gazette,* December 1902)

Apart from a trip to Holland to view a Rembrandt exhibition, Dorothy re-
mained with her family in London after leaving school, tied closely to
home in the Victorian manner, painting watercolors, doing needlework,
reading, and attending concerts and lectures with her mother. It was into
this quiet and somewhat restricted world that Ezra Pound abrupted in
early 1909.

We do not know the precise day when Ezra first met Dorothy. He was
introduced to Olivia Shakespear in January 1909, probably by the Aus-
tralian poet Frederic Manning, and on 31 January he wrote to his mother:
"Tea with Manning and a certain Mrs. Shakespeare [sic] who is undoubt-
edly the most charming woman in London." Three weeks later he reported
to his father that after luncheon at the Shakespears he had read from his
unpublished sequence of prose and poetry, *The Dawn* (see Appendix II).
But shortly before this reading there was the visit to the Shakespears re-
corded in the first entry that we print from Dorothy's notebook, when—as
Ezra proudly told Mary Moore of Trenton—he sat "on the same hearth
rug" where Yeats had sat, and talked of life and poetry.

A Note on the Text

Work on this edition has been guided by our belief that the editing of personal letters is an art which must take into account the character and style of each correspondent. We have aimed throughout at a readable and accurate text that retains the general appearance of the originals. Almost all the letters were written by hand; the few that were typed are clearly identified. In transcribing the letters we have avoided conjectural emendations and have placed a [?] after a few words we found doubtful or ambiguous.

We have printed all letters from this period, with two exceptions. (1) A few brief notes or post cards of a purely social nature have been omitted. (2) In those few instances when the letters become choked with trivial domestic details, we have treated groups of letters as a journal and have selected only those passages that are of special literary interest. This occurs when Dorothy is writing almost daily out of the boredom of a country-house visit, or when (in March 1914) Dorothy and Ezra are exchanging letters about wedding arrangements and the problems of setting up housekeeping. Omissions are indicated by [- - -].

The following guidelines governed our editorial decisions.

Abbreviations.

In citing Ezra Pound's poems, we have identified those retained in *Personae: The Collected Poems of Ezra Pound* (1926 and after) by (P); those not found in *Personae* but reprinted in *Collected Early Poems of Ezra Pound,* ed. Michael J. King (New Directions, 1976), are identified by (CEP).

Headings.

We have regularized the headings to all the letters. Editorial information in square brackets is from postmarks (many of the envelopes were saved) or from internal evidence.

Paragraphing.

Both EP and DS paragraph informally, using different degrees of indentation, or indicating breaks by spaces and symbols. We have tried to make the paragraphs conform to the internal logic of the letters.

Punctuation.

EP's letters are lightly punctuated: in many cases a dot or a pen-rest indicates either a comma, or a dash, or a full stop. Although DS uses more forceful punctuation, she is not always consistent. We have tried to preserve the original punctuation, but wherever exact reproduction would lead to ambiguity we have repunctuated slightly. Both writers frequently omit apostrophes in contractions and possessives. We have retained these irregularities to give the flavor of the original documents.

Spelling.

Spelling mistakes have been silently corrected, except where the original spelling seems intentional or is characteristic of the writer.

Authorial Revisions.

Most of the letters are written in a rapid, flowing manner, containing only routine small corrections of spelling and phrasing. These are not recorded. However, in those instances where the alterations are revealing (as in certain passages from DS's notebook, or in the drafts of Mr. Shakespear's letters to EP), we have recorded the canceled material in pointed brackets.

Foreign Languages.

Mistakes in spelling, accent, punctuation, and quotation have been allowed to stand; the correct version is supplied in square brackets or in an endnote. Translations are provided for all languages other than French. When a common word or phrase is used frequently in the letters, the correct version and translation are not repeated each time.

Annotations.

Persons, works, and places are frequently identified within the text in square brackets. Our usual practice has been to supply the full name when a person is first mentioned in a letter. More extensive annotations are at the end of each letter, keyed to a word or phrase in the text. Well-known people, works, and events are lightly annotated; more obscure references are fully annotated. Our aim has been to reconstruct the social and literary background of each letter. When the letters refer to previously unpublished or uncollected materials, especially writings by EP or reviews of his works, we have reprinted these in full in the endnotes.

Biographical Appendix.

This appendix contains biographical notices of people mentioned frequently in the letters. If a figure is not identified in an endnote, the reader should consult this appendix. Following our policy in the annotations, well-known figures are treated briefly. More space is given to significant but less well-known people (such as Olivia Shakespear and Frederic Manning) who figure prominently in the letters. The Biographical Appendix includes the following:

Aldington, Richard
CHARS
Cournos, John
Doolittle, Hilda
Fairfax, James Griffyth
Farr, Florence
Fletcher, John Gould
Fowler, Eva
Galton, Arthur
Gaudier-Brzeska, Henri
Hewlett, Maurice
Hueffer, Ford Madox
Hulme, T. E.
Hunt, Violet
Hyde-Lees, Edith Ellen
   (Mrs. Henry Tudor Tucker)
Hyde-Lees, Georgie
Leaf, Herbert
Lewis, Wyndham

Low, Lady Anne Penelope
Manning, Frederic
Mathews, Elkin
Maude, Nancy
Mead, G. R. S.
Monro, Harold
Monroe, Harriet
Moore, Mary
Pound, Homer Loomis
Pound, Isabel Weston
Rummel, Walter Morse
Sauter, Georg
Shakespear, Henry Hope
Shakespear, Olivia
Strutt, Hilda
Tagore, Rabindranath
Tucker, Henry Tudor
Williams, William Carlos
Yeats, William Butler

Family Charts.

The charts in Appendix I are simplified and include only the basic information needed to identify relationships adequately.

1909

1   From Dorothy's Notebook

16 February 1909

"Ezra".

Listen to it–Ezra! Ezra!–And a third time–Ezra! He has a wonderful, beautiful face, a high forehead, ⟨with a⟩ prominent over the eyes; a long, delicate nose, with little, red, nostrils; a strange mouth, never still, & quite elusive; a square chin, slightly cleft in the middle–the whole face pale; the eyes gray-blue; the hair golden-brown, and curling in soft wavy crinkles. Large hands, with long, well-shaped, fingers, and beautiful nails.

Some people have complained of untidy boots–⟨who⟩ how could they look at his boots, when there is his ⟨mobile⟩ moving, beautiful face to watch? Oh! fools, fools! They are the fools one cannot "suffer gladly". I do not think he knows he is beautiful.

At first he was shy–he spoke quickly, (with a strong, odd, accent, half American, half Irish) he sat back in his chair; but afterwards, he suddenly dropped down, cross-legged, with his back to the fire: then he began to talk– He talked of Yeats, as one of the Twenty of the world who have added to the World's poetical matter– He read a short piece of Yeats, in a voice dropping with emotion, in a voice like Yeats's own–He spoke of his interest in all the Arts, in that he might find things of use in them for his own–which is the Highest of them all.

"Have you ever seen things in a crystal?" I asked–And he looked at me, smiling, & answered "I see things without a crystal". He ⟨talked of⟩ suggested the Great Inspiration he was waiting for. That he wished above all things to be in readiness, open-minded and waiting, on the Great Day when it should come. For he evidently believes it will come to him. "You should never get up from a book tired"–he said.

He said Fred Manning had no sense of his relations to people–No idea that so-&-so was not the person to choose to talk to about such-&-such a thing. He said he would much prefer to take us to Spain than go back to his home.

Oh! Ezra! how beautiful you are! With your pale face and fair hair! I wonder–are you a genius? or are you only an artist in Life?

How *can* people look at his boots, instead of his face–It is they who are impossible, not he–not the beautiful Ezra. He said of one college, that it was only another tract of the barren waste he had lived in before. I think he has passed most of his life in tracts of barren waste—and suffered that which is untellable.

He is coming here again–I want to see him again–I want to remember his face–to know the mouth, and the brows better–The forehead & nose & chin, I know a little already; but oh! that elusive mouth!

And all the while clasping his ankles on the hearthrug, and smoking.

Fred Manning]   Frederic Manning, Australian-born poet and novelist. See Biographical Appendix.

one college]   Wabash College, Crawfordsville, Indiana. EP began teaching Romance languages at this Presbyterian college in September 1907, but was dismissed after one term for "Latin Quarter" behavior. There are various accounts of the events leading up to his dismissal: see Noel Stock, *The Life of Ezra Pound* (New York, 1970), pp. 36–43.

on the hearthrug]   In February 1909 EP wrote proudly to Mary Moore of Trenton (see Biographical Appendix) that he had been "sitting on the same hearth rug" where Yeats had sat.

2   From Dorothy's Notebook

[*16–26 February 1909*]

"Genius was priceless, inspired, divine; but it was also at its hours capricious, sinister, cruel;"

(genius) "is dealt out in different doses, in big cups and little," "we drink them down in the dark, and we can't tell their size until we tip them up and hear the last gurgle."

"And then I believe in the essential salubrity of genius–true genius."

from "Roderick Hudson".
Henry James.

Henry James]   *Roderick Hudson* (1875, revised 1879), a novel about an American artist whose "genius" is tested by the experience of Europe. DS is quoting from the Macmillan edition (London, 1883), Chaps. XI, pp. 165, 172; and III, p. 38.

3   From Dorothy's Notebook

26 February 1909

He (Ezra) has passed by the way where most men have only dreamed of passing. He has done with a Soul, that might be saved or damned–He has learned to live beside his body. I see him as a double person–just held together by the flesh.

His spirit walks beside him, outside him, on the left-hand side – He has conquered the needs of the flesh– He can starve; nay, is willing, to starve that his spirit may bring forth the 'highest of arts'–poetry. He has no care for hunger & thirst, for cold; of an ordinary man's evils he takes no notice– "It is worth starving for" he said one day. He has attained to peace in this world, it seems to me. To be working for the great art, to be living in, and for, Truth in her Greatness– He has found the Centre–TRUTH.

4   From Dorothy's Notebook

23 March 1909

Ezra took O.S. [Olivia Shakespear] & myself to tea after a concert, because it was the anniversary of his landing in Europe!

About three weeks ago I was living in the spirit – for some three days I went about in a dream, thinking, thinking, never ceasing to try & puzzle out the Truth – the Truth that Ezra has found. And I did not wish to find it *because Ezra* had found it–but because I knew that the Truth that I am searching for is the same that he has found. And for those days I lived with a veil, a thin, thin cobweb, between me and reality.

Then for a fortnight I was [*section missing*]

O.S.]   Olivia Shakespear, Dorothy's mother (see Biographical Appendix). In letters to his mother (31 January 1909) and to Mary Moore of Trenton (23 March 1909), EP called Mrs. Shakespear "the most charming woman in London."

5   From Dorothy's Notebook

2 June 1909

It is not friendship & love that I am wanting–it is that something beyond the horizon–friendship & love may help in the finding, but That Something is Life Eternal–my soul.

6   From Dorothy's Notebook

10 July 1909

"My soul"! It has not seemed to exist these last days–There is only an empty space when I try to feel for it–Nothing moves it, nothing even finds it.

Yes–One thing touched it, for an instant, and made it give a little cry– Ezra called me by a name that made me smile for joy–"You are Triste, Little Brother?" he asked three days ago. And again yesterday he said "Little Brother"–and it touches & shows me that I have something after all, hidden though it be, where my soul was–once.

But I have truly tasted of the Far Horizon once ⟨or twice⟩ and I cannot do without it now.

7   From Dorothy's Notebook

12 July 1909

Once it was the moon that watched ⟨and⟩ with the stars, and the heart that gave itself——

⟨Once⟩ Then the heart was lost & it was the moon with the stars, and the circle of eternity–

But now it is the circle of Eternity, ⟨the many coloured opal of knowledge, and the spreading wings of⟩

the wings of knowledge and the many-coloured opal of wisdom.

8   From Dorothy's Notebook

[12–24] July 1909

I have spoken a prayer to the Gods.
and I have asked
  That he may find love ⟨beautiful,⟩
  That he may find life ⟨beautiful,⟩
  That he may find his own soul–
  That the Gods ⟨keep him beautiful⟩
  have mercy upon him and pity,
  That they ⟨keep⟩ grant him to be beautiful
  in body and soul ⟨for ever⟩ alway
  until he return into The
  Ineffable Beauty whence he cometh.

9   From Dorothy's Notebook

24 July 1909

Each white poppy is a dream, and there are many whiles in which to dream. The white petals touch one another, clustering together; for when the circle is completed, each dream lives, and then has the soul found Life. But ⟨among⟩ the poppies are much Troubled, for certain blue forgetmenots still linger in their midst–⟨as opposing⟩ their whiteness; ⟨of the⟩ Even thus (as) ⟨the wreath⟩ the soul is ever troubled by the body.

10   From Dorothy's Notebook

8 October 1909

The poppies have grown shabby, they are no longer white: ⟨I have⟩ therefore have I thrown them away–saving the buds only and the yellow stamens of one which has fallen to pieces.

11   From Dorothy's Notebook

17 October 1909

Planh.

It is of The White Thoughts that he saw in
the Forest.

White Poppy, heavy with dreams,
  O White Poppy, who art wiser than love,
Though I am hungry for their lips
    When I see them a-hiding
And a-passing out and in through the shadows
—There in the pine wood it is,
And they are white, White Poppy,
They are white like the clouds in the forest of the sky
Ere the stars arise to their hunting.

O White Poppy, who art wiser than love,
I am come for peace, yea from the hunting
Am I come to thee for peace.
Out of a new sorrow it is,
That my hunting hath brought me.
White Poppy, heavy with dreams,
Though I am hungry for their lips
    When I see them a-hiding
And a-passing out and in through the shadows
—And it is white they are–
But if one should look at me with the
        old hunger in her eyes,
How will I be answering her eyes?
For I have followed the white folk of the forest.

Aye! It's a long hunting
And it's a deep hunger I have when I see them a-gliding
And a-flickering there, where the trees stand apart.

But oh, it is sorrow and sorrow
When love dies-down in the heart.

by Ezra Pound.
written for me between July 22nd and July 25th 1909.

Planh]   "Planh" (CEP), first published in *Exultations* (25 October 1909), and reprinted in *Provença* (1910) and *Umbra* (1920). On a fragment of a letter to DS, probably from July 1911, EP wrote: "that 'White Poppy' thing was made for you *definitely*." See Letter **38n**.

12   From Dorothy's Notebook

31 October 1909

I might perchance find the other. I desire that a man should kiss me–I desire that a man should hold me with both hands, and read in my eyes such Things as cannot be spoken: That a man should make me shiver and be silent–

That I may understand the chivalry and trust and joy of a great love.

Nevertheless I know that there be some souls who ⟨never⟩ do not learn these matters by experience–but ⟨who⟩ already know them by instinct– and that to such persons ⟨the⟩ to touch ⟨of hand⟩ hand with hand dims the vision, rather than reveals.

Also Revelation comes to a man when he is alone; and ⟨no man is alive⟩ until he has searched beyond others he will never be alone.

13   From Dorothy's Notebook

4 & 5 November 1909

"He (Ezra) is not as other men are – He has seen the Beatific Vision Which is an extenuating circumstance."

in a letter from FM [Frederic Manning] to OS [Olivia Shakespear].

14   From Dorothy's Notebook

4 & 5 November 1909

[*Final Text*]

Oh! Ezra! you leave me so far behind! You have passed through the wood–and the fear you felt in the darkness is even now vibrating in between the pine stems.

It is the only trace of your passing for yr. thoughts are so white, that the cobwebs cling across the path, as though none had gone through them. Yet I know that you went by once, long ago–

Sometimes in the loneliness I cry your name, hoping to dispel the fears which crowd behind me. Well I know that you do not hear my voice, that you cannot come back to speak with me–Yet I greatly desire some sign, when my faith fails me.

You have seen Visions that I shall never see–but when I shall have found my way through the wood, I shall be on the great plain where you are–and I shall hear the river that flows over the plain; whereat I shall kneel & drink of the water–may be the drops I drink come from beyond the horizon, will have touched your very hands as you trailed yr. fingers in the stream.

Meanwhile the cobwebs wreathe themselves into my hair, and catch against my fingers; also, because of my dismay, am I near to wishing you were still in sight.

[*Original Text with Revisions*]

Oh! Ezra! you leave me so far behind! ⟨Through the wood⟩ You have passed through the wood–and ⟨something of⟩ the fear you felt in the darkness is ⟨still⟩ even now vibrating ⟨on the left hand & on the right⟩ in between the pine stems. ⟨Each stem seems the same like another, each step seems over the same familiar,⟩
⟨Though each stem that I pass by mark one step forward–yet they all seem alike–all thin and tall, and wi⟩

⟨that⟩ It is the only trace of your ⟨having passed⟩ passing ⟨And yet I⟩ for yr. thoughts are so white, ⟨for⟩ that the cobwebs ⟨are are⟩ cling across the path ⟨as shining with the night's dew,⟩ as though ⟨no one⟩ none had gone ⟨by⟩ through them. ⟨ever⟩ Yet I know that you went by once, long ago–
⟨so long ago that you It was before⟩

Sometimes in the ⟨darkness⟩ loneliness I cry your name, hoping to dispel the fears which ⟨surround⟩ crowd ⟨about⟩ behind me. ⟨But⟩ Well I know ⟨understand⟩ that you do not hear my voice, that you cannot come back to ⟨help⟩ speak with me–⟨that That I must tread the path under the pines alone⟩–Yet I greatly desire some sign, ⟨because for⟩ when my faith fails me.

You have seen Visions that I ⟨can am not able to⟩ shall never ⟨be able⟩ see–but ⟨if⟩ when I ⟨can⟩ shall have found my way through the wood, ⟨I know that beyond⟩ I shall ⟨come⟩ be on the great plain where you ⟨still⟩ are – ⟨and one some happ day when the⟩ and ⟨when⟩ I shall ⟨have found⟩ hear the ⟨stream⟩ river that ⟨runs⟩ flows ⟨across⟩ over the plain; whereat I shall kneel & drink of the water — ⟨Knowing the perhaps⟩ may be the ⟨very⟩ drops I drink, come from beyond the horizon will have touched your very hands as you ⟨cooled your arms them at the source, resting within sight of⟩ trailed yr. fingers ⟨to cool them⟩ in the stream.

Meanwhile ⟨the wood I am struggling along the path,⟩ the cobwebs wreathe themselves into my hair, and ⟨half blind me twine⟩ catch against my fingers;
also, because of my dismay, am I near to wishing* ⟨that you had left some word not passed by is very long ago.⟩

Nov: 4. 09.

⟨that you had left some sign⟩
*you were still in sight.

Nov: 5. 09.

1910

1910

15   Ezra to Dorothy

[*Kensington*]

[*8 January 1910*]

Hail Grand daughter of Agamemnon! O breaker of hearts that deignst to dabble in mine ink, I fear that my hieroglyphics meant that Cavl: 29 & 30 are to be copied ⟨entier⟩ entire.

Much as it pains me to make this revelation I know that your ennui at receiving it will be greater than mine at making it. How beautiful is sympathy! (?)

I have written ten more lines of my canzone & Mrs Fowler is in an azure rage on the subject of azure ear-rings. How eventful is the life of the ⟨simple-minded⟩ guileless!

May the gods & uncle Hilary protect thee.

daughter of Agamemnon]   In the most common mythological tradition, Iphigenia is Agamemnon's daughter. EP may be recalling the opening address of the Chorus to Iphigenia in Euripides' *Iphigenia among the Taurians;* he was a member of the Chorus when the play was presented in Greek at the University of Pennsylvania in April 1903.

Cavl:]   Guido Cavalcanti (ca. 1255–1300), Dante's Florentine contemporary and a master of the *dolce stil nuovo* ("sweet new style"). Cavalcanti's technique fascinated EP, who made many translations, eventually publishing a critical edition with translations in 1932, and three additional canzoni in facsimile in 1949. *Sonnets and Ballate of Guido Cavalcanti* was first published in 1912, but the Introduction is dated 15 Nov. 1910. EP is asking DS to transcribe sonnets 29 and 30 from *Rime di Guido Cavalcanti, edite ed inedite* (Firenze, 1813).

my canzone]   EP published three canzoni in the *English Review,* 4 (January 1910): "Canzon: The Yearly Slain" (CEP), "Canzon: The Spear" (CEP), and "Canzon: To Be Sung beneath a Window" (CEP). EP may be referring to the "Canzon: Of Incense" (CEP), published in the *English Review,* 5 (April 1910).

Mrs Fowler]   Eva Fowler (Mrs. Alfred Fowler), a family friend. See Biographical Appendix.

azure ear-rings]   Probably a reference to the "single turquoise ear-ring" that EP wore at this time. "Ezra, with his mane of fair hair, his blonde beard, his rimless pince-nez, his Philadelphian accent and his startling costume, part of which was a single turquoise ear-ring, contrived to look 'every inch a poet'

. . ." [Douglas Goldring, *South Lodge: Reminiscences of Violet Hunt, Ford Madox Ford and the English Review* (London, 1943), p. 40].

uncle Hilary]   A small statue of the Buddha in the Shakespear home. It figures in Olivia Shakespear's novel *Uncle Hilary* (1910), a story about British life in 19th-century India. Early in 1909 EP wrote Mary Moore of Trenton that Mrs. Shakespear had invited him to meet W. B. Yeats: "it will be in a room all full of white magic where Uncle Hillary lives. Uncle Hillary . . . is also Mrs Shakespears next book."

16   From Dorothy's Notebook

[no date]

I have felt a great Peace upon my soul. Between you, my beloved, & me there must never be anything but Peace. There must be no sorrow, no anguish, no horror—nothing but gentleness—One can live as I have ⟨for⟩ these last days, floating above the world, untouched ⟨by any⟩—breathing only ⟨gentleness⟩ Peace; ⟨and⟩ giving ⟨you⟩ an ⟨gentle⟩ exquisite delicate love, instead of the hot-coloured passion which ⟨dies leaving⟩ dying leaves a blackness of Hell.

17   From Dorothy's Notebook

19 March 1910

Ezra! Ezra! beautiful face! I love beautiful things—and I know it more than ever, because when you made yourself nearly ugly by shaving off your joyous hair, I was miserable—I was angry also for I thought you understood the charm of your appearance altogether—Now that you know you have been a fool, I am sure of it again—but the time between was ⟨passed in⟩ touched with despair.

You are ⟨odd⟩ strange—elusive—of other habits of thought than I ⟨shall ever be able to⟩ can understand. You are all a dream—⟨all⟩ your ideas, ⟨all⟩ your knowledge, ⟨and⟩ your bluey eyes; all your great loneliness—

they do not belong to us, here–(And yet perhaps they belong to 'London' in some way.)

When you are gone away, I shall hardly ⟨like⟩ dare to speak of you, lest someone should say–You are dreaming–Who is he? I think I would enter the dream and touch the world no more, if it were possible–For such a dream is nearer to Truth than any existence can be. ⟨And⟩ One must live either calling the dream ⟨a dream⟩ nonsense, or shutting out all that ⟨makes⟩ renders it a dream. For it ⟨takes has⟩ exists in wonderful colours, wonderful forms, things that are no sooner said than ⟨forgotten⟩ they are enveloped in the cloud–All things you handle have a veil drawn round them, that draws them towards yourself, brings them to your dream land, your wonderful land of discovered Truth.

But whether to the world you are a dream or a Reality, to me you are ⟨what⟩ that which I desire–for you have given me understanding–perhaps your veil has floated past my hair–a little understanding–enough to make me crave more, and more, until I shall have attained your ⟨enough⟩ dream land; until I shall ⟨comprehend kno find⟩ live wrapt in the dream, touching the world no more.

18   From Dorothy's Notebook

22 March 1910

Ezra has gone—to Italy.
            7 P.M. March 22nd 1910

19   From Dorothy's Notebook

19 April 1910

. . . chiefly tenderness, which maketh every other excellence glow with its light——and tenderness is not what the common herd suppose it to be, namely, grieving at another's woe, which is rather a special effect of it, which is called pity, and is an emotion. But tenderness is not an emotion,

but rather a noble disposition of mind, ready to receive love, pity, and other charitous emotions.
(Pietà)

Dante's Convivio.
2nd Treatize.

Moreover, music so draweth to itself the spirits of men (which are in principle as though vapours of the heart) that they well-nigh cease from all operation; so united is the Soul when it hears it, and so does the virtue of all of them, as it were, run to the spirit of sense which receiveth the sound.

2nd Treatise, Convivio.

Convivio] The Convivio of Dante Alighieri, trans. Philip H. Wicksteed, Temple Classics (London, 1903). Second Treatise, Chaps. XI, p. 106, and XIV, p. 119.

20   Ezra to Olivia Shakespear

Hotel Eden
Sirmione am Gardasee
[Italy]
[15 April 1910]

Salve:

The last of the proofs is came, & I am 'old and grey & full of sleep'!

What I really want is to have someone–if angels dwell still upon this whirling sphere–is to have someone find out how "H. A. Rennart" spells his name. It means British Museum–if her highness went to look at japanese prints or mummies & got an emergency ticket–one could look at the catalogue for

H.A. Ren/ nart
/ art
/ ert
/ nert
Life of Lope de Vega.

Don't look under Lope 'cause there's miles of pages of him & you'd never find it.

I want badly a copy of 1. stanza of Arnaut Daniel's

"Sim fos Amors de joi donar tant larga".

to be found in, under, Daniel, Arnaut, ed. U. A. Canello, or perhaps more easily under Canello, U. A. 'Arnaut Daniel'. If one should by any miracle have strength to copy more than the eight lines of that stanza I'd welcome single stanzas of any canzone except the 1st, 2nd, 3rd, 10th, 11th, 12th, 16th, 18th, the I think 13th (*Sols sui qui sai lo sobrafan quem sortz*) and the one beginning "*L'aura amara*". These I have, or know they are un suit-able.

This leaves *eight*–begin at the 17th & take single stanzas working backward thru the book, that is after you've got the

"*Sim fos Amors de joi donar tant larga*".

I think thats the one we want–& I think the 4th & 5th probably wont do–but I'm not sure. Of course if one is merely human Dorothy's writing is more valuable than yours to any one desiring an accurate idea of the text.

I have been damnably explicit & I write with no confidence that the Griselda type has survived the Ibsen revolt and the last election. If however enough of the angelic matter dwells yet in the ways of London–If the divine signets of grace mercy & patience still wear white serge? We who have timely lifted up our necks for transcriptions of canzoni will not cease to offer thanks giving.

If anybody does arrive in that awful reading room & is in a hurry choose the canzoni with the longest lines. I don't know that thats any use either as Canello often prints a line in sections without regard to cadence.

The whole job means about 56 lines of transcribing–I only want one stanza of each canzone. (One might note the number of stanzas Daniel uses, & which rimes he repeats in the envoi). Of the things I have here nothing suits except the Incense form (& I'd rather not repeat) or a form of Ventadorns, which dont quite suit. I know I ought to have done it before I left London & I'm very sorry to howl over so many miles of interpolated land & water.

The specimen page of S. - R. [*The Spirit of Romance*] looks hopeful.

One more thing–dont bother with any canzon that doesn't carry the same rimes all through–from one verse to the next.

I know CHARS will object to this letter but they must consider.
"lo jorn qu'esperan donan".
I hope nobody will bother about this matter if it happens to be more than
usually inconvenient.

Yrs.

in Penitence

E.

proofs]   Of *The Spirit of Romance,* published 20 June 1910. *The Spirit of Romance* evolved from two courses of lectures that EP gave at the London Polytechnic in January–February 1909 and October–March 1909–10.

full of sleep]   From W.B. Yeats's poem "When you are old and grey and full of sleep," first published in 1892.

Rennart]   Hugo A. Rennert (1858–1927), author of *The Life of Lope de Vega* (1904), was one of EP's teachers at the University of Pennsylvania.

Arnaut Daniel . . . Canello]   *La Vita e le opere del trovatore Arnaldo Daniello,* ed. U.A. Canello (Halle, 1883). In *Purgatorio* XXVI the Provençal poet Arnaut Daniel (ca. 1180–1220) is referred to as *miglior fabbro del parlar materno,* "a better craftsman of the mother tongue"; hence the title "Il Miglior Fabbro" of the chapter on Arnaut Daniel in *The Spirit of Romance,* and T.S. Eliot's dedication of *The Waste Land* to "Ezra Pound, *il miglior fabbro.*" In Canello's edition "Sim fos Amors de joi donar tant larga" is canzone XVII, "Sols sui qui sai lo sobrafan quem sortz" is XV, and "L'Aura amara" IX. On this letter either DS or Olivia Shakespear wrote the correct numbers in pencil. EP's first translations of these canzoni were included in Chapter II, "Il Miglior Fabbro," of *The Spirit of Romance* (June 1910).

Griselda . . . Ibsen . . . the last election]   British women seeking the vote and social equality were increasingly active politically just prior to the general election of January 1910. The type for the New Woman of 1910 would be Nora Helmer, the heroine of Ibsen's *A Doll's House* who sacrifices conventional security for personal freedom, not the Lady of the Troubadours or the patient Griselda (the traditional figure of meekness and acceptance).

Incense form]   The verse form of EP's "Canzon: Of Incense" (CEP).

Ventadorns]   Bernart de Ventadorn (or Ventadour), Provençal troubadour (ca. 1150–1195). EP discusses Ventadorn in Chapter III, "Proença," of *The Spirit of Romance.*

CHARS]   See Biographical Appendix.

lo jorn . . . donan]   *lo jorn, qu' esper, denan,* "the day which I await before me". From Arnaut Daniel's address to Dante in his native Provençal (*Purgatorio,* XXVI, 144; Temple Classics edition).

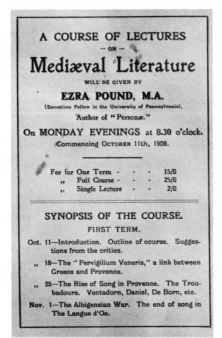

A COURSE OF LECTURES
— ON —
Mediæval Literature
WILL BE GIVEN BY
EZRA POUND, M.A.
(Sometime Fellow in the University of Pennsylvania),
Author of "Personæ."

On MONDAY EVENINGS at 8.30 o'clock.
Commencing OCTOBER 11th, 1909.

Fee for One Term	-	-	-	15/0
„ Full Course	-	-	-	25/0
„ Single Lecture	-	-	-	2/0

SYNOPSIS OF THE COURSE.
FIRST TERM.

Oct. 11—Introduction. Outline of course. Suggestions from the critics.
„ 18—The "Pervigilium Veneris," a link between Greece and Provence.
„ 25—The Rise of Song in Provence. The Troubadours. Ventadorn, Daniel, De Born, etc.
Nov. 1—The Albigensian War. The end of song in The Langue d'Oc.

Nov. 8—The Epic in France and Spain. The "Chanson de Roland." The "Poema del Cid."
„ 15—Narrative poetry in The Langue d'Oil, Crestien de Troyes "Romances." Marie de France "Lais from The Breton."
„ 22—Tristram and Ysolt. The Picard Text of "Aucassin and Nicollette."
„ 29—Tuscan literature derivative from Provence: Guido Guinicelli, Cavalcanti. Prose poetry concerning St. Francis of Assisi.
Dec. 6—Life of Dante.
„ 13—Dante "La Vita Nuova."

SECOND TERM.
Jan. 17—Dante "Inferno."
„ 24—Dante "Il Purgatorio."
„ 31—Dante "Il Paradiso."
Feb. 7—Francois Villon. Poet and Housebreaker. The End of Mediævalism.
„ 14—The Rise of the Romantic Drama from Church Services and Mystery Plays.
„ 21—The Drama in Spain. Lope de Vega.
„ 28—His Contemporaries. Cervantes "Don Quixote."
Mar. 7—The Rise of Portugal.
„ 14—Latin Poetry in Renaissance Italy.
„ 21—Metastasio and Leopardi.
„ 28—Summary. Avenues of the Tradition. The Preservation of the Texts.

21   Ezra to Dorothy

Hotel Eden
Sirmione am Gardasee
[22 April 1910]

Angelical Coz de los CHARS.
Os beso los manos.

Of course you were out of place in the reading room, but the room is *capable de tout*–most of the bloody sestina was written there. I wonder if you used the ensanguined desk.

Of course we were reared to believe that things should be used for that for which they were intended, but why apply it to people. Personally we think you fulfill your destiny most admirably and that to inveigle you into base utilities is a profanation. However the ultimate aim is poesia & therefore in accord with the graciousness of the serene CHARS coz.

Just as the barque with
blue and yellow sails

> Casts far ⟨that⟩ the splendour
>   on the waters round her,
> So hath she cast her
>   colours on my heart
> Till all its vanes grow
>   bright and gleam before her.

Not in the form yet but more or less the 'motif' I'm after.

Well your sainted mother says I ought to be grateful to CHARS coz–personally I think the advice unnecessary, but like the spanish king in Sordello's Sirventu

> "It is well known, to his credit, that he
> never does anything that displeases her."

Please tell your "Barnt" [Mother] that I have obeyed her injunctions and that my gratitude is doing nicely. It will last 'till you get to Brescia–after that it will depend on your behavior.

With the salaam of the four prostrations & due recognition to CHARS for their valuable services in commenting on your fitness for the toils undertaken.

    E.P.

Os . . . manos]   Formal, somewhat archaic Spanish, "I kiss thy hands."

bloody sestina]   "Sestina Altaforte" (P), first published in the *English Review*, 3 (June 1909), was partly written in the British Museum Reading Room. Its theme is the joy of war and slaughter.

Just as the barque . . .]   For the full text of this poem, apparently never published, see Letter **43**.

Sordello's Sirventu]   Sordello (ca. 1200–1269) was the most famous of the Italian troubadours. A *sirventes* is a poem in Provençal which is not a love poem. Written in a satiric, often vituperative manner, it deals with personal antagonisms and current events. EP "translates" Sordello's *sirventes* in Chapter III of *The Spirit of Romance*.

22   Dorothy to Ezra

12 Brunswick Gardens
Kensington
[*13 June 1910*]

In case I do not see you alone on Wednesday (if you are coming to tea), I take it that during your 'exile' you have been forbidden to write to me? That being so–if you have promised–don't break your word–don't write to me–but if anything happens write a word to my Cousin–I know he is to be trusted. I am having tea with him tomorrow afternoon–(a new thing, that has never been done before!). I will send the photo to you some day–in the autumn, I daresay. As yet, I have had no lecture–and have given no promise not to write to you–we pray I shall not be asked for the promise anyway.
I found this in "The King's Threshold".

> ". . . when we are driven out we come again
> Like a great wind that runs out of the waste".

also this:

> "The stars had come so near me that I caught
> Their singing."

I do beseech you to remain a poet–This letter–for crudeness–or is it merely simple-hearted–! But I have not your mouth to watch, and you have not my eyes to tell you things.

                                         Yours.

your 'exile']   EP sailed for the U.S.A. in mid-June 1910 and returned in February 1911.
   King's Threshold]   The quotations are from Yeats's play *The King's Threshold* (1904), lines 539–40 and 716–17.

23   Dorothy to Ezra

My dear;

I don't know what sort of mood you are in, so you must make the best of this. I am happier, I admit, now you are away: you in London, and a roomful of people between us, may have been delightfully ironical–but at the same time–I'd rather not!

I think you are pretty close to me sometimes–Last night I smiled philosophically to myself in bed: the philosophizings don't matter–but the end was this–that I was thanking you eternally, for you have given me Life in a way which I had no idea existed–For a thing *doesn't* exist, until one has felt it oneself.

To be fantastical–I lay my hair out over the pillow every night: so that perhaps you will find your way to me by it sometimes.

Meanwhile, your mouth, dear - - - smile!

£5000 a year not being found in a fortnight–

I am
Yours.

24   From Dorothy's Notebook

28 August 1910
Sunday

Surely you & I, Ezra, are both dreams; we are ⟨the⟩ subjective existences of some man or other, who little knows that we have met & loved–we–⟨his⟩ forms of his imagination! He ⟨dreamt⟩ formed you before he thought of me. You have had time to go ⟨further⟩ deeper into the Truth than I have been given.

But one day you & I met–all unbeknown to our Objective. We met in a blue, open, place–We saw each other's hair & knew that we both loved the Sun. Later we loved each other as well. But now, the Objective has taken you to the other side of the world & he has forgotten me–left me behind.

But because we are not real,–objective–it does not matter. We think we love–But that does not matter either, since we are both thin gray veils, having nothing in common with humanity ⟨or its physical properties⟩. We have touched, & twisted ourselves together, ⟨and⟩ floating in the blueness–And by that touch we have found our own souls, ⟨our⟩ the only Realities of which we have any need.

Dearest, whatever happen[s], what the Objective may do with us, ⟨together⟩ in contact or separately, we have ⟨touched⟩ come together & slipped one round the other–and thereby tasted of the Truth & Life Eternal, which kills sorrow & the power of the Objective.

25   From Dorothy's Notebook

15 October 1910

"Sara" told my hand.

"You are very broad-minded–too much so. Very artistic. All for colour. Very sensitive–over-sensitive. At a very great turning point in life–the change will be great–will come soon–quite soon–Eight–weeks–months– months I think.

You will marry twice & have two children. You will live abroad. Travel is connected with you–Someone is coming to you, or you are to make a long journey, connected with yr. marriage. I see travel & movement all the time–Has he travelled much? I see the letter F. underneath it all– (no) It may be *Fz.* (yes) and a good-looking man–with clear-cut classical features. You'll have a fever when you are about 30: perhaps you'll have had to go to a hot climate. But yr. life line is strong.

Have you or those nearly connected with you had money trouble. I see colour again very strongly. Are you liable to colds? The best part of yr. life is after marriage–You'll live away from your native place. You are n't English, are you? Very adaptable–good-natured. Double head-line later in life. Psychic possibly–intuitive."

26   From Dorothy's Notebook

8 November 1910

Anything more difficult than to write a letter which will have no answer,
I can't imagine.
Its altogether useless.

———————————

Today it has suddenly come upon ⟨with⟩ me that you once said "and if
ever you want me, I will come, at once".

This evening I have almost made up my mind to do a really serious
thing. To ask you to come back next summer–After all She [Olivia Shake-
spear] cannot forbid your coming to London–She can only forbid your
coming to the House–

True, she can forbid our meeting, too–Well–then I shall surely be
strong enough by next summer to say–"I will have my own friends–I am
old enough to choose my own friends–I will not bring him to the House if
you don't want to see him–" We could meet - - - anywhere. I saw two
people the other day at the [British] Museum in the Greek part; evidently
discussing some tiresome problem. You & I would at all events look more
in place there than they two! And the Greeks would keep us ⟨sound⟩ sane.
⟨True to⟩ They are so clean and exquisite.

27   Dorothy to Ezra

[? London]
November 1910

My dear.

You have been with me very much lately–I wonder if you are writing
me another poem. The Gods be praised I have inspired you to write
poems–After all that's as much as one ought to desire. If I have given you
anywhere near the amount you have given me–I am–not satisfied, perhaps–
but greatly contented. I hope I shall never be satisfied with life–and I know
you never will be.

But let there be between us, always, Peace–the sort of peace one finds,
at the moments when one is sure the world & other folk don't exist. Mozart

at present exists for me–I am battling with a d–d song–oh! so exquisite–
of his

"Viene, non tardar, gioia bella:
Ti vo' la fronte incoronar di rose," etc:

Don't slip that information in a letter to O.S. [Olivia Shakespear]! She
generally shows me yours, so send salutations.

Meanwhile, I ask of you this–that if my letters cease to be of use to you–
you will tell me so.

Meanwhile
Believe me yours

Viene . . . di rose]   From Susanna's aria in *Le Nozze di Figaro* (Act IV,
Scene 10) about her love for Figaro. DS has combined two separate passages:
Deh vieni non tardar, oh gioia bella . . . vieni, ti vo' la fronte incoronar di rose
. . . ("O come do not delay, my beautiful joy . . . come, I wish to crown your
forehead with roses").

28   Dorothy to Ezra

[*? London*]
December 1910

My dear:

A thousand thanks for the book of poems. I sent a word of thanks by
O.S. [Olivia Shakespear]–I had thought of enclosing a note, but her voice
"have you any message" forbade such a piece of independence. My copy
is at present with Lady Low: who calls me "dear Dorothy"!

I wish we could have some of your cold over here–Its done nothing but
rain, rain, rain–oh! awful! The sun is a matter for deep faith–like so many
other things.

This is to wish you luck for 1911, with much inspiration.

A Toi.

I wish you would translate a set of Arnaut Daniel & print them with the
original alongside. I am longing to see the Cavalcanti.

book of poems]   *Provença* was published in Boston on 22 November 1910.
Lady Low]   A friend of the Shakespears; EP lectured in her home in 1913
(Letter **139n**). See Biographical Appendix.
Cavalcanti]   See Letter **15n.**

29   From Dorothy's Commonplace Book

December 1910

For genius is, in fact, life and the faculty of engendering life in others.

from Butcher's
"Some aspects of the Greek genius."

Butcher's]   S.H. Butcher, *Some Aspects of the Greek Genius* (London:
Macmillan and Co., 1893), p. 198.

1911

24 January 1911

I went to Sara for a fuller reading. She told me:–

You are sensitive–too sensitive: & tremendously broad-minded: idealist, artistic: strong colour sense–apt to catch cold–very honest–good friend. Strong line of life–health good in middle life–much better than beginning or end. ⟨Old⟩ long-lived people on one side of family? I could make myself a name if I chose–artistically:–between 30 & 35. I should do so possibly.

I am to marry twice–to have two children by the first–rather quickly.

My brain will concentrate easier on things when I am a little older, 30 to 35 again.

The man I am to marry is to have a change in his life within the next four–weeks–or months. A *great* change for me is coming–I shall go abroad (live abroad, I understand) & travel about.

At present the difficulty of money seems insuperable. I shall always be guarded from real poverty–but it seems to trouble him. He will nearly drop out of my life–then suddenly & quite quickly things will be settled. He will make a great name & have renown.

We shall not be well-off at first–but it will come later–I asked her if I could paint: Yes: I might do something if I chose. She also said I could hypnotize away pain or "bad habits"–I was a little clair-voyante & might make a good palmist. I asked for the health of my family.

A slight operation, perhaps to one–⟨Both⟩ Two (were there two?) would be ill: One worse than the other–in fact one would get better for a little while and then the line dies ⟨away⟩ out altogether: I asked should I go abroad? Yes: not with my family–Possibly with two or three other people. It would not affect my career: just go there & back.

I see all the time the number 27 (she said) remember it, out of curiosity.

31   Dorothy to Ezra

St. Catharine's Court
Bath
[20 April 1911]

My dear:

You are still in the gay city [Paris], I suppose? The sun has been lovely here for three days–but not hot enough–nearly. I have been reading Petrarch sonnets and J. M. Synge's translations, which are really exquisite.

Also an entrancing book on 'Mysticism' by Evelyn Underhill. We were partie carrée over Easter–quite pleasant.

I wonder if you are coming to London? Also if you are better of yr. illness.

Yours.

Synge's translations]   John Millington Synge, *Poems and Translations,* with a Preface by W.B. Yeats (1909). Contains translations from Petrarch, Villon, de Musset, Walter von der Vogelweide, and Leopardi.

'Mysticism' . . . *Underhill*]   Evelyn Underhill, *Mysticism: A Study in the Nature and Development of Man's Spiritual Consciousness* (1911).

32   From Dorothy's Notebook

7 May 1911
6 P.M.

To-night (and all yesterday) I have had a feeling you were "about"– Is it possible you are coming back to me? And yet the news is bad–For Mercy's sake come back to me–I shall never rest until I have seen you again, & settled that one thing in my own mind. How can I rest?

I have only lived by you; You have taught me all I care about–about poetry & Revelation–Inspiration. And you are exquisite, body & soul–that I swear. And troubled in both–And then I must love someone, soon–Life is no good for a girl, without love. Life is monotonous, or boring or maddening–but ⟨never⟩ not happy–Enjoyable sometimes may be–but never happy. I think I have never been happy–really happy–all my life–except that one short time–which can never come again. And soon I shall be saying 'Oh! my lost youth!'

And Youth is a wonderful thing–& I would use it–and yet I cannot–by myself all alone–I need somebody to push me on–somebody to use it for– Oh! my dear–come back to me–and let us spend our Youth in dreaming dreams together. If only you would come back & fold away the veil between me & Life! Once I swore to serve Beauty always–but I have lost the Vision entirely, & the memory is faded–Come back & give me the Vision again–because it was always yours, I saw.

'Oh! Heart of me' come back! Its Spring–& May–& a year ago.

'Oh! Heart of me'] From the second stanza of "Canzon: The Vision" (CEP), first published in *Provença* in November 1910.

> Dream over golden dream that secret cist,
> Thy heart, O heart of me, doth hold, and mood
> On mood of silver, when the day's light fails,
> Say who hath touched the secret heart of thee,
> Or who hath known what my heart hath not known!

May . . . a year ago] In late April 1910 DS and Olivia Shakespear joined EP at Sirmione on the Sirmio promontory at the southern end of Lago di Garda, celebrated for its natural beauty and its associations with Catullus. On May 6 EP escorted them to Venice. The days at Sirmione influenced both Dorothy and Ezra profoundly. In " 'Blandula, Tenulla, Vagula' " (P), first published in *Canzoni,* Ezra equates Sirmio with Paradise:

> If at Sirmio
> My soul, I meet thee, when this life's outrun,
> Will we not find some headland consecrated
> By aery apostles of terrene delight,
> Will not our cult be founded on the waves,
> Clear sapphire, cobalt, cyanine,
> On triune azures, the impalpable
> Mirrors unstill of the eternal change?

And in "Prologomena" [*Poetry Review*, 1 (February 1912)]] he says he "would much rather lie on what is left of Catullus' parlour floor and speculate the azure beneath it and the hills off to Salo and Riva with their forgotten gods moving unhindered amongst them, than discuss any processes and theories of art whatsoever."

For Dorothy this visit to Sirmio was a personal and artistic transformation. "Truly my life was lived then," she wrote in her diary a year later (see Letter **33**). Many of her most finished and original watercolors from 1910 through the 1930s are of scenes on or around Lago di Garda, and late in life she told Noel Stock that the 1910 visit "was the first time I ever saw colour" [Noel Stock, *The Life of Ezra Pound* (New York, 1970), p. 86].

33 From Dorothy's Notebook

2 July 1911

Its the same again: I felt all yesterday you were "about". I feel so today. I feel quite sure today that you & I shall come together again–soon. I have not felt it much lately–Last night I remembered all S[Sirmione] so well. I lived those exquisite days again: more clearly than I have for months been able to see anything. The Tower, & the two other afternoons. Truly my life was lived then.

Oh! I vow you'll be back soon! You are thinking of me now: and I love you–At this moment, I dont see everything against us: that you are a poet–that I am incapable–that– – Oh! all the world is against us–but still, I believe with a great belief in the wonderfulness of our souls.

I shall know more when your new poems come. I shall find out through them: "Alas, the hurt, Belovèd". Life is terrible.

   new poems]   *Canzoni*, published in July 1911, and dedicated "To Olivia and Dorothy Shakespear."

34   Dorothy to Ezra

[*London*]
[*13 July 1911*]

[*missing*] Canzoni "with the Author's compliments" have just come. I have been waiting for them for some while. I did not realise there would be so many new ones. You have done a lot of work this last year–as I gather you have been translating Guido [Cavalcanti] & [Arnaut] Daniel–as well.

Canzoni have given me courage again. I have found much in them. I am thanking you from my heart.

You may "not understand" neither do I, neither can one, ever–but I think that state is nearer Il Paradiso than most contentment. I have been re-reading Il Paradiso–your copy–and the marker is in Canto XXX. I cannot criticize your poems: they are too near me.

I wish I could have been at Sirmione with you this summer. I shall probably never go there again–being a woman one cannot wander alone–though I prefer to be alone than with most people.

I shall get great calm from "Abelard"–and I do not think you are afraid much–I have puzzled over "Excuses" a good while. I believe I have got it now:–Life is made up of the days when one cries "I don't understand" & the days when one realizes it doesn't matter if one doesn't understand.

Later

I do not know whether you are still at Sirmione–but if you are–will you build a little altar of stones down where your "perch" was? And think that your prayer for my peace has been felt by the High Gods too–not the Cthonic (spelling?).

At last you have (or E.M.?) [Elkin Mathews] achieved the right binding.

I could write of many things tonight–of the great & fast friendship between O. [Olivia] and Lady Low–of a visit to the Cottage, Brasted, & how I slept in the little room on the ground-floor & watched a large yellow moon–Of a certain Apuleius I have just read–Of Il Maestro di Toccar–who is a very wonderful person–& to be "counted among the immortals", I fancy.

If you come to London you will come to see me, won't you? Meanwhile, dear, write well, & may the triune azure envelope you.

Yours.

P.S.

Since I wrote the above Olivia has told me I had better write to thank you for my copy–& given me your address–So you can send back a message if you have any to send.

I love "To Our Lady of Vicarious Atonement"–It was of course in the other volume [*Provença*]. It is very exquisite. For The Vision I have already thanked you.

I will surely meet you at Sirmio–where we will pause awhile–then perhaps Riva will call–after we are rested. This phantasy pleases me–

> "That is the starlight woven into strings
> whereon the Powers of peace make sweet accord."

I fancy [Walter] Rummel has helped you a good deal? He played us some of his String quartet–I thought it beautiful–I must find out which of yr. songs he has set. No. IV of the Heine is delightful!

I think "The Flame" is very fine:

> "O thou anxious thou,
> Who call'st about my gates for some lost me;"

–and all that last stanza.

I told you I couldn't criticize–& I have just washed my hair–Think of the confusion in my brain!

A Toi.

Guido . . . Daniel] EP's work on the *Sonnets and Ballate of Guido Caval-canti* (first published in April 1912) must have been nearly completed by July 1911, since the manuscript and proofs were circulating in the latter part of 1911. As early as February 1911, when the contracts for the *Guido Cavalcanti* had been signed, EP started work on an edition of Arnaut Daniel, and by 13 October 1912 he could refer to "*The Canzoni of Arnaut Daniel* (now in publisher's hands)" [*The Letters of Ezra Pound, 1907–1941*, ed. D.D. Paige (New York, 1950), No. 8]. Ralph Fletcher Seymour, who had also arranged to publish *Patria Mia*, contracted for the *Arnaut Daniel*, and even issued a prospectus (see page 199); but the book was never published. Later, in 1917–18, EP revised the translations for publication by the Rev. C. Clinch Bubb, who ran the Clerk's Press in Cleveland, Ohio, and published works by Lionel Johnson, Richard Aldington, F.S. Flint, Hilda Doolittle, and John Cournos. The manuscript was mailed to Cleveland in January 1918 but never arrived; EP at first thought it had been intercepted by the American censor, but later concluded that it had been "sub-marined." For further details on the fate of *The Canzoni of Arnaut Daniel* see Donald Gallup's *Ezra Pound: A Bibliography*, Revised Edn. (Charlottesville, 1983), pp. 446–47.

During 1911–12 various translations from Arnaut Daniel appeared in "I Gather the Limbs of Osiris" (*New Age*, 28 December 1911 to 22 February 1912). *Instigations* (1920) and *Umbra* (1920) incorporated many translations of Arnaut Daniel, reprinted in *The Translations of Ezra Pound* (1953).

Canto XXX] This canto of the *Paradiso* contains the apotheosis of Beatrice.

"Abelard"] Part III of "Victorian Eclogues" (CEP). This poem and all others referred to in this letter are from *Canzoni.*

"Excuses"] Part I of "Victorian Eclogues" (CEP).

a little altar] See Letter **144n.**

Elkin Mathews] Publisher of *Personae, Exultations,* and *Canzoni.* See Biographical Appendix.

the Cottage, Brasted] One of Mrs. Eva Fowler's houses, also known as "Daisy Meadow."

Apuleius] "Speech for Psyche in the Golden Book of Apuleius" (P).

Il Maestro di Toccar] "Maestro di Tocar" (CEP). This poem is dedicated to "W.R.," Walter Morse Rummel, the American composer and pianist who was a close friend of EP. See Biographical Appendix.

triune . . . azure] See " 'Blandula, Tenulla, Vagula' " (P).

"To Our Lady of Vicarious Atonement"] Appeared only in *Provença* and *Canzoni* (CEP).

The Vision] "Canzon: The Vision" (CEP).

Riva] A town on the northern shore of Lago di Garda. See " 'Blandula, Tenulla, Vagula' " (P), which closes with:

> Soul, if She meet us there, will any rumour
> Of havens more high and courts desirable
> Lure us beyond the cloudy peak of Riva?

"That is the starlight . . . sweet accord."] From "A Prologue" (CEP), first published in the *Sunday School Times* (Philadelphia), 52 (3 December 1910) as "Christmas Prologue." The lines come from the section "In Heaven," where we hear an "Echo of the Angels singing 'Exultasti' '':

> Silence is born of many peaceful things,
> Thus is the starlight woven into strings
> Whereon the Powers of peace make sweet accord.

Rummel . . . yr. songs] *Three Songs of Ezra Pound for a Voice with Instrumental Accompaniment by Walter Morse Rummel* was published on 19 September 1911, containing "Madrigale" (CEP), "Au Bal masqué" (which appeared only in this volume), and "Aria" (CEP). A fourth song, "The Return" (P), was added in 1913. Rummel's *Hesternae Rosae, Serta II* (1913) contains nine Troubadour songs of the 12th and 13th centuries set for piano and voice, with French and English texts. EP supplied the English versions.

No. IV of the Heine] Part IV of "Translations from Heine, Von 'Die Heimkehr' '' (P).

> I dreamt that I was God Himself
> Whom heavenly joy immerses,
> And all the angels sat about
> And praised my verses.

"O thou . . . lost me"] From the last section of "The Flame" (P), Part VIII of "Und Drang" in *Canzoni.*

> If I have merged my soul, or utterly
> Am solved and bound in, through aught here on earth,
> There canst thou find me, O thou anxious thou,
> Who call'st about my gates for some lost me . . .

35   Ezra to Dorothy

[Desenzano]
[Lago di Garda]
[16 July 1911]

Dearest Coz:

There aren't so many 'new ones'. I realize it's a bit confusing. The masterpiece was to have been the table of contents but some of the poems got on my nerves & I cut out 15 pages of 'em at the last minute. I tried to get an arrangement that would do a little of what Hugo botched in his Legend des Siecles. Artistically speaking its supposed to be a sort of chronological table of emotions: Provence; Tuscany, the Renaissance, the

XVIII, the XIX, centuries, external modernity (cut out) subjective modernity. finis. (& advs. of early work added by E.M. [Elkin Mathews]–the binding my own). I dont suppose any body'll see it–the table of contents–in this light but when my biographers unearth this missive it will be recorded as an astounding proof of my genius. The plan is filled in, as you see, with translations & old stuff more or less revised. The Abelard was done two years ago, I think.

Bill's brother lent me a Browning with an introduction that says "clear the vision of the inexperienced reader by setting this animating moral idea before his mind". *Cave!* I dont much believe a good poem can be gotten back into a formula–but what you say is very good "philosophizing"–yes. I'm writing a new prose book. Seriously. The Guido [Cavalcanti] is the part of last years work that has most in it, I'll bring you the proof sheets when I come, that is, I think I'll have 'em then. Mrs F. [Fowler] has heard some of them. Arnaut [Daniel] is not so important as poetry but the eagle [Yeats] was interested & I've writ a monstrous long introduction. I go to Milan next week to look up a *mss* that's said to have some music in it. Of course nothing could have done so much for my own work, technically, as the two translations. The Canzoni is a sort of Purgatorio with the connecting links left out. I feel now with it done & the 2 translations done, as if I were 'sul monte' [on the mountain] & out where I could breathe. No I'm not ill here. I've lived in the sun & water & am physically better than I've been ever, or at least for as long as I can remember.

I'm glad you like the 'Vicarious Atonement'–its one of the best, most real that is, that I've done but no one ever sees it. The 'Eclogues' are I think over-strained & morbid but part of my criticism of emotion, the whole book is in sort that–to the working out from emotion into the open. Walter [Rummel] & I had two weeks at Swarthmore that mattered, but he has doubted my sanity or respectability or both ever since I took him to New York & housed him in a flat I'd borrowed from a mad lady from Colorado. The expression on the face of that eminently proper young man as he retired for the night into the midst of most of her personal belongings, is one of those historical effects, those *aurorae boreales* of emotional psychology, which are forever to be treasured by the empiric & the connoisseur. In Paris we mostly jawed technique. CHARS think this letter is getting monstrously long & foolish–My address after Aug. 1st. is c/o F.M. Hueffer, 15 Friedrichs Strasse, Giessen, a/L. Germany.

Ezra.

cut out 15 pages] EP had originally intended to include in *Canzoni* five additional poems with notes. This material was set up by the printer, but later canceled. The canceled poems—"Leviora" (Sonnets I, II, and IV), "To Hulme (T.E.) and Fitzgerald (A Certain)," and "Redondillas"—are reprinted in CEP. Sonnet III of "Leviora" was retained in *Canzoni* as "L'Art" (CEP). In 1916, when Elkin Mathews asked EP to delete or alter sixteen poems in *Lustra,* EP recalled the "cutting" of *Canzoni* in his plea that Mathews "think of the book as a whole, not of individual words in it."

> This shaping up a book is very important. It is almost as important as the construction of a play or a novel. I neglected it in 'Canzoni' and the book has never had the same measure of success as the others. It is *not* so good as the others. I was affected by hyper-aesthesia or over-squeamishness and cut out the rougher poems. I don't know that I regret it in that case for the poems weren't good enough, but even so the book would have been better if they had been left in, or if something like them had been put in their place.
>
> [EP to Elkin Mathews, 30 May 1916, in *Pound/Joyce,* ed. Forrest Read (New Directions, 1967), p. 285]

Legend des Siecles] *La Légende des Siècles* (1859, 1877, and 1883), by Victor Hugo (1802–1885), an epic poem in three series which ranges from the Creation to the Last Judgment. Hugo portrays man's spiritual and social development in scenes drawn from different periods of legend and history.

Bill's brother . . . Browning] Edgar Williams, the younger brother of William Carlos Williams. The Browning is the Everyman edition (London and New York, 1906), with an introduction by Arthur Waugh. "And, perhaps, if ever an introduction to a volume of poetry is justified, it may be held to be justified in the case of Browning, in making some attempt to clear the vision of the inexperienced reader, by setting this animating moral idea before his mind" (Vol. I, p. xiii).

new prose book] The "renaissance affair" of Letter **39,** which was planned but never written.

Guido . . . Arnaut] See Letter **34n.**

the eagle] In April 1910 Yeats became a founding member of the Academic Committee of the Royal Society of Literature. The letterhead of the Royal Societies Club, St. James's Street, used by Yeats in some of his correspondence, has the telegraphic address: "Aquilae, London." Hence "the eagle" may be an affectionate but somewhat ironic comment on Yeats's new-found responsibilities, although it can also be an allusion to one of Yeats's favorite images in his poetry of this time: the lofty and aristocratic eagle who gazes directly at reality. In some of the later letters both EP and DS use a simple "V" in lieu of "the eagle."

Milan . . . mss] In Canto 20 EP recalls his discovery in the Ambrosian Library of two poems by Arnaut Daniel with musical notation.

'sul monte'] Perhaps an allusion to Dante's progress from the Inferno to the Mount of Purgatory.

'Vicarious Atonement']   "To Our Lady of Vicarious Atonement" (CEP).
'Eclogues']   "Victorian Eclogues" (CEP).
Swarthmore]   In September 1910 Walter Rummel visited EP in New York;
they then spent about two weeks in Swarthmore, Pennsylvania.
F.M. Hueffer]   Ford Madox Hueffer (later Ford), English novelist, editor,
and critic. See Biographical Appendix.
The following letter from DS to EP, 24 July 1911, was sent to Giessen,
Germany, care of F.M. Hueffer. For the impact of this visit with Hueffer on
EP's style, see Letter **156n.**

36   Dorothy to Ezra

12 Brunswick Gardens
Kensington
24 July 1911

Thank you–

It is burnt.

Yours
D.

37   Dorothy to Ezra

High Hall
Wimborne
[Dorset]
26 August 1911

Dearest Ezra;

These terrible people have breakfast at 8 A.M. so I stuck to my bed–
I tried to read the Guido [*Cavalcanti*] trans: but there were too many
wasps buzzing round–so no remarks are to the fore on the m.s.s.

I heard the name of Leopardi last night–but couldn't follow it up–but
the household is learned in languages so perhaps I will show your Guido
[*Cavalcanti*] & hold my own tongue.

I suppose you are now interviewing Madame ma mère?–Here I had a deal of conversation–about foreigners & their habits. There is a charming Swedish girl staying here: An excellent actress & most amusing–I hear that there if the girls are not married by 22–they are considered "terrible failures". It seems full young.

Yours
Dorothy.

No ambiguities, are there?

Leopardi] Giacomo Leopardi (1798–1837), Italy's greatest 19th-century poet. EP's poem "Her Monument, The Image Cut Thereon" (P), first published in *Canzoni,* is from the Italian of Leopardi.

charming Swedish girl] A young Swedish girl, Blenda Lundstrom, was visiting High Hall, Wimborne, August 10–28.

38   Dorothy to Ezra

High Hall
Wimborne
[Dorset]
30 August 1911
Wednesday

My dear–

I salute you. Thanks for two very welcome letters.

Nobody has seen the Guido [*Cavalcanti*]: & I have not read them all yet. What on earth are you "objecting" to Augener about? Is it poems W. R. [Walter Rummel] has set to music? I hope no other will be allowed to touch them.

I wish I had seen you at Brasted, refusing to play parlour tricks! Eva [Fowler] gave me quite a serious warning (oh! so subtly) against "the artistic temperament". You might have thought she had been caught by it herself & suffered severely. Someday I will tell you various remarks she made.

My Ezra walked in the garden? I suppose the Dorothys are not flowering still. They threatened to be many when I was there.

You see the moon has nothing to do with *us*—It happened to be full when I was there: that's all. Now the Sun is much more likely to go out of his course when we meet - - - I am wearing my sun-frock tonight: it was made that some day you might rejoice–Its yellow with green-&-yellow-shot stuff over it & has certain string-coloured Venetian lace down the front.

Yes, dear: I always knew the White Poppy was mine–But I always in my mind underlined so strongly the "I am come to thee for peace" (I can't quote) that it meant to me a ⟨very cold⟩ friendship–rather cold & blue.

The Swede is awa'–& we have a most attractive Canadian in her place– I am to be replaced by an American–I go tomorrow (Thursday) to

> Stanswood
> Fawley
> Southampton.

until the 9th. We are to be in Town 9th–11th–but I don't much see how we can meet - - -

I have found a trans: of "Theophrastus"–Characters–most entertaining and totally modern. A novel of Gertrude Atherton's about a poet——I was very firm about it–& told 'em the psychology was all wrong.

Does me getting into my coat amuse you? Of the man–more anon.

A laurel leaf held in the mouth averts evil, I read. Again–& yet again–

I,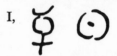

Salute thee.

Augener]   Augener Ltd., London, published *Three Songs of Ezra Pound for a Voice with Instrumental Accompaniment by Walter Morse Rummel.* See Letter **34n.**

Ezra walked in the garden] In "Und Drang" XII (P), subtitled "(Au Jardin)," EP twice quotes the first line from Yeats's "The Cap and Bells" (1894): "The jester walked in the garden." In the original manuscript EP commented that "This page will naturally be comprehended by none but true lovers" (CEP, p. 310).

White Poppy] "Planh" (CEP), first published in *Exultations* (1909), contains the line "Am I come to thee for peace." See Letters **9–11n.** The undated fragment containing EP's declaration "that that 'White Poppy' thing was made for *you definitely*" may have been saved from the "burnt" letter referred to in Letter **36,** or from another of the same period.

The Swede is awa'] See Letter **37n.**

"Theophrastus"–Characters] *The Characters of Theophrastus,* translated by R.C. Jebb (1870; new edition, 1909).

Gertrude Atherton's] *The Gorgeous Isle* (1908). Set in the British West Indies in 1842, the novel tells of a poetic genius, Byam Warner, whose talent can only be stimulated by alcohol. He reforms in order to marry, but his wife soon realizes that he cannot accomplish his great work in domestic tranquillity. The novel ends with a melodramatic gesture of self-sacrifice as she places a decanter of brandy in front of him. In her autobiography Gertrude Atherton says that the novel was inspired by meeting Theodore Watts-Dunton, who (she was told) had stifled Swinburne's genius by depriving him of "the stimulation of liquor" [*Adventures of a Novelist* (New York, 1932), pp. 386–87].

39   Ezra to Dorothy

> [*24 or 31 August 1911*]
> *Thursday*
> [*By hand*]

Dearest:

My last two letters were probably quite foolish & it seems likely that this one will be worse. I am trying to read the seven prefaces to Valla's "Elegantiae" but I really don't see how I can be expected to feign an interest, and it is a matter of utter indifference to me whether the latin tongue is to be regarded as a great sacrament or great pest.

> Magnum ergo Latini sermonis sacramentum est . . .

I could however agree with Pico *"animum sacra invadent"* if he'd change the number of his verb–which would in consequence modify the interpretation of *sacra*. This whole renaissance affair seems quite pointless as it is quite certain the proceeds will not buy a house in Mayfair and no Etruscan god has as yet consented to be caught in a wicker basket. Fairies are perhaps cheaper & some people might manage to live with one, but they *are* frightfully neo-celtic & one *must* "keep up the tone".

Of course nobody *does* know much about Etruscan gods and its hardly Etruscan gods that I mean—but nobody seems to know *at all* what kind of gods did inhabit "that section". Its my own belief that they matched up with a metallic architecture that Pater hints at (ref. Lacedaemon in his "Plato"); but this is a needless digression.

I wasted yesterday morning clawing the insides out of the rented spinet (rented with the *casa* that is). I've got several octaves in working order but can't say that it sounds much better than the grand piano.

Mr(?) Yone Noguchi sends me two volumes of poems from Kamakura, he says "as I do not yet acquainted with your work, I wish you will send me your book, which you like to have me read": he also assures me that although "This little note may sound quite business like," he "can do better in" his "next letter to" me. His poems seem to be rather beautiful. I dont quite know what to think about them. The line

> "Fill me a cup with the tea ancient-browed"

is I suppose a printer's error. But he seems "to do better" in his "next".

> "She is an art (let me call her so)
> Hung, as a web, in the air of perfume.
>
> . . . .
>
> Is her own self not the song of dream & beauty itself
> (I know she is tired of ideal & problem & talk.)
> She is the moth-light playing on reality's dusk
> Soon to die as a savage prey of the moment;
> She is a creation of surprise (let me say so)."

———————

His matter is poetic & his stuff not like everything else, he is doubtless sent to save my artistic future. I was in doubt about his genius but I am now convinced - *Eccovi!* [There you are!] here is the refrain to the poem on p. 42.

> "Min, min, min, min, minminminminmin . . ."

———————

I am dining with a scotch poetess this evening, have you any message?

How frequently are you allowed to receive letters, i.e. envelopes in the same handwriting? Is there anything you want to know, details, minutiae, etc. I cant see that anything much matters except that you're out of London & I ain't, & that don't so orfully matter 'cause it can't go on forever, but then - - - besides its quite certain we'll never get time to *talk* about unimportant detail- -fond illusion that–yes, dearest coz. on p. 43. 1.3. of my last work insert, or rather amend to "3 CHARS". I'd have done it in your copy only as you before noted the book was sent from Welkin [Elkin Mathews] direct.

It seems a long time since I wrote to you, and this is I presume most reprehensibly soon to repeat the operation.

Boaz

Valla's "Elegantiae"]   The treatise *Elegantiae linguae latinae* ("On the Elegance of the Latin Language"), by the humanist and philologist Lorenzo Valla (1407–1457), was reprinted nearly sixty times between 1471 and 1536. EP owned a copy of the Aldus edition (Venice, 1536), which is inscribed with his name and dated 1911. The quotation ("Great, therefore, is the holy mystery of the Latin language") is from Valla's first preface. In his preface to the *Poetical Works of Lionel Johnson* (1915) EP says that "Lorenzo Valla wrote invectively as Johnson might have written elegiacally, 'linguam latinam magnum sacramentum est.' " In the chapter of *Make It New* (1934) entitled "Cavalcanti: Mediaevalism." and dated 1910/1931, EP remarks that "Lorenzo Valla somewhat altered the course of history by his close inspection of Latin usage. His prefaces have here and there a burst of magnificence, and the spirit of the Elegantiae should benefit any writer's lungs" [*Literary Essays of Ezra Pound,* ed. T. S. Eliot (New Directions, 1954), pp. 362–63 and 192].

Pico]   This reference to Pico della Mirandola (1463–1494), the Renaissance humanist, is obscure. EP may have garbled a passage from Pico's *De Hominis Dignitate* ("Oration on the Dignity of Man") which reads: *Invadat animum sacra quaedam ambitio, ut mediocribus non contenti anhelemus ad summa . . .* ("Let a certain holy desire invade our mind so that, not content with mediocre things we aspire to the highest ones . . .").

renaissance affair]   In July 1911 EP told his father that he was "working on a book about the Renaissance and I think in my mild way that it will give me a chance for a little straight hitting." But in the same month he wrote to his mother from Sirmione that the "prose book was to have been about philosophy from Richard St. Victor to Pico della Mirandola, or more or less so, but I'm casting about for something more lucrative—the manufacture of false teeth or something of that sort."

Pater . . . "Plato"]   Walter Pater, *Plato and Platonism* (1893). Chapter VIII is entitled "Lacedaemon."

Yone Noguchi]   Yone Noguchi (1875–1947) was a well-known popularizer of Japanese literature and culture. His volume of verse, *The Pilgrimage,* was published by the Valley Press in Kamakura and by Elkin Mathews in London (1909). The first quotation is from "Meditation on a Chinese Tea Cup" (p. 26) where "ancient-brewed" appears as "ancient-browed," and the second from "The New Art" (p. 3).

Min, min, min, min, minminminminmin]   The refrain of Noguchi's "To the Cicada" (pp. 42–43). The "Min-Min," an imaginary animal akin to a squirrel that Dorothy drew at an early age, figured largely in the private mythology of the Shakespear family. The name derived from the sound of train wheels going over the ties on the track.

scotch poetess]   Rachel Annand Taylor (1876–1960). Elkin Mathews published two volumes of her poetry: *Rose and Vine* (1909) and *The Hours of Fiammetta* (1910). She shared with EP an interest in the Italian Renaissance and the Scottish "Chaucerians."

insert . . . 3 CHARS]   Line 3 on page 43 of *Canzoni*, "The dark dwarfs blow and bow there," would then read: "The 3 CHARS blow and bow there / Small horn and violin" [Part VII of "Translations from Heine" (P)].

Boaz]   The following appeared in *Punch*, 141 (16 August 1911), pp. 122–23.

> A new poet is about to swim into our ken in the person of Boaz Bobb, a son of the Arkansas soil, who has long been resident in London studying Icelandic literature for the purposes of a new saga of the Wild West. Those persons who have been privileged to see Mr. Bobb's lyrics in MS. say that they can remember nothing like them for their simplicity and candour. Mr. Bobb, with the delightful lack of restraint and false shame that is so marked a characteristic of the age, takes the reader into his confidence with complete unreserve, even when he runs the risk of suffering in reputation from so doing. The title of the little volume is *Naked and Unashamed*. It will be printed on hand-made paper, with the widest margins of recent times.

40   Dorothy to Ezra

Stanswood Cottage
Fawley
Southampton
[2] September 1911
Saturday

Dear Heart:

I chuckled a good deal over all your brilliant suggestions–But let me say at once they won't work. Chiefly this reason–that I would do nothing about you here except you came as O.S.'s [Olivia Shakespear's] friend & I think she had better have a holiday. Also its singularly impossible because we depend entirely on the elements, so that nothing is ever settled until somebody has been "to the front to see what the sea is doing" about 10 A.M. Also Southampton is a mere 17 miles.

Go to Lady Low's straight via Bournemouth Central (I believe) on 8th, and you will see some queer Dorset country–very very beautiful. I have seen Netley & Beaulieu–the latter charming–I should love to sketch there (!) but you see if I love architecture–so does H.H.S. [Henry Hope Shakespear] from whom I get it–& he's "on the holiday" & indefatigable.

The library with chained books at Wimborne, I have also seen! Do you begin to understand how bloomingly well-educated I am?? We, all of us, should only be in London just Sunday, & packing at that - - -

I fancy that this autumn perhaps I might do a thing I have long thought about–& that is, a set of sketches in the old London churches - - - I must think about it - - - again.

The plural "we" *are* all here–but Fawley is not Stanswood–3 miles separate them–& many more elapse before any railway. It's useless. Partie carrée (spelling correct) would mean here "one man & three who aint". They dont have men here much, except brothers. There is the beautifullest boy in the world here–a cousin–but he wouldn't do for one side of a square being 10½ years of age. You might nevertheless have got on.

"Dorothy's" are a small pink rambler rose–quite nice–their surname is Perkins.

What a crazy letter. I meant to write to you from ship-board–But at the chosen moment I had to stay on deck to survive the wash of a huge American liner on her way to Noo York. I am afraid I must leave it to you as to whether you are to show consideration in what you send me–but anything that comes I will try "to give my best attention to". My attention is not easily concentrated–but I hope it will be better soon.

I am reading Hueffer [Ford Madox Hueffer]. On the 'leventh O.S. [Olivia] & I go to the East Coast to Harry & Nellie. H.H.S. [Mr. Shakespear] to Scotland.

Go happily to Lady Low–She's a blessed woman with a brain. I am duly grateful for having met her. I have never before realized what a God-forsaken place this is.

I know Eva [Fowler] is death on psychic things: I talked to her like a mother when I was down there about it all.

Bless you.

I'll be hanged if we won't enjoy ourselves this autumn.

A Toi.

H.H.S.]   Henry Hope Shakespear, Dorothy's father. See Biographical Appendix.

Harry & Nellie]   Henry Tudor Tucker, Olivia Shakespear's brother, and his wife, Edith Ellen ('Nellie'), widow of Gilbert Hyde-Lees. See Biographical Appendix.

Olivia Shakespear (from *The Literary Year-Book*, 1897).

"Who ever had a like profile?—
a profile from a Sicilian coin."

—W. B. Yeats in a letter to Olivia Shakespear, 6 December 1926.

41   Olivia Shakespear to Ezra

[August–September 1911]

[In envelope with previous letter]

[missing] with the realities of life–& marriage does that. Failing that, couldn't you persuade her to go [to] the studio! What distresses me is that I see her becoming always more fundamentally selfish and self-absorbed. Of course this does not show on the surface, as her manners are too good– but I really don't believe she would stir a finger to help her dearest friend if it cost her a moment's trouble or inconvenience–she seems to have a perfect horror of being of any use to anybody.

I know I have spoilt her, but with the best intentions, because I was so afraid of not letting her develop on her own lines. Of course I know, further, that she has modelled her social life quietly[?] on mine–but she has not the sense to see that what is suitable for a worn out woman of my age, & a girl of hers, is very different.

You will probably think all I say very brutal, because you are in love with her; but you are quite intelligent enough to get outside that if you choose, & see that she is not perfection. Nobody is more aware of the fact that she has excellent & charming qualities than I am, & I am only anxious that she shd develop them, & not the imperfections that being human, she is bound to have.

I will write again later on & fix a day for you to come next week.

Yr. affctly
O. Shakespear

42   Dorothy to Ezra

Stanswood Cottage
Fawley
Southampton
[5 September 1911]
Tuesday afternoon

The heat being about 90° in the shade– –

I started a letter to you in bed last night–but somehow inspiration failed: so did sleep unfortunately for a while. I had been telling the children Celtic tales–& read them the Vision of Hanrahan–which the Beautiful Boy, anyway, thoroughly appreciated. Also a Fiona McCleod–about a seal-man. My head therefore was turned by such unwarranted success & so many kisses– not alas! the ones I wanted. Fiona McCleod is really very exquisite often.

Yesterday, at five minutes' notice I was whirled in the morning to Southampton–& at ten minutes' notice in the afternoon through Beaulieu– It's an ironical world.

And I got yr. Monday's Good morning on Sunday (country postmen have either better souls than Town ones or else they are nigligeable [sic]) & so had to use it again on Monday–This morning I went without–& only looked at yr. portrait which is excellently well painted–Its a somewhat savage (I mean angry)–no–perhaps it's really savage–conception of you! But awfully like too!–Did you ever suspect me of paying compliments? I find they are generally a trifle sharp on the other side too.

6.45 P.M.

I half hoped for a letter by the 2nd post. What brilliant ideas and plans are you concocting!

I hope, really, that it's the azure transparent poem.

I sent back the 'carton' wrapper - - - I nearly wrote a letter to go inside– but if you hadn't found it - - - !

I have shown CHARS privately yr. portrait: but their aunt [Olivia] has not seen it yet. They were a trifle scared. I am awfully bored here: if it weren't for the pine woods I should go crazy.

Do write:

Vision of Hanrahan]   Either "The Vision of Hanrahan the Red," first pub- lished in Yeats's *The Secret Rose* (1897); or "Hanrahan's Vision," first published in *Stories of Red Hanrahan* (1904) and reprinted in Vol. V of Yeats's *Collected Works* (1908).

Fiona McCleod]   "Fiona Macleod" was the pseudonym for William Sharp (1855–1905), who wrote many stories and plays in the Celtic Twilight mode. See "Sea-Magic" in *The Works of "Fiona Macleod"* (1910), Vol. V.

azure transparent poem]   This may be a reference to the following lines, found on the undated fragment of a letter where EP states that the "White Poppy" poem ("Planh") was made for Dorothy (see Letter **38n.**).

> & there shall be scarce sound at all
> In all our music
> & silent dances with no sound of feet
> More than the light makes on pale azure waters.

yr. portrait]   In Paris in the spring of 1911 Eugene Paul Ullman painted EP's portrait. It is reproduced as the frontispiece of Donald Davie's *Ezra Pound: Poet as Sculptor* (1964). EP had a photograph of the portrait made to send to his parents.

43   Dorothy to Ezra

> *Stanswood Cottage*
> *Fawley*
> *Southampton*
> [*7 September 1911*]
> *Thursday: aft:*

I have seen one or two lovely things these last days. Yesterday the sea & sky were all one grayish surface, because it was so hot: & the sun dropped Dantescan rain on the waves–silver, though, not gold. In the evening six large silent gray destroyers took up their moorings just outside here: & they signalled from the mast-head to each other for ages. We feared a night attack but they were gone away without a word by this morning. I saw, too, the sunrise, quite by mistake. A yellow & gold fan of light behind the pine-stems, & then the sun–red–the world in a gray even mist, & the liners all blowing fog-horns. Last night, the harvest moon presided over the waters–I am afraid of the moon.

———————

Thank you for your letter. I am sorry if I teazed you to write. And you were a trifle mixed. It isnt *yet* "8.55 P.M. Thursday"! Anyway I gave O.S. [Olivia Shakespear] the Criticism to read–& she is glad you are looking at Sapphic metres. I reverted immediately to the Swinburne.

Do you remember this little flower nel giardino Eden? "Love-in-a-Mess"? Thanks also for the White moths.

Friday 9 A.M.

Letters posted before 6 p.m. in London generally reach the country by the first post. So your second came with my morning glass of milk–& got me up.

I have often thought of Vicenza's finest rose. It having died, I suppose Ezra his mark is now suspended in the air for ever! I don't want to go back to Vicenza–

I wonder what confusion the stodgy old Times made about you? The cutting you sent in yr. last but one gave me a panic! The back page said you had married young–or something. Yes. "On June 18th we find 'He married'——".

We had a tremendous excitement last night about dinner-time–The Common not far off was blazing–Great bouffées of smoke kept on rising up over the edge of the wood–& for a while we wondered if our own wood were going to catch fire–It was simply lovely to watch–Unfortunately we couldn't, for ½ doz. reasons, go to the place.

Montaigne has many wise sayings (quoted by Miss Sichel) about style. "For my part I hold . . . that whoso hath in his mind a vital & lucid thought, will produce it". And he likes "a succulent, nervous speech, short & compressed, not so much combed & curled & coddled as vehement & brusque"–"Force & nerves cannot be borrowed; you can only borrow cloaks & furbelows."

In answer to yr. last–Do you remember in a Wilde play the Lady who had been married to so-&-so for ten years? "An eternity" injected her friend–"Eternity with Time thrown in" she retorted.

Well–well–my philosophical calm was always an outward grace (not much at that!) & no true inward light–except by infrequent flashes.

If you like long ramblings–here you are! Re Catullo–I wonder if I shall find it in mine–which I can't read–(perhaps it's as well?). I have a dear little C [Catullus]–Propertius & someone else that I got in Bath for 6d. I couldn't get any further in Propertius than Elegiae Lib iii 25–& yours in Canzoni is 26–Please explain. I like the said 26 enormously. Revenir à nos moutons (there is a french gov: [governess] in the house). The Catullus I can imagine well stickied over with pale honey (not even heather-honey) Yes: vertige.

I don't know our Southwold address yet–& O.S. [Olivia] is asleep at this moment–If you write home it will be forwarded all right–& I'll send it to you tomorrow probably. I have never suspected yr. artistic temperament of carrying you as far S.W. as Chelsea–Its too far from the [British] Museum for instance.

I had a letter from [Walter] Rummel a while since with an enchanting diagram of something he improvised to us one day. I am duly shocked to hear he is insolent. Oh! I must stop this babble–Is yr. formal "Suo" en revanche for my more familiar A toi? If so I immediately sign myself A Toi. If you see fit give my love to Lady Low–She may know my hand writing.   D.

[A single sheet in EP's hand, found in the envelope with this letter]

Candido lepido

Here two white moths went up against the sun
& shone with flaked silver/fire, like two stars
Sirmio June 1911

⟨Just⟩ as the bark with, blue & yellow sails
Casts far their splendour on the waters round her
So hath she cast her glamour on my heart.
Lo it is gold & deeper azure where
It casteth back the lustre of her hair
or bath ta'en on the shadows of her eyes

— — —

Tis the last word of beauty
& the thing
th' unhappy cycles have been searching for.

the Criticism]   Probably a reference to some of the pieces in the "I Gather the Limbs of Osiris" series, published in the *New Age* between 30 November 1911 and 22 February 1912.

Sapphic metres]   "Apparuit" (P), which appeared in *Ripostes* (1912), is written in Sapphics. Edward Marsh's unreliable memoir, *A Number of People* (1939), contains a satiric account of EP reciting an inaccurate translation of Sappho's "Ode to Aphrodite." See Letter **47n.** In "I Gather the Limbs of Osiris, XI" (*New Age* 10, 15 February 1912), EP compares the first line of Catullus 51 with the original in Sappho.

Swinburne]   Perhaps a reference to Swinburne's "Sapphics," in *Poems and Ballads* (1866); or to "Salve Pontifex (A.C.S.)" (CEP), first published in *A Lume Spento* (1908) but revised somewhat for the *Poetry Review* (February 1912) and *Ripostes* (1912).

White moths]   The poem enclosed with this letter. The title may be EP's rendering of "White moth" on the analogy of "lepido," "lepidoptera." Or it may mean "white, agreeable." For an earlier version of the poem, see Letter **21.**

Vicenza's finest rose]   See "Rosa Sempiterna" (CEP), published only in *Canzoni.*

stodgy old Times]   This is an obscure allusion. The only reference to EP in the London *Times* during the summer of 1911 appears to have been a one-sentence notice of *Canzoni:* "These Canzoni reveal Mr. Pound once more as a scholar whose poetic work has a real individuality of its own, expressed in finely-chiselled, somewhat austere verse" [*Times Literary Supplement*, 27 July 1911, p. 279]. DS may be mistaken about the source of the cutting, as she was later [Letter 52] when she confused the *Daily News* with the *Daily Mail*. It is possible that EP sent her a cutting of the favorable review of *Provença* that had appeared six months before in the *New York Times Book Review* ["A Triad of American Poets: Mr. Ezra Pound's 'Provença' Reveals a New Planet on the Literary Horizon," 12 March 1911, p. 134]. On the back of this particular cutting DS would have found part of a humorous note about Shakespeare and Bacon containing the phrases "the future Mrs. Shakespeare" and "man she was to marry."

Montaigne . . . Miss Sichel]   Edith Sichel, *Michel de Montaigne* (London: Constable and Co., 1911). DS's quotations, both from *Essais* I, 26 ("De l'Institution des Enfants"), are on pp. 154–55.

Wilde play]   Unidentified.

Re Catullo]   The following version of the first seven lines of Catullus 51 is found on an undated fragment of a letter from EP to DS.

Ex Catullo:

God's peer that man is in my sight
Yea, & the very gods are under him,
He sitting opposite to thee & near thee
Seeing & hearing

Thee. And thou smilest. Oh woe upon me!
Quenched all my senses - - -
Drawn close to thee, Lesbia, there is
Nothing above me.

& someone else]   Tibullus. Several single-volume school editions of the three poets were published in the 19th century.

Elegiae . . . Please explain]   "Prayer for His Lady's Life" (P), first published in *Canzoni*, is subtitled "From Propertius, *Elegiae*, Lib. III, 26." EP used the 1892 Teubner text (ed. Mueller), which has a different numbering from that found in the Loeb and other texts.

44   Ezra to Dorothy

> *Sea View*
> *[Wareham]*
> *[Dorset]*
> *[10 September 1911]*
> *Sunday*

Sea View (only you can't see it).

Dearest:

You are very lovely & I am very stupid. One of which facts I have mentioned before, & the other is self evident. In fact I think they are both each way. Yesterday 'we' went down to the 'edge' (front?–whatever it properly is–at least in "Darset") it was proper bleak & gray–& "very odd" = very unpleasant, very poetic, & strong beyond anything. There is no place for senses in this scheme of things–only for feelings that last life out–deeper, more intense than all Italy, and silent. There are several of my family names about here–but that apart it is like getting back to the roots of things.

It is a place that would be very strong on one.

> *Later*

I have been submitted to "service"; charming relique of Temporis aet: [times past], whose only anachronistic feature was his speech. He should have accommodated himself to his surroundings & spoken anglo-saxon. He had a beautiful head plagiarized from some Roman cameo–a true mystic. [*rest of letter missing*]

45   Dorothy to Ezra

Glan-y-Don
Southwold
[Suffolk]
[12 September 1911]
Tuesday

Glan-y-Don. ?–Strong my shoulders.

My dear–

"What you mail after noon Monday - - -" & I haven't written a word since Sat's postcard–oh! dear. But I am loving you for feeling all that about the cliffs & Darset. I only know that part of it (the wild part) from Hardy. I know of course Sherborne & Wimborne, & have driven a good deal about–It has always seemed to me unlike the other counties I know. I should greatly mistrust that £35 house! It probably has no drains (or few, which is worse) & no water-supply–but sounds nice with its gate-posts. Or else its horribly haunted.

I have no news: & not having read any Montaigne (intelligently, anyway) I can't tell you if he has any theories on the use of "quantity".

I went out to sketch this morning–was severely repulsed by an old woman in a cottage, The Keeper of The Keys of the Church, when I desired to draw the font–However the Vicar remains & my courage is undamped–The air is wonderful here & I think will cure me of my cough–my milk-cure is fattening me–I have had to abandon one skirt as unbearable.

I believe "Walter" [Rummel] is near the truth–& that we return to my beloved London on about Oct: 4th–not before, I fear. But as I have hardly put brush to paper this summer its perhaps as well. I will try to enjoy my Youth–of course you don't know of my sins. Do tell me severely to paint hard while I am here–

I am glad you lay in the sun–I know by experience its an exceeding wonderful thing to do. Only you were probably devoured by harvest-bugs? Rub damp soda on 'em, if so.

I have read nothing & am about to read nothing. The only lit. here is detective stories. How therefore should I have an idea as to what you are to write? Aren't you embarked on a Great prose-work?

I dreamt last night of a queer street on a curve & then a great Cathedral, with snow all piled up on the roof–but the snow fell in five minutes feet thick & then melted in humps from underneath–a strange bedroom I suppose induced such queer fancies.

Of course the Vicenza rose died–young, too–the honour was more than it could bear.

Yes. How are intimacy & mystery combined? Therein lies the whole root of the matter.

I might perhaps "get took" on the pier–I'll see.

The geranium is only aesthetic–to give you a new sensation instead of only recalling an old one.

Depraved taste for fr. [French] fiction–*me*? It was once O.S. [Olivia Shakespear] if my excellent memory serves me well.

I don't know when I'll ever get to a post-box–I will wait for the unreadable N—— until I am back–please. Don't write too often: Letters are laid about here terribly–& I can't help it. You might send a line to O.S. [Olivia] if you are pining to write. I address faithfully to 2A [Granville Place].

Sua.
D.

£2–part of my yearly income–just arrived.

The geranium]   A watercolor by DS.

the unreadable N——]   Probably Max Simon Nordau (1849–1923), whose *The Interpretation of History,* translated from the German, was published in 1910.

46   Dorothy to Ezra

Glan-y-Don
[Southwold]
[Suffolk]
14 September 1911

25 mortal years have I been on this planet & only lately met you! For goodness' sake don't be middle-aged yet!

I am sorry for you about yr. teeth–Our dentist is quite expensive, I fear; About 1 guinea for stopping a tooth I believe. His name is A. Cutler & he lives at 1, Gloucester Place, Portman Square, W. Then there is a man called Cadwallader-Jones, I know is good, but not so dear, somewhere at the top (Bays[water] Rd. end) of Queen's Rd. None of which will much help you–I think it must be yr. illness of last winter.

Didn't you know I wanted you to write poetry? Or were you uncertain? But I don't want you to write Greek to me–because I hardly know the alphabet even!

Blessed be Sappho who has shown you a path towards Truth.

I have been sketching gaudy bathing-houses–The effect was meant to be pale Conder–but isn't. I've done two other brutes of things–but the weather has been stormy & my brain unimaginative.

I have had two delightful presents: from H.H.S. ¡Henry Hope Shakespear, Dorothy's father] a travelling clock–& from H.T.T. (Bunkle) [Henry Tudor Tucker] a pewter box for - - -

> cigarettes
> or   hairpins
> or   jewels
> or   buttons–

They sell lovely yellow cornelians (my stone) here very cheap: I shall get some–earrings possibly.

The sea & sky have been beautiful–but blowy & cold.

Never mind *me*–write, if you want to–When I am back–*when*–we'll talk about the incoronare [coronation]. I fancy red roses are out of season. D—— its raining.

I have nothing to tell you–except that I am fairly reconciled to being here–The sea is wonderful: & there is a long curly line of foam round the coast, not a lighthouse. [sketches]

Georgie's face *is* square: but she is very handsome, I think, as well. She is awfully intelligent, & I believe admires yr. poems–what more can be said? Alarmingly intuitive at 18. There is no one I am likely to tell about your rhythmic triumphs.

Oh! yes! Anent style! The old churchkeeper man told G. [Georgie Hyde-Lees] she didn't mean she wanted "to paint the font" but "to take a painting of it"–quite sharp? G. chuckled, & I remarked that he was the more correct. He then showed us, hidden away, a most beautiful carved oak chest. The choir screen is gilded & painted oak–most lovely: & the ceiling, unfinished, in squares of blue (Italian).

> I must rest
> put Harlene on my hair
> dress for dinner.
> through all of which
> Je suis à toi.

Yes: once: because you are happy.

middle-aged] Possibly a reference to an early version of EP's "Middle-Aged, A Study in an Emotion" (P), first published in *Poetry* (Chicago), 1 (October 1912).

Conder] Charles Conder (1868–1909), English-born Australian artist noted for his delicate fin de siècle colors.

Bunkle] "Bunkle" (uncle) or "Bunk" were nicknames for Henry Tudor Tucker, Georgie Hyde-Lees's step-father.

Georgie] Georgie Hyde-Lees, a close friend of Dorothy who married W.B. Yeats in 1917. See Biographical Appendix. Because of her square face, EP and DS used a private shorthand □ for her in many letters. She, in return, signed cards to Dorothy: "Yr. Step-pest."

47   Dorothy to Ezra

Southwold
[Suffolk]
16 September 1911
Saturday

Dearest:

I am supposed to be resting from 2–4 P.M. but have procured this writing-pad & a ld. bottle of ink–so you shall have a line. Yours came at glaring midday–but with a covering p. card from an Aunt. Besides, I don't care, now. Everyone here has known for the last fifteen months, why I loved [Lago di] Garda.——Intuition——! Which, when combined with intense discretion is quite a decent faculty.

I ordered to be made, yesterday, a pair of earrings, as a present from O.S. [Olivia Shakespear] three cornelians–perhaps I might sarruptiously get one to hang round my neck–"from you"? I won't ruin you! My earrings will only be 10/6. - - - Thanks for the gray side of the 2 olive-leaves. Hadn't you better keep the rest–lest the affair should be too one-sided? (I have nothing here to send you–unless sand or pebbles would suit?).

'Harlene' smells just of hairwash. It will be over when you see me next probably.

Oh! dear! It isn't 'cloak', its *clock*–or did *you* do the misspelling? I have already had, ages, a divine gray cloth military *cloak*.

The Provence is better than Greek but my capacity is limited.

For goodness' sake don't make D.'s. this way–as on yr. envelope. [sketch] I can't bear it. Its chiefly on account of yr. ordinary ones that I send information as to Harlene, clocks, etc: etc:

I happen to be in good temper–have you discovered it? I did two hours good painting in the gilded church this morning. All the rest has been un-concentrated rot. I *will* paint a little better than a beastly girl–'Don't mind me'!

I got what we believe to be a 1st ed: of Meredith's "Amazing Marriage" yesterday for 1/6–two vols:

Mercy on us its 3. ocl: & I haven't had a wink of sleep for seven hours.

Good night.

The sunset last night–wonderful. My paint-box–inadequate. Good luck with yr. dentist, & later, with the Sapphic Ode. I daresay they *won't* combine!

Yours D.

P.S. You see the initial is a point of resemblance: of which I see few.

Meredith's "Amazing Marriage"] George Meredith's novel *The Amazing Marriage* (1895).

Sapphic Ode] In his often unreliable memoir *A Number of People* (N.Y. & London, 1939), pp. 328–29, Edward Marsh recalls a dinner with EP at a Soho restaurant.

> . . . This author has of late been discovered in the *New Statesman* and elsewhere as less of a scholar than he had given the public to understand: he seems to be like the character in George Eliot who 'knew Latin' in general, but was apt to be defeated by any particular piece of Latin . . . In the middle of dinner he asked me if I was up in the new system of quantitative verse; and as I had studied William Stone's paper on the subject and been further indoctrinated by Robert Bridges, I admitted that I was. Thereupon he produced a version of Sappho's ode to Aphrodite, and begged me to tell him if he had made any mistakes. He had; and when I pointed them out, he put the paper back in his pocket, blushing murkily, and muttering that it was only a first attempt. 'Judge of my surprise' when some weeks later the piece appeared in the *Poetry Review* without a single amendment.

"Δώρια" (P) appeared in the *Poetry Review*, 1 (February 1912); "The Return" (P) and "Apparuit" (P) in the *English Review*, 11 (June 1912). None could be called a "version of Sappho's ode to Aphrodite."

48   Dorothy to Ezra

> Southwold
> [Suffolk]
> [19 September 1911]
> Tuesday

I began a Goodnight last night - - - & sent you a blessing for each eye-lid - - - I then wrote some rot on the other side, so its torn up–Yours came last night, for a sleeping-draught (I dreamt awful dreams) & this morning I sent off the Guido [Cavalcanti]: does the Dormouse [Elkin Mathews] publish it over here? I can't keep pace with yr. two countries.

I am here for anyway another fortnight - - - I suppose October will turn up some time. Though according to H.H.S.'s [Mr. Shakespear's] clock it won't ever: the clock won't go–(Divine Fecundity? don't seem enough to go round?).

If you go as butler to E.F. [Eva Fowler], I shan't go as housekeeper: though I doubt whether I should be less competent than you.

I don't fancy the play at all. I am glad it won't ever be finished.

Have you had a tooth crowned? or all of them, or what? If so, its a point more of resemblance.

Don't *you* be "nebulous to the Nth" about yr. Troubadour psychology–or [G.R.S.] Mead won't be pleased. Say you're a re-incarnation so you *know*. Are you? do you?

I do happen to know the Wallace [Collection]–The Watteau & Co. are lovely there: & some of the finest Rembrandts in the world also are there. I cant remember the Velasquez for the moment. Some beautiful Van der Velde's I seem to remember too.

What the devil is 'catamosity'? Vile word, anyway! Its just dawned upon me (*comatose*). I have it!! Southwold is good for bodily vigour–not so much for that of the mind.

After I had posted yr. G: [*Guido Cavalcanti*] I routed out a whole "fancy Bazaar" & procured the enclosed, for 8d; sent to show what mine are like. No: I shall get the pendant "from myself"

¼ size approx.   [sketch]

Who in heaven's name is "L.C.S"?–chief inexplicability (what a long word for you to spell) in yr. letter.

Yes: I know I'm cross. Its because I've nothing to do. The only Meredith you need read is "The Shaving of Shagpat"–or have you already done so?

?? [the question-marks] seem to dance today–I feel what O.S. [Olivia Shakespear] calls "desoeurée"–I've no doubt S. [Southwold] is a charming place–O.S. went yesterday to see 33 submerged churches.

I am reading again [Dante's] La Vita Nuova; in fragments only.

Lets pretend its Eternity until Oct: then perhaps we shall be surprised–

(I wonder what you are?)

Wednesday, 3 ocl. P.M.
resting-hour.

Dear: the post before 6. experiment works out well: arr: 1st post here. Perhaps I felt so awfully cross yesty: in sympathy with your molars. I am sorry for you, whatever the devil-dentist may be doing.

(There's a funeral-bell tolling. Hah! work!).

Did a drawing this morning (incorrect) of the font in the gilded church– & tipped the verger: who gave us last week, two huge Harvest-Offering apples, stolen by him from the said font. We leave this house on Monday 25th & go to the Marlborough Hotel, equally at Southwold.

Montaigne also says "Above all things avoiding fear, that great disturber of reason. The thing in the world I am most afraid of is fear."

Au revoir à bientôt
Yours.

the play]   At this time when EP was working energetically to advance his literary reputation (and income) he made attempts at both a novel and a play.

Troubadour psychology . . . Mead]   On 17 September 1911 EP wrote to his mother: "I have spent the P.M. with G.R.S. Mead, edtr. of *The Quest,* who wants me to throw a lecture for his society which he can afterwards print. 'Troubadour Psychology,' whatever the dooce that is." The lecture was delivered in early 1912 and printed later that year in the *Quest,* 4 (October 1912). It was later (1932 and after) reprinted as Chap. V of *The Spirit of Romance.*

G.R.S. Mead, a student of hermetic philosophy and the occult, was a frequent guest at Yeats's Monday Evenings. See Biographical Appendix. He was President of The Quest Society, whose announced aims were: "1. To promote investigation and comparative study of religion, philosophy, and science, on the basis of experience," and "2. To encourage the expression of the ideal in beautiful forms." *The Quest,* a quarterly review edited by Mead, was devoted mainly to articles and reviews that promoted these aims, but Mead had eclectic taste and opened the journal to literary contributions from Pound, Yeats, Laurence Binyon, and a wide variety of artists and scholars.

L.C.S.]   An error for "C.L.S.," Charles Lancelot Shadwell (1840–1919), the translator of Dante and editor of Walter Pater. See Letter **67**.

Meredith]   George Meredith, *The Shaving of Shagpat: An Arabian Entertainment* (1856).

Montaigne]   From *Essais* I, 18 ("De la peur"). Not in Edith Sichel's *Michel de Montaigne* (see Letter **43**).

49   Ezra to Dorothy

> [*London*]
> [*22 September 1911*]
> *Friday*

Dearest:

From hence henceward you will find my stock of small talk limited, the chief topic being ended, i.e.–Dr. Bacon [dentist] has come to a finish with four blastings & a fine display of speed. There remains nothing but the Sapphic ode.

They tell me I'm likely to meet the Bahi next week in order to find out whether I know more about heaven than he does. Whatever the decision, I bet I can give him points on "Helsewhere".

I am quite convinced of the possibility of all miracles. All they need is a decade's practise & a modicum of intelligence. Example of amateur job. (divide silver as silv-er).

> Surely strange art was in the secret, subtle
> Stronger craftsmanship in the woven wonder
> Made in deathless woof of the rain of heaven,
>   Silver unfeignèd.

Its stupidly done, without variety & with no skillful disturbance of the accents.

Saturday

The sun to you.

My one comfort is this sapphic affair. Surely all systems of metric since have been a vulgarity & a barbarism, and their beautiful results have been due to genius & accident & not to any virtue inherent in the 'system'. 'melos' "is compounded out of 3 things, speech, music & rhythm." Montaigne–or rather Plato. And unless you write in quantity (by intent or accident) those three things mean mess (with little, very little love in it). Sappho would unlike W.B.Y. [Yeats] have rejoiced in the piano because it wouldn't have interfered with the song method.–& en revanche–your musician simply cant muck you up, he can do you more or less well or more or less expressively, but he cant knock your words out of shape or obscure them.

the Bahi]   The London *Times* of 6 September 1911 announced that Abdul Baha (Abbas Effendi) had arrived in London for a fortnight's stay. "Abbas Effendi is a son, and the generally recognized successor, of Mirza Hussein Ali, the so-called Baha-Ullah ('the Splendour of God'), the founder of the larger, or Bahai, section of the Bahi sect." EP met the Bahi on September 28. See Canto 46, where EP recalls meeting with Abdul Baha.

Surely strange art . . . Silver unfeignèd.]   This appears to be both an exercise in alliterative form, at a time when EP was translating "The Seafarer" [first published in the *New Age,* 10 (30 November 1911)]; and an anticipation of the Sapphic meter in "Apparuit" (P), which was first published in the *English Review,* 11 (June 1912).

Montaigne–or rather Plato]   *The Republic,* Book III (398 D): "the song is composed of three things, the words, the melody, and the rhythm." EP refers to this passage twice in the "I Gather the Limbs of Osiris" series [*New Age,* 10 (21 December 1911 and 8 February 1912)].

50   Dorothy to Ezra

Southwold
[Suffolk]
23 September 1911
Saturday

My dear:

There's nothing to say. Do you expect, or hope, to be crowned by W.B.Y.'s academy?? W.B.Y. being a quarter of a century younger than any of the other members, perhaps they need younger blood.

I sketched this morning a most CHAResque booth, of sweets & lemonade–result not special.

Sun
Mercury
Venus
Moon
Jupiter.

Here you have my astrological knowledge in a nutshell. I must have the Guido [*Cavalcanti*] again–because I have n't properly read the last ones.

(Yr. spelling vocabulary in the animal-line seems shaky? Hoarse?–doormouse?!). I believe you have a *most* "unconquerable aversion to simple statement"–& I don't think letters should contain–what? Anyway yours was fairly lucid, with Yeats' help.

Its all very well–Life will be d——d serious when I'm back! And how we shall manage our behaviour, I can't quite see. Oh! damn! never mind.

Also in the Summer, in a fit of despair, I implored my Aunt to take me in the autumn for a week's motor-tour somewhere. Now you bet she'll remember it, & I shan't know what excuse to give–oh! dear! What a rotten world it is! And I have ordered "Paris Fashion" & the beasts won't send it–one thing & another. However, Harlene progresses nicely: half a 1/– bottle done.

Oh! yes! I have achieved my cornelian earrings–very pretty is the verdict–& also the pendant.

(this at dinner).
  "Who is the pendant from?"
  "Myself".
  "Do let me give it to you" from Nelly [Georgie's mother].
  "I shall be charmed" from me.

So there! Sold again! No: I couldn't let you give me a thing you hadn't seen or chosen. You've a birthday yourself some time in the blessed month of October?

☐ [Georgie Hyde-Lees] & I go to London on Oct 2nd. We are busy on Tuesday: I am occupied with Hilda [Strutt] on Wd: & on Thursday 4th [Walter] Rummel is coming to us–& may bring you if it suits you both–Voilà (You may not know about 4th as yet?). But I *am* busy until then–

Good-night–

Sunday noon

not only blowing, but blowing a gale: the sea has come over the shingle & made a great lake along the shore. CHARS find it a great delight. I have just been packing to go to the Marlborough tomorrow. One more week, & I shall be packing for home.

I must post now or never.
D.

W.B.Y.'s academy]   In April 1910 Yeats became a founding member of the Academic Committee of the Royal Society of Literature. On 12 April 1910 he wrote to Edmund Gosse, who had been campaigning for an English Academy, that "an English Academy would save us, perhaps, from the journalists, who wish to be men of letters, and the men of letters who have become journalists" [*Letters of W.B. Yeats*, ed. Allan Wade (New York, 1955), p. 549].

Hilda]   Hilda Strutt went to school with Dorothy. See Biographical Appendix.

51   Dorothy to Ezra

[*Southwold*]
[*Suffolk*]
[*26 September 1911*]

I started a letter to you dated Tuesday 1.15 P.M. on a bank by the river, Blythborough, but I went to sleep instead.

My dear. Thanks for the Guido [*Cavalcanti*] again & your letter. I had a good paint this morning–I am glad Sappho is so entrancing. I understand it will have "to simmer" for some while. Meantime: is it perlite to call O.S. [Olivia Shakespear] & self a gang of women? Rummel I believe to be a musician, certainly.

I think you had better come early on 4th & discuss the woman question with me upstairs, before Maestro di Toccar disturbs our nervous systems. So be it–mutual friends–I've none to give you. Lady Low is our best at present. If "Dorothy" & her poet-husband (I wonder which he is primarily?) are interesting: very well.

I wouldn't bet about what "that beast W.R." [Walter Rummel] hasn't an idea of, in the way of playing Fate.

Tell me the substitutes for

"milk, water, & piety"
Honey, wine, & what?

Life dawdles along here: the people are negligeable–weather decent.
This word to say Good Morning–no, it won't–Blessing on the Sapphic Ode Trouble.

Yours–

Maestro di Toccar]   The poem "Maestro di Tocar" (CEP), published only in *Canzoni,* is dedicated to Walter Rummel.

> You, who are touched not by our mortal ways
> Nor girded with the stricture of our bands,
> Have but to loose the magic from your hands
> And all men's hearts that glimmer for a day,
> And all our loves that are so swift to flame
> Rise in that space of sound and melt away.

"Dorothy" & her poet-husband]   This may be an oblique reference to Hilda Doolittle and her companion Frances Gregg (see Letter **113n.**), whom DS had not yet met. H.D. would be an earlier "Dorothy" because she was at one time engaged to EP. In the summer of 1911 H.D. traveled to Europe with Frances Gregg and Mrs. Gregg; and after a stay in Paris, they arrived in London around the end of September. DS may have misunderstood "Frances" as "Francis."

52   Dorothy to Ezra

Southwold
[Suffolk]
[27 September 1911]
Wednesday 5.15 P.M.

Dearest: "Yours to hand".

My mistake: I apologize: I mean this: that W.R. [Walter Rummel] is asked to tea on *Thursday 5th:* & can't you come too? The 4th I am busy. My head has been in such a muddle about dates.

Is McConnel "E.McC"?

You are in this week's "Punch": they love you! Also D. [Daily] Mail (was it?).

We have been for a very dull drive: & I feel I shall be at Southwold all
the rest of my life.

My dear:

Yours–

Is McConnel "E. McC"?]   In a previous missing letter EP must have referred
to a "McConnel," perhaps Thomas Leo McConnell (1882–1922), a classmate at
the University of Pennsylvania. DS wonders whether the poem "For E. McC."
(P), first published in *A Lume Spento* (1908) and reprinted in *Personae* (1909)
and *Provença* (1910), was dedicated to him. "For E. McC." was actually written
for Eugene Stock McCartney (1883–1959), a classmate at the University of
Pennsylvania who—as EP says in the subtitle to the poem in *A Lume Spento*—
"was my counter-blade under Leonardo Terrone, Master of Fence." McCartney
received a Ph.D. from Pennsylvania in 1911 and had a long career as a classicist.
The lost friend of the poem (and of the "Rejected Stanza" in the San Trovaso
Notebook, CEP p. 250) was almost certainly EP's "first friend," the young
painter William Brooke Smith, who died in 1908 and to whom *A Lume Spento*
is dedicated.

this week's "Punch"]   The following parody appeared in *Punch,* 141 (27
September 1911), p. 227.

A BALLADE OF DRIVEN GROUSE.

Ye say that your gun's fair gone gyte,
    That you're missin' the coveys a' through,
An' your language is that impolite
      Fowk wad think ye'd the de'il in your moo;
      Here's a ferlie I'd bring tae your view,
(Though aiblins professors 'ud froon,)
      An' ye'll kill once ye ken the way hoo–
It's aye best tae haud into the broun!

They grouse has a gey nesty flight,
    Yin that fair gies a body the grue,
When they link doon the win' quick as light,
      An' ye never could shoot when it blew,
      Though ye're fine at a hare on the ploo
Or a craw when he's branched up aboon;
      Ay, there's mony a lad that's like you,
An' he's best haudin' into the broun!

There's some has a skill an' a sight
    That can pick their birds oot o' the blue,
Be the braes in their braws, or in white
      Wi' snaw-wreaths o' winter-time's brew,
      Come they single, or packed in a crew,
Clean killed, I wad wadger a croon,
      But the likes o' that kind is gey few,
Ye'd be best tae haud into the broun!

ENVOY

Losh, Prince, but ye've got it the noo,
  Yon's a brace an' a half ye ca'd doon,
You're right gin ye ken whit tae do–
  It's aye best tae haud into the broun!

In the same issue (p. 230) is an anonymous poem called "The Modern Orpheus; or, A New Way for Troubadours," based on the report of "a lady farmer [who] has discovered that she improves the condition of her cows and the quality of their milk by playing the mandoline to them daily." One stanza begins:

Hard by the portals of their house
Or in the dewy mead
I'll play them little lumps of STRAUSS,
And bits of EZRA READ . . .

D. Mail]   See Letter **53n.**

53   Dorothy to Ezra

Southwold
[Suffolk]
[1 October 1911]

Dear:

The rain & wind are awful. I shall be glad to be home again. I go on Monday, if you write, to

16. Montpelier Square
Knightsbridge.

Sunday 2 P.M.

Verily October is, for some, begun. Yesterday afternoon the wind & rain were such that all the fishing boats had to be beached, & yours affectionately went out without a hat & helped pull on a rope, with (as Byng would say) several other men. It really was great fun: & then after tea I dragged out □ [Georgie Hyde-Lees] & we helped to move bathing-clothes etc: from a greatly-imperilled hut. Altogether I felt by dinner, that I had earned it. (Vanity oh! vanity!).

This morning, thanks for yours. Lady Low sent us the D. [Daily] Mail cutting about your works, so refer to her: I can't tell you the date, & am not sure it was the D.M. (a typical state of mind with me).

I must pack–the Lord be praised! I could so easily develop a passion for Ming & Famille Rose, jade and ivories–much more easily than for J.G.F. [J.G. Fairfax]–besides he should marry a title to give the £.s.d. raison d'être. I'm talking rubbish. Hurrah! yr. Infallible One is talking rubbish!

I shall try to hypnotize the dragons into well-wishing, and they won't comprehend your yellow head in the least.

Thank you for the olive leaf.

"Prima Vera" bound in black! How agitated & foreign Mrs. Fowler would become.

Your eyelids dear, and
Au revoir.

16 Montpelier Square]   The residence of DS's uncle, Henry Tudor Tucker.
Byng]   One of the Shakespear cats.
D. Mail cutting]   The following unsigned review of *Canzoni* appeared in the *Daily News,* 25 September 1911, p. 3, under the title "A Modern Troubadour."

Mr. Ezra Pound is much more of a troubadour in the present volume than he has managed to be hitherto. His interest in Provençal poetry has always been conspicuous, but in his previous volumes this interest in the most precise and formal of all modern literatures was queerly mingled with an ineffective, jerky kind of expression; his work seemed not so much poetry as the uncompounded elements of poetry. Here, however, in these 'Canzoni,' as the title implies, Mr. Pound has learnt from Arnaut Daniel and the others how to effect the beauty of close, precise, poetic form; and where the troubadours are ruling him his songs are free from the vague explosiveness of his earlier work. As a set-off to that, we miss those sudden moments of bright vision which used to surprise us in the midst of his most violent crudity; the verse is much more level than it was; but if it is more governed, it is certainly more listless; and the imagery sometimes comes perilously near to mechanics. It seems as if Mr. Pound were imitating, whether consciously or not, Provençal poetry in more things than its construction. For the troubadours wrote poetry which was, more than any other poetry, simply the exquisite manners of language. Intricacy of rhyme, delicacy of metre, and the natural beauty of the Langue-d'Oc itself were elements more important to the troubadour's art than sentiment and idea; and even more important than any of these was the music to which the poetry was sung.

We do not know whether Mr. Pound intends his 'Canzoni' to be sung; if he were a real troubadour he would, of course, invent the airs for them himself. Moreover, the troubadour verse was the direct expression of a civilization in which life was elaborated into a formality almost inconceivable to us. Nowadays, therefore, these verse-forms, lacking the music, lacking the flowing Provençal vowels, and lacking the very real inspiration of a beautifully artificial manner of life, can only seem to us strange curiosities of poetry, for Mr. Pound has hardly attempted to pour into these delicate shapes of verse any reality of sentiment or idea. He seems to us rather a scholar than a poet, and we should like to see him giving his unusual talent more to direct translation from the Provençal. Nevertheless, Mr. Pound's canzoni will show the reader a good deal of the troubadour poetic manner, and that is certainly something worth showing.

The author of this review may well have been R.A. Scott-James, the literary editor of the *Daily News*. In the "Literature" section of *The Daily News Year Book* for 1910 (p. 284) he declared that "One new poet stands to the credit of this year, Mr. Ezra Pounds [sic]. In spite of his artificial archaisms, there is a quality of confidence and exaltation in his ideas, added to a striking originality in his vigorous rhythms, which will make it a matter of great interest to watch his promising future." Scott-James had reviewed *Personae* in the *Daily News* of 9 July 1909.

J.G.F.]   James Griffyth Fairfax, the Australian-born journalist and poet. See Biographical Appendix.

"Prima Vera"]   EP had forwarded to DS a post card from Hilda Doolittle which reproduced a detail from Botticelli's "La Primavera."

54   Dorothy to Ezra

> *12 Brunswick Gardens*
> *Kensington*
> *[10 October 1911]*
> *Tuesday evening*

My dear:

Yes: if we are to continue meeting, not à trois or à quatre, I think you should interview H.H.S. [Henry Hope Shakespear, Dorothy's father]–He is, I believe, much more likely to be perfectly sensible than not; possibly he will ask us to take breath until the New Year? I don't know. My only advice to you is, that you will, I am sure, find plain businesslike statements much the most efficacious.

I will tell O.S. [Olivia Shakespear] before 3.45 P.M. on Thursday. For goodness sake meet me then–

This seems to seal my fate to be.

à Toi.

Posted Wednesday morning.   D.

55   Henry Hope Shakespear to Ezra

[Draft letter from H.H.S.'s office files: sent substantially in this form]

> *[Shakespear and Parkyn]*
> *[8 John Street]*
> *[London]*
> *[12 October 1911]*

Dr Mr. Pound:

The subject of our interview yesterday took me quite by surprise & I was not ⟨in a position to⟩ prepared to go at all fully into the statements you made to me as to your financial position & prospects.

I am now writing a purely business letter, & you will I am sure recognise that these are matters which must be carefully gone into by me. I confess I am wholly ignorant of the sources from which a man in your position ⟨gets⟩ derives ⟨his⟩ an income & I shd like you to ⟨give me an idea of⟩ let me know what you have made in, say, the last 12 months & from what sources; also ⟨what⟩ to give me an idea as to what you can reasonably expect to make in the near future.

I understood you to say that from some source ⟨outs⟩ & independent of your own exertions you could calculate on £200 a year. If ⟨you care⟩ I cd satisfy ⟨me⟩ myself that any such sum is or would be secured to you in any event it wd go far to meet the most obvious & glaring difficulty ⟨is that in the case of a man living I feel⟩ which presents itself.

I think it will help to clear the air for both you & me if you give me a reply in writing to these remarks before we discuss the matter further viva voce.

56   Dorothy to Ezra

> *12 Brunswick Gardens*
> *Kensington*
> [*13 October 1911*]
> *Friday*

My dear.

You are to come to tea on Monday, 16th, apparently–Tuesday is some-
one else's day; Wednesday you are out–Thursday is a week away.

You will have got The Letter [see Letter **55**]–which I have not seen:
but am told was in no way unkind. My dragons think the situation in China
terrible: a Presidency–ugh!

Come after 3 ocl. on Monday–& up to me. Good luck for yr. tea party.

> Yours.

Bring those proofs.

situation in China]   The 1911 revolution in China led to the formation of a
Republic with a President.

proofs]   Probably proofs of *Sonnets and Ballate of Guido Cavalcanti* (1912).

57   Henry Hope Shakespear to Ezra

[*Fair copy of original, from H.H.S.'s office files*]

> [*8 John Street*]
> [*London*]
> *16 October* [*1911*]

Dear Mr Pound,

I regret not having replied sooner to your letter, but I was very much
"rushed" on Friday & Saturday.

I thank you for having written to your Father & shall await the pleasure
of a letter from him. I think you will agree with me that the rest of your

letter doesn't carry the matter much further. Macmillan's letter, which I return, is a pleasing recognition. I also return the book of counterfoils from which I am glad to see that you have a balance to your credit.

Yrs. very sincerely
H. Hope Shakespear

If you write here please mark your letters "private" on the outside.

Macmillan's letter . . . book of counterfoils]   As evidence of his financial stability, EP gave Mr. Shakespear a letter from the publisher Macmillan (presumably concerning future contracts) and a record of his bank account. On 22 July 1911 EP boasted in a letter to his mother that Macmillan "is at my feet."

58   Dorothy to Ezra

12 Brunswick Gardens
Kensington
[15 October 1911]
Sunday

Dearest:

Yes: come in tomorrow for tea. I have read the F.M. Hueffer–a queer tale.

I hear from Olivia that you had an amicale meeting at the Office!

Yours
D.

F.M. Hueffer–a queer tale]   Ford Madox Hueffer's *Ladies Whose Bright Eyes* was published in July 1911. Modeled after Mark Twain's *A Connecticut Yankee in King Arthur's Court,* the romance tells of a modern man "thrown back" into the Middle Ages. But the "queer tale" is more likely to be "Riesenberg" [*English Review,* 8 (April 1911)], a fantastic allegory of a "forbidden valley" inhabited by two giants who are described by a German doctor as "survivals of a time which went before the foundations of our splendid Teutonic race." Hugh Kenner has suggested that EP is referring to "Riesenberg" in the famous elegiac passage from Canto 74:

> Lordly men are to earth o'ergiven
> these the companions:
> Fordie that wrote of giants
> and William who dreamed of nobility

59   Dorothy to Ezra

12 Brunswick Gardens
Kensington
[18 October 1911]
Wednesday

My dear:

Please come on Friday. O.S. [Olivia Shakespear] is somewhat reluctant - - - *"Twice* a week?"

If that letter from America ain't satisfactory - - - I shall have to ask you myself.

Yours
D.

letter from America]   EP had asked Homer Pound to send a letter to Mr. Shakespear confirming his son's financial resources. On 14 November 1911 Homer Pound wrote that he had the greatest confidence in his son, and that to the best of his knowledge EP had an income of $1000 per year in addition to royalties from his books. On 28 November 1911 Mr. Shakespear replied:

> I thank you for writing to me–I fear that your Son has somewhat misunderstood something I said to him. He stated to me that he was at present in receipt of an income of $1000 [£200] a year outside anything he made by his literary work.
>
> I never for a moment doubted the accuracy of his statement: but he gave no information as to the source from which he received this sum, nor did he seem prepared to say that it was of a permanent nature; & *this* is of course the most important thing. Literary work of the kind for which he is, no doubt, eminently suited is not likely for some years to furnish him with the means of supporting a Wife.
>
> We like him personally very much, & consider he has great abilities; but until he has some regular income in addition to a permanently secured £200 a year, it is obvious that he is not in a position to marry.

60 Dorothy to Ezra

12 Brunswick Gardens
Kensington
[22 October 1911]
Sunday

Dearest:

At present I have ascertained that O.S. [Olivia Shakespear] is expecting Nelly [Georgie Hyde-Lees's mother] to tea tomorrow (Monday)–So I think we must be fairly safe? I will be there anyway–& if you don't feel you had better come–why, I'll go look at Greek things by myself.

What a gale–
Yours.

61 Ezra to Dorothy

[London]
[28 October 1911]

Dearest:

I forgot to bring away 'Il Paradiso' as you may have noticed. Will you bring both copies.

As for the rest I wonder if we can not look at the beginning of things as a sort of divine phantasmagoria or vision or what you will and the 'vagueness' etc as a sort of smoke–an incident in the much more difficult process of drawing down the light, of embodying it, of building it into the stiffer materia of actualities. The whole thing a process of art, of the more difficult art in which we are half media & half creators.

CHARS think this getting orfully polysyllabic.

I have written some preface but I had this ready before I started the preface, so it aint wholly the result of a plethora of prose.

A toi–& Tuesday is infernally distant & the park was very crisp & pleasant this morning.

"All-golden mercy in the golden flare
of the great trees our seven lights in chief".

E.

some preface]   This could be a rewriting of the "monstrous long introduction" to Arnaut Daniel mentioned in Letter **35**.

"All-golden . . . lights in chief"]   These lines pick up the tone, imagery, and two of the rhyme-sounds of "Canzon: The Yearly Slain" (CEP), a reply to Frederic Manning's "Korè" first published in the *English Review,* 4 (January 1910).

62   Dorothy to Ezra

12 Brunswick Gardens
Kensington
[2 November 1911]
Thursday 10 A.M.

Dearest:

No: I'm afraid I can't 'venture'! "Until something is settled" as Olivia says ("settled", I ask you!). She would evidently so much rather we didn't do anything of that sort–anything for a quiet Life–& as you don't even say what the lecture is about–it can't be over-exciting? I'll be home by three ocl. tomorrow afternoon (Friday)–

Saw W.R. [Walter Rummel] last night at Bechstein.

Step-cousin comes next Tuesday–her name is [Georgie] Hyde-Lees.

I have made a rough idea of the tryptich–to get started on–

Yours
D.

10.30 P.M.

Mrs. [Hamilton] Fletcher & I have just arranged a profession for me–to be most remunerative–flower-decorator at private-houses–Think it'll do? I might surreptitiously leave your poems lying about, you see (which I have *not* mentioned to her) every now & then.

Bechstein]   A London concert hall, later known as Wigmore Hall.

Mrs. Fletcher]   Mr. and Mrs. Hamilton Fletcher, who owned Leweston Manor, near Sherborne, Dorset, were old friends of the Shakespear family.

63   Dorothy to Ezra

Lee Priory
Littlebourne
Canterbury
[*25 November 1911*]
Saturday

Mercy! *Two* letters from you awaiting my arrival–everybody quite discreet until this morning–curiosity got the better of my arnt [sic], who said lightly "Two letters in the same hand, weren't they?" So I refrained from looking self-conscious with a noble effort of will & said it was important information etc: etc: Meanwhile yours is great news, if the naïve one's contract seems all right.

I came yesterday evening & have already talked through with my cousin all the things that the arnt would think most *un*suitable conversation for two girls.

We were perhaps unnecessarily discreet on Wed. Even: but I feel sure somebody or other must have noticed the wrapt expression on my features & [Walter] Rummel's!! I saw him on Thursday & duly thanked him–O.S. [Olivia Shakespear] radiated disapproval - - - her judgement lately has gone astray a little. I meant the toothbrush– –I upset □ [Georgie Hyde-Lees] by whispering confidentially that the toothbrush had arrived & so on–She thinks your flippancy terrible–She is used to mine.

How can I write you a decent letter when I am in the girls' sitting room & there is desultory chatter going on. The cold is awful.

The post goes shortly, so yr. name & address may yet be concealed! Not that I care!

My dear:
Yours.

"Reincarnation" quotha. I never *have* believed in it!

naïve one's contract]   Probably a reference to Charles Granville and EP's
contract with Stephen Swift and Co., the publishers of *Sonnets and Ballate of
Guido Cavalcanti* (May 1912) and *Ripostes* (October 1912). See Letter **69n.**

64   Dorothy to Ezra

> *Lee Priory*
> *Littlebourne*
> *Canterbury*
> [*27 November 1911*]
> *Monday*

Dearest.

Come in to tea on Wednesday if you can? I get up to Victoria [Station]
just before 3 ocl. so should be ready for you about 4 ocl. Or else on Thurs-
day 2.30 to *my* room (some one to lunch, & Bergson 4.30)? Or both! No
answer needed.

Have just been motoring: to Canterbury: a fine Cathedral.

> *Tuesday*

I shall be glad to be home again–I hoped to hear from you–but expect
you've no special news. *I* have none.

> Yours
> D.

Bergson]   T.E. Hulme (see Biographical Appendix) gave several lectures
on Bergson at a private house in Kensington in November/December 1911. At
the same time he was publishing articles on Bergson in the *New Age*.

65   Dorothy to Ezra

12 Brunswick Gardens
Kensington
[2 December 1911]
Saturday

Dearest.

1 ocl. upstairs Hill's: and if you can come back to tea, tant mieux. You were very cheerful at 124 Kn. [Knightsbridge] weren't you? I can't get my fill of sleep this week. W.R. [Walter Rummel] was here playing to Nelly [Georgie Hyde-Lees's mother] last night & we had the Schumann again: its splendid.

My friend Nancy [Maude] came to lunch–looking so handsome & full of so many things–married life has agreed with her well.

☐ [Georgie] comes to Dante [Yeats] on Thursday, after all. I must go to shop.

A Toi.

Hill's]   A music shop in Bond Street.
124 Kn.]   124 Knightsbridge: the address of Mrs. Eva Fowler's town house.
Nancy]   Nancy Maude. See Biographical Appendix.

66   Dorothy to Ezra

12 Brunswick Gardens
Kensington
[5 December 1911]
Tuesday

My dear:

Yes, come back to lunch on Thursday & if you [can] face Hulme–Bergson again we can go down together.

I am sorry I was a fool yesterday. I suppose I was more tired than I knew–I have been leading the strenuous life lately: & shall have to continue it until Xmas. After that, I think I shall have a rest-cure, & see no one but you.

O.S. [Olivia Shakespear] remarked this morning that "your Hilda" was a Hamadryad–which hits it, doesn't it?

> Dearest
> a toi.

Hulme–Bergson]   See Letter **64n.**

"your Hilda" . . . *Hamadryad*]   Hilda Doolittle, the American poet who had known EP and William Carlos Williams when she was a student at Bryn Mawr College near Philadelphia. See Biographical Appendix. EP called Hilda Doolittle the Dryad, and "The Tree"—later the first poem in *Personae: The Collected Poems* (1926)—was part of *Hilda's Book,* a collection of poems made for her in 1906–07. Olivia Shakespear transformed the initials "H.D." into "Hamadryad," a wood nymph said to live and die with the tree that she inhabits.

67   Dorothy to Ezra

> *Leweston Manor*
> *Sherborne*
> *Dorset*

[Selections from letters of 22–28–30–31 December 1911]

> *Saturday 5.30 P.M.*

Such a lovely day–roamed about the Garden by myself in the morning, & tried to make friends with a Shetland pony. The house is decorated with holly & mistletoe: I feel the latter doesn't concern me–and I can't reach it to send you a leaf! I am reading a trans: of Cellini's Life. [- - -]

No! no! I don't want a large country-house–I should ask all my guests & then go away myself: they would drive one distracted–

The really nice people are the spaniels–two. The room mine (an inside one) opens into is haunted, too: & I imagine things in the night.

I don't much fancy the Castle–no: its a mill–above the Lakes: perhaps you have methods of exorcism?

Last night I tried drawing [a five-pointed star]–then there's a more complicated one with seven points–O.S. [Olivia Shakespear] makes an 8 & puts the good at the top–white: & the black is forced into the bottom circle– but I feel afraid of it. Fact is–hum! hum!

Sunday

Oh! that female–She was the wife of a genius (Linly Samborne) &, become a widow, she reads Ella Wheeler Wilcox–& babbles–not of green fields–but of every imaginable folly that doesn't matter–

Heaven defend & preserve me from picking up *any* arts' claptrap, by which to deceive the innocent & madden the wise.

I am delighting in Lionel's Essays. I have only read the Pater ones as yet–I had not found out that that strange quality in Pater was a discreet humour–I daresay it is–I must read "Marius" again.

Thursday

I have been hearing a lot about the Loire Chateaux & the south of France places–Nîmes, Arles, etc: do you know any of them?

Friday

I hope you will have had a good poetical influence on Fred [Frederic Manning]–& he a good prose on you!

Saturday 10.30 P.M.

Ah ha! at least I have come upon the serious subject treated frivolously–Mark Twain's "Christian Science" is, as the boys say, "priceless". Its the most entertaining work I have read for ages–& withal no Tom-foolery whatever.

I think that "Purgatorio" of Shadwell is the one with the Pater introduction, isn't it? [- - -]

You would have smiled to see my afternoon promenade yesterday–one queer dog on a string, strangely reluctant; a white Pekinese under the other arm: a spaniel pup round about, & four carrots, as bouquet, for the Shetlands. [- - -]

I am trying to like George Herbert–but don't much.

Sunday

I am sure I have no suggestions for your long poem. You might damn the Commonplace–and all the unemployed, (meaning myself). [- - -]

Now I am to go to church–& *such* a church. Pray for me–it's more than I'm likely to do for you there.

trans: of Cellini's Life]   Several translations of *The Life of Benvenuto Cellini Written by Himself* appeared in the late 19th and early 20th centuries, including one by John Addington Symonds.

Linly Samborne]   Linley Sambourne (1845–1910), artist and illustrator, who was for many years chief political cartoonist for *Punch*.

Ella Wheeler Wilcox]   An American poet (1850–1919), perhaps the most widely read and quoted versifier of her generation. When *A Lume Spento* was published in 1908 EP asked Ella Wheeler Wilcox to review it, and her notice appeared in December 1908, copyrighted by the American-Journal-Examiner syndicate. A clipping in Homer Pound's scrapbook (now at Yale), which does not include the name of the newspaper, is headed "New York, December 14, 1908." The review was also published in the *Chicago Evening American* on 17 December 1908, and may have appeared in other newspapers. The title of the review sets its tone: "A New Singer of Songs: The Greeting of a Poetess of Established Fame to a Newcomer Among the Bards." After a description of the book and its dedication, Mrs. Wilcox strikes a personal note.

> The name of the poet is 'Ezra Pound,' and when I realize that this poet is grown to the age of manhood it makes my own youth seem far and far away; for somewhere among my souvenirs of a Springtime of life there is a little tintype picture of several youths and maidens; and the father of this poet is among the number; and so am I.
>
> And then I stop and remember that my own wee son, who tarried so short a time on earth, would be also man-grown were he here; and he too, might be writing verses, even as the son of my friend of long ago.
>
> And so, with more than the interest of an older writer in a young singer, I give these strange, and weird, and new songlets a setting here, that 'those who love what he loves after his own fashion' may read.

This is followed by extensive if rather jumbled quotations, and a final flourish: "Success to you, young singer in Venice! Success to 'With Tapers Quenched.' "

EP's father, Homer Pound, had known Ella Wheeler Wilcox when he was a young man. Marian Culver, the first wife of the poet Basil Bunting, interviewed Homer in Rapallo in 1931 and reported that he "had photographs of each of the twenty-five young ladies in Eau Claire [Wisconsin]. The most precious picture, however, is that of Homer Pound with the late lamented Ella Wheeler Wilcox, taken in Chicago in 1880. Mrs. Wilcox never recovered from a sentimental interest in Homer Pound as some of her poems testify" [*Chippewa Herald-Telegram*, Chippewa Falls, Wisconsin, 29 April 1931].

Lionel's Essays]   Lionel Johnson (1867–1902), critic and poet, a first cousin of Olivia Shakespear. His poem "Lines to a Lady Upon Her Third Birthday" (1889), written for Dorothy, concludes:

> And I,
> Despite all dark fates, Dorothy!
> Will prove me thine affectionate
> Cousin, and loyal Laureate.

In 1911 Elkin Mathews published *Post Liminium: Essays and Critical Papers by Lionel Johnson;* the first section, "Notes on Walter Pater," contains four essays written between 1893 and 1900.

"Marius"]   Walter Pater, *Marius the Epicurean* (1885).

Mark Twain's]   *Christian Science: With Notes Containing Corrections to Date* (1907).

"Purgatorio" of Shadwell]   *The Purgatory of Dante Alighieri,* translated by Charles Lancelot Shadwell, with an introduction by Walter Pater (1892).

your long poem]   Further evidence that EP was planning a "long poem," ultimately the *Cantos,* as early as 1911.

1912

68   Dorothy to Ezra

[Kensington]
[21 February 1912]
Wednesday

Dearest.

It seems an unnecessary while until Friday.

I was deeply interested in [G.R.S.] Mead–so, I think, was G. [Georgie Hyde-Lees]. I liked the picture of the seaweeds (⟨in N. Age last week⟩ (I cracked) P. Review)–It has the same movement, swinging, trying to get up, but held by the stalk, that Debussy's "Mouvement" always gives me: Only your green colour is more pleasant.

I thought I had several things to say–but apparently not. If by any chance I hear Friday wont do–Will you come up on Sat. Morning 11 ocl? No answer needed.

A Toi–

N. Age . . . P. Review]   DS first thought *New Age,* then corrected this to *Poetry Review.* "Sub Mare" (P), which contains the lines "Algae reach up and out, beneath/ Pale slow green surgings of the underwave," was first published in the *Poetry Review,* 1 (February 1912).

69   Ezra to Henry Hope Shakespear

10 Church Walk
[London] W.
[12 March 1912]

Dear Mr. Shakespear:

I am sorry to bother you again with my affairs, nevertheless they have somewhat advanced–to about £400 per. year, with reasonable chance of increase. This would not go very far in England but Dorothy seems to think she could live abroad for a year or so. This seems feasible and she could see a number of things & places which she probably could not see if I were tied to an educational position. At any rate the idea seems to interest her more than the prospect of keeping house in one set locality.

I dare say you think it a rather mad-cap scheme but there is a chance she might enjoy it. As to my assets above the £200, about which I have already written–there's the £100 per. yr. from my publishers for work *"in book form"*. I've had inserted the clause about returning any *mss.* not used by them, as you suggested. The minimum of 60,000 words per. yr. as required is ⟨only what⟩ not more than what I could do comfortably in two months, so I don't think it likely that I shall fail on that score–even if I did have a break down. The son of some rather solid people has just gone in as junior partner, so I feel fairly confident about the firm.

Income from other sources could I think be reasonably counted at £100. pr. yr. Actual receipts, Nov. 1 to Feb. 29, £38. I shall not offer this month's (March) receipts for average as the returns from my lectures are more than what seems to me fair for purpose of gauging an average.

Sincerely yours
Ezra Pound

my publishers]   Stephen Swift and Co., publishers of *Sonnets and Ballate of Guido Cavalcanti* (May 1912) and *Ripostes* (October 1912). The company had agreed to publish EP's books for a period of ten years, giving him £100 per year as an advance against royalties, but on 5 November 1912 EP wrote to his father that " 'Swift' is busted. They caught the *mgr.* in Tangier with *some* of the goods." On 29 November 1912 he reported to his mother that he was "getting satisfactory terms out of Swift's liquidator."

son . . . as junior partner]   Possibly Charles Granville, the proprietor of the *Freewoman* (see Letter **172n**). "His firm, Stephen Swift, published in the main unorthodox writers, free-thinkers and mystics, but their list also included Katherine Mansfield" [Jane Lidderdale and Mary Nicholson, *Dear Miss Weaver* (New York, 1970), p. 55]. Charles Granville himself wrote several volumes of poetry, essays, and fiction.

my lectures]   Early in 1912 EP gave his lecture on "Psychology and Troubadours" to the Quest Society (see Letter **48**). On March 14, 19, and 21 he gave three lectures on Mediaeval Poetry in Lord Glenconner's "private gallery." The first was on Guido Cavalcanti, the second on Arnaut Daniel, and the third on Anglo-Saxon Verse. Admission was £1. 1s. for the course of three lectures, or 10s. 6d. for a single lecture.

By the kind permission of
LORD AND LADY GLENCONNER.

EZRA POUND, M.A.

(Author of " Exultations," " Canzoni,"
" The Spirit of Romance ")

WILL GIVE

THREE LECTURES ON

MEDIÆVAL POETRY

AT

34 QUEEN ANNE'S GATE, S.W.,

AS FOLLOWS, AT 3.30.

THURSDAY, MARCH 14TH.

TUSCANY, A.D. 1290 : GUIDO CAVALCANTI.
In the Chair—FREDERIC MANNING.

TUESDAY, MARCH 19TH.

PROVENCE, A.D. 1190 : ARNAUT DANIEL.
In the Chair—

THURSDAY, MARCH 21ST.

ENGLAND, A.D. 790 : ANGLO-SAXON VERSE.
In the Chair—W. B. YEATS.

The Three Schools will be considered in part, in their possible
relation to the Art of to-day.

TICKETS may be obtained on application to LADY LOW, 23 De
Vere Gardens, Kensington, W.

For the Course of Three Lectures, £1 1s.
Admittance to Single Lectures, 10s. 6d.

As Audience is limited to FIFTY an early application is desirable.

70   Dorothy to Ezra

[*Kensington*]
[*19 March 1912*]
Tuesday

Dearest.

Yes. Come in on Thursday morning–& if you can stay to lunch, O.S.
[Olivia Shakespear] asks you–let me know. She doesn't understand your
methods of pursuing life: & thinks we might as well know about yr. con-

tract–but I have told H.H.S. [Dorothy's father] we won't bother him at present. She also says that there is a "Society for the Protection of Authors" which, if you join, will give you legal advice– –(free, I understand)– She says she has heard W.B.Y. [Yeats] speak of it–in the event of yr. wanting any more contracts.

She evidently thinks we are a somewhat crazy couple–which is just what we aren't. Perhaps you wish we were.

I am just off to the dentist: & this evening 8.30 go to the Bechstein Hall to hear Marinetti lecture in French, about les Futuristes.

Yours   D.

"Society for the Protection of Authors"]   The Society of Authors was founded in 1884 by leading men of letters to promote reform in the copyright laws and to maintain "friendly relations between authors and publishers, by means of properly drawn agreements."

Marinetti lecture]   The following report of the lecture appeared in the London *Times,* 21 March 1912, p. 2.

> The Aims of Futurism.—At the Bechstein Hall [now the Wigmore Hall] on Tuesday Signor Marinetti, the founder of the Futurist Movement, gave a lecture on Futurism in literature and art. He read his lecture in French with such an impassioned torrent of words that some of his audience begged for mercy, and of his sincerity there can be no question, but his doctrines are a morbid form of destructive revolution. There is no beauty, according to the Futurists, except in violence and strife: every museum and all the great works of the past should be utterly swept away.

71   Dorothy to Ezra

12 Brunswick Gardens
Kensington
[2 April 1912]
Tuesday

Dearest.

The roses are delicious–As I go in a fur coat & mean to travel 1st Class (crowds) I think they will look well in my front! Did you see a fine eclipse of the moon last night about 10. ocl?

I will send you a p. card or so! That's probably all. And, thank Heaven, I don't know my destination, except Wells tomorrow night.

Yours

D.

72   Dorothy to Ezra

South Western Hotel
Southampton
[8 April 1912]

My dear.

I am glad I am not sailing for America from here, I confess! It's cold & windy–& the hotel is so magnificent, it scared me into changing for dinner & having a bath! The food though is delicious, & the bill no affair of mine.

I am enclosing wild thyme from a neolithic Camp [Maiden Castle] near Dorchester (where we lay yesterday morning) & also a cowslip from one of the same camp's earthworks. We saw a Roman amphitheatre there, which was probably a Temple of the Sun before that: a very wonderful shape. [sketch]

I am de trop in this room–which is being swept–so with my thyme my love.

I am with the Leafs until Thursday–so perhaps you can tea on *Friday?* We go to Romsey & Winchester today.

à Toi

the Leafs]   Rose Mary La Roche Shakespear, Hope Shakespear's youngest sister, married Herbert Leaf, a wealthy Assistant Master at Marlborough College. See Biographical Appendix.

73   Dorothy to Ezra

12 Brunswick Gardens
Kensington
[13 April 1912]
Saturday

Dearest–

Please come in on Monday. And one shall be charmed to see Pavlova one evening; any evening except Monday or Tuesday. But O.S. [Olivia Shakespear] says she wishes to pay for our tickets–
I am just going to have my hair washed, oh! woe!

Yours
D.

Pavlova]   Anna Pavlova (1882–1931), the great Russian ballerina who made London her permanent home in 1912. See Letter **95**.

74   Dorothy to Ezra

[Kensington]
[20 April 1912]
Saturday 1.15 P.M.

My dear

What am I to do about Miss Mary Moore? I dont know her address– nor any reason why I am to ask her to tea. Will you tell her the New Century Club on Tuesday at 4. ocl? Has she never been in London before?
Oh! yes. Olivia says you really must *not* wear in London that turn down collar, with a black coat–I have no doubt she is right - - - but I myself never know about men's clothes.

Yours
D.

Put tea on Tuesday nicely for me to M.M.

Miss Mary Moore]   *Personae* (1909) bears the dedication: "This book is for Mary Moore of Trenton, if she wants it." See Biographical Appendix.

75   Dorothy to Ezra

[*Kensington*]
26 April [*1912*]
8.15 P.M.

Dearest:

No time this afternoon to ask you for Mary Moore's address. Will you
send it along before you go to Cambridge? I hope W.B.Y. [Yeats] is duly
grateful & impressed about his books!

Don't be more tired than need be for Cambridge. And if you can come
in here on Monday at 2.30–tant mieux. *If* you go up to Yeats tomorrow
morning–I left cards for labels–but no pins–the latter are in the "attache"
case.

A Toi–

W.B.Y. *. . . . about his books*]   EP and DS may have helped Yeats in wrap-
ping and mailing copies of his books which had been published in the autumn
and winter of 1911–12, when he spent most of his time in Dublin working with
the Abbey Theatre. *Plays for an Irish Theatre* and Theatre Editions of *The Pot
of Broth, The Green Helmet,* and *The King's Threshold* appeared in November–
December 1911. It is also possible that prepublication copies of *The Countess
Cathleen* (revised version) and *The Land of Heart's Desire,* published in June
1912, were available in late April.

for Cambridge]   On Saturday, April 27, EP read a paper to an undergradu-
ate literary society at King's College, Cambridge. T.E. Hulme took Edward
Marsh (the future editor of *Georgian Poetry, 1911–1912*) to hear it.

76   Dorothy to Ezra

[*Kensington*]
3 May 1912
Friday morning

My dearest.

I of course thought, until I had read it twice, that the wreck of the
Calais boat Train was the one you were in (She ran off the rails or some-
thing).

The weather has broken: it is raining hard, so I shall have to go out & roll in the new gravel. The day you left M. Moore [Mary Moore of Trenton] came to lunch & Tubby did not: She & I went on to the Wallace [Collection]. The little boy with his arms folded up his sleeves is very charming, but too large somehow: there are two exquisite very tiny pictures by Watteau, of clowns & harlequins.

Yesterday Mat-Mat [Arthur Galton] came to lunch–so he & O.S. [Olivia Shakespear] & I rushed up to the Zoo for a while. We watched the King Penguin for ages. He is most lovely: gray shawl, yellow shading down his lovely front & yellow near his eyes. His cousin called to him for five minutes in a persuasive voice & he came slowly to speak to her–four steps at a time & then a rest: all the ordinary little penguins were sitting on a rock above his path, watching him intently & quite awe-stricken by his royal manner! Mat-Mat will stand for hours in front of nice creatures while their aunt & Coz [Olivia and Dorothy] talk folly to them.

There is a great plan afoot that O. [Olivia] & self, Mat-Mat & Fred [Manning] should go to Oxford for a week later. I believe it would be most delightful. Apparently old [Selwyn] Image gets some £400 a year for his Slade Prof: & has only to give twelve lectures a year there.

Last night W.B.Y. [Yeats] & Mat-Mat dined together at Eva's [Eva Fowler], with O.S. & Miss Aimée Lowther (have you met her ever?). There was nearly (as Taffy [Mr. Fowler] put it) "a scrap"–A. Lowther suddenly & for no reason attacked the innocent Eagle [Yeats]–She hates Poets & Irishmen–the two combined were over-much for her. *She* was very rude, & the Eagle *nearly* lost his excellent Temper!!

On Tuesday we go to
    c/o Miss Hayes
        Broomhill Hotel
        West Malvern
        Worcestershire.

Oh! yes! H.H.S.'s [Mr. Shakespear's] only comment on your early visit on Wedy. was "I thought he was going abroad". I believe he had been under the impression, for a week at least, that you were safely awa'.

The little Byng [the Shakespears' cat], as usual, understands his cousin, & has been up two mornings & slept on her lap–a great honour–

Saturday

Glad to have yours: I thought you would write first, being the traveller. We had tea yest. with "Richard" [Aldington]. But exactly as I supposed, he asked us when feeling lonely, & then when we came didn't a bit want to see friends–also there were some other fools there.

I have read "The Shepherd's Life"–It has nice tales in it, & I liked the stout cat who fished every day.

I wish I were in Paris: it must be exquisite–& the ducks adorable. But nothing can be so nice as the penguin.

I like the Verlaine.

Byngdy interrupted here–

With love, my dear,

Ever yours, D.

P.S.

Byng has settled on my lap & I *have* such a lot of things to do.

Tubby]   Possibly Robert Emmons Rogers (see Letter **170n**), whose nickname was "Tubby."

Mat-Mat]   Rev. Arthur Galton, a friend of the Shakespear family who was called "Mat-Mat" because he took pride in having known Matthew Arnold. See Biographical Appendix.

Image . . . Slade Prof]   Selwyn Image (1849–1930), artist and poet, co-edited the *Hobby Horse* in the 1890s. EP met him in February 1909, and later that year they both contributed to *The Book of the Poets' Club* (Christmas, 1909). In section VII of the first part of *Hugh Selwyn Mauberley,* "Monsieur Verog" speaks of "Image impartially imbued / With raptures for Bacchus, Terpsichore and the Church." Image was Slade Professor of Fine Art at Oxford, 1910–16.

Aimée Lowther]   On 31 January 1909 EP wrote to his mother that he "had lunch with Miss Lowther at the house of a lady with wonderful sapphires." When she died in 1935 a friend wrote to the London *Times* (12 February 1935): "Aimée Lowther will not be forgotten by those who enjoyed her friendship. Her genius was for conversation, and its distinctive trait was intellectual vitality. It was by no means monologue, nor was it argumentative. . . . Her taste in literature . . . was for French writers . . . . Perhaps she would not suffer fools very gladly, but what she said in their absence was nothing compared with what she said to their faces."

"Richard"]   Richard Aldington, the English poet, novelist, and critic who married Hilda Doolittle ("H.D.") in 1913. See Biographical Appendix.

"The Shepherd's Life"]   In *A Shepherd's Life* (1910) the travel and nature writer W.H. Hudson (1841–1922) tells of the people and animals of the Wiltshire Downs.

the Verlaine]   Not identified. At a recital on 1 March 1910 Miss Florence Schmidt (Mrs. Derwent Wood) sang four songs with texts by Paul Verlaine. EP supplied translations for the program sold at the recital.

77   Dorothy to Ezra

Broomhill Hotel
West Malvern
Worcestershire
[8 May 1912]

Dearest.

We came yesterday–and immediately rushed out & walked wildly round the School Grounds–outside. Everything is lovely; all pale green; and the views for miles & miles so blue. I had quite forgotten how far one could see–right into Wales & on & on.

This morning early we went to St. James' & attacked Miss Baird [the Headmistress]—with the result that we have now the run of the grounds for when & as long as we like! There is an orchard of apples–very pink– There are tulips–and such azaleas–flame coloured, near a pond. Old Lady de Walden was no fool when she planted her garden.

In answer to yours. No–of course, I can't manage Paris–as you say–a "strange female" and then I'm *here!* Of course I should love St. Jean de Luz. (My grandfather–O.S.'s f.–used to sternly pronounce it St. Jeen de Luz). But really I don't see that that is possible either. You see if we were officially engaged it might do - - - But as Father "won't recognize" our engagement - - -

You might thank "Margaret" [Cravens] very much though for proposing to invite me–it's extraordinarily good of her anyway. And don't talk to too many of your best friends about me. I have had to suppress M. Moore [Mary Moore of Trenton].

I am glad the Hamadryad [Hilda Doolittle] is not lost. Is 'Richard' [Aldington] preferred to W.R. [Walter Rummel] at present?

I have gathered a very country bouquet of cowslips, "cuckoo" flower, bluebells & an autumn scarlet blackberry leaf.

Three other people in the pension–Who will try to talk of course. G. [Georgie Hyde-Lees] & I hope to be in the Garden all day or on the hills.

Its lunch Time & I am starving. I wore the Ring round my neck last night! I am glad to be in the country–& such country too as this.

A Toi.

I enclose a piece of sweet scented briar rose.

D.

St. James']   St. James's School was originally in Hampshire, and then in Crowborough, Sussex (1900–02). On 28 November 1902 the school reopened in West Malvern, Worcestershire, with the four Baird sisters the " 'one man' manager of the school," as the local newspaper put it.

Lady de Walden]   Previous owner of the house and grounds that became St. James's School. When the gardens were first laid out in 1894 she employed seventy gardeners.

"Margaret"]   Margaret Cravens (1881–1912), an American pianist living in Paris, who studied under Ravel. EP met her through Walter Rummel in Paris in March 1910. She committed suicide in June 1912: see Letters **86–92.**

78   Dorothy to Ezra

Broomhill Hotel
West Malvern
11 May 1912
Saturday

My dear–

I have just got some gold paint which excites me rather. I must do something with it: I wish I had an idea how to design–Have you anything for me to try to make a pattern for? I have done two sketches & a half: the half hopes to be finished tomorrow. We have also decided that the 66 girls at St. James' are like ants swarming busily round in their heap.

There is a Tempio in the Garden called "The House of Fame" where names are put up when a girl leaves, with her dates. I meant to do an allegorical painting of it–but it won't do: the Fame isn't worth talking about, and the Tempio is in a hollow instead of on a hill. True, there is a cypress avenue leading to it–but - - -

I have just been for a long walk–found a new flower, very blue indeed,

& a charming bird, which may have been a lark, quite close: it hopped along beside me, & we had much conversation: it was feigning a broken wing–so I imagine it had a nest somewhere near.

Sunday
After a heavy lunch!

We went for a fine discovery walk this morning: found lovely fields & flowers, and a magnificent quarry to sketch in–(it pouring with rain now). At the quarry we were invited into a shed & shown six retriever pups: one week old, three tan & three black–oh! so very fat & adorable!

It is very pleasant to be away from one's family & "on the loose"–Also I feel most robust–quite an energetic Coz! Georgie [Hyde-Lees] wants to know what Spanish to read beside Lopez [Lope de Vega] & Calderon. She has tried some modern verse, but seems to have pitched upon rubbish. So I said I'd ask you.

I have been trying to read Tolstoi's "What is Art". Perhaps Grenell would find it interesting–I can't be doing with it. Silly old white bearded prophet.

So now I am on to Renan's "Vie de Jésus". Of course–delightful: I have never read any of his before. He speaks of the "Carrière vagabonde" of Jésus - - -

Your robust feeling Coz.   D.

Tolstoi's "What is Art"]   *What Is Art?*, by Leo Tolstoy (1828–1910), first appeared in 1897. Arguing that great art must have moral and religious purposes, Tolstoy rejects as "bad art" his own early works, as well as some masterpieces by Shakespeare and Wagner.

Grenell]   Charles Edward Grinnell (1841–1916), a Boston lawyer and author. Grinnell graduated from the Harvard Divinity School in 1865, and was pastor of the Harvard Church in Charlestown, Mass., from 1869 to 1873. He then turned to the law, and was admitted to the bar in 1876. His publications include sermons and several books on legal matters. In 1881–82 and 1907–09 he was editor of the *American Law Review*.

On 21 February 1912 EP told his mother that "Old Grinnel is back from Russia & very enthusiastic & disenclined to agree with Tolstoi & the general squalor & pessimism of the advertised russian litterati." In Canto 93 EP links "Old Grinell" with the hokku he had quoted in his essay "D'Artagnan Twenty Years After" [*Criterion,* 16 (July 1937); *Selected Prose,* p. 453]:

"The waves rise, and the waves fall
But you are like the moon-light:
Always there!"
Old Grinell had remembered that.

Renan's "Vie de Jésus"]   Ernest Renan (1823–1892), French philosopher
and historian of religions. His *Vie de Jésus* (1863), which treats Jesus as an
"incomparable Man" and shows how early Christianity was shaped by the popu-
lar imagination, was denounced by the Church as "atheistic."

79   Dorothy to Ezra

> *Broomhill*
> *West Malvern*
> *[19 May 1912]*
> *Sunday*

My dear.

This should catch you in Paris before 21st–if you go that day. A horrid
Man has come for Sunday & so we have had to give up the smoking room,
which we were allowed to use, to him: he has a bad face & his wife a very
"tight" one: I suppose he tries her severely: & there is a swarm of their off-
spring, all red-headed & sickly-looking: I believe they hail from Birming-
ham.

I had pleasantly picturesque dreams last night–one I shall try to paint
later. The other was of a Nijinsky–Amor dance: A bow & arrow–but the
arrow came back boomerang–fashion to near where it started from: and
one was let fly & came back to me, changed into a golden oak-leaf–& no-
one understood it was for me except myself & Nijinsky.
Ha! Work!!
(My late mistress [at school] says I am sentimental–but then *she* is–hope-
lessly).

I hate scholarly methods–so Renan without contemporary literature is
delightful. I always supposed somehow the Christ was interesting: but
school & Protestant methods are boring. *You* can be scholarly: I'll be sur-
face: I can't be anything else! But nevertheless I am painting quite half-
seriously. And I love it very much.

I will send the Guido [*Cavalcanti*] off when I go home the end of the month–if they have arrived.

Yours, dear.

P.S. Angleterre, not Anglaterre!

Nijinsky–Amor dance]   Vaslav Nijinsky (1890–1950), the leading dancer of Diaghilev's Ballets Russes. A symbol of the *avant-garde,* the Russian Ballet was one of the great intellectual and social events in the London of 1911–12.
Renan]   See Letter **78n.**

80   Dorothy to Ezra

Broomhill
West Malvern
[*21 May 1912*]
Tuesday

My dear.

Our letters crossed I imagine. I have just been asleep after an exhausting morning painting up at the quarry–The pups are so fat & delightful–There's a thunderstorm brewing in the South and a heath-fire on the West–The hedges are white with May–I did a telegraph pole in a stretch this morning & its quite decent!

I am enjoying myself very much altogether very much–I hope you will find Provence equally congenial. Liberty & the country certainly are very nice sometimes. I have got a piece of so-called "victor's laurel" to show you. It has a queer little extra leaf growing out of the middle of each large one. I have been promised some in a pot.

Renan continues quite delightful, but I have very little time for reading–just fancy!

Thursday

It poured all yesterday & we were somewhat bored. I have been using this pen for gold ink, & it now shines a little–I tried to do the Laurel in gold & black–on brown paper–a fine colour scheme.

The old lady in the room below mine announced this morning that something had *bumped* heavily in the early dawn over her head: She had evidently had a panic. But as it was quite certainly not from me, I haven't been able to at all reassure her! My room was full of some unpleasant personality when I came but its getting better.

Today wonderful clouds & a raging wind–so cold. There isn't anything whatever "to tell you". I have put my late head mistress on to one of Francis Galton's books– –lots about heredity, the vision habit, & also visualization in all forms: so I hope she'll talk about it all the next time I go to tea.

I can't imagine your giving lectures there! Sixty girls in a heap are awful. They are savage & unpleasant.

I am reading some of St. Gregory: I like the man who "met a footstool"!

You will tell me when & where you go after Paris? Meanwhile I am your devoted

Coz.

one of Francis Galton's books] Francis Galton (1822–1911), English anthropologist and founder of the school of "Eugenics." His *Inquiries into Human Faculty and Its Development* (1883) was reprinted with significant changes in the Everyman Library (1907).

St. Gregory . . . "met a footstool"] *The Dialogues of Saint Gregory . . . with an Introduction and Notes by Edmund G. Gardner* (London: Philip Lee Warner, 1911). In Chapter II ("Of Libertinus, Prior of the same Abbey") St. Gregory tells how the Abbot in a rage struck the venerable Libertinus with a footstool; but the humble Libertinus forgave the Abbot, and when asked how he came by "such a swollen and black face," he replied: "Yesterday . . . at evening, for punishment of my sins, I met with a footstool, and gat this blow which ye see." See Letter **86n.**

81   Dorothy to Ezra

Broomhill
West Malvern
22 May 1912
Wednesday

Dearest.

A very wet morning: so we have a fire & are doing a little book-work instead of painting. I have been intensely excited over another of [G.R.S.] Mead's–"The World-Mystery". It is full of interesting things, and I have "correlated" several to vaguenesses of my own! Also a footnote fit for Walter [Rummel], about a "dodecagonal pyramid" with a door of many colours–the pyramid "in a sphere of the colour of night"–

I have been needing Il Paradiso to refer to–but must wait until I get home again. I feel I might now read it a trifle more intelligently–only a little, but still - - - I go home Tuesday 28 & on Wed 29 to

Lee Priory
Littlebourne,
Canterbury,
Kent.

Hilda [Strutt] & her Frank [Deverell] are coming down to the hotel for Whitsuntide–I wonder how she & Georgie [Hyde-Lees] will get on. Perhaps H. will be too busy with her young man.

Do you know Bacon's "Wives are young Men's Mistresses; Companions for middle Age; & old Men's Nurses"? It somewhat pleased me. I have been reading some of his Essays.

I had hoped for a letter from you today–but I must content myself with the Ring. It likes, I believe, being worn every night: I love it very much.

I had a line from O.S. [Olivia Shakespear] saying that The Eagle [Yeats] wishes for your *birth date*. Do you know it? If so will you send it to her or him–The Eagle [Yeats] must be positively interested in your career if he goes for yr. horoscope. Do try to know it (the date)!

Oh! I can't send this until I have yr. address.

I find Renan an excellent antidote to G.R.S. Mead & his numbers & Mysteries.

Friday

Yours from the Bibliothèque [Nationale] came–Thanks. I have given Georgie [Hyde-Lees] yr. information about Spanish. London is again messed up with Strikers–It is a rotten time.

The hills were so lovely this morning: we scrambled on them for two hours & a half & I found cold spring-water, with which I bathed my hands & eyes & your hands & eyes.

I am reading a little book on Mediaeval Eng: Lit: by Dr. Ker.

There is such a delightful conveyance going about here–a donkey, with two wheels behind him, on which is a water-barrel–in which two small black-eyed boys stand to their shoulder-blades & drive. I haven't tracked them far enough to see them get in or out!

Coz must sleep: there is a great thunderstorm coming up.

I think some day you & I will come to stay in W. Malvern: the hills are green & plain: there are woods below, & a British Camp in the distance. Was the "Ashwood at Malvern" here? I have just gathered that Piers Plowman begins on Malvern Hill.

Yours, dear,

D.

Mead's–"The World-Mystery"]   G.R.S. Mead, *The World-Mystery* (1895); "entirely revised and largely augmented" as *The World-Mystery: Four Comparative Studies in General Theosophy* (London and Benares: The Theosophical Publishing Society, 1907). In a footnote on p. 119 of the revised edition, Mead says that in "one of the books of the Peratae Gnostics mention is made of a dodecagonal pyramid . . . in a sphere of the colour of night . . . . This pyramid— every side of which was a regular pentagon—had a door leading into it . . . of many colours, like Joseph's coat, for what we call colours here below are the witnesses to very real powers or forces in spiritual nature."

Frank]   Frank Deverell married Hilda Strutt on 17 July 1912.

Bacon's . . . Essays]   Francis Bacon (1561–1626). From Essay VIII, "Of Marriage and Single Life."

Strikers]   The spring of 1912 was a time of social and political unrest in Britain, including a long strike by coalminers. On May 24 the Transport Workers at the London docks were on strike.

book . . . by Dr. Ker]   *English Literature: Mediaeval* (1912), by the well-known scholar W.P. Ker (1855–1923).

"Ashwood at Malvern"]   "La Fraisne" (P), first published in *A Lume Spento* (1908), is subtitled: "(Scene: The Ash Wood of Malvern)." *A Lume Spento* was originally entitled *La Fraisne*.

82   Dorothy to Ezra

Broomhill
[West Malvern]
27 May 1912
Monday

My dear.

Thanks for Poste Restante address. Your weather should be lovely for walking if its like ours. We scrambled miles on the hills yesterday & eventually parted company to come home–I took the High Rd (over the hills) & G. [Georgie Hyde-Lees] the low round the base. My Hilda [Strutt] & her young man are roaming about here: they are staying in a cottage belonging to the School–quite unchaperoned–which amuses me so much!

I have no news: Your coz was locked out last night! She strolled at 8.30 P.M. up to school–met people & talked until 10.45–when she came home & had to rouse a maid to unlock & light up! *Sounds* bad! On Sunday night too–after never having been near the church either!

The Garden is lovely: May etc: full of sunny smells & a Japanese-rose hedge all crimson. Also lots of nice birds about–fat & shiny & soft. Some day I shall "take to Nature" & never come back.

Meanwhile I am trying to pack scientifically–to go home for a night & on to Lee Priory. O.S. [Olivia Shakespear] is at Daisy Meadow [with Mrs. Fowler]. I haven't heard from there though.

Oh! this morning in the most frequented spot in the Garden we saw a squirrel–He came through the balustrade & walked quickly up a dozen steps & through the balustrade again–He was so lovely: all bright beady eye & tail–*such* a *tail!* I was glad the Min-mins weren't about–or there might have been trouble.

Lunch Time

London apparently will be starved out–besieged–I know not what horror–soon–all begun all over again worse than ever. I haven't read the papers for three weeks–so don't know whether its really bad–Georgie [Hyde-Lees] mayn't stay there–but has to go on to the country again.

With much love & a smelly leaf

from your
Coz.

Min-mins]   See Letter **39n.**

83   Dorothy to Ezra

12 Brunswick Gardens
Kensington
28 May 1912
Tuesday

Dearest.

They *have sbagliato* [blundered]. I arrive & find three packages from Small, Maynard & Co: containing in all *ten* vols. of Cavalcanti. I am sending one to Miss Cravens–keeping one for myself & one for the Hueffers– Et puis———? What shall I do with the remaining seven? They are charming to look at–gray & white.

Also there has come a vol. of poems by Florence Wilkinson–"The Far Country". Voilà–I must do 1001 things. I spent 7d. on the Conrad & Hueffer "Romance".

Wednesday

Having just helped Louisa [the housemaid] put back all the books, I am aweary. But have to go out before I leave,

So–dear
with love
à Toi.

quote 7749. Apr. 26. 1912 when writing (if you do) about Cavalcanti.

Cavalcanti]   *Sonnets and Ballate of Guido Cavalcanti* was published in Boston by Small, Maynard and Co. on 27 April 1912, and in London by Stephen Swift and Co. in May. Although EP had asked that the author's copies of the American edition be sent to his father, "those fools in Boston sent all my copies of 'Guido' to London" (EP to Homer Pound, [May] 1912).

vol. of poems by Florence Wilkinson]   *The Far Country* (1906), by Florence Wilkinson (Evans). Born in Tarrytown, N.Y., Mrs. Evans spent the latter part of her life in England.

Conrad & Hueffer "Romance"]   *Romance* (1903), a novel written in collaboration by Joseph Conrad and Ford Madox Hueffer.

quote 7749. Apr. 26. 1912]   The invoice number of the Small, Maynard shipment.

84   Dorothy to Ezra

Lee Priory
Littlebourne
Canterbury
1 June 1912

Dearest

I'm a trifle crazy, that's all–I wrote twice to what I supposed (without being able to get at an atlas) was yr. address & it was obviously wrong. I wrote chiefly a line from home to say that they have sent 10 copies of Guido [*Cavalcanti*]–instead of the three: I have taken one for myself–I sent one to Miss Cravens, and am keeping one to send the Hueffers when you say–What else am I to do? Also there was a book of verses by one Florence Wilkinson (?) which has come up to 12. B.G. [Brunswick Gardens].

There's no news–There never is–The butler has had a stroke & so there is only the Boy. I sketched vilely this morning & Tore it up. I paddled through the river–which was nice: & we picked yellow irises growing wild.

All the drawing books had to be put back the morning I was in Town: There are a great many & poor Louisa [the housemaid] looked so helpless over it alone! A terrific thunderstorm is coming rapidly nearer:

Dear. Here I was interrupted & since I have discussed Oneness & Nothing-ness & have recommended [G.R.S.] Mead etc. etc:

& now I shall be late for dinner.

With great love.
Yours
D.

85   Dorothy to Ezra

Lee [Priory]
[Littlebourne]
[Canterbury]
3 June 1912

Dearest.

You are really a beast. Why didn't you tell me about Walter's [Rummel] marriage?? You must have known! Meanwhile I have had the extreme shock from O.S. [Olivia Shakespear]. Do you know Thérèse Chaigneau, & like her? O.S. says the Dryad [Hilda Doolittle] writes approval of her. I suppose you'll get married next without telling me anything about it. Then I shall have to make up to J.G.F. [James G. Fairfax] & like inferior verse.

Yours came this morning with the Minerve. I will keep anything you send. She is a delightful being–but I don't see any way of utilizing her for my next evening frock!

I am painting a little here: but its pouring wet part of most days. I hope you haven't caught yr. death of cold yet: its as well yr. sac [rucksack] was carefully lined!

Walter married–I can't get over it.

I don't make out about posts–but hope this will reach you. Yr. foreign stamps & bright yellow envelope created a great excitement here–It looked *so* indiscreet among the other correspondence–but I volunteered no information about it. Curiosity is a singularly unpleasant & tiresome trait, always to be found in stupid people, I believe.

I must go to tea or there'll be more of it. Good luck to yr. book. I will keep anything coming for you.

Dear! dear!

Think of W. a married man!

A Toi.

I go home the end of this week.

Walter's marriage]   Walter Rummel married Thérèse Chaigneau, a professional musician, in the summer of 1912. The marriage was eventually annulled.
the Minerve]   A postcard showing Minerva wearing a helmet.

86   Dorothy to Ezra

Lee Priory
Littlebourne
Canterbury
[7 June 1912]
Friday

My dear.

I have just heard, through Walter [Rummel], about Margaret [Cravens].
It sounds very terrible–but perhaps if she had no wish to live - - - I am so
sorry for you–I sent her the Guido [*Cavalcanti*] when I was in London, so
she had it before - - - Perhaps also it will not be altogether a shock to you?
I am sad not to have met her. There's nothing else to be said–

8 June
Saturday

Thanks for some more cards–The Clocher at Poitiers is lovely.

I can't remember whether I told you that W.B.Y. [Yeats] wants your
birth hour for horoscopic purposes? Will you send it if you know it.

I have heard a genuine story down here about a ghostly bloodstained
floor. The old woman said she couldn't get it out–although she scrubbed &
scrubbed–& even had the carpenter in to plane the boards!

I go on writing to Limoges–although you seem to be south of it.

My little cousin here is rejoicing in St. Gregory's Dialogues which I have
with me. I really do go home on Tuesday.

I enclose a leaf of the laurel, I spoke of before.

Much love
Yours

about Margaret]   Margaret Cravens (1881–1912) was an American pianist
living and studying in Paris. EP first met her in March 1910 through Walter
Rummel, whom she knew well. Her father had committed suicide a year earlier,
and Rummel's sudden marriage to Thérèse Chaigneau may have been too much
for her.

St. Gregory's Dialogues]   See Letter **80.** EP wrote a short unsigned review
of the *Dialogues* for the London *Daily News,* 20 November 1911, p. 5.

This is a great book–and we do not use the term lightly–perhaps *the* great book
of the sixth century which has come down to us. Speaking in the modern sense, it
will interest few people. It will interest students of Dante and of the Middle Ages,

and it will interest such general readers as can put themselves into its atmosphere, into a leisurely and inquisitive state of mind. The pleasure of it is the difficult pleasure of getting at the point of view of that indefatigable invalid Pope Gregory the First. He is hardly mediaeval. In his belief that the Bishop of Rome was the supreme ecclesiastic, and that the Church was subject to the State in temporal affairs, we have the Roman bias. Caesar or Cicero would have held the same. In these dialogues he discusses most matters of interest. His thought precedes the mediaeval writings and gives tone to them. With him the cult of misery is not a perversion, but a heroic endeavour–an endeavour to give courage to an age of ruin in which one could not logically expect anything from the future. His saints, as he presents them, are more like human beings as we know them than are the characters in "The Fioretti," but to get at them we must realise that manners of speech vary, and that when Gregory speaks of St. Bennet as "desiring rather the miseries of the world . . . than to be exalted with transitory commendation," he refers to an impulse which a modern writer would define somewhat in this fashion: "desiring rather to get at the real values of life, to find out actualities."

The book will come to life if one can make these substitutions. And there is in Gregory's mind a profundity mixed with a curious naïveté, which repays one, and a heritage from the humanity and breadth of "the classics." The historical background is concisely presented by Mr. Edmund Gardner in his introduction to the translation of the Dialogues made by "P.W.," an unidentified writer of the time of King James I. The publisher's name is sufficient guarantee for the beauty of the format, and the illustrations and notes are particularly well chosen.

87   Ezra to Dorothy

[*92 rue Raynouard*]
[*Paris*]
[*10 June 1912*]

Dearest Coz:

A whole lot of mail came to Limoges with your letters and sudden news. I have come back here to Paris as you see.

Sadness and nobility and so many things are in the web that it is hard to exercise so wooden a Thing as my profession, that is, words–even to you. Someday we will talk, perhaps - - - if, that is, the Thing comes near you.

Write to me, dear, and I will answer as best I can. I won't say, "don't write me trivial things", but write to [me] gravely for a little.

yours.
yours.
Ezra

88   Dorothy to Ezra

12 Brunswick Gardens
[Kensington]
[12 June 1912]
Wednesday

Dear.

I got two letters from you on arriving home. I was afraid you would feel Margaret Craven's death a great deal. I am glad she left you a letter. You shall talk about it all to me 'some day'–when you want to do so. It *has* come near me in a way–but not having known her personally - - - it can't so much.

Has she "any people"–or was she alone - - - No: that is idle curiosity. I was wondering for which of several reasons I can imagine, you went back to Paris.

We saw the Irish Theatre Co. last night–a new play of Mr. [Lennox] Robinson's–fine I thought–tragic, & in these days appropriate. There's nothing to write about–there's a tea party & a wedding shortly–ugh!

I wish I were with you–I send a petal from a yellow rose.

A Toi.

Irish Theatre Co. . . . Mr. Robinson's]   On 4 June 1912, p. 7, the London *Times* reported that "The Irish National Theatre Society—which we know better under the name of the Abbey Theatre—began its season last night." The new play by Lennox Robinson (1886–1958), Irish actor, playwright, and director, was *Patriots*.

89   Dorothy to Ezra

12 Brunswick Gardens
[Kensington]
12 June [1912]
Evening

Dearest E.

W.B.Y. [Yeats] was in at tea–He is very much pleased with yr. two Eng. Review Sapphics–read them to us with due music. He prefers the first. By

THEIR LETTERS   1912   111

the bye you mean "aureole" not "oriel" I am sure: do alter it ⟨if you can⟩–
(unless there is some far-fetched theory of spelling!?). The Eagle [Yeats]
named the first–The Return–"distinguished". They are beautiful.

The English ed. of Guido [*Cavalcanti*] is here now–six vols., one of
which I have given to O.S. [Olivia Shakespear]. May I give one to Bunk
(an American). I will in time send back the Americans to the addresses you
gave me. Meanwhile I await further orders.

Also the enclosed was enclosed in a copy of "The Human Fantasy"
Wheelock. Anche [Also] M.S.S. returned from S. Swift & enclosed. Shall
I forward proofs to 92 r. R. [rue Raynouard]? They seem very correctly
printed on the whole–but one or two things want looking at - - - The punc-
tuation in "Apparuit".

W.B.Y. has been induced to take an interest, O.S. [Olivia] sends message,
in [Harold] Munro & the P. Review.

Shall I send the two lots of proofs & yr. own M.S.S. or how much? I am
sorry not to know without asking what you want.

This must go at once.

My dear: all my love & write me a "business letter" if no other.

A Toi.

two Eng. Review Sapphics]   "The Return" (P) and "Apparuit" (P) were
published in the *English Review*, 11 (June 1912). In the fourth stanza of "Ap-
paruit" EP uses the word "oriel" in the sense of a portal or entrance-hall, but
"aureole" would also make sense in the context.

Bunk (an American)]   Henry Tudor Tucker, Dorothy's uncle, was to re-
ceive a copy of the American edition of *Cavalcanti*.

"The Human Fantasy" Wheelock]   *The Human Fantasy* (1911), by the
American poet John Hall Wheelock (1886–1978).

M.S.S. . . . proofs]   The original manuscript and two sets of proofs for
Ripostes were sent to EP at 10 Church Walk on May 30.

Munro & the P. Review]   Harold Monro founded the *Poetry Review* in
1912. His Poetry Bookshop in Bloomsbury was a meeting-place for writers. In
December 1912 he published the first of five anthologies of *Georgian Poetry*.
See Biographical Appendix.

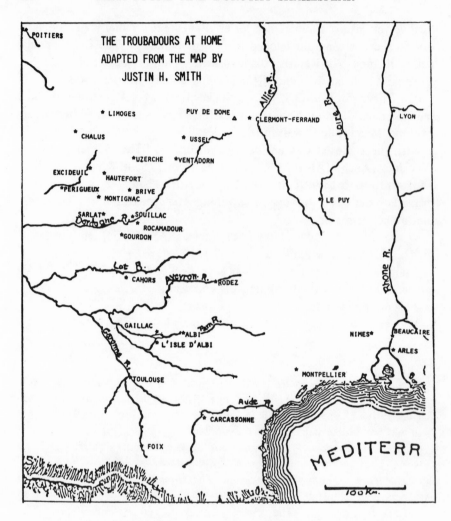

THE TROUBADOURS AT HOME
ADAPTED FROM THE MAP BY
JUSTIN H. SMITH

90   Ezra to Dorothy

[Paris]
[France]
[16 June 1912]
Sunday

Dearest:

When I said send *mss* & both proofs, I didn't expect your wild debauch of registration, "proofs" as mail count as junk, old iron, etc. They never *do* get lost but if they did, there'd be–probably–the type set up at the printers from which to get more. Of course the foundry might be blown up by strikers at the same time and in that case it *would* be inconvenient. Thanks for sending 'em with care–as if valuable.

I've got myself in hand again & and did a real days work at the Bibliothèque [Nationale] yesterday. Most of which you'll see in the blooming opus, in which I've somehow or other acquired a faint interest. The big print in "Ripostes" is very easy to read but there are so many lap-over lines that one cant see a verse form–where there is one–the wretched sapphics, of course, bear the brunt of it.

I am very reprehensible with "sleight". I mean "magic", and I revert to the "Shakespearian" practice of using a noun for an adjective when I want to. Of course, I *do* spell so many words wrong–it was a habit of my period.

This letter reads very severely but I've just corrected those evil proofs. I haven't answered any questions from your letters because it would take too long to say everything, & nothing else is worth while.

The Eagle [Yeats] is welcome to my dashed horoscope tho' I think Horace was on the better track when he wrote

> "Tu ne quaesaris, scire nefas, quem
> mihi quem tibi
> Finem dii dederunt"
> etc.

Roughly about 3 P.M. Oct 30, 1885 at Hailey, Idaho, *Etats Unis*. Hailey is a little east of Boise–which is perhaps visible on a scale map. He will find Venus well dignified and the rest of the horoscope a blank. He will find the horoscope for London at the same hour very interesting. It is to be noted that nothing did happen to me in Hailey, as the love of adventure & metropolitan life led me thence at the age of 18 months. It will be observed that

I smother if I move westward or inland in the U.S.A. That I have or have had literally a sense of drowning or gasping for breath–west of the Alleghanies. That I have some sense of stellar magnetism, & that the bonum regnum Saturni is not for me.

I shall probably stay here in W.R.'s now spacious dwelling [Rummel's Paris flat] until I copy my notes. Then I suppose I'll go to Uzerche and down the valley of the Dordogne.

I kiss your eyes.

E.

reprehensible with "sleight"]   "Green come the shoots, aye April in the branches, / As winter's wound with her sleight hand she staunches. . ." ["A Virginal" (P), lines 11–12; first published in *Ripostes*].

Tu ne quaesaris . . . dederunt]   Horace, *Odes,* I. xi:

Tu ne quaesieris (scire nefas) quem mihi, quem tibi finem di dederint . . .

(Ask not—we cannot know—what end the gods have set for me, for thee. . .)

Uzerche . . . valley of the Dordogne]   For place names in France mentioned in this and following letters, see the map on p. 112.

91   Dorothy to Ezra

12 Brunswick Gardens
[Kensington]
16 June [1912]

My dear.

I saw Walter [Rummel] today for a few minutes–which is better than nothing. He gave me yr. love & said you are feeling better again than when you came to Paris. He himself is looking well I thought.

I sent off your proof, & M.S.S. yesterday–and gave Bunk [Dorothy's uncle] a vol: today (he had asked me ages ago to give it him when it came out).

The Meads [G.R.S. Mead] here at tea yesterday: they both have so much, & such pleasant, personality. I expect you are seeing the Hamadryad [Hilda Doolittle]? Give her my best love–Tell her Mead says Centaurs can't have existed "in the flesh" because if so by now we should have "found skeletons".

Pardon about oriel [see Letter **89**]. Being wrong, I put it back to the original, who was W.B.Y. [Yeats]–Who read it to me before I read it to myself. Walter seems troubled as to his nationality–& is now rapidly becoming English–Of course the English won't appreciate the fact at all. O.S. [Olivia Shakespear] was pleased with the "Portrait d'une femme"– The pencil remarks in yr. proofs were my gentle queries–the ink–St: [Stephen] Swift (I imagine).

I am not really feeling the least gay. I *am* feeling glad if Walter is happier. And please don't be too miserable. I *am* understanding why you should be–and that it was all an awful shock to you, & I can't send you any help through letters:

Give me your hands–& I'll stroke them gently for you & not say a word: & you'll feel rested.

h'è vero?

à Toi.

Monday

Dearest: I shall hope to hear from you soon– –

Meanwhile

My love.   D

P.S. Fortunately I had the gump to wait for the 11 ocl: post–by which yrs. turned up. My spelling remarks seem to have been unfortunate: I told O.S. you might mean "sleight"–& now I have lost the Context.

I debated awhile on the extravagance of registration, but felt a trifle anxious & Martha-ish. You see–I am not used to literary habits!

Yes–the Sapphics don't look so nice in broken lines.

Letters are–the devil. I know–"Nothing else is worth while". Some day we shall meet again after all.

I have just sent back to U.S.A. the three copies [of *Cavalcanti*] you asked me to. I will give the Eagle [Yeats] one–also yr. horoscope. What I wonder is the "bonum regnum Saturni"? I don't know Saturn's attributes - - - but have hitherto suspected him of melancholy & blackness. The Horace I actually can read.

There's thunder about–& I go to the Stage Society with 'Erb [Herbert Leaf] today.

I feel quite interested–having found an incantation in Mead beginning "Iaô, aôi, ôia". I find a book of Walter's here on the Voyelles & their significances.

Also I have just been amused by a washing-cart–whose Master left the large black dog in charge–the latter holding whip & reins in his mouth.

I believe we don't go to Oxford until the second week in July–& Ilfracombe, north Cornwall (or Devon?) seems to be looming for September with the Bunk & Co.

I hear–but have not seen–The Observer has a scathing review of Guido [*Cavalcanti*]–Some fuss about Rossetti–Never mind. W.B.Y. says The Return is "flawless".

Yours–

"Portrait d'une Femme"]   "Portrait d'une Femme" (P), first published in *Ripostes* (1912).

h'è vero]   *è vero*, "Isn't it true."

might mean "sleight"]   See Letter **90.**

"bonum regnum Saturni"]   See the reference in Letter **90,** and EP's explanation in Letter **92.**

Stage Society]   The Incorporated Stage Society, founded in 1899 to produce plays of artistic merit that would not have commercial appeal. Productions were on Sunday nights when West End theatres were available.

incantation in Mead]   G.R.S. Mead, *The World-Mystery* (London and Benares: The Theosophical Publishing Society, 1907), p. 65. See Letter **81.**

Among prayers to the Supreme Principle are specially to be remarked the mystic invocations in the Coptic Gnostic MSS., brought back from Upper Egypt, and preserved in the Bodleian Library, Oxford, and in the British Museum. These are largely Christian overworkings superimposed on a basis of Egyptian Gnosticism. In the concluding section appended to the *Pistis Sophia* document headed "Extract from the Books of the Saviour," the Saviour, the First Mystery, thus addresses the Hidden Father in the mystic celebration of an initiatory rite of which a dim memory remains in the Eucharist of the Churches. The Prayer is in the mystery-language, untranslatable by the "profane," and runs as follows:

"Hear Me, My Father, Father of all Fatherhood, Boundless Light:

"Aeēiouō· ïaō· aōï· öïa· psinōther· thernōps· nōpsiter· zagourē· pagourē· nethmomaōth· nepsiomaōth· marachachtha· thōbarrabau· tharnachachan· zorokothora· ïeou· sabaōth."

book . . . on the voyelles]   Perhaps *Principes de phonétique expérimentale,* by L'Abbé Jean-Pierre Rousselot (Paris-Leipzig, 1897–1901), which contains several long sections on *Voyelles.* In Paris in the early 1920s EP spoke "The Return" (P) into Rousselot's "machine for measuring the duration of verbal components": see *Polite Essays* (London, 1937), pp. 129–30; and Canto 77, where EP remembers "old Rousselot/who fished for sound in the Seine."

The Observer . . . Guido]   Under the title "Mr. Pound Translating," a review of *Sonnets and Ballate of Guido Cavalcanti* was published in the *Observer*

(London), 16 June 1912, p. 5. The anonymous reviewer begins by misquoting the opening lines of "Cino" (P), which first appeared in *A Lume Spento* (1908) but was not collected in *Exultations* (1909).

> 'Bah!' wrote Mr. Ezra Pound on one occasion in his 'Ejaculations,' 'I have written of women in three climes. Now I will sing of the sun.' And now he has turned his attention to the work of Guido Cavalcanti, Dante's friend, many of whose sonnets and ballads Rossetti most beautifully translated, and the translations are to be found in the volume of Rossetti's works entitled 'Dante and His Circle.' Rossetti had a wonderful command of language and rhythm, and his translations from the early Italian poets contain some of his very finest work. Mr. Pound has taste in ejaculations, as is proved by his staccato preface and his heading of one sonnet, doubtless with authority, 'Hoot Zah!!!'; but he has small taste in words and a dull ear for rhythm. The beginning of the little Ballata 'Of his lady among other ladies,' which in Rossetti's version runs: —

> > With other women I beheld my love—
> > Not that the rest were women to mine eyes,
> > Who only as her shadows seem to move.
> > I do not praise her more than with the truth,
> > Nor blame I these if it be rightly read.

> becomes under Mr. Pound's harsh and ungainly handling: —

> > Ladies I saw a-passing where she passed;
> > Not that they seemed as ladies to my vision,
> > Who were like nothing save her shadow cast.
> > I praise her in no cause save verity's,
> > None other dispraise, if ye comprehend me.

> In his preface, in which Mr. Pound writes bigly of 'the science of the music of words and the knowledge of their magical powers,' he assures us that 'in the matter of these translations and of my knowledge of Tuscan poetry Rossetti is my father and mother,' and he goes on to explain why he has been at pains to make the present version and not carry out his 'first intention to print only Guido's poems and an unrhymed gloze.' The reason he gives is, 'I cannot trust the reader to read the Italian for the music after he has read my English for the sense,' and yet he ends by quoting an *envoi* from one of Guido's Canzone: —

> > Thou mayest go assured, my Canzone,
> > Whither thou wilt, for I have so adorned thee
> > That praise shall rise to greet thy reasoning
> > Mid all such folk as have intelligence;
> > To stand with any else, thou'st no desire.

> Some folk who have intelligence will, however, be content with Rossetti's translations, incomplete as they are, and will suppose that Mr. Pound's work must be meant for those Americans who find Rossetti's English distasteful to them.

The Return]   "The Return" (P) was first published in the *English Review,* 11 (June 1912).

92   Ezra to Dorothy

92 rue Raynouard
[Paris]
[18 June 1912]

Dearest:

I jawed with Margaret's aunt [Drusilla Cravens] up till about 2 A.M. last night and am this day exhausted, after the manner of a rag's limpness. There is to be no funeral here, and what M. [Margaret] wrote of so blithely, in one of her last notes, as "The remains" will be conveyed to the U.S.A. As M. is by now a small, fat, brown god sitting in a huge water-lily, splashing over the edge, the performance will probably amuse her. Said image may sound ridiculous, but it is a great comfort to one, and is so unanswerably true that I don't dare mention it to anyone else. It is however the solution of the whole affair, and we rest of us who are not yet ready for such damp white-petaled beatitude may as well continue with our *paradise terrestre*. [G.R.S.] Mead's Holy Hierotheos would consider her present spiritual attitude lax, but I as a "humanist to the last" defend it.

As for Saturn's *bonum regnum* it was in theory a time when the quiet life was not a will-o-the-wisp but an objective fact and no man fought with his brother or his wife's relations.

The "Observer" won't bother me much–besides it is highly improbable that the reviewer has read either me or Rossetti.

The 'Bunk' [Dorothy's uncle] and 'M' [Margaret Cravens] are, now that I for once come to think of it, not so unalike in certain phazes. As for dear Walter [Rummel], a marriage licence in France costs 200 francs, so England at 7/6 needn't feel so dam' flattered.

Richard [Aldington] & the Hamadryad [Hilda Doolittle] met W.R. just after he had discovered the above fact, and they gave thanks to me & god, in private, that they were neither of them going to marry [here].

S.v.p. Send me the adverse reviews of Guido [*Cavalcanti*], that sort of thing occasionally draws down the muse if I read it before dinner. I shall end this to send it forth by the "bonne"–yes'm, now that W.R. has left me I am employing a servant–very *odd*!! Now–I wonder if I'll get any more notes copied, today, than I did yesterday–Stevensonian [R.L. Stevenson] charm *etc*.

E.

I'll give your love to h-d-d [Hilda Doolittle] but Mead's remarks on centaurs will displease her greatly & she is sure to be sceptical. Besides there were very few and there is no reason why their bones should be so d—n permanent–THEY [CHARS] Think–Some one will deny the existence of the unicorn next & then the British Empire WILL go to pieces.

small, fat, brown god]   From "His Vision of a Certain Lady Post Mortem," *Blast No. 1* (1914), printed in *Personae* (1926) as "Post Mortem Conspectu":

> A brown, fat babe sitting in the lotus,
> And you were glad and laughing,
> With a laughter not of this world.
> It is good to splash in the water
> And laughter is the end of all things.

Mead's Holy Hierotheos]   In March 1912 EP wrote to his mother that "Mead's lecture on 'Heirotheos' [at the Quest Society] was very good." G.R.S. Mead published the lecture in *Quests Old and New* (1913) under the title " 'The Book of the Hidden Mysteries' by Hierotheos." The lecture was based on a description of the British Museum manuscript; the full text of *The Book of the Holy Hierotheos*, with a translation, did not appear until 1927. Mead believed that "Hierotheos" was the pseudonym of a monk of the early Syrian church who wrote about the mystical stages in the ascent of the soul toward the Supreme.

93   Dorothy to Ezra

12 Brunswick Gardens
[Kensington]
[21 June 1912]

Dear.

The British Empire appears to be in a state, an unpleasant state, of decay, unicorn or no unicorn. Every one is wild about this blooming Lloyd George's Insurance Act & H.H.S. [Henry Hope Shakespear] is in legal despair. Mat-Mat [Rev. Arthur Galton] is going to live without servants as he *won't* be Ll. G's tax-gatherer–& poor Fred [Frederic Manning]–is to be away for a while–then I suppose he'll be inadequate housemaid at Edenham [The Rectory].

Walter [Rummel] was here to dinner last night & so was Bunk [Dorothy's uncle]–They went home together–or started anyway–W. played nicely–two new Debussy's. (He told me to tell you for future reference that it is all spelt in one–"Debussy".)

Today its about 100°–in the shade & Byngdy [the cat] is on my lap. He spoke pleasantly to Walter last night. The latter was tired–*said* he had "spent five hours in Harrods [department store] trying on pyjamas (& night-dresses for my wife)". I washed my hair yesterday & was in consequence cross & depressed. So I went to interview the Sellaio–& the Crivelli.

Walter is sending you "The Observer" he said.

I have done Renan's "Jésus" (he never uses the word "Christ" at all). I mean soon to read some Voltaire.

Thursday

Have just read a disgusting book of Maxwell's. I wonder whether the right people will take the sermon to heart. Its about egotism.

I send a snapshot of me taken on the river near Canterbury. We had an entertaining time: (Edie & I) because I had only steered with a tiller before, & got very mixed. We met several dead-nesses floating down & a brute of a man snapshotted us from his garden at the most difficult spot– E. [Edie] said he was going in for a "Happy Holiday" Competition!

I must go out & search for a wedding present for Hilda [Strutt]–*my* Hilda–Its to be "copper"–a trifle vague. I seem to feel it will *cost* more than "copper-s".

I am glad about the "fat brown god".

Friday

This must & shall go this morning. "Yrs. to hand", for which thanks. No: don't send the note: read it to me some day. I can't think what you have been trying to convince Mrs. Sill & L'Abbé [Dimnet] of–Anyway you probably haven't done it.

I have a row of lovely pink sweet peas out on my window ledge. The weather hot–& thundery. My head in a fuzz.

My love, dear.

Where is Mary Moore [of Trenton]? I sent her a card for the tea parties– but she is probably in Amurrika–

Yours.

Lloyd George's Insurance Act]   The National Insurance Bill of 1911, introduced by David Lloyd George, sought to improve the conditions of the working class through social insurance. This idea caused great concern in Britain, especially among the professional classes.

the Sellaio–& the Crivelli] Jacopo del Sellaio (1442–1493). His "Venus Reclining" in the National Gallery was the inspiration for "The Picture" (P) and "Of Jacopo del Sellaio" (P). Published for the first time in *Ripostes,* they both repeat the line: "The eyes of this dead lady speak to me." During the nineteenth century the National Gallery acquired several paintings by the Venetian painter Carlo Crivelli (*ca.* 1457–1493).

disgusting book of Maxwell's] *In Cotton Wool,* by William Babington Maxwell (1866–1938), published in March 1912. Maxwell was a prolific and popular novelist. The reviewer for the *Times Literary Supplement* (11 April 1912, p. 146) called the hero of *In Cotton Wool* "a mere outward man." In this book about "the cotton wool of environment," Mr. Maxwell has spared his hero nothing; it is "because he has allowed destiny—and destiny alone—to rattle the dice box, that his book bristles with 'lessons.' " When we reach the end of the novel "we may wish even we had not read it—its last chapter, at any rate. But no wishing will make us forget it."

Maxwell stressed the novel's "lessons" in a brief foreword:

> I would say that one of the greatest evils of our modern civilisation is the steady increase of egoism. As society is now constituted, a man with a moderate but assured income can find people who in exchange for his money will perform for him nearly all the duties of manhood; and, as though he were something infinitely delicate and inestimably precious, he may thus wrap himself in cotton wool and evade the shocks and perils of active existence. And the fact that within the packing of cotton wool all the best of the man has perished, and only the husk of a man remains, seems of no consequence to any of the parties to the bargain.

Edie] Edie M. Wood, a Shakespear cousin who was very close to both DS and Olivia. She lived much of her life in Hampshire, and on Olivia's death in 1938 was given the statue "Uncle Hilary" as a memento (see Letter **15**).

Mrs. Sill & L'Abbé] Mrs. Louise Morgan Sill (1868?–1961) was the first woman editor of *Harper's Magazine.* She moved to Paris in 1908 where she lived for many years, contributing articles to various American journals. L' Abbé Ernest Dimnet (1866–1954) taught English literature at Stanislaus College in Paris, and wrote extensively in English and French. Mrs. Sill published a translation of his study of the Brontë sisters (1910) in 1927. They were in the same literary and musical circles as Miss Cravens and both attended her funeral.

94   Ezra to Dorothy

> *92 rue Raynouard*
> *[Paris]*
> *[24 June 1912]*

Dearest

I'm mailing you Chap. I of "op[us] 411", you're not exactly expected to read it. Some one may want to print it in sections. It seems unlikely but if they do, it will have to be where one of us can get at it, and I can't take it with me, nor could I correct proofs, which same I should commit to your mercies.

Will you give W.R. [Walter Rummel] a copy of the Guido (American), & tell him its my wedding present to Thérèse [Chaigneau] (not to him, I'll deal with him later, if I'm able). Also do give O.S. [Olivia Shakespear] her copy–we've woefully neglected that act–either edtn. she wants, the Eng. Edtn. is a bit more correct, but there's not a great deal of difference.

If I want a really fat & comfortable tea I shall have to go out towards now.

> I kiss your eyes.
> E.

Chap. I of "op[us] 411"]   On 18 August 1912 EP wrote to Harriet Monroe that he had "been working for three months on a prose book" [*Letters*, No. 5]. This book was a study of the Troubadours and the conditions—both physical and intellectual—that shaped their art. First called simply "the Opus," by the end of July EP was referring to it as "Gironde" (see Letter **103** and after). On August 27 he wrote to Homer Pound that his "walking tour" would appear in volume form. But EP was never pleased with the shape of "Gironde," and after Ford Madox Hueffer had criticized it (see Letter **117**) he decided to abandon the project. EP's rough draft of "Gironde," made during the walking tour, is in the Pound Archive at the Beinecke Rare Book and Manuscript Library, Yale University. Notes on the manuscript indicate that EP returned to it about 1959, possibly with the intention of revising it for publication.

Work on *Patria Mia,* which began to appear serially in the *New Age* in September 1912, must have reinforced EP's doubts about "Gironde," since it is much more consistent with the new style and attitudes evident in *Ripostes.* On 2 October 1912 EP reported to his mother that *Patria Mia* was meeting with considerable success, and added—perhaps not too seriously—that he would be able to cut short "Gironde" and use *Patria Mia* as the second half of "Studies in Mediaevalism Past & Present."

95   Dorothy to Ezra

12 Brunswick Gardens
[Kensington]
24 June [1912]
Monday

Dearest.

I have writen a word to M. Moore [Mary Moore of Trenton]–without any explanations or comments. So you can write later on yourself when you feel inclined: but need not until then.

I am glad to hear "Thérèse" [Chaigneau] is no fool. Of course you couldn't tell me about it under the circumstances: I find O.S. [Olivia Shakspear] was in the secret!

Have you heard Walter [Rummel] has got an engagement to play on Wed. night at the concert of a certain Mrs. Macmillan (an American, I believe)? He is very proud of himself.

We went to the Sauters (know or not?) yesterday & saw the Hueffers. Mrs F.M.H. was evidently pleased at the dedication of the Guido. I lay low: & didn't say *I* had sent them the copy! "My name first, too" said V.H. [Violet Hunt]. I should hope it was put first.

Awful Storm raging.

The Sauters have got an awful & terrific Rodin, a great clenched hand. He said "it keeps me Good"–& I wasn't surprised: it is terrifying.

Walter & my Hilda [Strutt] go with us to the Irish play soon–to see a Synge: & we go alone to "Countess Cathleen": Craig production.

Mr. [Lennox] Robinson was here on Saturday: (party) someone took Mrs. Fagan for Harry's new wife: & Walter played at the end to "the elect".

Jim [James G. Fairfax] comes to tea. Eva [Fowler] has given me a white satin frock of hers–& I have been reading "Candide" & "Prince Otto". Now you know all.

Tuesday

I went to Pavlova last night: she is lovelier than ever, & danced as a gypsy with brown rags & a crimson petticoat.

Yrs. to hand & the M.S.S. which I will cling to, & read perhaps at my leisure - - - which isn't *this* week. Hilda [Strutt] is to be married in July & I am to be a bridesmaid oh! dear! but I think a pretty frock–pink & blue & a large plain "garden" hat.

I have given O.S. [Olivia] an Eng. vol. of Guido [*Cavalcanti*] without waiting to ask you. Jim [Fairfax] didn't seem to care much about them - - - but really I couldn't discuss the question at length with him. I think he was feeling a little "catty" about them! He said something later to O.S. about all the poetry being at present produced being unnecessary–I think he is beginning to find his *own* is unnecessary–& it makes him feel uncomfortable.

A Toi.

Sauters]   Georg Sauter, the Bavarian painter, and his wife Lilian, the sister of the novelist John Galsworthy. See Biographical Appendix.

the Hueffers . . . dedication of the Guido]   *Sonnets and Ballate of Guido Cavalcanti*, published in April 1912, has the dedication: "As much of this book as is mine I send to my friends Violet and Ford Maddox [sic] Hueffer." For the relationship between Violet Hunt and Ford Madox Hueffer, see Biographical Appendix.

Irish play . . . a Synge]   J.M. Synge's *Riders to the Sea* was playing at the Court Theatre on June 27–29, and *The Playboy of the Western World* on July 1–3.

"Countess Cathleen": Craig production]   The first London production of Yeats's revised *The Countess Cathleen* opened on 11 July 1912. The producer was Nugent Monck, who staged the play as a mediaeval pageant, using the famous "screens" that Gordon Craig had first devised for his Moscow Art Theatre production of *Hamlet*. Gordon Craig (1872–1966), designer and director, rejected naturalism and sought to make the theatre a visionary experience. Yeats had been impressed by Craig's method as early as 1901, and in 1909–12 he introduced Craig's designs at the Abbey Theatre. See Letter **101**.

Mr. Robinson]   Lennox Robinson (1886–1958), the Irish playwright who was associated with the Abbey Theatre throughout his career as writer, producer, and director. See Letter **88**.

Mrs. Fagan]   The wife of James Bernard Fagan (1873–1933), Irish actor, manager, and playwright.

"Candide" & "Prince Otto"]   Voltaire's philosophical satire (1759) and a romance by Robert Louis Stevenson, *Prince Otto* (1885).

Pavlova . . . danced as a gypsy]   See Letter **73n**. The *ballet divertissement* in which she appeared as a gypsy was *Amarilla*.

M.S.S.]   The manuscript of *Ripostes*.

96   Ezra to Dorothy

[*92 rue Raynouard*]
[*Paris*]
[*26 June 1912*]

Dearest:

The second chapter is done, and is more diverting than I had expected, and that means that a little more than 1/4th of the opus is off my virile chest, and as I had sweared a swear not to write a word until July, I am duly impressed with myself.

The enclosed from Richard [Aldington] has followed me down & up the land and it reminds me so of Mat-Mat [Arthur Galton] that I feel I must share it–not the face but the attitude–also the portrait of Wm. Blake, left fore-ground seems an odd coincidence.

As to W.R. [Walter Rummel] I suspected that the anonymous house was that of one Lucy McMillan "of Pittsburg, now living in Hill St." He won't be nearly so proud of himself when he gets there and finds the front hall full of stuffed tigers and lions and elephants and 'sich' Trophies of the jungle.

V.H. [Violet Hunt] is probably pleased that the AM. Edtn. got published before her name was Hueffer, tho' be it afar from me to suggest that same audibly.

"Keeps who good?" that [Rodin] hand at the Sauters. I thought Sauter was reformed by Father Kneip (yes, Kneip curé *allè sameè*.)

Poor Jim-jim-jim-jam [James G. Fairfax], as if by virtuously translating the ancients one didn't refrain from, *ipso facto* refrain from adding to the already excessive bulk of written speech. Of course I don't exactly catch him in the act of spotting the *virtu* ascending or of understanding anything much about G.C. [Guido Cavalcanti] except the rime schemes–which are unimportant. However I was really unpleasant about his "Shipwrecked Pool". [Harold] Monro is suffering the same sort of relapse. I find the british university dilettante is capable of sustained admiration only when this produces a counter current of the same nature.

[G.W.] Prothero of the very Quarterly writes that he is full up till October, but will be glad to consider stuff when I come back–don't mention the matter, for, never having read the Quarterly, I still have a naive respect for it and wish very much to entrench myself behind its covers, and shall be horribly mortified if it don't come off.

Did you see Hewlett's "Gaubertz" in the May "Fortnightly"? If not never mind, I'll read it you when I come back. I rather like it. Now must I shave me and go forth. Tomorrow it's Uzerche & then the road for a week.

Yrs

E.

Next address is *Poste Restante* in *Cahors* (of evil name).

second chapter]   Of "Gironde." See Letter **94n.**

The enclosed . . . Mat-Mat . . . Wm. Blake]   EP enclosed a post card from Richard Aldington and Hilda Doolittle which shows "Le Curé de Pontoise" in his pulpit, denouncing a woman who has deceived her husband. The point of the joke is that Arthur Galton ("Mat-Mat") was a minister. In the crowd around the pulpit there is a figure that looks remarkably like William Blake.

Lucy McMillan "of Pittsburg, now living in Hill St."]   Lucie Fairbanks Webber, of Northampton, Mass., married William Northrup McMillan (1872–1925), of St. Louis, Mo. After a business career in St. Louis—not Pittsburgh—McMillan moved to London in 1898. His hobbies were exploration and big-game hunting in Africa, and after 1905 he maintained a ranch in British East Africa. *Who's Who* for 1914 gives his address as "Nairobi, British East Africa; 19 Hill Street, Berkeley Square, W." Mrs. McMillan's address is on a list that EP sent to Wyndham Lewis on 30 April 1914 naming those to whom Lewis should send a Prospectus for the Rebel Art Centre.

V.H. . . . AM. Edtn.]   The American edition of *Sonnets and Ballate of Guido Cavalcanti* (1912) bears the dedication: "As much of this book as is mine I send to my friends Violet and Ford Maddox [sic] Hueffer."

Father Kneip]   Sebastian Kneipp (1821–1897), pastor of the Roman Catholic church in Wörishofen (Bavaria). In his many writings Mgr. Kneipp popularized a water cure that involved barefoot walks in the wet grass or snow. "Kneipp Societies" flourished in Europe and America at the turn of the century.

"Shipwrecked Pool"]   EP is playing on the title of James G. Fairfax's volume of verse, *The Troubled Pool* (1911).

Prothero . . . Quarterly]   G.W. Prothero (1848–1922) was editor of the *Quarterly Review,* which published "Troubadours: Their Sorts and Conditions" in October 1912.

Hewlett's "Gaubertz"]   Maurice Hewlett's "Lai of Gaubertz" [*Fortnightly Review,* 97 (1 May 1912)] has the acknowledgment: "I owe the substance of this *lai* to my friend Ezra Pound, who unearthed it . . . in some Provençal repertory." Gaubertz de Poicebot figured in Chapter II of "Gironde" (see Letter **98**).

Cahors (of evil name)]   In the 13th century Cahors was a financial center with a colony of Lombard bankers. Hence the term "cahorsin" came to mean "usurer." EP almost certainly has in mind *Inferno* xi, 50, where Dante links Sodom and Cahors as emblems of violence against Nature. The editor of the Temple Classics edition that EP used comments: "Cahors, in the South of France, was so notorious for its usurers in the Middle Ages, that 'Caorsinus' was frequently employed as a synonym for 'usurer.' "

97 Dorothy to Ezra

12 Brunswick Gardens
[Kensington]
29 June 1912
Saturday

My dear–

I have just been reading Chap 2. of the Opus. It is very interesting: the fair must have been enchanting: One should be able to paint such things: and I have no doubt the Castle belonged to the young thing with one goat & one cow–of course it did.

I cannot find Uzerches on the map. Is it by any chance a certain "Ussel" I see marked?

So you are now the proud possessor of an umbrella! A green & white gamp–or a real black umbrella?

Walter [Rummel], my Hilda [Strutt], O.S. [Olivia Shakespear] & I went to the Court [Theatre] last night to see [J.M. Synge's] "Riders to the Sea" and a Comedy, quite entertaining by one William Boyle. W.M.R. [Walter Morse Rummel] & W.B.Y. [Yeats] met at tea here & discussed music for Countess Cathleen (or am I betraying state secrets?) & W.B.Y. sang us a little song, to our amusement & his embarrassment. W.M.R. & [Lennox] Robinson have also met, & I think liked each other.

I *shall* go on a walking tour some day: I know I should like it.

Sunday even:

Mrs. Emery [Florence Farr] was here the other day: she is going in August to Ceylon–to be head of some college, or something queer! I gave her back her "Sappho" which she was glad to see again: evidently had wondered where it was–She says she is leaving the psaltery with W.B.Y. and out there can get a lovely instrument with quarter-tones to play & sing with.

Also she is going to dress in blue (blanketing) bath towelling made loose - - - mercy! how odd! really odd!

Monday

I am going out with the Bunk [Dorothy's uncle] to see Pictures and lunch. Also to fit bridesmaid's dress–Yr. cousin is to have a frock of blue over pink with a purple belt, & then purple ribbons on a floppy garden hat? Do you care?! It will probably be a best evening frock when you come back.

Dont trouble to write much next week when I shall be at Oxford (9–13th) & I can't give you my address there. Unless second post brings a letter this shall go.

Yours.

the Opus] "Gironde." See Letter **94n.**

Comedy . . . William Boyle] The first production of *Family Failing,* by the Irish playwright William Boyle (1853–1923).

music for Countess Cathleen] In Yeats's *Four Plays for Dancers* (1921) the music for "The Dreaming of the Bones" is by Walter Rummel. A note signed "W.M.R." is dated Paris, September 1917. There is no evidence that Rummel composed music for *The Countess Cathleen.*

Mrs. Emery . . . leaving the psaltery] The actress Florence Farr (Mrs. Edward Emery) worked with Yeats in developing his theories of how verse should be spoken to music. Yeats's essay "Speaking to the Psaltery" (1902), first collected in *Ideas of Good and Evil* (1903), was a result of their co-operation. Arnold Dolmetsch (1858–1940), who restored and recreated early musical instruments, made for them an instrument "half-lyre, half-psaltery." See Biographical Appendix.

98   Ezra to Dorothy

Sarlat
[*Dordogne*]
[*France*]
[*1 July 1912*]

Dearest:

If the whim strikes you, you might look at chap. II. near the end, in fact just before the notice of Gaubertz Poicebot, and see what places or people Sordello visited in Provence. The 2nd chapter is rather diverting anyhow, tho' you mightn't expect it. Also, I don't suppose you've inspected the little Hullah, not that it matters, but if you should see a copy of "The Troubadours at Home" by Justin Smith– –British Museum or elsewhere– you might see in what part of the map he puts Ventadorn or "Ventador"– its marked in the index of chapters & I'd like to know where he thinks it is (or was???). I've arrived here via Uzerche, Brive, Souillac.–I am sick of names ending in -ac, the first 50 are interesting but after that it becomes a bore.

Rodez

I missed your note this a.m. at Cahors but suppose it will follow me to Toulouse–anyhow try P. Rest. [Poste Restante] Toulouse on your answer to this, and after that "Carcassonne". This scribble is very dull, but you'll be inundated with details later. This Rodez is really good but I your humble serviteur am also a-weary. One is finally, here, in what are I presume mountains. Gourdon also a small but pictish strong hold with "Fourgons" & "Cavaignac" but faintly disguising the real orthography. If I'd written this p.m. I'd have said I hadn't yet the tang of things, but my dinner seems to have restored me.

That swine W. [Walter Rummel] has not sent my reviews & I shall go to bed almost at once.

I kiss you–if you permit it.
E.

notice of Gaubertz Poicebot]   This has survived in a passage on Gaubertz de Poicebot in EP's "Troubadours: Their Sorts and Conditions" (*Literary Essays,* pp. 95–96).

little Hullah]   Annette Hullah, *A Little History of Music* (1911). Annette Hullah had a special interest in Provençal poetry and music.

"The Troubadours at Home"]   Justin H. Smith, *The Troubadours at Home: Their Lives and Personalities, Their Songs and Their World,* 2 vols. (New York & London, 1899). Justin H. Smith was a professor of modern history at Dartmouth College. EP consulted this learned travel book in the British Museum while planning his trip to the south of France.

For further information on Provençal texts, compiled by EP's former teacher at Hamilton College, see *The Oxford Provençal Chansonnier* by William P. Shepard (Princeton University Press & Les Presses Universitaires de France, 1927). For an excellent modern catalogue of troubadour castles and strongholds, see the *Dictionnaire des Châteaux et des Fortifications du Moyen Age en France* by Charles-Laurent Salch (Editions Publitotal, Strasbourg, 1979).

Ventadorn or "Ventador"]   See Letter **20n.**

"Fourgons" & *"Cavaignac"*] In "Gironde" EP describes his arrival at Gourdon: "As I come in by the street of Cavaignac Fourgons past the restaurant of *Fourgons* I feel shure [*sic*] the last pict is not dead here." A *fourgon* is a wagon or ammunition-carrier; *les fourgons,* the wagon train. Both Jacques-Marie Cavaignac (1773–1855), the general who commanded the French cavalry in the retreat from Moscow, and Jean-Baptiste Cavaignac (1762–1829), an enthusiastic supporter of the revolution of 1789, were born in Gourdon.

99   Ezra to Dorothy

> Gaillac
> [*Tarn*]
> [*France*]
> *5 July 1912*

Dearest,

I finished the Rodez-Albi affair with a 30 mile sprint yesterday & This place is on toward Toulouse, slap in the Midi, by the feel of it.

I'll strike Toulouse day after tomorrow and at that rate this trip wont last forever. Its much too hot to think or to move on to L'Isle d'Albi until the sun shifts a bit. Said Isle being where I intend to *riposar.*

Dearest:

Your letters are, in this weary land, a comfort–even if I'm not to burst out into responses for a week or so. This is Toulouse, two days before schedule. 90 pedestrated miles in the last four days, I shall become boresomely athletic if I'm not careful. I train to Foix & walk presumably from there to Carcassonne. I'm glad you find the "prose" diverting. Uzerche is MILES east of Ussel–it's about 30m. south of Limoges, in a straight line for Cahors or Toulouse.

The umbrella is black–going greenish.

As for F.F. [Florence Farr] Ceylon ought to suit her. I wonder if she'll see her portrait before she goes. Of course she always did dress in towling made loose–chez elle, that is–or in remnants of stage properties & improprieties. Yes–I'm glad if you like it blue over pink, clouds at sunset–& the rest of it. God knows it'll be years before I ever see you in an evening frock. I've more than ever reverted & positively *no* one will invite me out after I get back to London. Please gracious heaven I shall turn my talents to *drarma,* & spit in the social face completely.

Nîmes
13 July

This country abounds in heat & is not devoid of fleas. I have done about everything except the little stretch between Le Pui [Le Puy] & Clermont [Clermont-Ferrand], and am rather worn with the job. You will probably have me back in August as I can't see any reason for dallying about here any longer. I corrected Mead's proof in Arles. The thing is bad but has paragraphs. It is utterly–as a whole–incomprehensible–but that was necessary. One can not write & convey information at the same time.

That parasite [Harold] Monro seems to have displayed one more of the traits of ⟨such vermin⟩ his species, still it was very well done in its way– & A. de R. got a good deal out of six misprints. The rest is malignant buncomb. If [Edmund] Gosse or some one in authority had done it I should have great glee in replying to *the P.Rev.* [*Poetry Review*]. The noble Richard [Aldington] has withdrawn his contributions in a state of pious rage. The Hamadryad [Hilda Doolittle] sent you her affections by the post to Arles or Carcassonne. You might send what other girarations of the press you fall upon–to P. Restante, Clermont-Ferrand.

I've just come in from a very amusing bloodless bull fight in the blooming roman arena. Yesterday at Aucassin's Beaucaire which is *really* charming, I nearly sat down for a week there. I'm not sure that the large fox-terrier, foremost among the bull's assailants, wasn't the maddest part of the show–now fore–now aft–nose to horn etc. One skittish bull seems a sort of village pet and apparently enjoys the affair as much as any one. He had his horns in mittens. But the other two were *au natural*.

I must rise with the blooming rooster. So enough of this. I've been completing my education on Murger, de Maupassant, Turgenieff–Murger's preface to "Le Vie de Boheme" is surprisingly strong. For the rest they amuse me less than Henry [James] & Anatole [France] & "Our Frederic" [Manning].

Buenas Noches.

E.

F.F. . . . her portrait]   This reference confirms the speculation that EP's "Portrait d'une Femme" (P), first published in *Ripostes,* is a "portrait" of Florence Farr. See Letter **100n.**

corrected Mead's proof]   Proof for "Psychology and Troubadours," which appeared in G.R.S. Mead's journal *The Quest,* 4 (October 1912). The essay was later (1932 and after) reprinted as Chapter V of *The Spirit of Romance.*

Monro . . . & A. de R.]   Arundel del Re's review of *Sonnets and Ballate of Guido Cavalcanti,* which appeared in Harold Monro's *Poetry Review,* 1 (July 1912), charged EP with carelessness and a complete disregard for textual accuracy. "Either Mr Pound knows very little about the Italian language, or he is totally lacking in that critical judgment necessary to the translator."

Aucassin's Beaucaire]   In *Aucassin et Nicolette,* an early 13th-century fable, Aucassin, son of the Count of Beaucaire, falls in love with Nicolette, a captive Saracen who has converted to Christianity.

Murger]   Henri Murger (1822–1861), French journalist and novelist. His *Scènes de la vie de bohème* (1848) was the source for Puccini's opera *La Bohème.*

100   Dorothy to Ezra

[*London*]
[*5 July 1912*]
Friday

Dear.

Letters seem complex things–I posted to Cahors last Monday 1st July, & yrs. has postmark 2nd & reaches me on 5th–so no wonder you didn't find my last. I am looking at Chap ii which I really don't seem to have had time & inclination (together) to do yet. I am busy getting my bridesmaid's frock etc. Also my friend in Japan has sent me £1.1. to buy him books! He is sending the same to two other friends– –is, I think, developing an interest in psychology! They are to be "modern": so I send the Conrad "Under Western Eyes"–a certain very clever work "Mr. Perrin & Mr. Traill"–Chesterton's "Ballade of the White Horse" which is pleasing–Masefield's Ballads & some 1/- Irish plays!!!

Chap ii of the opus only mentions that Sordello went to "the court of the Count of St. Boniface" & eventually he "went into Provensa", where he was honoured by all, especially the Count & Countess - - - And I haven't possibly time to hunt at the [British] Museum for Ventadorn.

I hope mine to Cahors will be forwarded: I believe it had some news in it: (of Mrs. Emery [Florence Farr] going to Ceylon for five years.) Just read a new book by "Florence Farr". *Such* a Sargasso Sea muddle. Every body divorced several times, & in the end going back to their originals: & a young man called "Dorus Callando" who lay among lilies all night & is Oscar [Wilde], without the bitter-sweetness.

Later

Spent a strenuous morning hunting wedding presents–for my Hilda [Strutt] & yr. Walter [Rummel]. I arrived at a large MSS book for the latter, made of Italian papering outside: he should be able to make use of it I think–or else "Thérèse" [Chaigneau] must! Hilda is having some Sicilian drawn-thread work & two copper bowls.

This must go, to try & catch you.

Much love, dear,
Yours.

P.S. I haven't read Chap ii properly yet: I had to go out.

Conrad . . . Masefield's Ballads]   Joseph Conrad, *Under Western Eyes* (1911); Hugh Walpole, *Mr. Perrin and Mr. Traill* (1911); G.K. Chesterton, *The Ballad of the White Horse* (1911); John Masefield, *Salt-Water Ballads* (1902).

Museum for Ventadorn]   See Letter **98.**

new book by "Florence Farr"]   Florence Farr (Mrs. Edward Emery) left London for Ceylon in 1912. Her novel *The Solemnization of Jacklin: Some Adventures on the Search for Reality* (1912) is a pastiche of semi-autobiographical experiences. The publisher's advertisement described the situation in "this extremely modern novel" as "one of increasing occurrence in the lives of modern couples today. The solution attempted in all seriousness, is novel and daring." DS is alluding to EP's poem "Portrait d'une Femme" (P), which was intended as a "portrait" of Florence Farr (see Letter **99**).

> Your mind and you are our Sargasso Sea,
> London has swept about you this score years
> And bright ships left you this or that in fee:
> Ideas, old gossip, oddments of all things,
> Strange spars of knowledge and dimmed wares of price.

–   –   –   –   –   –   –

> These are your riches, your great store; and yet
> For all this sea-hoard of deciduous things,
> Strange woods half sodden, and new brighter stuff:
> In the slow float of differing light and deep,
> No! there is nothing! In the whole and all,
> Nothing that's quite your own.
>   Yet this is you.

101   Dorothy to Ezra

12 Brunswick Gardens
[Kensington]
14 July 1912
Sunday

Dear.

It seems a long while since we have communicated?

The heat here is quite surprising–as terrific as some of those days last August. Thank goodness we are all going away for next week end - - - and all separate–H.H.S. [Henry Hope Shakespear] yachting. I have had the pleasure of having " 'Erb" [Herbert Leaf] up in my room to pay me a private visit, this morning. We discussed aesthetics, languidly: and he told me I wore my finger-nails in an American fashion i.e. he disapproved.

We went to see "Countess Cathleen" last night, staged by Nugent Monk. It was very very lovely; against a plain, folded, curtain: with no footlights, but lantern-light thrown from the back of the dress-circle.

We had a pleasant time at Oxford. Mat-Mat [Arthur Galton] was a trifle severe at first–but we were hopelessly frivolous: F.M. [Frederic Manning] was in excellent health & most amusing. He is now with Jim G.F. [James G. Fairfax] & goes to Daisy Meadow soon. Every one is away. Eva [Fowler] goes soon. Lady Low is in the North. The Montpels go to Ilfracombe tomorrow–where I believe we join them in Sept. Hilda [Strutt] goes honeymooning on Wednesday.

There is a Prize of £30 "for the best poem, long or short, published in the (Poetry) Review during the year 1912." Adjudication to be made by committee to be announced in Dec. Wouldn't you like to send up? I feel [Harold] Munro will go bankrupt in December– –however.

Tuesday the 16th

Yrs. from various places has come: for the which thanks. It must be terrible-hot walking if you are having the New York heat-wave that we are. I have spent the afternoon & evening helping my Hilda pack her box and things of that kind. Tomorrow is THE DAY, and on Thursday, when they are honeymooning–*I* am to go & make lists of china and glass & watch men pack it all up–I won't *ever* do such a thing as have the conventional wedding & party: it's really too too unspeakable–And they are all exactly alike–and it's insufferable. ! ! ! an exclamation from each CHAR.

I have been making some Lavender bags and my room smells so very good: It's the best smell in the world.

I shall be delighted to see you back in August–We shall be going away for a week on 6th or 7th I believe to the [Hamilton] Fletchers, and I suppose from 3rd to the 6th somewhere (Bank Holiday) to give H.H.S. [Henry Hope Shakespear] an airing. I wrote to you at Carcassonne: but it's difficult to tell what you have had.

A wonderful (bad) new novel by our poetly cousin, Harty–I'm in it as an innocent girl of 19 called Fay: who was on the whole tactful but washy. It is about a woman called "Averil" (born under Venus) & a poet whose wonderful (bad) verses are interjected here & there–spoken by himself or others–Such a work!

> I must to dinner.
> My love dear
> Yours.

"Countess Cathleen" . . . *Nugent Monk*]   See Letter **95n.** Nugent Monck (1878–1958) was a well-known actor and director.

The Montpels]   Mr. and Mrs. Henry Tudor Tucker. Mrs. Edith Ellen Hyde-Lees, Georgie's mother, married Henry Tudor Tucker on 1 February 1911. They lived at 16 Montpelier Square: hence "the Montpels."

the Fletchers]   The Hamilton Fletchers, old family friends, lived in Leweston Manor, near Sherborne in Dorset.

wonderful (bad) new novel by our poetly cousin]   Harriet Louisa Childe-Pemberton, a Shakespear cousin, published *The Silent Valley* in 1912 (London: Constable & Co.). Throughout the novel Fay (Dorothy) appears as a minor character.

The author also has one of her characters speak of Constantia (Olivia Shakespear) thus: "Everybody confides in her;—you will, before you've known her twelve hours. Oh, she never asks for confidences; she'd much rather not be bothered with them; but people will tell her things,—especially when their lives are—shall we say — tangled?" (p. 21).

102   Ezra to Dorothy

Hotel de Londres
Rue Bonaparte
Paris
[*23 July 1912*]

Dearest:

That being the case, I suppose I had better call either before the third or after the fourteenth. I have been writing out [the] book with great velocity for the past three days. I doubt if the *'suite'* is as good as the beginning, but then it'll be reviewed on the first chapter. Tomorrow I go to the library to crib some interpolative chapters.

I have seen Walter's mama [Mrs. Rummel] and she thinks the service was legal. She addressed me an announcement and said it was the last she would address to anyone, *positively any one.*

Tuesday

I believe my coffee will ascend in a moment or two. Beyond that my head is hollow as a drum. I go to the library - - - (said that last night). Shall I bring the Hamadryad [Hilda Doolittle] back to England? Richard [Aldington] has been recalled to his "domestic den". She sent you her affections by letter ten days ago, but I probably forgot to transmit 'em.

I should have been afield an hour ago.

Os beso los ojos.
E.

Os beso los ojos]   Formal Spanish for "I kiss thine eyes."

103 Ezra to Dorothy

Thos. Cook & Son
Waiting Room
1 Place de l'Opéra
[Paris]
27 [July] 1912
Saturday

Dearest:

I'll be over in a day or so, but don't bother to have me in until its convenient. Have been scribbling at W.R.'s [Walter Rummel's] beastly "provencal for music"–he seems to have lost, eaten or mislaid certain *opii* in the excitement of his nuptuals.

What news there might be can wait. I've done more than the next quarter of "Gironde" but the temper is not thereby improved. May the gods scatter roses before you. They ought to at least, in recompense. Everybody seems to want this desk.

Salutations to Byng, *lo nero* [The Black One].
Yours.
E.

W.R.'s . . . "provencal for music"] Walter Morse Rummel, *Hesternae Rosae, Serta II. Neuf Chansons de Troubadours des XIIième et XIIIième Siècles . . . Adaptation anglaise par Ezra Pound,* published in London by Augener Ltd. on 26 March 1913. In the Preface, dated 1912, Rummel says that "The writer with the help of Mr. Ezra Pound, an ardent proclaimer of the artistic side of mediaeval poetry, has given these melodies the rhythm and the ligature, the character which, from an artistic point of view, seems the most descriptive of the mediaeval spirit."

104   Dorothy to Ezra

Holly Lodge
Burnham
Bucks
4 August 1912

Dearest.

This should be "The Cat's Home"–There are three mamas & five young–
& TWO fathers–and nobody knows whose is which–& everybody cleans
the thing next it regardless of generation–all Siamese–and all lovely. They
are a pleasant interlude to the boredom from which I always inevitably
suffer in this house. A straw amuses several for a long time.

I have done a deal of needlework, and eaten some good food. Also I
am reading "Little Brother" which is quite interesting. I shall *not* go to
the village church, though it is expected of me. Please come in on *Wed.*
aft. as we arranged: I shall be packing–but what matter?

Much love–no news.
Yours.

"Little Brother"] *Little Brother* (1912), an autobiographical novel by
Gilbert Cannan (see Letter **121**).

105   Ezra to Dorothy

[London]
[9 August 1912]
Friday

Dearest:

Mary's [Mary Moore of Trenton] new name is James Frederick Cross,
Jr. and THEY [CHARS] think you'd better remember the "jr." in order
to dee-stinguish 'em from old Charing X and the rest of that family. In
any case they'll be known as the crusaders or something yet more sacri-
ligious will be said of the affair. Jesus Maria, Mater dolorosa *und so
weiter*. And we shall have to turn Taoists to mention them without blas-

phemy. Her née address is 136 W. State St., Trenton, N.J., U.S.A. and you may as well write there as she don't seem to have broken with her family.

Played tennis with F.M.H. [Ford Madox Hueffer] yesterday A.M. and saw Florence Farr in the P.M., have breakfasted this A.M. It seems unlikely that I will do much else.

I don't see how to do without the cat in the last line. The rest comes out of drawing [out of focus] if there isn't something of that sort. I don't see how you can get the necessary *mépris* and *dépit* etc into the affair without some such objectionable remark. One might be pre-raphaelite and say Cameleopard or simply 'pard' which is American argot but any of these animals seem too elaborately zoölogical for my simple sensuous purpose and Byng [the Shakespears' cat] would see quite as well thro a dark sub-consciousness as they would. Besides the T at the end of KaT is more acute phonetically than 'cameleopard'. Besides KaT is very sacred in Egypt and doth more fit the atmospheric conditions. No cameleopard was ever embalmed. Whereas the KaT the Ka and the King might decently inhabit the same sepulker with no violence to the most egyptian comme-il-faut-ness.

Yesterday I invited a divorced countess to have tea here with me on Monday, (by letter), supposing from hers that she was a male friend of Wyndham Lewis's–we await developments. I mean I invited her by letter. If I'd seen her I'd have known she was a divorced countess, or at least that she wasn't a male friend of W.L. I can't think of anything else that has happened. It remains to see whether she'll have sense enough to know that a letter addressed "Esq." is meant for her. Enough of this.

The gods attend thee.

E.

Mary's new name]   Mary Moore of Trenton married James Frederick Cross, Jr., on 19 July 1912.

the cat in the last line]   EP's poem "Middle-Aged: A Study in an Emotion," which he described to Harriet Monroe as "an over-elaborate post-Browning 'Imagiste' affair" [*Letters,* No. 5.], ends with the couplet:

> The which, no cat has eyes enough
> To see the brightness of.

First published in *Poetry* (Chicago), 1 (October 1912), the poem was not included in the 1926 edition of *Personae.*

a divorced countess]   Probably Frida Strindberg, reportedly "ample," who was the second wife of August Strindberg. She operated the Cabaret Theatre Club, also known as the Cave of the Golden Calf. See Letter **190n.**

Wyndham Lewis]   Percy Wyndham Lewis, the artist and writer who was one of the founders of the Vorticist movement. See Biographical Appendix.

106   Dorothy to Ezra

Leweston Manor
Sherborne
Dorset
[*10 August 1912*]

Dearest–

Thanks for yours & Mary's name & approximate address. I can't remember when she was to be married–never mind.

There are six black spaniel pups here very young–& all over lumps because their Mama won't clean them properly! I went 40 miles with the boys yesterday in the car, to a cricket-match–and began a dull sketch this morning–of the font here in the chapel. I am onto another Anatole [France] "Barbe-Bleue" and am doing a certain amount of embroidery. It's a lovely place, this, full of cedars. There is a german, *no*–Austrian gov: [governess] here for the boys' benefit–& I know none–O.S. [Olivia Shakespear] struggles–at times. Somebody's eye has been cut by a cricket ball - - - & there's a doctor wandering round wondering if he will ever get away–the household being vague about matters of Transport.

à toi.

The lavender here is exquisite.

"Barbe-Bleue"]   Anatole France, *Les Sept Femmes de la Barbe-Bleue et autres contes merveilleux* (1909).

107   Dorothy to Ezra

Leweston Manor
Sherborne
Dorset
[*11 August 1912*]
Sunday

Dearest.

Everyone else except O.S. [Olivia Shakespear] & I/me gone to church. The dog having been given an old emerald-green collar to chew, has been 'ick of it!

This is [to] wish you luck of the Countess if she comes. I shall be amused to hear what happens about her. I wonder if she is in the habit of writing manly letters? & of receiving hers "Esq". There is an engaged couple in the house–HE seems colonial and horribly shy–SHE is given to hunting & good works in due seasons.

I am "sorry I spoke" about KAT.

There is to be a fête here on Wed: some stupid affair about money needed for a village nurse or sommat. We return I conclude the next day.

Yesterday I watched cricket again–here–local talent: It was really most amusing & extremely midgey. Oh–this rain is dreadful. I wanted to go to meet Mervyn [Fletcher] (No.II) & relieve him of the engaged couple whom he has escorted to Church. I am amused: There are two old family (Fletcher) friends here, who have never before met–One is jealous & the other doesn't care–Its quite entertaining to watch!

Yours.

"sorry I spoke" about KAT]   See Letter **105n.**

108   Ezra to Dorothy

[*London*]
[*13 August 1912*]
Tuesday

Dearest:

The countess, after having sent a telegram which led me to believe she would not, came twice yesterday, P.M. in my absence and sat on the doorstep 15 minutes. It's only a german countess and I am beginning to lose interest.

[T.E.] Hulme & I discussed the metaphysics of art until 11.30.

'Jack' the terrier has departed Church Walk, and possibly this life. *Rural notes* A♭. I found an egg in the dog kennel, which same Langley [the landlady] describes as "Louisa's"–Sarah's eggs being of a lighter complexion. And that's all I've got to balance the fourteen spanielletti. Mrs Langley says the countess is about as broad as she is long, that she probably wouldn't "own to forty", that she wished she (Mrs. L.) had her (die Furstin's) hat.

This prose book is a dam'd nuisance & I've sent the songs to W.R. [Walter Rummel]. Hope I wasn't too severe about the KAT. The poem is very bad anyhow. Kat or no Kat.

[J.C.] Squire is coming this P.M. but I feel very uncertain about his ability to amuse me. "Madame Bovary" is the only oasis in this waste of ennui.

The gods preserve you
E.

the countess]   See Letter **105n.**
prose book]   "Gironde."
songs to W.R.]   See Letter **103n.**
the KAT]   See Letter **105.**
Squire]   J.C. Squire (1884–1958), poet, critic, and journalist who edited the *London Mercury*. He had reviewed *Canzoni,* not unfavorably, in the *New Age,* 10 (21 December 1911).

109   Ezra to Dorothy

[*Kensington*]
[*25 August 1912*]
Sunday

Dearest:

[A.R.] Orage has arranged tomorrow 4.P.M. (Monday) to see me, so I suppose I'd better come in to you Tuesday–if that suits. R.& H. [Richard Aldington & Hilda Doolittle] routed me out this A.M. and we have spent the idlest of days. Et nunc, I shall read my borrowed Horace & retire:

> Inter ludere virgines
> Et stellis nebulam spargere candidis.

or something of that sort. It will take my Villon longer to arrive so I've been reading him at the [British] museum and trying to memorize some of the things I either dont know, or have forgotten. He is worth if not all at least half the classics–⟨*sottise!*⟩.

> Toulù m'as la haulte franchise
> Que beaultè m'avoit ordonnè
> Sur clercs, marchants et gens d'eglise.
>   etc.

He is so much more vital than the unconcerned greek lyrists peut être, what nonsense I go on scribbling. V'la [Voilà].

bonne nuit.
E.

Orage]   Alfred Richard Orage (1873–1934), editor of the *New Age* from 1907 to 1922.

Inter ludere . . . candidis]   Horace, *Odes,* III. xv. 5–6.

inter ludere virgines
et stellis nebulam spargere candidis.

(Cease to play among the maidens and to cast a
cloud over the shining stars.)

Toulù . . . gens d'eglise]   François Villon, *Le Testament,* 48. The readings vary, and we do not know which edition EP consulted at the British Museum.

Tollu m'as la haulte franchise
Que beaulté m'avoit ordonné
Sur clers, marchans et gens d'Eglise . . .

(You have taken from me the great power that
beauty granted me over clerks, merchants, and
churchmen. . .)

110   Dorothy to Ezra

11 Larkstone
Ilfracombe
[Devon]
2 September [1912]

Dearest.

Its a pleasant place. G. [Georgie Hyde-Lees] & I sketched in a wood
inland this morning–And this afternoon their two aunts & Coz's went for
a long drive to a village which was full of brand new villas–the old har-
bour was very pretty & a nice church. The rocks here are fine - - - [sketch]
kind of scratchy shape. There is a Parade, where every one goes about
(on Sundays) in white satin frocks & terrific ostrich feathers!

Here I tried to paint you a sky–the result totally unlike a sky - - - & I
have sucked such a lot of nasty paint off my brushes. We have a pianola–
G. [Georgie] plays it beautifully & we have Brahms & Schumann (oh *dear*
Walter!) in the evenings.

We saw a delightful hill called " 'Angman 'Ill" today during our drive:
it was like a slumbering dragon with his large paws laid on the sea [sketch]–
& it was covered with heather. I must write to the Hamad–d [Hilda Doo-
little]. And it is getting dark–and as usual Coz can't write a decent let-
ter - - -

à demain.

Tuesday

A fine paint this morning: the rocks are lovely – silvery-gray & in streaks
& very difficult. Coz hasn't read a word of anything: its a thick mist now.
Humanity bathing is entertaining: –& maddening. It spoils the rocks a lot
& is *so ugly.*

Yours
D.S.

111   Ezra to Dorothy

[*Kensington*]
[*3 September 1912*]

Dearest:

I like to have the pictures here on the wall. And I will [have] more of them. They keep my mind off of various things, and on various things, and the exchange is satisfactory. I think we have wasted a good deal of time–mentally.

I have finished my 6th philippic and have writ a note on "Bill" [William Carlos Williams] which I believe to be a masterpiece of tactful iniquity. I was heartened thereto by the heroic behaviour of Ellen Terry [the actress]. I told you I was being taken to see "Rebecca of Sunnybrook Farm" and so I was. And it was fairly amusing, yes quite except in the serious parts, and from the end of the third act on it got steadily worse, and at the end of the fourth there was a hush and gradually the friends of the authoress regained their presence of mind, and there was Mary Anderson in the authoress's box nearly weeping with anxiety when she ought to have been weeping with some thing else. (I don't quite know what)–and there was the house relapsing–despite its earnest and kindly intention–into silence, and the authoress had rushed behind the scenes but there wasn't time for her to get before the curtain and silence grew denser, and then did the aforesaid Ellen rise in the front row of the stalls, and with a gesture of imperial and unparagonable command begin to clap, it wasn't the noise but the motion, that renewed the ⟨subsiding⟩ subsided ⟨applause⟩ disturbance–ah, yes, 'tis little to write of, gord wot! but splendid to see.

My "Heine" & "Villon" have come so I suppose I shall get nothing done for a day or so–Yes, I like the Sirmio, the light in the hill (Baldo).

I can't remember that I've done anything except dine with the Dryad [Hilda Doolittle], and read 'Henry' [James] and write prose, and this is Tuesday, God save you.

Io ti baccio gli occhi.

E.

6th philippic]   The sixth installment of *Patria Mia*, which was published in the *New Age*, 11 (10 October 1912). Serial publication of *Patria Mia* had begun on 5 September 1912. EP was able to work so fast because he was re-shaping material recorded during his visit to the U.S. in 1910–11.

a note on "Bill"]   The introductory note to a selection from William Carlos Williams's *The Tempers* [*Poetry Review*, 1 (October 1912)].

"Rebecca of Sunnybrook Farm"]   The play Rebecca of Sunnybrook Farm,
by Kate Douglas Wiggin and Charlotte Thompson (adapted from Kate Wiggin's
popular novel of 1903), opened in London on 2 September 1912. The next day
the Times ended its review with this comment: "It is a quaint medley of American
ruralisms and sentimentalisms that will probably from its sheer strangeness prove
acceptable to many London playgoers."

the Sirmio]   A watercolor by DS which captured the light on Monte Baldo.

112   Dorothy to Ezra

> *11 Larkstone*
> *Ilfracombe*
> *[Devon]*
> *[3 September 1912]*
> *Tuesday even:*

Of course as I was so lazy–yours has crossed mine. I am sure something
is wrong with us both - - - I am glad the two sketches are pleasant to live
with. I do hope I shall do some here that you will care about. I did a
pale-gray rock against a dark-gray sky today. Thank goodness there isn't
much need here for mental efforts–I paint & eat & hold desultory con-
versations with G. [Georgie Hyde-Lees]. They think I am cross, or dull or
queer–accordingly–but if I can do the rocks I don't care! And really when
I "think" I only get into tangles & make myself miserable - - - *not* about
my soul!–but about my body: so here with wind & mist & sea I just enjoy
them all. The engaged & honeymooning couples are a word of warning–all
over the place & they walk about leaning towards each other [2 sketches].
Good-night.

> *Wed or Thurs evening*

Coz has gone fair crazy on the rocks here! She sketched them here in the
morning yesterday, & then in a "sweet-pretty" (Louisa's expression) place
we drove to in the afternoon– –She can't do clouds or sea though. This
afternoon at very low tide we scrambled onto some rocks & sat–most pain-
fully–& painted for a while– –The fisherman who superintends that cove
came alongside & talked gentle Devon to me. He had never seen anybody
paint those particular rocks before, he said (? compliment) & "you got
them in well, haven't you" he said–I had only got in some heavy shad-
ows - - - did he approve or was it mere conversation? I never knew such

a place for trippers who stand solidly beside one & watch. Yesterday a young man stood two yards behind me for ten good minutes. Hardly anyone here seems to paint. There's been a lot of sea today–& wind–& Coz loves it–& has wanted this scenery all her life.

a toi.

113   Ezra to Dorothy

[*London*]

[*early September 1912*]

"Daily she goes out a-walking
With two damnable old ladies"

H. Heine, Esq. animadverting on the "Tuilierien garten" (jardins des Tuileries).

Various books have arrived so I am thereby diverted, and shall get nothing done. The beginning of Patria Mia VII is in better prose than the earlier sections. The Kennedy-Fraser lady's gaelic was very interesting.

> Nun da bin ich.
> Just so weit wie einst Petrarcha.

We all dined with the Hamadryad's [Hilda Doolittle's] she-poet last evening. Richard [Aldington] has just brought me a bad poem and departed with dampened spirits. As I have before remarked,–I have a growing perception that I shall end as a sort of Pietro Bembo to this *saeclum inane*, i.e. 'this rotten age'. My one present consolation is that I am making six enemies per paragraph by the Patria Mia.–Also your clouds in the water keep one from meditating on the curse of accursedness.

I've just (i.e. an hour or so later & after lunch) received a long and affectionate epistle from the more highly respected segment of my grandmother's (maternal-grandmother's to be exact) family. There's supposed to be a society propaganda started in New York to get me into a nonextant "chair" of something or other.

My most diverting cousin seems to have married out [of] his difficulties so I suppose they've got leisure to consider mine.

And so forth.
E.

"Daily . . . old ladies"]   From Heinrich Heine's "Die Unbekannte" ("The Unknown"), No. 16 of the "Romanzen" sequence in *Neue Gedichte* (1844), which opens:

> Meiner goldgelockten Schönen
> Weiss ich täglich zu begegnen,
> In dem Tuileriengarten,
> Unter den Kastanienbäumen.
>
> Täglich geht sie dort spazieren,
> Mit zwei hässlich alten Damen—
> Sind es Tanten? Sinds Dragoner,
> Die vermummt in Weiberröcken?
>
> (My adored and golden-haired one,
> Every day I'm sure to meet her,
> When beneath the chestnut branches
> In the Tuileries she wanders.
>
> Every day she comes and walks there
> With two old and awful ladies—
> Are they aunts? Or are they dragons?
> Or dragoons in skirts and flounces?)

The Kennedy-Fraser lady]   On 3 September 1912 EP wrote to his father that "Marjorie Kennedy Fraser is coming tonight to sing us some gaelic folk songs. You may have come on her collection of Hebridean Songs." Mrs. Marjory Kennedy-Fraser (1857–1930) compiled several collections of Scottish songs, including *Songs of the Hebrides and Other Celtic Songs from the Highlands of Scotland* (1909).

Nun da bin . . . Petrarcha]   From the penultimate stanza of Heine's "Die Unbekannte":

> Laura heisst sie! Nun da bin ich
> Just so weit wie einst Petrarcha,
> Der das schöne Weib gefeiert
> In Kanzonen und Sonetten.
>
> (She is Laura! I'm as great now
> As was Petrarch when he chanted
> And extolled his lovely lady
> In those canzonets and sonnets.)

she-poet]   Hilda Doolittle's friend Frances Josepha Gregg (1884–1941). In *End to Torment* H.D. tells how Frances Gregg "filled the gap in my Philadelphia life after Ezra was gone, after our 'engagement' was broken. Maybe the loss of Ezra left a vacuum; anyway, Frances filled it like a blue flame. I made my first trip to Europe with her and her mother, summer 1911. Frances wrote, about a year after her return to America, that she was getting married. . . . She said that one of the objects of her marriage to this English University Extension lecturer—or in fact the chief object—was a return to Europe so that she could join me; we would all go to Belgium together where 'Louis' was lecturing." But according to H.D., EP persuaded her not to join Frances and her husband. In H.D.'s autobiographical *HERmione,* completed in 1927 but not published until 1981, EP figures as "George Lowndes" and Frances as "Fayne Rabb." *HERmione* is dedicated "To F . . . . . for September 2nd"; the 2nd of September was Frances Gregg's birthday [*End to Torment,* ed. Norman Holmes Pearson and Michael King (New Directions, 1979), pp. 8–9; *HERmione* (New Directions, 1981)].

The "Louis" that Frances Gregg married was Louis Umfreville Wilkinson (1881–1966). After being sent down from Pembroke College, Oxford, for "blasphemy," Wilkinson was admitted to St. John's College, Cambridge, where he formed lasting friendships with John Cowper Powys and Llewelyn Powys. Between 1905 and 1919 he lectured frequently in the United States, often in Philadelphia, and from 1909 to 1945 he was a University Extension lecturer in literature for Oxford and London universities. He wrote a number of novels, two under his own name and the rest under the pen name Louis Marlow, which was also the name he used when he published his study of the three Powys brothers, *Welsh Ambassadors* (1936; new edition 1971, with a biographical introduction by Kenneth Hopkins).

Wilkinson married Frances Gregg in 1912, and they had a son, Oliver, and a daughter, Elizabeth Josepha. But the marriage was not successful, and Frances obtained a divorce in 1923. Louis subsequently married three more times. Frances and her daughter were killed in the blitz on Plymouth in 1941.

In 1911–12 Frances Gregg was thought of as a promising young poet. Four of her poems appeared in the *Forum,* 46 (December 1911), two in the *Cerebralist,* 1 (December 1913), and two in *Poetry* (Chicago), 5 (January 1915). She also published a highly revealing group of "Contes Macabres" in the *New Freewoman,* 1 (1 December 1913); and an essay on Strindberg in collaboration with J.C. Powys [*Forum,* 55 (January 1916)]. Some years later she published two stories in *The Second American Caravan,* ed. Alfred Kreymborg, Lewis Mumford, and Paul Rosenfeld (New York, 1928). In a Biographical Note to this volume she is described as a contributor to "The Forum, The Dial, Poetry, The Smart Set, The Adelphi, The Monthly Criterion, and the London Mercury."

Pietro Bembo]   Pietro Bembo (1470–1547), Italian humanist and historian of Venice.

most diverting cousin]   William Wadsworth, the son of Charles David Wadsworth, had married Helen Tweed, a daughter of Charles Harrison Tweed, a well-to-do banker-lawyer, on 23 May 1912. EP refers to his cousin (under the pseudonym Edward) in *Indiscretions* (1923): "Edward, from being a gentleman, has had great difficulty in discovering how to be anything else: he has somewhat drifted about the professions—in a charming manner. . . . Edward had taken the Exchange as a bore and an imposition; it had bored him for forty years. . . ." [*Pavannes and Divagations* (New Directions, 1958), p. 26].

114   Ezra to Dorothy

[Kensington]
[9 September 1912]
Monday

Dearest Coz.

I have read a little Montaigne, and embellished my opening to 'Gironde' by certain speculations on the new paganism and I may have done a little more 'Patria Mia' tho' I think that was done before my last letter. And I have conversed and had meals with Richard [Aldington] & Bridgit [Patmore] & the Dryad [Hilda Doolittle] and I think that is about all that is pleasant. And the worst that can be said of things is that I am mildly apathetic and not sufficiently discontented with anything to burst into valuable lyrics. I am more inclined to suspect my liver than the state of the universe at large–still a revolution would be consoling. I have found one good poem by Verhaeren.

Quiller-Couch has brought forth a volumn & dedicated it to M.H. [Maurice Hewlett].

> "Hewlett as ship to ship
> Our ensigns dip"

and etc. The quotations from which may be held as matter for mirth. I don't think he has got anybody on "The royal bench of British Themis" but the Observer assures us that the verse is "luscious as the buds of Spring".

I had last night a most gorgeous dream about the marriage in Cana of Galilee, it began in symbolical patterns on a rug and ended in a wedding dance to exceed the Russians both in grace, splendour & legerity–convincingly naive and oriental!!

I wonder if the eagle [Yeats] is back or anywhere near? God save you, and keep the winds & clouds in order and present you with sun enough to bring out the colour.

Yours

E.

Bridgit]   Brigit (Ethel Elizabeth Morrison-Scott) Patmore (1882–1965), a vivacious young woman from Ulster who married John Deighton Patmore, the grandson of the Victorian poet Coventry Patmore. In the years immediately before the first World War she was part of the literary circle that included Violet Hunt, Ford Madox Hueffer, Hilda Doolittle, Richard Aldington, and EP. See *My Friends When Young: The Memoirs of Brigit Patmore,* ed. Derek Patmore (1968).

Quiller-Couch] Arthur Thomas Quiller-Couch (1863–1944), the popular anthologist. On 22 October 1912 EP reported to Harriet Monroe that "Q" wanted to put him "in the *Oxford Book of Victorian Verse.* This is no small honor—at least I should count it a recognition. Nevertheless he had hit on two poems which I had marked 'to be omitted' from the next edition of my work, and I've probably mortally offended him by telling him so. At least I haven't heard from him again" [*Letters,* No. 9.]. The poems "Q" included in the anthology were "Portrait" (CEP), first published in *Exultations* (1909), and "Ballad for Gloom" (CEP), which first appeared in *A Lume Spento* (1908). The "volumn" EP refers to in this letter is *The Vigil of Venus and Other Poems by "Q"* (1912). The dedicatory poem, "To Maurice Hewlett," opens with this stanza:

> Hewlett! as ship to ship
> Let us the ensign dip.
> There may be who despise
> For dross our merchandise,
> Our balladries, our bales
>   Of woven tales;
> Yet, Hewlett, the glad gales
> Favonian! And what spray
> Our dolphins toss'd in play.
> Full in old Triton's beard, on Iris' shimmering veils!

The anonymous review of *The Vigil of Venus* in the *Observer* (8 September 1912) opens: "This volume contains Sir Arthur Quiller Couch's rich and scholarly translation of the Pervigilium Veneris—a poem luscious as the bursting buds of spring."

dream about the marriage in Cana of Galilee] The inspiration for "Dance Figure, for the Marriage in Cana of Galilee" (P), first published in *Poetry* (Chicago), 2 (April 1913). See Letter **117.**

115   Dorothy to Ezra

11 Larkstone
Ilfracombe
[Devon]
[11 September 1912]

Dearest,

We have just got a new "book-box" from the Pianola Coy. & have had great fun–one Cui a modern Russian who seems tuneful, simple, & belated.

THEIR [CHARS] Bunk has been simply dreadful these last days: he swore they–THEY–were going to be married–to one Mildred Sawford–a nice girl who paints in the old-fashioned stipple style–CHARS have been nearly persuaded into belief, because he went on so about it–I found him giving their aunt (OS) a list of their wedding presents forsooth!–And now he pretends *he* never suggested it, & has got them out of a scrape–ugh! *And* they "once inclined to the female sex" *any*way. It's been very agitating.

We leave here on 23rd & go for a fortnight to Lynton, near Exmoor. Cold wind has made sketching rather difficult–& awful gales of it too. Yesterday we created a sensation in The Harbour by sketching there–nobody has been seen to do such a thing before, we conclude.

Nelly [Mrs. Tucker, Georgie Hyde-Lees' mother] has given me a pair of earrings that don't suit her–pearly & silver–very pretty. I had a charming letter today from H-d-d [Hamadryad: Hilda Doolittle].

I must to bed–its 10.30.

A toi

12 September

Its the coldest, bleakest, grayest day that ever was. So we are spending the morning in. One really can't sketch in a "northerly wind that blows from behind" & brings along with it clouds of sand. Georgie says she had a great tip from your head about coiffure!! She has done it this morning & looks nice! Yesterday we went to the Kinema–most entertaining–and in front were two CHAR-children: they were stout & active, with fair curly heads & gray eyes–aged anything between 3 & 300 years. Such loves, & full of wickedness. I have been reading an old H.G. Wells "Mr. Polly"–rather pleasant–not very.

Too cold & sunless to write any more
A toi.

"book-box" . . . *Pianola Coy.*]   Probably a boxed selection of sheet music, not rolls for a player-piano.

Cui]   César Antonovich Cui (1835–1918), Russian military architect and composer.

THEIR Bunk]   In this fantasy about CHARS Henry Hope Shakespear is imagined as their uncle (Bunk) and Olivia as their aunt.

"Mr. Polly"]   H.G. Wells's novel *The History of Mr. Polly* (1910).

116   Olivia Shakespear to Ezra

> *11 Larkstone*
> *Ilfracombe*
> *[Devon]*
> *13 September 1912*

Dear Ezra–

As I never have any opportunity of seeing you & discussing matters, I must write what I have got to say.

You told me you were prepared to see less of Dorothy this winter. I don't know if you wd rather leave it to me to say I don't think it advisable she should see so much of you etc. or whether you wd rather do it in your own way– –I suppose I cd trust you to do it? I don't want to put the onus of it on your shoulders if you don't want me to–on the other hand, it seems to be a sort of surgical operation with her before she can say anything to me about you & of course, we *might* have a row over the business–for I don't intend to give way about it–She has never mentioned you to me, & I don't know if she still considers herself engaged to you– but as she obviously can't marry you, she must be made [to] realize that she can't go on as though you were her accepted lover–it's hardly *decent*!

There's another point too–which is the personal inconvenience & bother to myself–I had all last winter, practically to keep 2 days a week for you to come & see her, which was all very well whilst there was some chance of yr marrying her, & I put up with it, but I really can't put up with it for the remainder of our lives–it gets on my nerves.

The most serious thing about the whole business is that she isn't the least likely–she can't in decency–"transfer her affections" to anyone else whilst you are always about–& you'll be doing her a great injury if you stand in the way of her marrying–She *must* marry–She & I can't possibly go on living this feminine life practically *à deux* for ever, & we haven't money enough to separate–& should have less than we have now if her father died–indeed, in the latter event I should probably marry again, & she wd be very much de trop– –raison de plus for her marrying.

You *ought* to go away–Englishmen don't understand yr American ways, & any man who wanted to marry her wd be put off by the fact of yr friendship (or whatever you call it) with her.

If you had £500 a year I should be delighted for *you* to marry her (no nonsense about waiting 5 years etc.) but as you haven't, I'm obliged to say all this–as her mother I can't see it any other way–I've seen too much of girls wasting their lives on men who can't marry them, & they generally end by being more or less compromised demivierges. I only *hope* you have not talked about her to your friends. I trusted, perhaps wrongly, to your honour in the matter–but I know that Mme. Hueffer, for one, knows you have an affair with somebody–Think all I have said well over before answering–& remember you will gain nothing by being cheeky!

I shouldn't mind yr coming to see her once a week, but she can't go about with you American fashion– –not till she is 35 & has lost her looks. Dear Ezra–I'm sorry for you–really–but you are a great trouble, & my anxiety about her is always there. Tomorrow is her birthday, & all I can feel is that I wish she had never been born. She chose her parents very unwisely.

Yrs O.S.

117   Ezra to Dorothy

[*Kensington*]
[*14 September 1912*]
Saturday

Dearest:

Tis this day your Kalends, whereon one should erect altars and offer wreaths, *halentia serta* and pour forth honey and milk (a sticky mess one would imagine) and *pede libero pulsanda est tellus* and one should offer verses in the neo-classic style and so on with due form and ceremony. Cartels and protocols from your mother!!

It is also a season wherein I should offer you philosophical counsel

from the ancient authors–*far buon tempo e trionfare,* no that's not suffi-
ciently scriptural. I should rather get me to Montaigne–who has so far as I
have read, said little of women–or to Tullius [Cicero] who says of them
almost nothing at all. Also I should have prepared you an ode and I have
done nothing but a semitic "vers libre" on the "Marriage of Cana in Gali-
lee" *à la* my apochryphal dream–and writ a few modern epigrams to keep
Richard [Aldington] from the blues–one on the tea-shop rewritten de-
cently–and one on a porcelain bath-tub which is held for a marvel of
precision.

I went over the first 80 pp. of 'Gironde' with Ford [Madox Hueffer]
yesterday, he says its as bad as [R.L.] Stevenson and that is very violent
for him, he is however pleased with the Ripostes–and his criticism of the
prose is very helpful, and the stuff is not precisely hopeless or past re-
vising.

> Cara vorrei che tu sola ed io
> Fossimo presi per incantamento
> E messi ad un vascel

> – – – – – – – –

> Sicchè fortuna od altro tempo rio
> Non ci potesse dare impedimento
>   etc

Only as the great Tuscan later remarks its not all skittles and moonshine.

I'm to be let in *once* a week unless you go to Italy with the Dryad
[Hilda Doolittle] which seems unlikely. However - - - Sufficient unto the
day is the damnability thereof.

I've got to get some tennis balls sent to F.M.H. [Ford Madox Hueffer]
or they wont be there in time for this P.M. Who the deuce is Ray Lan-
kester? that I'm to meet at a luncheon tomorrow? Not that you can answer
in time–Is it male or female, or only an unmarriageable CHARS. I really
dont think THEY [CHARS] Kan–it wouldn't be legal.

The gods avail you, eat as much open air as you can and don't worry.
I doubt not that life is as the sages have agreed "Just one damn thing after
another" and our only recourse is to watch the procession as stoically as
possible.

Yours
E.

Kalends]   September 14th was Dorothy's birthday.
halentia serta]   *halantia serta,* "fragrant garlands."
pede libero . . . tellus]   Horace, *Odes,* I, xxxvii, 1–2.

> Nunc est bibendum, nunc pede libero
> pulsanda tellus . . .
>
> (Now is the time to drain the flowing bowl, now
> with unfettered foot to beat the ground with
> dancing . . .)

far buon . . . trionfare]   The epigraph to "Elegia," Part IV of "Und Drang" (CEP), which was first published in *Canzoni* (1911). In connection with Dorothy's birthday it means "to be happy and celebrate."

"Marriage of Cana in Galilee"]   See Letter **114n.**

modern epigrams . . . tea-shop . . . porcelain bath-tub]   "The Tea Shop" (P) was published in *Lustra* (1916); "The Bath Tub" (P) first appeared in the *Smart Set,* 41 (December 1913).

'Gironde' . . . Stevenson]   The travel writings of Robert Louis Stevenson (1850–1894) were noted for their "charm." His *Travels with a Donkey in the Cévennes* (1879) tells of his experiences in southern France.

Cara vorrei. . . impedimento]   Adapted from the first two quatrains of Dante's Sonetto VI.

> Guido, vorrei che tu e Lapo ed io
> Fossimo presi per incantamento,
> E messi ad un vascel, ch' ad ogni vento
> Per mare andasse a voler vostro e mio;
>
> Sicchè fortuna, od altro tempo rio
> Non ci potesse dare impedimento,
> Anzi, vivendo sempre in un talento,
> Di stare insieme crescesse il disio.
>
> (Guido, I would that thou and Lapo and I were
> taken by enchantment, and put in a vessel, that
> with every wind might sail to your will and mine;
>
> so that tempest, or other ill weather could give
> us no hindrance, rather, living ever in one mind,
> our desire might wax to abide together.)

This sonnet is the opening of the *tenzone* or competition between Dante and Guido, of which four sonnets by Guido have survived. Lapo Gianni belonged to the group of poets that included Dante, Guido, and Cino. EP translated Cavalcanti's reply to this sonnet in *Sonnets and Ballate of Guido Cavalcanti* (1912); for his personal "answer" to Guido's "answer," see "Guido Invites You Thus" (P), first published in *Exultations* (1909).

Ray Lankester]   Edwin Ray Lankester (1847–1929), director of the natural history departments of the British Museum from 1898 to 1907. He was twice Vice-President of the Royal Society, and it is likely that EP met him through Yeats, who was a member of the Academic Committee of the Royal Society of Literature. Lankester was noted for his artistic and literary abilities.

118   Dorothy to Ezra

> *11 Larkstone*
> *Ilfracombe*
> *[Devon]*
> *15 September [1912]*
> *Sunday*

Dearest.

The sea is such lovely colours–blues & greens, & brown near in. We found such a place at very low tide: it was like a great Roman road of shingle (gray) with rocks on each side, and it went over apparently into the sky. I want to try & paint it, but its so near low tide mark that I am afraid of being drowned. Georgie [Hyde-Lees] has gone off this morning to paint alone: it is a queer uncanny place down, down, at the bottom of Cliffs and I simply *daren't* go there to paint [sketch]–Its chiefly because it makes me horribly giddy–but slightly because its so cold & alarming.

We had awful adventures the other day: we scrambled round at low tide among such gorgeous places which are certainly 10ft. & more, under water at High [Tide]. It scares me all the time–but G. [Georgie] seems calm & leads the way, & there's really no danger, I know.

We had a day out yesterday: a long cliff walk; lunch (not much!), a cliff exploration, sketching, tea & the family–HOME. Net result–shells in a matchbox for the H-d-d [Hamadryad: Hilda Doolittle].

Thanks for your birthday letter: I am looking forward to the Cana poem. It sounded lovely: the dream. Also I am glad the tea-shop is changed.

Once a week be hanged - - - Which of many reasons that might be, is given?

Yours with Love.

G. is very depressed with life, I fancy–But we paint a lot & take as little notice as possible of the Family–which I am not sure they don't think nasty tempered of us. Nelly [Georgie's mother] said yesterday à propos some frivolous remark, that she would "believe anything of the Young" (that's us).

Dio Mio!

Once a week be hanged]   See Letter **116,** where Olivia tells Ezra: "I shouldn't mind yr coming to see her once a week, but she can't go about with you American fashion."

119   Ezra to Dorothy

[*Kensington*]
[*17 September 1912*]
Tuesday

Brava!

Et les jeunes, indeed? It is a terrible generation but Georgie [Hyde-Lees] shouldn't be too depressed about it.

I have revised pp. 1–82 of Gironde & on counting up the rest of my *mss* find that the book is about done–in the rough–which is some relief. I play tennis with Ford [Madox Hueffer] in the afternoons and dine with Richard & the Dryad [Aldington & Hilda Doolittle].

F.M.H. [Ford Madox Hueffer] finds my prose as bad as [R.L.] Stevenson, so I've made some alterations and inserted a soliloquy on fat middle-aged gentlemen in armchairs. F. [Hueffer] has just returned from instructing the ⟨cabinet⟩ personnel of your respected cabinet, so he is a little out of hand.

Wednesday

Have translated a sonnet of Carducci's, and thought about beginning to rewrite some more Gironde. The thought is thoroughly exhaustive, so thoroughly exhausting, in fact, that it is now high noon and I am not yet tubbed. The American Bookman states that I am a "rude, dominant man" and advertises me to the extent of 4¾ columns.

Don't crawl down a cliff-hole and get Desdamona'd by the tide. I must quit this and get mobilized or luncheon and tea etc will be upon me incontinent.

à toi.
E.

sonnet of Carducci's]   Giosuè Carducci (1835–1907), the Italian poet who won the Nobel Prize for Literature in 1906. EP's translation was never published.

American Bookman]   In an omnibus review entitled "A Panel of Poets" [*The Bookman,* 35 (April 1912)] Milton Bronner devoted considerable space to EP's *Personae, Exultations,* and *Provença.* The review is quite favorable ("he will sing you one song or ten in honor of his beloved,—exquisite things, cast into new moulds, with the freshness of manner that comes in a real poet who is breaking away from his teachers and models"), and the passage from which EP quotes is one of high praise.

> It speaks much for Pound that, despite the fact that his three books of poems are very small and despite the various experiments we have glanced at, he nevertheless manages to convince one that he has the right Promethean fire. Not only that, but he makes one feel, too, that he is a big personality, one who is both lover and thinker, a rude dominant man, almost burly, hewing out his own proper effects in a strikingly original manner. . .

120   Dorothy to Ezra

11 Larkstone
[Ilfracombe]
[Devon]
[21 September 1912]
Saturday

Cher.

Just think! I found a whole heap of four–& five-leafed clovers yesterday! G. [Georgie Hyde-Lees] found some too - - - all in a field with a well worn path through it. It was so exciting - - - & its supposed to be very lucky! We tested some of our luck by taking a long, rather dull, drive in the afternoon–were well rewarded, as we saw the finest bit of coast I've seen up to now–a place called Morthoe. It has a most remarkable situation & *such* a Cat/Kat at the Pub: G. [Georgie] & I are thinking of going there perhaps for few days to sketch–after Lynton.

We go on Monday 23rd to:–

> Gordon House
> Lee Road
> Lynton
> N. Devon.

for a fortnight.

Sunday

Packing wildly for Lynton. And such a vol. of [G.R.S.] Mead to go in still! F. of a F. Forgotten. Also, a delightful book published in '71 or so, printed on blue paper called "The Blue Ray of the Sunlight". All about electrical currents & why things (*any* Thing) grow faster under Blue Glass. I mean to paint my window blue! It cures rheumatics etc. by the heat generated.

I must continue to pack–

Au revoir. D.

Are you moving from Piazza [10 Church Walk]?

Morthoe]   A village on the coast of north Devon, near the dangerous Morte Point, about five miles from Ilfracombe where DS was visiting. Her drawing of the cliffs has survived.

Mead . . . F. of a F. Forgotten]   G.R.S. Mead, *Fragments of a Faith Forgotten. Some Short Sketches among the Gnostics Mainly of the First Two Centuries* (1900).

"The Blue Ray of the Sunlight"]   *Influence of the Blue Ray of the Sunlight and of the Blue Colour of the Sky, in developing animal and vegetable life; in arresting disease, and in restoring health in acute and chronic disorders to human and domestic animals, as illustrated by the experiments of Gen. A. J. Pleasonton, and Others, between the years 1861 and 1876.* Addressed to the Philadelphia Society for Promoting Agriculture (Philadelphia, 1876). An earlier version, *On the Influence of the Blue Color of the Sky . . .*, was published in 1871.

121   Ezra to Dorothy

> *10 Church Walk*
> *[Kensington]*
> *[23 September 1912]*

Dearest:

No I'm not moving. The rain has destroyed the crops of the father of my landlady so we're not taking a larger maison this season. Richard [Aldington] & I did think of taking a rather diverting cottage in Duke's Lane overlooking the monastery gdn. but we decided it would be too much bother.

I've become a 'foreign correspondent' or 'foreign edtr.' or something of that sort–for a Chicago "Poetry" magazine–about the time you were finding four-leaf clovers.

They're printing the 'Kat' and a note on Whistler in their opening number. And they'll be a little more lucrative than the "P. Rev." [*Poetry Review*]. I'm sending them some "Richard" [Aldington] and a denunciation of everybody except Yeats & [Padraic] Colum for their next number.

Lady Low approves of the "Alexander Hamiltons" in the N. Age [*New Age*]. Gilbert Cannan appeared on Sat. with *two* elephantine dogs. The great bohemian poet Vrchlicky is *morto*. I don't know that it will much affect you. Had I seen Selver's anthology of "Modern Bohemian Poetry" before you departed–Good stuff done into very bad english??

The Dryad [Hilda Doolittle] is much depressed at the prospect of returning to its parental bosom.

I've hung about the 1st. ⅓rd. of 'Gironde' on my west wall as a sign that I'm dam'd if I bother much more with revising it.

I've found some fine things in Gautier's "Emaux et Camées" and alternately bless & curse my education which has kept me from so much modern continental stuff & which has *en revanche* allowed me so much that it I would never have bothered about if I'd known the modern stuff first.

F. & V-M.H. [Ford Madox Hueffer & Violet Hunt] have just come into the 'Pyat*zaa*' and summoned me to tea. And I've already had 5 cups of my own. Nathless I think I will go up, as they are off tomorrow for somewhere or other.

à toi

E.

Chicago "Poetry" magazine] Harriet Monroe, the editor of *Poetry* (Chicago), began corresponding with EP in the summer of 1912, and the November issue of *Poetry* announced that "Mr. Ezra Pound has consented to act as foreign correspondent of POETRY, keeping its readers informed of the present interests of the art in England, France and elsewhere." EP's "Middle-Aged, A Study in an Emotion" [the "Kat" poem] and his note "To Whistler, American. On the Loan Exhibit of His Paintings at the Tate Gallery" appeared in the first issue of *Poetry* (October 1912). Three poems by Richard Aldington were published in the second issue (November 1912), but EP's "Status Rerum" did not appear until the fourth (January 1913).

"Alexander Hamiltons"] The *Patria Mia* essays in the *New Age*. EP is alluding to *The Federalist*, a series of essays in defense of the U.S. Constitution (over two thirds written by Hamilton) that appeared in the New York newspapers in 1787–88.

Gilbert Cannan]   Gilbert Cannan (1884–1955), novelist, dramatist, and dramatic critic, lived near EP in Kensington.

Vrchlicky]   Jaroslav Vrchlický (1853–1912), the Czech poet and translator.

Selver's anthology]   Percy Paul Selver (ed.), *An Anthology of Modern Bohemian Poetry* (1912). EP reviewed the book for *Poetry* (Chicago), 1 (November 1912). The character Eli Peck in Selver's novel *Schooling* (1924) is based on EP. "Eli Peck was the artist as portrayed in the comic papers. A velvet jacket, a tuft of beard and a far-away look were the chief items in his get-up."

Gautier's "Emaux et Camées"]   Théophile Gautier (1811–1872), the French poet whose collection *Emaux et camées* became for EP a touchstone to the "hard" and precise in modern poetry. Writing to Felix E. Schelling in July 1922, EP said that the "metre in *Mauberley* is Gautier and Bion's 'Adonis'; or at least those are the two grafts I was trying to flavour it with" [*Letters*, No. 190].

the 'Pyatzaa']   The "piazza" in front of 10 Church Walk.

122   Ezra to Dorothy

[*Kensington*]
[*1 October 1912*]
Tuesday 11 P.M.

Dearest:

De Goncourt (both of 'em) is (are) dead, but De Gourmont isn't, & "De Gourmand" is unknown in the serene plaisaunces of The *Art*. Gautier is also dead (physically) but I've been reading him.

I'm to meet [Rabindranath] Tagore tomorrow (si fas est).

The family of Mond has evidently descended on [Austin] Harrison, so I've got £4.4. and he has had a mauvais ¼ d'heure and that is food for glee. The N.A. [*New Age*] articles are so well received that I can stop Gironde about where it is and use "Patria Mia" as a second "Mediaeval Study". My humor ergo improves. I may be tolerable company by the time you get back.

Hewlett's last is the worst bilge I have *ever* seen.

Friday

These days have been as the weaver's shuttle. I dined with Tagore on Wed.–discussed meetres etc. Spent most of yesterday P.M. (2–6) with him. Discussing prosody, watching [William] Rothenstein paint his portrait, listening to him read & sing. Have arranged to print 6 poems [by Tagore] in "Poetry" unless somebody raises a fuss. We manage to keep the American copyright by this process, so its a jolly good thing for all concerned.

I have written for Deah Walter [Rummel] to come play before King ⟨Saul⟩ Rabindra [Tagore], so we may have some real soirées artistique during October. (We have assumed that some one will provide a piano.) I believe I am to go read to him some time or other. He is very fine & makes me feel like a painted pict with a stone war club–Naturally I've done nothing else.

You have seen the eagle [Yeats] in a state of exhultation over this matter and you may readily judge the condition of my lighter & more volatile spirits. I send this off before I go into another fit of meditation.

Yours.

E.

De Goncourt (*both of 'em*)]   Edmond de Goncourt (1822–1896) and Jules de Goncourt (1830–1870), brothers and literary collaborators, whose monumental *Journal* was begun in 1851. EP greatly admired the rationale for the realistic novel put forward in the Preface to their novel *Germinie Lacerteux* (1864).

De Gourmont]   Remy de Gourmont (1858–1915), the French philosopher and critic whose ideas had a profound impact on T. S. Eliot and EP. On 2 October 1915 EP wrote to Harriet Monroe that "De Gourmont is dead and the world's light is darkened" [*Letters,* No. 75].

Tagore]   Rabindranath Tagore (1861–1941), the Bengali poet who won the Nobel Prize for Literature in 1913. See Biographical Appendix. EP was deeply impressed by Tagore: "I speak with all gravity when I say that world-fellowship is nearer for the visit of Rabindranath Tagore to London" [*Poetry* (Chicago), 1 (December 1912)].

si fas est]   "If the Fates are willing."

Mond . . . Harrison]   Austin Harrison was the editor of the *English Review,* which was sponsored by the wealthy industrialist Sir Alfred Mond. "Mond killed the English Review / and Ford went to Paris (an interval)" [Canto 104].

N.A. articles . . . second "Mediaeval Study"]   See Letter **94n.**

Hewlett's last]   Some of the poems included in Maurice Hewlett's *Helen Redeemed and Other Poems* (1913) were published in whole or in part during 1912. In his review of the volume [*Poetry* (Chicago), 2 (May 1913)] EP praised several of the poems in the collection but said that the long title poem is "in the regular pentametric couplets, with the usual inversions, sometimes for the rime's sake, the long similes, etc., *cui amet.*"

Rothenstein] William Rothenstein (1872–1945), the English portrait painter who was a close friend of Yeats. In 1915 he published *Six Portraits of Sir Rabindranath Tagore.*

6 poems in "Poetry"]   Six poems by Tagore were published in *Poetry* (Chicago), 1 (December 1912), with a commentary by EP.

123   Dorothy to Ezra

[Lynton]
[Devon]
[5 October 1912]
Saturday

Dearest.

I am glad for your Tagorean days. W.B.Y. [Yeats] is here & we all return on Wednesday I hope. Perhaps he is here privately–I mean he may not want to be bothered by anybody's knowing–he has proofs & things I fancy. We have been told many tales of Tagore père going up the Ganges & fleeing from Goorkah regiments etc:

Is Walter [Rummel] likely to come over? It would be East & West meeting with a vengeance. Is Walter to play Debussy to him–I have many questions–all futile–to ask.

I shall hardly expect to hear from you again–I will write telling our plans. Life is sometimes interesting? h'è vero?

Yours–

124   Ezra to Dorothy

[Kensington]
[28 November 1912]

Dearest:

I don't know that my abstractions & generalities were of any use to you. I'll try to go into things definitely on Thursday *si ti piace* [if it pleases you]. If not don't bother.

E.

125   Dorothy to Ezra

[*Kensington*]
[*30 November 1912*]
Saturday

Dear

I am keeping Bill's [William Carlos Williams's] mental processes until Thursday–they are quite illuminating - - - but I have only hurried through them yet. Of course it will "mi piace" [please me] to have light thrown on yours, by yourself instead of W. Carlos W. Ton fils [Walter Rummel] was very charming yesterday.

I am so cold I must go out.

A toi.

D.

Yesterday, also, we heard Cernikoff. Today, I pine for Walter. Don't any day say so to Eva [Fowler]!

Bill's mental processes]   In a brief undated note to DS, EP says that he is sending "Bills epistle. It may divert you if you can make head or tail of it. I want to keep it, anyhow, as its an interesting sign board to Bill's mental processes. Incidentally some of it seems to be correct."

Cernikoff]   Vladimir Cernikoff (1882–1940), concert pianist.

126   Ezra to Dorothy

[*Kensington*]
[*16 December 1912*]

Dearest:

There is a little jade at 31 Edgeware Rd. There is more & better jade at 55 Long Acre. Nothing that I should care much for at either place. But 33 Cranbourn St. off Leicester Sq. interests me. It was shut this P.M. but I think they'd have good things. There was good stuff in the window, at least its the most promising place I've seen. The Long Acre place is a "fence" I should say, at least its got an atmosphere *tout vilain*.

I am dentisting & on Monday & Probably Friday. I'm lunching late on Tuesday & have a vague suspicion that you intend to invite me on that day. Please let me know when I'm to come–by return post if you can as I want to have the Wilkinsons or at least one of 'em to Tea before they go. As a matter of fact I shall invite F. ["Frances"] who most certainly won't invite her husband.

I have written 3 *impossible* poems in the course of the afternoon. One addressed to Eva [Fowler].

We are considering a complete edtn. of my poems in 2 vols.–not the new stuff. That is hardly, as yet, encycled–full-orbed or whatever the victorian term is.

Homages.

E.

jade]   EP had been looking for jade at the shops of Charles Collier, antique dealer, 31 Edgware Road; William John K. Clark, pawnbroker, 55 Long Acre; and Samuel Fenton, curiosity dealer, 33 Cranbourn Street.

Wilkinsons]   Frances Gregg and her husband, Louis Wilkinson. See Letter **113n.**

One addressed to Eva]   Probably "The Garden" (P), first published in *Poetry* (Chicago), 2 (April 1913).

complete edtn . . . 2 vols.]   In May 1913 Elkin Mathews published *Personae & Exultations* and *Canzoni & Ripostes* as "Ezra Pound's Poems, Volumes 1 and 2."

127   Ezra to Dorothy

10 Church Walk
[Kensington]
[22 December 1912]
Sunday

Dearest:

I shall not go to Paris as I'm going down to Burnham Beeches or some such for a week with Ford & V. [Ford Madox Hueffer & Violet Hunt]. The Eagle [Yeats] read me his diary up till 2 this morning–I figure it @ 6d per hr. counting cab fare home–and quite worth it.

The inimitable Tancred aroused me to meet the beau soleil & lunched with me. I have writ a favourable review of Jouve and a scathing one of the Georgian anthology. Tagore is at Urbanora Illinois, of all recesses!! Merci, for the Hachette's. I will deal with them at leisure. R. [Rummel] descants on the clarity of the Italian illumination.

The De Gourmont is fine, but the "Jouve" which I snaked from W.B.Y. is more alive than the Verhaeren.

I haven't O.S. [Olivia Shakespear's] copy of W.B.Y.'s plays. I've the copy he lent me to get some typing done from? has he hers? Her gift of Theophile Gautier has bien arrivè and I will write her my gratitudes.

What am I to say to Nancy [Maude]. Jouve talks much of an *enfant*, long & gravely, but d-d-d if I can. He says:

> "Il a la face concentrèe
> Du tres viel homme d'affaires."

He says

> "Il est vif et dejà solide"

he also says (to another one)

> "Tu seras mobile ainsi qu'une goutte d'huile."

— — — — — — — — — — —

What *am* I to say about le p'tit Jesu irlandais?

The "Poetes d'aujourd hui" I have already.

To save my soul I can't remember what has happened since when. F. & V. [Ford Madox Hueffer & Violet Hunt] had a box for "The Younger Generation" & it was very diverting, with a curtain raiser "Aristide Pujol" and a sentimental [J.M.] Barrie one act to finish. F. & I groaned so as to be heard all through the theatre. Thereafter I met G. [Gilbert] Cannan leaning over his front gate & he walked his dogs down to my room & drank tea until 2 A.M. (its the thaw that keeps 'em all so alert) and assured me that Barrie's humour in this play was unintentional. Well, he ought to know!

Met Mrs Napier at the Woods (not Derwent W's–The "Valiant, the master of the Temple", Woods) and she is always worth meeting. "Henry" [the landlady's dog] is better.

The eagle [Yeats] groans that "no one" could read the georgian anthology with pleasure, & yet he forbids me to remove [it] from 18 W. blds.

[Woburn Buildings] as he "ought to know something about these people".
uugh! May *Les bons anges* protect you platonically.

Bon Noel.

E.

Tancred]   Francis Willoughby Tancred, whose *Poems* were published in
1907. He and EP were members of the 1909 "Secession Club," and both con-
tributed to *The Book of the Poets' Club* (Christmas, 1909). Tancred's poem
"To T.E. Hulme" appeared in *Poetry Review*, 1 (December 1912).

review of Jouve]   A review of *Présences* (1912), by the French poet Pierre-
Jean Jouve [*Poetry* (Chicago), 1 (February 1913)].

Georgian anthology]   On 28 September 1912 EP wrote to Marsh, who had
asked him to contribute to the anthology *Georgian Poetry, 1911–1912:*

> I'm sorry. I can't let you have *that* poem as I'm just bringing it out in a volumn
> of my own.
> Is there anything in the earlier books that you like? "Canzoni" is the only one
> that comes within yr. 2 years radius. (not the Goodly Fere, as it don't illustrate
> any *modern* poetic tendency).
> Also I'd like to know, more or less, what gallery you propose to put me into.
> I'm usually in on Tuesday evenings if you care to talk over the matter.

In his biography of Marsh, Christopher Hassall speculates that the new poem
about to appear in *Ripostes* was "Portrait d'une Femme," and that Marsh found
nothing suitable in *Canzoni* [*Edward Marsh: Patron of the Arts* (London, 1959),
p. 193].

When *Georgian Poetry, 1911–1912* was published in December 1912, EP
immediately sent a hastily-scrawled "review" to Harriet Monroe. Intended for
the notes and reviews section of *Poetry* (Chicago), it was never printed. The
one-page manuscript was saved by Miss Monroe and is now in the *Poetry* maga-
zine archive at the University of Chicago Library.

> *An Anthology of* ⟨Gregorian⟩ *Georgian Verse.* Edited by E. Marsh published
> at the Poetry Bookshop: London
>
> ---
>
> This collection of verse printed since 1910 will reveal to the American reader
> about all the younger London points of view in poetry which are likely to be
> unrepresented in my notes.
> The work of Lascelles Abercrombie is about the best in the book, though the
> poem by D. H. Lawrence stands in pleasing contrast to its neighbors.
> Those who have read the *Lyric Year* with interest will peruse this anthology with
> deepest admiration.
>
> E.P.

The poem by Lawrence was "The Snapdragon." In a letter to Harriet Monroe
of March 1913 EP suggested that he might do a review of Lawrence's *Love
Poems and Others* (1913):

Lawrence has brought out a vol. He is clever; I don't know whether to send in a review or not. We seem pretty well stuffed up with matter at the moment. (D. H. Lawrence, whom I mentioned in my note on the *Georgian Anthology*.) Detestable person but needs watching. I think he learned the proper treatment of modern subjects before I did (*Letters,* No. 15).

The review appeared in *Poetry* (Chicago), 2 (July 1913).

In the ironic last sentence of his note on *Georgian Poetry* EP is referring to *The Lyric Year: One Hundred Poems,* edited by Ferdinand Earle (New York, 1912), "a selection from one year's work of a hundred American poets . . . . Ten thousand poems by nearly two thousand writers of verse have been personally examined by the Editor for this competition."

Urbanora Illinois] Urbana, Illinois, where the oldest Campus of the University of Illinois is located.

Hachette's] A bill from the London branch of the famous Parisian bookseller and publisher.

Verhaeren] Emile Verhaeren (1855–1916), the leading Belgian poet associated with the Symbolist movement. His *Poèmes* (*nouvelle série*) were published in 1911, and *Les Blés mouvants* in 1912.

Nancy] Nancy Maude, a school friend of Dorothy who married the Irish poet Joseph Campbell (1879–1944). See Biographical Appendix. She published a book of poems, *The Little People* (1910), and *Agnus Dei* (illustrated by Joseph Campbell).

Jouve talks . . .] The first two quotations are from the second and third stanzas of Jouve's long poem "Enfant."

> Il est vif et déjà solide
> En plusieurs forces qu'il sait bien.
> Dans le poids rouge de ses joues
> Se serrent ses lèvres humides.

> Et sous la mèche couleur de lin
> Qui domine son front léger,
> Il a la face concentrée
> Du très vieil homme d'affaires.

The third quotation is from Part II of "Hymne à un Enfant."

> Puis tes gestes se détacheront de ton corps;
> Tu essaieras de te répandre par tes membres
> Sur la peau adoucie des choses qui t'entourent;
> Tu seras mobile ainsi qu'une goutte d'huile.

[P.-J. Jouve, *Présences* (Paris: Georges Crès, 1912), pp. 77, 12].

le p'tit Jesu irlandais] The young son of Joseph Campbell and his wife Nancy (Maude).

"Poetes d'aujourd hui"] *Poètes d'aujourd'hui,* edited by Adolphe van Bever and Paul Léautaud. First published in 1900, this popular anthology of modern French poetry had gone through twenty-five editions by 1913.

"The Younger Generation"] A play by Stanley Houghton (1881–1913).

"Aristide Pujol"]   *An Adventure of Aristide Pujol,* by William John Locke (1863–1930).

sentimental Barrie]   *Rosalind,* a comedy by J.M. Barrie (1860–1937), the author of *Peter Pan.*

G. Cannan]   See Letter **121.**

Mrs Napier]   Probably Eva Marie Louisa Napier (1846–1930), Lady Napier of Magdala, the author of several novels including *Muddling Through* (1912). Daughter of the 4th Baron Macdonald, she was married to Robert William Napier, 2nd Baron Napier of Magdala and Caryngton.

the Woods]   Not the home of Francis Derwent Wood, the sculptor, and his wife the singer Florence Schmidt (see Letter **76n.**); but the home of the Rev. Henry George Woods (1842–1915) and his wife Margaret Louisa Woods (1856–1945), the poet and novelist. The Rev. H.G. Woods was "Master of the Temple," i.e. Master of the Temple Church, a "royal peculiar" whose Master was appointed by the two legal societies, the Inner Temple and the Middle Temple. See Letter **199.**

128   Ezra to Dorothy

[Farnham Common]
[Buckinghamshire]
[28 December 1912]

Casa di Jiovanni Miltoni, Burnham Beeches (or some such–heaven knows what the P.O. address is–Write to 10 Church Walk.)

Dearest:

Of all places for *me* to have landed. I can fairly hear the lion ramping about the dining-room–Beastly dark low-ceilinged hole. I suppose IF one had always lived in such a place–in an unenlightened age one might have writ rhetorical epics about original sin–all sin *is* unoriginal–mais quoi donc!

Have had a note from [Charles] Vildrac who wants to know what he is to send me–(for Potery).

3 days later

Its quite impossible to get a letter written in this place. Chiefly because the tables are in demand & there is such paucity of ink pots–I might, it is true, have used a type writer, but it didn't occur to me.

We walked to Taplow yesterday in frightful slush. I've been reading De Maupassant & Nordau–This latter is as stupid as the former is intelligent–or rather his conclusions are fairly sound, but his reasons for 'em are idiotic. If he had sense enough to dogmatize he might easily pass for a sage.

I should think–*etc*. I don't know that I should either. I intended some moralizings on life in town & country–yrs. The 'Serene Aphorist' etc. Richard [Aldington] has intelligence enough to prefer North Italy to Rome, which surprises me–pleasantly. He says "your mediaeval duffer is better, any hour, than a sham classic"–so now we know.

A week of country at this time of year is about five days too much, one should try rather a week-end. However this is Saturday so I've only got the week-end before me & Mrs McKenzie has gone and taken her decrepit dog with her so the place is more enjoyable. That! my dear is the sort of thing one shouldn't say. I say it to you. Ten to one I say it to someone else and ultimately I get myself disliked (reflection on life no. 4,500,321,826).

> Now I shall be good & write to mother.
> Mille baisers
> E. Catullo

Casa di Jiovanni Miltoni]   On 24 December 1912 EP wrote to his mother from "Slowgh (more or less)" that he was "down here for a week with the Hueffers in a dingy old cottage that belonged to Milton. F.M.H. and I being the only two people who couldn't be in the least impressed by the fact, makes it a bit more ironical" [*Letters*, No. 32; misdated 24 December 1913].

Vildrac]   Part IV of "The Approach to Paris" [*New Age*, 13 (25 September 1913)] is on the poet and dramatist Charles Vildrac (1882–1971). Vildrac and Georges Duhamel published in 1910 *Notes sur la technique poétique*, mentioned by EP in "A Few Don'ts by an Imagiste" [*Poetry* (Chicago), 1 (March 1913)].

Nordau]   See Letter **45n.**

Mrs McKenzie]   The novelist Compton Mackenzie and his wife were members of the house party. See Arthur Mizener, *The Saddest Story: A Biography of Ford Madox Ford* (New York, 1971), p. 229.

1913

[*Kensington*]
[*2 January 1913*]

Dearest:

Relieved of the damp & the ghost of Milton my spirits have arisen. The Eagle [Yeats] read more poems to me on Tuesday, & said my criticism was much more valuable than Sturge Moore's: I should *hope* so!!!

Dined with [Victor] Plarr on sunday. Had tea with Ever [Eva Fowler] yesterday. Dine with the Heron-Allens this evening which is odd–presumably some country cousin or something wants to meet me–judging from the appearance of the place, the one time I have been there, the food should [be] excellent & fastidiously chosen–not quite so conducive to the increase of adipose as Eva's. The Eagle, by the way, must be putting most of his pension into a cellar.

Have not yet found you a suitable gew-gaw–but then, I've been plugging at the type-writer and reading a book of V.H.'s [Violet Hunt's] most of the time since I got back. There's been another note in the Times. "Ripostes" etc.

The estimable Ghose may be coming in to tea with me. And what more? g—od blessmysoul. Oh yes, Mr. [Harold] Monro invites me to the opening of his shop. And I am unavoidably prevented. And H.L.P. [Homer Loomis Pound, EP's father] considers you a sensible young woman, *no,* "sensible young lady", and Mary [Moore of Trenton] writes that she loves me and wishes you a happy Xmas. And Richard [Aldington] sends me some bad poems and seems to exult in having horrified Miss [Phyllis] Bottôme whom he describes as a Meredithian female–whatever that may be.

I saw a decent jade pendant but it was £16.16. and a nice bit of lace for 40 ditto, & praeterea nothing that I'd be bothered to carry home. I must drop literature for a day & really take to hunting - - - What colour goes with a Chinese skirt?

Oh yes, I've written some more verses but nothing decorative. Eva [Fowler] likes the [Laurent] Tailhade. I think I must read 'em all, *etc.* You'll be sleeping off the more indecorous dance and much too sleepy to read any more of this.

I kiss you your eyes, with the salutations of the sun.

E.

ghost of Milton]   See Letter **128.**
Sturge Moore]   Thomas Sturge Moore (1870–1944), poet, designer, and wood engraver. Moore and Yeats met in 1898 and remained close friends until Yeats's death. Their published correspondence extends from 1901 to 1937.

Plarr]   Victor Gustav Plarr (1863–1929), a member of the Rhymers' Club whose only volume of verse, *In the Dorian Mood,* was published in 1896. From 1897 until his death he was Librarian of the Royal College of Surgeons. He appears in section VII of the first part of *Hugh Selwyn Mauberley* as

> M. Verog, out of step with the decade,
> Detached from his contemporaries,
> Neglected by the young,
> Because of these reveries.

Heron-Allens]   Edward Heron-Allen (1861–1943), a late-Victorian polymath whose interests (and publications) ranged from violin-making and rare books to geology, zoology, and marine biology. He translated the *Rubá'iyát of Omar Khayyám* from a Bodleian manuscript, and published an edition of Fitzgerald's *Rubá'iyát* with a Persian text (1899). In *Who's Who* he listed his recreations as "Persian Literature; Marine Zoology; Meteorology; Heraldry; Bibliography; Occasional Essays and Scientific Romances; Auricula and Asparagus Culture."

The Eagle . . . his pension]   In 1910 Yeats was awarded a Civil List pension of £150 per year by the British Government.

note in the Times]   In a notice of nine recent volumes of poetry [*Times Literary Supplement,* 12 December 1912, p. 568], an anonymous reviewer [Harold Child] singled out *Ripostes of Ezra Pound* and Evelyn Underhill's *Immanence* as volumes with "individuality of flavour." In contrast to Evelyn Underhill's unfashionable mysticism, "Mr. Ezra Pound's originality is of a different kind."

He begins with a challenge—

> When I behold how black, immortal ink
> Drips from my deathless pen—ah, well-away!
> Why should we stop at all for what I think?
> There is enough in what I chance to say.

Do you bite your thumb—or, rather, do you cock your hat—at me, Sir? He ends with a poem headed 'From a thing by Schumann.' They are fine, careless fellows, these poets. And in between come brilliant examples of cleverness, magical use of words, proofs of sound learning, metrical triumphs–mixed up with more cockings of the hat, 'things' that remind us of nothing so much as the defiant gestures of retreating small boys, and essays in what we will call by the gentle name of wilfulness. At the Post-Impressionist exhibition some spectators may be seen dancing with fury, others quaking with laughter, others indiscriminately worshipping, and a few using their brains coolly. Mr. Ezra Pound's book will have the same effect, no doubt, upon its readers. Now and then it is hard not to join the first group. Perhaps, on reading 'from a thing by Schumann,' it is safer to pass by, as one might pass by a bust in its third stage by Matisse, with the polite reflection that we do not understand its aim and therefore cannot see the art or the beauty of it. There is enough, we understand, in what Mr. Pound chances to say; but why should a poet have chanced to say this 'thing,' when he can write such 'things' as the poem to Swinburne, 'Salve Pontifex,' or the fine, harsh 'Seafarer,' or the exquisite 'Thou keep'st thy rose-leaf'—each of which has its little bursts of wilfulness to give flavour to beauty, but is not the cocking of a hat, not a vulgar gesture of defiance?

The *Times Literary Supplement* had published a joint review of EP's *Sonnets and Ballate of Guido Cavalcanti* and a new edition of Rossetti's *Poems and Translations* on 21 November 1912, and EP had replied with a letter published on December 5 claiming that "there could be no possible clash or contention between [Rossetti's] aesthetic method and my scholastic one; he was as avowedly intent on making beautiful verses as I am on presenting an individual."

Ghose]   Kali Mohan Ghose, one of Tagore's pupils. EP worked with him in translating "Certain Poems of Kabir" [*Modern Review* (Calcutta), 13 (June 1913)]. EP recollects this in Canto 77 with the refrain, "Thus saith Kabir."

Monro . . . opening of his shop]   Harold Monro's Poetry Bookshop had its official opening on 8 January 1913.

Miss Bottôme]   Phyllis Bottome (1884–1963), novelist. Her book of memoirs, *From the Life* (1944), contains a chapter on EP. EP has indicated the preferred pronunciation of her name with a circumflex.

the Tailhade]   Laurent Tailhade (1854–1919), poet and man of letters. EP commented on his work in part five of "The Approach to Paris" [*New Age*, 13 (2 October 1913)], but the reference here is probably to EP's poem "Our Respectful Homages to M. Laurent Tailhade," which appeared only in *Blast*, 2 (July 1915).

read 'em all]   EP intends to read all his new verses at one of his forthcoming "lectures" in Eva Fowler's drawing room (see Letter **130n**). In Letter **138** DS says she is enjoying reading the new poems to herself, "after having heard them."

130   Ezra to Dorothy

[Kensington]
[4 January 1913]

Dearest:

Have spent the day in searches–fruitless & otherwise. Liberty's makes me feel as if I'd got into somebody's dressing room by mistake.

I contemplated mediaeval japanese prints at the [British Museum] & feel ages older & wiser. The Paradisal calm & *aura dolce*. Bin-Bin [Laurence Binyon] *adest* lamenting that England will never have a collection comparable to the "Fuller" lot in the U.S.

I suppose your abbreviated H.H. means 'igh 'all [High Hall, Wimborne] not H.H.S. [Henry Hope Shakespear]. And, you silly person, Chewsday is the 7th not the 6th and the country is very damp.

Dansa! Dansa! Fanciulla! etc. I believe I corruscated properly–or with proper impropriety last evening—I dine *S., M., & T.* [Sunday, etc.] so my evenings are provided for. I've ordered lecture announcements, so I presume I've got to go thru' with it.

R. [Richard Aldington] thinks that he, the HD. [Hilda Doolittle] & I have money enough to send him to Sicily.

God save Thee.

E

Liberty's]   Liberty & Co. Ltd. of Regent Street, designers and manufacturers of artistic fabrics.

aura dolce]   *Purgatorio*, xxviii, 7–9.

> Un' aura dolce, senza mutamento
> avere in sè, mi ferìa per la fronte
> non di più colpo che soave vento . . .

> (A sweet breeze, itself invariable, was
> striking on my brow with no greater force
> than a gentle wind . . .)

Bin-Bin]   Laurence Binyon (1869–1943), poet and connoisseur of Chinese and Japanese art. He was on the staff of the Department of Prints and Drawings at the British Museum from 1895 to 1933.

"Fuller" lot]   EP has misunderstood "Freer" as "Fuller." The Detroit financier Charles Lang Freer (1856–1919) formed a great collection of Oriental art which Ernest Fenollosa called "the finest and best unified group of masterpieces by the greatest Chinese and Japanese painters of all ages that exists outside of Japan, with the possible exception of that in the Boston Art Museum." In 1906 Freer gave his entire collection to the Smithsonian Institution in Washington, D.C. The collection was in place by 1920, but the building was not formally opened until 1923. Laurence Binyon's *Painting in the Far East* (2nd edn., 1913) is dedicated to Charles L. Freer, and in the Preface (p. ix) he refers to "the marvellous collection of Mr. Freer at Detroit." Freer often visited Whistler in Paris or London and acquired a spectacular collection of his works now at the Smithsonian.

Dansa! . . . Fanciulla!]   "Dance! Dance! Young girl!" Properly *danza*, but in the Venetian dialect "z" is reduced to "s."

lecture announcements]   On 12 December 1912 EP wrote to his father that he was "going to lecture in Mrs. Fowler's new chinese drawing room in January" (Eva Fowler had recently moved from 124 Knightsbridge to 26 Gilbert Street, Grosvenor Square). The first lecture (January 21) was on "The Normal Opportunity of the Provençal Troubadour"; the second (January 23) on "Rabindra-nath Tagore"; and the third (January 28) on " 'Vers Libre and Systems of Metric,' with reading from the Lecturer's own work."

By kind permission of
Mrs. FOWLER

EZRA POUND
Will give THREE LECTURES

At 26 Gilbert Street, Mayfair, as follows,
at . 3.30 p.m.

Jan. 21st, Tuesday : " The Normal Opportunity of the Provençal
                     Troubadour."
Jan. 23rd, Thursday :   -   -   " Rabindranath Tagore."
Jan. 28th, Tuesday : " Vers Libre and Systems of Metric," with
                     reading from the Lecturer's own work.

Tickets for Single Lecture, 7/6
For Three Lectures   -   £1

---

131   Ezra to Dorothy

10 Church Walk
[Kensington]
[8 January 1913]

Dearest:

Gracious salutations. I send you a shower of petals - - - Further, I have seen two beautiful lacquer mirrors if you insist on toilet sets. I would rather drape you in useless & gaudy fabric but we will arbitrate.

I had a tranquil and charming tea with O.S. [Olivia Shakespear] yesterday. Also I went forth and bought a book on ancient colours. And dined with the eagle [Yeats], who was tired–and who gave me another poem for "Poetry". I've also extracted one from [F.S.] Flint, who is doing an intelligent article on me chiefly at my own dictation.

I went to Eva's [Eva Fowler's] this P.M. to address my obituary notices. F.M. [Frederic Manning] there, very much "of the Spectator" and a heavy Thackeronian from Oxford, most oppressive, & O.S. [Olivia] mildly amused at the Eagle who insisted on talking ghosts. F.M. says that after the "Quest" lecture, the title of the first one of this series is wholly indecent. Also he advises me to placate [John St. Loe] Strachey–oh là là.

I am reading "Education Sentimental" and find it the most readable of Flaubert. I send you kisses by mail since you are too indolent to come to town to receive them. Et quoi donc. I have just bought a huge history of Hindoostan for 4d.

I seem to have spent the rest of the time in useless activities. [John] Cournos came this A.M. before I was wholly awake. I am having coffee with Mrs Patmore because B.P. [Brigit Patmore] is going to the theatre with someone else.

Old Gould has sent me a volumn of essays–looks like religious biology, eheu fugaces.

W.B.Y. is writing a poem on Mabel Beardsley. I'm going to see some [Charles] Condors with O.S. [Olivia] demain. The Oxford Essay Society wants me to deliver a paper–apparently for the love of hearing myself keep serious. I'm going to dine with a curious club "Phratry"–"chiefly of civil servants", said the very grave cleric who invited me. I shall take my poem of the crocuses.

Dieu te garde, m'amie.

E.

poem for "Poetry"]   Yeats's "The Grey Rock," *Poetry* (Chicago), 2 (April 1913).

one from Flint . . . my own dictation]   F.S. (Frank Stewart) Flint (1885–1960), poet and translator. Unable to afford an advanced education, Flint learned Latin and French in evening schools and at age nineteen gained entry to the Civil Service, where he eventually became chief of the Overseas Section of the Ministry of Labour. His first volume of verse, *In the Net of the Stars,* was published in 1909 by Elkin Mathews, and in that year he and EP joined with other young writers to form the "Secession Club." Flint's essay on contemporary French poetry, published in the *Poetry Review* for August 1912, strongly influenced EP and the other Imagist poets. EP included five poems by Flint in the anthology *Des Imagistes* (1914).

A note on "Imagisme," signed by F.S. Flint, was published in *Poetry* (Chicago), 1 (March 1913), alongside EP's "A Few Don'ts by an Imagiste." EP actually drafted the note or "interview," and many years later Flint said that "his own part in it was confined to correcting a few stylistic idiosyncrasies for which he could not, with a clear conscience, take the responsibility" [K.K. Ruthven, *A Guide to Ezra Pound's 'Personae'* (Berkeley, 1969), pp. 10–11; for background on the composition of Flint's "Imagisme," and on the relationship between Flint and Pound, see Christopher Middleton, "Documents on Imagism from the Papers of F.S. Flint," *The Review*, No. 15 (April 1965), pp. 35–51]. The poem mentioned in this letter was probably one of the "Four Poems in Unrhymed Cadence" published in *Poetry* (Chicago), 2 (July 1913).

my obituary notices] Announcements of EP's forthcoming lectures at Mrs. Fowler's.

"Quest" lecture . . . first one of this series] EP had delivered a lecture on "Psychology and Troubadours" (later Chapter V of *The Spirit of Romance*) to G.R.S. Mead's Quest Society in early 1912 (see Letters **48** and **69**). The first lecture in this 1913 series may have been "Troubadours: Their Sorts and Conditions" [later published in the *Quarterly Review*, 219 (October 1913)].

Strachey] John St. Loe Strachey (1860–1925), editor and proprietor of the *Spectator* from 1898 until 1925. "Salutation the Second" (P), first published in the "Contemporania" series [*Poetry* (Chicago), 2 (April 1913)], contains the aside: "(Tell it to Mr. Strachey)." Writing to his father on 3 June 1913, EP explained that " 'Strachey' is actually the edtr. of *The Spectator*, but I use him as the type of male prude, somewhere between Tony Comstock and Hen. Van Dyke. Even in America we've nothing that conveys his exact shade of meaning. I've adopted the classic Latin manner in mentioning people by name" (*Letters*, No. 20). For an example of Strachey's prudery, see Dorothy's letter to EP (Letter **138**) noting that one of Fred Manning's poems has been rejected by the *Spectator*.

"Education Sentimental"] Flaubert's novel *L'Education Sentimentale* (1869).

Cournos] John Cournos (1881–1966), poet, playwright, novelist, reviewer, and translator. See Biographical Appendix.

B.P.] Brigit Patmore. See Letter **114n.**

Old Gould] Not Gerald Gould (1885–1936), the poet and critic who taught Richard Aldington at University College, London; but George Milbry Gould (1848–1922), the Philadelphia ophthalmologist who wrote a number of important medical textbooks. Gould held advanced theories about the connection between eye-strain and ill-health, and he published six volumes of *Biographic Clinics* (1903–09) in which he interpreted the personalities of writers such as De Quincey, Carlyle, and George Eliot in the light of his theories about eye-strain. EP consulted Dr. Gould about his own eye trouble when he was an undergraduate at the University of Pennsylvania and later recommended him to James Joyce. Gould took an active interest in the career of Lafcadio Hearn and wrote an analytic study *Concerning Lafcadio Hearn* (1908). He also published a volume of verse, *An Autumn Singer* (1897). The "volumn of essays" sent to EP was either *The Meaning and the Method of Life: A Search for Religion in*

Biology (1893) or *The Infinite Presence* (1910), "a search for religion in biology."

eheu fugaces]   *Eheu fugaces . . . labuntur anni,* "Alas, the years pass swiftly by" (Horace, *Odes,* II, xiv, 1–2).

W.B.Y. . . . on Mabel Beardsley]   Mabel Beardsley was the sister of Aubrey Beardsley (1872–1898), the leading artist of the Aesthetic movement who had been Yeats's close friend. She died in 1916 in her early forties, after a long illness. Between January 1913 and her death Yeats wrote seven poems about her courage and nobility, which were published in 1917 under the title "Upon a Dying Lady" (in the *Little Review* and the *New Statesman* of August 1917, and later that year in *The Wild Swans at Coole*). The poem referred to in this letter is either the first or second in the sequence, since they are based on a visit described in Yeats's letter to Lady Gregory of 8 January 1913 [*Letters of W.B. Yeats,* ed. Allan Wade (New York, 1955), pp. 574–75].

Condors]   Charles Conder, the artist. See Letter **46n.**

Oxford Essay Society]   EP delivered a paper on Cavalcanti to the Essay Society of St. John's College, Oxford, on 2 February 1913. For an account of the evening see Stock, pp. 131–32.

"Phratry"]   In ancient Greece, a phratry was a subdivision of a phyle (a tribe or clan based on kinship).

poem of the crocuses]   "Coitus" (P), first published in *Poetry and Drama,* 2 (March 1914), which begins: "The gilded phaloi of the crocuses/ are thrusting at the spring air."

132   Ezra to Dorothy

10 Church Walk
[Kensington]
[21 January 1913]

Dearest:

What a life! Mind you get up and see me tomorrow for you're not a french marquise of the XVIIIme siecle and you won't be let receive me otherwise.

Ma mignonne
Je vous donne le bon jour etc.

I have hammered the typewriter from breakfast to 6 P.M.–a "little shirt for Rawdon" or rather a little kindergarten course in Ars Poetica for

Chicago. And then Eva [Fowler], and then the eagle [Yeats] up till half an hour ago.

Miles of letter from Chicago–utterly illegible–I suppose they put the part I was intended to read in the typewritten part. Tagore is being boomed by the Chicago newspapers. He's sent me 25 new poems–some of which I shall read on Thursday–a nice one about ducks. [F.S.] Flint is also doing an article on Imagism. One of the eagle's poems has been translated into Bengali. The lectures are going to pay a little after all. And Strecker has forked up for the W.R. [Walter Rummel] Troubadour stuff, etc. And [John] Cournos has gone to a hospital so we didn't dine together tonight. And his article has appeared in the "Philadelphia Record" with more than oriental splendour so my august progenitors are for the nonce contented. And Eva has ordered the cook on pain of death not [to] have anything for lunch that will pervade the celestial halls. And my gloves have come back from the cleaners and one cuff is missing from the week before last's laundry. There–I guess I've given you "all my mind a while". "All, all, the bottom of the bowl" as the Eagle write it.

The Eagle has done two more poems to Mabel Beardsley, and I object to his having rimed "mother" immediately with "brother" and I wish he wouldn't ask me for criticism except when we're alone. *One* of [the] lyrics is rather nice, but he cant expect me to like stale riming, even if he does say its an imitation of an Elizabethan form. Elizifbeefan. vey [CHARS] know BETTER. Its just moulting eagle, they think, AND THEY'RE DAM well right.

This epistle is getting too fat. I shall tear off the other half of this sheet and retire.

E.

Ma mignonne . . . le bon jour]   EP may have had in mind Ronsard's poem addressed to "Mignonne" (Livre I, Ode XVII).

"little shirt for Rawdon"]   From the scene in Chapter 44 of Thackeray's *Vanity Fair* where Becky (Mrs. Rawdon Crawley) is trying to impress Sir Pitt with her domestic virtues:

> . . . she gave him her hand and took him up to the drawing room, and made him snug on the sofa by the fire, and let him talk as she listened with the tenderest kindly interest, sitting by him, and hemming a shirt for her dear little boy. Whenever Mrs. Rawdon wished to be particularly humble and virtuous, this little shirt used to come out of her workbox. It had got to be too small for Rawdon long before it was finished.

course in Ars Poetica for Chicago]   "A Few Don'ts by an Imagiste," *Poetry* (Chicago), 1 (March 1913).

letter from Chicago]   From Harriet Monroe, editor of *Poetry*.

Tagore . . . read on Thursday]   Evidently EP intended to read some of Tagore's poems as part of one of his "lectures" at Mrs. Fowler's home.

Flint . . . on Imagism]   See Letter **131n**.

Strecker . . . Troubadour stuff]   Payment for EP's translation of the Troubadour songs in Walter Rummel's *Hesternae Rosae, Serta II* (See Letter **103n**).

Cournos . . . "Philadelphia Record"]   John Cournos's article on EP appeared in the *Philadelphia Record* on 5 January 1913.

NATIVE POET STIRS LONDON

Ezra Pound Wins English Critics' Praise

In years to come Philadelphia may brag of having furnished the world a great poet. It is not even within the limits of impossibility that the Browning Society of that city may pause long enough from its libations to the memory of the dead to discover the existence of one live and gifted, if prosaically named, Ezra Pound. For the present, however, Mr Pound has been taken to the bosom of his adopted mother, that city of cities, London.

It is no small achievement for so young a man. Only 27 now, his poetic utterance first met instant fame three years ago; this fame has grown steadily with the advancing maturity of his wares. The word "instant" is used advisedly; the reader must not be inveigled into the belief that the "Personae," the little volume which received this sudden recognition, was Pound's first work. Let it be known that the poet's apprenticeship to his Muse involved the preliminary destruction of at least three hundred and fifty poems—it would be pertinent to mention that two of his novels were subjected to a similar fate.

Mr. Pound has been his own most rigorous critic. He possesses that now rare trait, a literary conscience, to a powerful degree. Couple to it another quality, a tireless industry, and you have a combination that is like an electric dynamo, which harnesses mood and temperament and converts emotion into a finished and concentrated product ready for distribution—via the printing press.

In the short space of these years this poet has published no less than five volumes of verse and one of prose—and has two volumes in preparation. His prose, by the way, is not what one would call "a poet's prose;" it can hardly be said to flow, is in fact rather angular; still, it is not ordinary, has something to say and is marked often by audacity of expression. It is perhaps Mr. Pound's chief outlet for his Americanism—and by that we mean American snap, not American English. The fact is he hates to write prose, and only does so because he has certain theories and convictions which demand expression outside the bounds of the poetic form.

He concentrates his energies on poetry, which he indeed considers neither as a luxury nor as "an escape out of life," as some poets do, but as a natural utterance of life and as a daily need not alone for the poet, who is the creator, but for the people for whom he creates. He argues that if poetry has fallen into disfavor it is the fault of the poets themselves who do not express themselves naturally, but are content to over-indulge in rhyme and rhetoric. He holds that "as long as the poet says not what he, at the very crux of a clarified conception, means, but is content to say something ornate and approximate, just so long will serious people, intently alive, consider poetry as balderdash—a sort of embroidery for dilettantes and women."

He pleads for "a simplicity and directness of utterance," different, however, from the simplicity and directness of daily speech in that it is "more 'curial,' more dignified." "This difference, this dignity cannot be conferred by florid adjectives or elaborate hyperbole: it must be conveyed by art, and by the art of the verse structure, by something which exalts the reader, making him feel that he is in contact with something arranged more finely than the commonplace."

This idea, and incidentally another—involving a new scheme of scholarship, concerning which I will speak presently—Mr. Pound develops at length in the introduction to his forthcoming volume containing his translations of Arnaut Daniel, the best of the Troubadours, whose poetry is distinguished for its elaboration and fineness of harmony, the emphasis given to the music and the arrangement of words. These Provencal poems, containing "subtleties of rhyme blending that Swinburne never thought of," have never before been translated into English in their original form—and in trying to achieve this feat Mr. Pound was tempted chiefly by the quality of the art structure which shaped so exquisitely the simplest combination of words. This rendering of the Provencal forms in English—Pound employed no less than four of the forms in his original poems—was one way of demonstrating to his critics the importance and possibilities of the poetic art as an art. The value the Provencals attached to form may be judged from the fact that in those days it was considered as much a plagiarism to use another man's form as well as the content. All poetry was made to sing to music, consequently to steal a man's form was to steal his tone.

This realization of the importance of form will explain Pound's indefatigable experiments in versification resembling almost the method of a scientist in his laboratory: it is quite amazing to go through his several volumes of verse and observe the startling variety of forms he has attempted. When you grasp this experimental nature of the man, ever seeking the secret of the most perfect poetic structure, you can readily understand that, though only three years have elapsed since his first two slender volumes of verse—"Personae" and "Exultations"—were published by Elkin Mathews, he already looks back upon them as early, if not altogether unworthy, efforts.

[The main body of the review is a long survey, with extensive quotations, of EP's works from *Personae* through *Ripostes,* ending with this paragraph.]

It is perhaps not to be wondered at that a kindly editor of one of the "better" American magazines returned Pound's verses with some such missive as this: "Your work, etc., is very interesting, etc., but you will have to pay more attention to conventional form if you want to make a commercial success of it." Pound, by the way, recently embodied his impressions of America, partly as a result of his visit a year ago, in a series of papers published in the New Age under the title of "Patria Mia." Without being great prose they had the merit of being terse and alive, and kindly if critical. In his own particular domain of poetry, however—to judge from the discontented, progressive nature of the poet—no one need be astonished if, after having passed through the various stages of his wide-ranged development and manifold experiment, he shall achieve something altogether new and distinctly his own, just as in the art of painting a certain distinguished countryman of Pound's succeeded in being Whistler, despite Velasquez and the Japanese.

"all my mind . . . the bowl"] From Yeats's *The Shadowy Waters: A Dramatic Poem* (1906 version), lines 117–18. Forgael is speaking:

> If you will give me all your mind awhile—
> All, all, the very bottom of the bowl—
> I'll show you that I am made differently . . .

two more poems to Mabel Beardsley] Poems IV and V of the sequence "Upon a Dying Lady" (see Letter **131n**). Poem V originally contained the following passage, where Yeats rhymes "mother" with "brother."

> Although she has turned away
> The pretty waxen faces
> And hid their silk and laces
> For Mass was said to-day
> She has not begun denying
> Now that she is but dying
> The pleasures she loved well
> The strong milk of her mother
> The valour of her brother
> Are in her body still
> She will not die weeping
> May God be with her sleeping.

> [A. Norman Jeffares, *A Commentary on the Collected Poems of W.B. Yeats* (Stanford, 1968), p. 194]

133   Dorothy to Ezra

12 Brunswick Gardens
Kensington
[30 January 1913]

The Eagle has been inspired. "Every external weakness has a corresponding internal strength".

12, Brunswick Gardens,
Kensington.

The Eagle

has been

inspired

134   Ezra to Dorothy

[*Kensington*]
[*31 January 1913*]

The lone coyote in its wilderness has also taken to aphorism. [sketch]
   "The external use of the ballanced senctence [*sic*] shows a corresponding internal unballance (vide. in the mind.)"

135   Dorothy to Ezra

[*Kensington*]
[*9 February 1913*]
Sunday

Dearest.

   I go to
        at Lee Priory
            Littlebourne
                Canterbury
                    Kent
until I believe Sat. 15. You might write me one letter there? I have written a long letter to Dear Walter [Rummel]: in spite of yr. not having brought the song.

   I am now reading a trans: of one Philostratus "Apollonius of Tyana". Amusing at whiles. There is a long & charming, & authentic, description of a lot of dragons in India–"russet brown backs" they have–and some are "serrated" and the mountain kind are golden with a terrible eye. He also met a woman whose upper half was white & lower portion black–and then yesty: Evening H.H.S. [Henry Hope Shakespear] read out of the paper of a whole family in America somewhere who are parti-coloured–like pigs– but not neatly divided in the middle–although I have seen pigs so [sketch].

   Louisa [Crook, the housemaid] has spilt & broken my new bottle of medicine–Quite clever of her!

   Coz □ [Georgie Hyde-Lees] to lunch today. It is *so obvious* that you are the person we want for Tivoli–but–alas!

                                        A toi.
                                        D

Your cold gone?

Walter . . . the song]   On 21 October 1911 EP wrote to his mother that
he had "done nothing useful for some weeks except correct a few proofs and
translate an old French song for W.R. Very dull song at that, only he wants to
print it in both languages." In his *Bibliography of Ezra Pound* (item B8) Donald
Gallup concludes that this song is the "Slumber Song (Berceuse) From the
French" in Walter Rummel's *Ten Songs for Children Young and Old* (1914).

Philostratus]   Flavius Philostratus, "the Athenian," wrote a life of the
Pythagorean philosopher Apollonius of Tyana. Several English translations of
Philostratus were available in 1913, including the most recent by F.C. Conybeare
in the Loeb Classical Library (1912), reviewed in Mead's *Quest,* 4 (July 1913).
In 1901 Mead had published a "critical study" of the *Life.*

for Tivoli]   DS and Georgie Hyde-Lees were planning their April visit to
Rome. See Letters **141ff.**

136   Dorothy to Ezra

> *Lee Priory*
> *Littlebourne*
> *Canterbury*
> [*13 February 1913*]
> *Thursday*

My poor dear! And I have been comparatively happy in the woods all
today. Primroses, bursting buds, and daffodils in the gardens. Also I am
reading Nathaniel Hawthorne's "Marble Faun" which is most exciting &
very beautifully written.

> *Friday*
> (instead of going down
> to prayers).

I am going home tomorrow—and will write a pc [post card] Sunday when
we can meet. I go to the Stage Society on Sunday night with 'Erb [Herbert
Leaf]—but daren't say so here.

We saw a queer old church yesterday in Canterbury—which used to be
for Lepers. But the old man who took us round was 88 and toothless, so
Edie [Edie M. Wood, a cousin] & I arrived back with somewhat different
views as to what he had said! I enclose a "palm" flower. The woods are
lovely, and inches deep in mud.

Prayers is over.

Edie is mad over hens. She & I spent a whole sunny morning in the copse carpentering old hen coops into new. She gives them filthy looking messes, which they seem to enjoy–making queer noises.

Is Mrs. F.M. Hueffer established?

> Much
> Love
> Dear
> Yours.

P.S.
Letter from O.S. [Olivia Shakespear]. Come in on Monday.

"*Marble Faun*"]   Hawthorne's romance *The Marble Faun* (1860) is set in Rome.

Stage Society]   See Letter **91n.**

Mrs. F.M. Hueffer]   Violet Hunt. See Biographical Appendix.

137   Dorothy to Ezra

12 Brunswick Gardens
Kensington
[*Selection from letters of*
18–22–27 February 1913]
Tuesday

We should like to go to see the Russians: Any night next week except Wed: or Thurs. I want to see the Debussy "Faune". O.S. [Olivia Shakespear] will pay you back for our tickets later.

Saturday

Venez Lundi. I have obtained an admission to the Print Room [British Museum]–& have seen a portfolio of Utamaro. I wonder which you liked so much?

Thursday

Please meet us 8.20. in the Main Entrance on Sat. and bring the tickets with you. I saw "The Pretenders" yesterday. Interesting.

the Russians . . . Debussy "Faune"]   Claude Debussy's "Prélude à l'après-
midi d'un faune (after Mallarmé)" was produced by Diaghilev as a ballet in
1912, with Nijinsky as choreographer and dancer. Nijinsky and Karsavina
danced the ballet at the Royal Opera House, Covent Garden, on Saturday eve-
ning, 1 March 1913.

Utamaro]   Kitagawa Utamaro (1753–1806), the Japanese artist known
especially for his wood-block prints of beautiful women.

"The Pretenders"]   Ibsen's *The Pretenders* (1863) was playing at the Hay-
market Theatre.

138   Dorothy to Ezra

[Kensington]
[14 March 1913]
Friday

Dearest.

An interesting, but exhausting day. Began by reading yr. poems in the
morning. Then helped O.S. [Olivia Shakespear] choose two summer hats.
Lunched with Frederic Manning, Mr. & Mrs. Sargeant, Charles Whibley:
who is very round and pet–& full of ironic humorous anecdotes. Then we
went to tea with R. & C. Shannon. Saw all sorts of lovely Greek & Egyp-
tian things–also Jap: prints. There we met Glyn Philpot (who paints my
Jew family) & some other people came in to tea. A yellow head–going the
other way from yours: a sculptor was under the drooping locks.

The Spectator has refused a poem of FM's [Frederic Manning's] as be-
ing improper: Whibley merely commented "To the Pure *all* things are im-
pure", with no accent on the *im- - -* !

I am enjoying reading yours to myself, after having heard them. Their
value changes in one or two cases. The Bellaires still bore me. And for
God's sake don't you get the sex mania–or I shall despair–with all my
friends newly married & therefore impossible.

I still love dearly your "impertinent", "shameless" songs–one I like so
much "To Kalon". In One–I can't find it–you say at end it was (Millwins?)
"worthy of comment"–I thought it sounded very unnecessarily egotistical.

My dear:

I shall keep the M.S.S., unless I hear to contrary, until you come.

Yours–
D

Tagore lectures at the Quest early in June.

Mr. & Mrs. Sargeant]   Edmund Beale Sargant (1855–1938), a friend of Frederic Manning, was the author of *Songs, and Other Poems* (1911) and *The Casket Songs* (1912). A poem from the latter volume, "The Cuckoo Wood," was included in the first anthology of *Georgian Poetry, 1911–1912* (1912). A South African educated at Rugby and Trinity College, Cambridge, he served for a time after the Boer War as Director of Education in the Transvaal. Later he moved to London and in 1910 married his second wife, Marie Don Sargant.

Charles Whibley]   Charles Whibley (1859–1930), author among other volumes of *The Book of Scoundrels* (1897). Olivia Shakespear reviewed Whibley's *The Pageant of Life* in the *Kensington* (March 1901), commending him for "the faculty of seizing the essence of a man's personality; only giving us such details as are essential." Whibley assisted W.E. Henley on the *Scots Observer* and the *National Observer,* and for many years wrote a monthly article, "Musings Without Method," for *Blackwood's Magazine.*

R. & C. Shannon]   Charles De Sousy Ricketts (1866–1931) and Charles Haslewood Shannon (1863–1937) met at the City and Guilds Technical Art School and remained close collaborators until Ricketts' death. From 1889 to 1897 they owned and edited *The Dial,* a periodical devoted to painting and literature. A fine painter, printer, and writer, Ricketts was also an innovative designer for the stage, and Yeats admired his work. Shannon is best known for his delicate lithographs. Together Ricketts and Shannon built up a remarkable collection of drawings, prints, and art objects.

Glyn Philpot]   Glyn Warren Philpot (1884–1937), the painter (and later a Trustee of the Tate Gallery) who was especially noted at this time for his portraits.

The Spectator]   See Letter **131n.**

The Bellaires . . . "To Kalon"]   "The Bellaires" (P) and "Tο Καλόν" (P) were first published in *Poetry* (Chicago), 4 (August 1914).

"impertinent", "shameless" songs]   In "Salutation the Second" (P), first published in *Poetry* (Chicago), 2 (April 1913), the poet urges his "little naked and impudent songs" to "Go and dance shamelessly! / Go with an impertinent frolic."

"worthy of comment"]   "Les Millwin" (P), first published as part of the "Lustra" series in *Poetry* (Chicago), 2 (November 1913), concludes:

> Let us therefore mention the fact,
> For it seems to us worthy of record.

Tagore . . . the Quest]   Most of Tagore's lecture was published in the *Quest,* 4 (July 1913), under the title "The Realisation of Brahma." The conclusion, however, did not appear until the next issue ["Lead Me Across," *Quest,* 5 (October 1913)], with this note from the editor: "This fine fragment is really the conclusion of Mr. Tagore's paper . . . added at the last moment when the paper was read to the Quest Society, and the sheets of the last number had already been run."

139   Dorothy to Ezra

> *Holly Lodge*
> *Burnham*
> *Bucks*
> *[21 March 1913]*
> *Friday*

At Holly Lodge until Tuesday–Heaven help us.

I don't know what you may be feeling– But with a Lopez [Lope de Vega] play on hand–I defy you to feel the boredom I am now enjoying. Hot-cross-buns have been a slight, very slight alleviation at breakfast and tea time–Its pouring wet–& there's a faint odour of CAT everywhere!

All the wickedness of the past generations seems to be here–all the boredom of my aunts, and the rebellion of one and the utter squashing of individuality of another. The conventionality of '60s–all the things you hate most of all–And then to defy the conventions, one of the best Siamese mothers has had 6 "rainbow-coloured" kittens! Only two still surviving–very tabby & pet– large & vulgar.

The Hamadryad [Hilda Doolittle] won't stay with us at T. [Tivoli] but may come for the day. So there is still room for you & one other!

It's a perfectly damnable world. I have done so much already of my needlework that it will be finished tomorrow if I am not careful–*then* I shall go mad. I think I shall go to Paris with FM [Frederic Manning]! Or the Lago [di Garda] with you, or the next world alone–I might go to London for the week-end.

Thank you–I feel better–a little.

> *Saturday*

Wet again: ugh!

I have been reading your Mallarmé. He seems to me (the prose) worse than dear Henry James. Its all upside down. The Vers I haven't tried yet.

All the Cats seem very well today & spry–

Poetry has just been forwarded to me–the March No: The "don'ts" amuse me–I wonder will anybody take profit by them.

There is really nothing of interest to say. I go out with the Beagles this afternoon possibly. Come in on Wednesday please.

I hope Lopez goes well.

Yours
D.

Lopez]   Lope de Vega (1562–1635). EP had intended to write his doctoral dissertation on the Spanish dramatist, and in *The Spirit of Romance* (1910) he devoted a chapter to "The Quality of Lope de Vega." The play referred to may have been *El Desprecio Agradecido,* "Thanks to the Despised" [A Comedy in Three Acts], which he began translating as early as February 1910. A summary of the play and translations of a few passages appeared in the chapter on "The Quality of Lope de Vega" in *The Spirit of Romance* (1910). EP's continuing interest in Lope de Vega may be seen in "The Condolence" (P), first published in *Poetry* (Chicago), 2 (April 1913), where the epigraph is taken from a poem by Lope ("La Doreata") that he had translated in *The Spirit of Romance.*

Poetry . . . The "don'ts"]   "A Few Don'ts by an Imagiste," *Poetry* (Chicago), 1 (March 1913). On 18 March 1913 EP gave a lecture at 23 De Vere Gardens, the home of Lady Low. We do not know the subject, but it may have been Imagism. On an admission card to this lecture Wyndham Lewis later jotted down a reminder that EP was to lecture on Imagism at the "Cubist Academy" [Rebel Art Centre] on 30 May 1914.

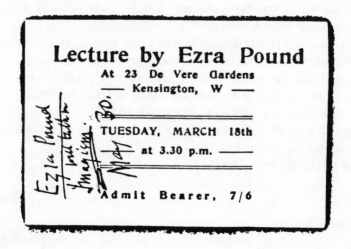

140   Dorothy to Ezra

12 Brunswick Gardens
[30 March 1913]
Sunday

Dearest.

Our address at T. [Tivoli] is

Villa Sant'Antonio
Tivoli
Rome.
HITALY
(CHARS think.)

We are packed–thats about all the news. Frederic [Manning] is coming home on Monday, so we only see Walter [Rummel] for dinner.

Oh! yes! Irony this! my respected aunt Florence [Tucker] (O.S.'s sister) sails for America on June 9th! It makes me smile. She goes to Boston & then to California. Of course she might die & leave me her income: but I doubt its happening yet (or ever): & in the Californian climate she'll last for ages!

Let me know your address–I shan't write to you until I have heard from you. Do you want a Roman scarf to tie round your waist? Just think what a "give-away" it would be.

Of course its rot your not coming too - - -

Yours
D.

If you want your Mallarmé–or any of those other books–come for them: I'll tell Louisa [the housemaid] to let you in. You may of course have anything from my room but *not* from the drawing room.

141   Dorothy to Ezra

Villa S. Antonio
Tivoli
Rome
[*5 April 1913*]

Dearest

It certainly is a lovely old house–but I loathe the "Cascate" [waterfalls], which are opposite. This moment they are foaming a handsome brown, as there has been rain–rain– –more rain than ever I have seen! We have had queer adventures about the housekeeping–but a dictionary helps some. The Olives are wonderful–They are *much* larger than Sirmione ones, & very beautiful. There is nothing much else to paint, as the hills around are scrubby & speckley. Rome 20 miles across the Plain is suggested by [sketch] St. Peters above the horizon.

Tivoli is pretty–a trifle uninspiring, & more than a mile away, along what ought to be a very dusty hot road, but is a very muddy messy one. Above us on the hill is a farm: the remains of an old monastery with cloisters evidently. It has a lovely campanile, and attractive pear-shaped cactuses (pl. cacti, or cactūs?). G. [Georgie Hyde-Lees] & I are on the verge of sui-cide–We have been out one afternoon to draw olives, and this, we have tried to paint indoors.

There is a chapel next door to the hall, filled with crutches & imitation arms & legs. Service tomorrow I imagine. (Sunday ps: Thank Heavens no–). All the rooms are pale colour-washed, & with heavy brown wood ceilings; also chilly but lovely crisscross red tile floors [sketch].

I can splash my bath water as much as I like & nothing matters!

I am painting simply vilely–Oh! dear! What ever else do you suppose I came here for, except to paint & sit in the sun. The few glimpses of the SUN have been so hot & heavenly.

The posts here hardly exist. Yours of Monday 31st arrived on Thursday, so I feared I could not catch you in London even by return–Hence this 'orrible delay!

What I feel about the Pomes? It is hard to say without them at hand, as I keep on forgetting them. They strike me as being slightly protesting - - - one or two very charming. The Bath Tub kind interest me, because of the baldness of outline which just isn't ugly–But its not very everlasting, as you say. A book of Sapphics & suchlike would be a great work.

(If you watch a waterfall long enough, it seems as though you saw creatures climbing up the rock behind a thin veil of water—which is by-the-way.)

As you know: I care for the more delicate exquisite kind of poem the best–(Sentimental Coz)–and find it very hard to criticize the others. But I find them very good for me all the same! There is one very CHAResque one, that is full of joy & humour, and *not* Post-Imp: [Post-Impressionist].

Sunday

No ink–Much Love–I am glad to think of you in Italy soon–This morning the sun was out–& hot–& we sketched. I find it so difficult to paint any new way–& the old way bores me. (The Children round about find it interesting!!). I suppose two or three fit to be seen is all one can do in a month?

I send a golden olive leaf–

Yours
D.

The Bath Tub kind]   Crisp, ironic poems like "The Bath Tub" (P), which was first published in the *Smart Set,* 41 (December 1913). In early March 1914, when Yeats (who was then on an American lecture tour) received a note from EP about the forthcoming marriage, he wrote to Lady Gregory [unpublished letter of 8 March 1914] that everybody thought the engagement had been broken off, especially since EP had written a number of satiric poems like "The Bath Tub" about his beloved. But these poems were actually written before the estrangement of June 1913 (see Letters **162–168**).

one very CHAResque one]   Probably "The Study in Aesthetics" (P), first published in *Poetry* (Chicago), 4 (August 1914).

142   Dorothy to Ezra

S. Antonio
Tivoli
Rome
8 April 1913
Tuesday

Cher.

We made a thrilling discovery yesterday. Below the house is a wonderful old Roman "Nymphaeum". Its huge & with a rounded roof and old mosaic flooring–used for the wood. It is called "La Villa d'Orazio". Our refectory & monks cells are over it. It is square with an apse at one end, and all square stone work - - - Where oh! Where is Mat-Mat [Arthur Galton]!? Also we hear from dear Walter [Rummel] that he has been to Debussy–(perhaps while you were in Paris?) and was accueilli with great friendship. I am so very glad, as he was in such a fuss about the meeting. Debussy & his Chinese things must be charming. Thanks for yr. letter from 10 C.W. [Church Walk]–and the Arnaut [Daniel] notice. I shall hope to be given one then!?

We found more Roman remains yesterday about 2 miles away: Probably belonging to Hadrian; and the hills are covered with white-flowering bushes (not May) and the wet places are pink wtih wild cyclamen possessing a strong aromatic smell. I wish you were here: it is whitewashed & lovely and would calm you nicely. Unless the cascades drove you wild. They *are* ugly–except when brown with rain & mud.

Oh–the weather! We have sketched twice so far & today its worse than ever. What black magic can we use?

I am reading Lanciani on Pagan Rome–and "Baed." [Baedeker]

There are two nice cats here, both awfully hungry; both are much tamer & less fiercely ravenous than when we came. "Pizzagarone" & "Cappuccino" are their names.

I do hope you at all events will get some sun. Its maddening–because the sun is so hot when it does appear–& the garden & loggia so nice to sit & bathe in. Not so many beasties as might be. The oxen are gray & silver, & one hardly sees them among the olives. They appear soft-nosed & gentle.

Wednesday

Wet AGAIN. I shall go mad. Really to come here & then go & be arctic-cold & pouring wet is too vile & disgusting. We have found a cupboard full of books about Rome, etc: so are reading a lot–I have taken up with Augustus, & E. [Edie M. Wood] with Domitian–and we three "young gals" hope to go into Rome tomorrow–We have spent hours looking up maps & trams! I am fearfully excited to see Roman remains.

Here a newspaper came, & we find there may be European War at any moment–but what it's all about–heaven only knows.

"La Villa d'Orazio"]   Horace's Villa. Most of DS's information about Rome was drawn from standard sources, such as those mentioned in this letter.

the Arnaut notice]   The announcement for Ralph Fletcher Seymour's projected edition of *The Canzoni of Arnaut Daniel*, which was never published. See Letter **34n.**

Lanciani . . . "Baed."] Rodolfo Amedeo Lanciani's *Pagan and Christian Rome* (1892), and the standard Baedeker guidebook of the period. Lanciani wrote a number of books on Roman antiquities.

TO THOSE INTERESTED IN THE BOOKS ISSUED BY RALPH FLETCHER SEYMOUR COMPANY AT THE ALDERBRINK PRESS

ANNOUNCEMENT

The Canzoni of Arnaut Daniel

Translated by Ezra Pound, with original music transcribed by Walter Morse Rummell.

WE have received a valuable and beautiful translation of the songs of an early Provençal poet, who, preceding Dante, was his acknowledged mentor, and whose canzoni, although typical and expressive of the best of that school, are here first translated into English.

The volume contains an introduction; the Provençal text, with translation, retaining the original forms and rime schemes: also the original music for the canzoni, and a transcription of it into modern notation. The writings exist in early XIV century MSS.

Few such opportunities present themselves to draw from original sources such rich and hitherto unused material. A creative and inspired appreciation and critique by the translator is included in the work.

To formulate, print and publish this volume, which entails considerable care and expense, we shall have to ask for the co-operation of those whose interest will make the work possible. Therefore, we wish to ask if you will sign and return the enclosed order blank, assuring us that you will be one of one hundred

and fifty to purchase this book when issued at the price of from $4.00 to $5.00, complete.

The edition will be limited to three hundred copies on hand-made paper, and ten copies on Japan Vellum paper. It will be designed and printed with the greatest care and in the style of the fifteenth century printers. It will consist of about one hundred and eighty pages and the size will be 8 x 11.

If you are interested, a response at your early convenience will be appreciated.

RALPH FLETCHER SEYMOUR.

March 1, 1913.

To RALPH FLETCHER SEYMOUR COMPANY
THE ALDERBRINK PRESS
FINE ARTS BLDG., CHICAGO

Date................

I wish to subscribe for.................[Japan vellum] [paper] copies of the book entitled "The Canzoni of Arnaut Daniel," to be delivered when completed to the following name and address.

The price of this book to be $4.50 on hand made paper, and $15.00 on Japan Vellum (subject to slight change if necessary).

Name of subscriber................

Address of subscriber................

Name of one }
to receive book }

Address of one to receive book................

The Alderbrink Press prints and sells fine books in limited editions, made for those who enjoy the best. Write for list of editions.

143   Ezra to Dorothy

[Lago di Garda]
[12 April 1913]

Dearest:

The sun has been out for a little, long enough to show up the water on the tree tips. The bust of Giuseepi Verdi or who ever it is has been put in a private garden & they are putting up a chapel in the Campo Santo, concrete in imitation of S. Zeno. En route, I found four of the inhabitants (of Sirmio, not of the C.S.) loudly & excitedly instructing a fifth who was catching snails. It is cold & grey and full of tears and very wonderful, all the olive grove, and a few more little bits of stone have fallen from the grotte, and your altar is still pink slablet uppermost.

Domenica [Sunday]

Clear. MA! un vento, un vento del norte, that would cut the ears off an ivory ape (Job IV.ii) or else (Scenes & Portraits). The surf has been splashing all night. "quidquid est *domi cachinnorum*" which we may as well render "with whatever of splashiness it possesses". Also it shades out greenish & then goes very dark blue with white foam.

?? re/ yr. second letter: [No. **142**] How do you know its a "nymphaeum"? Horace did of course have a villa at Tivoli & doubtless all the nymphaea that Maecenas would permit, but it seems unlikely that he and St. Ant. [Saint Anthony] would have occupied the same quarters - - - or - - - "Hence the Temptation". You can have it either way you like. I met three spirits in the olives yesterday & they took me to where the trees had been stripped and pruned & we all of us were wholly indignant. The shoots were white on the ground, like the carnage in Sturge Moore's "Amazons".

Later: The aqua almost black out from the cliffs, & the mountains some of 'em snow down to their middles.

According to Cracco [the proprietor] there will be no posta oggi because of the cattivo tempo. Since then the wind has gone down & they have put me "up stairs" where I belong and whence I can get some sort of outlook on the lago & the peninsula, etc. It was very fine and savage & icy on the cliff this A.M., very "different".

I am now reduced to the problem of 'la barba'–if I go out first, I shall get cold in my face & my fingers (too cold for the operation), and if I shave now the sun will be lower when I go out.

La! La!! This place is purely emotional & it was not intended that one should here indulge in intellectual gymnastics.

yours.

E.

S. Zeno] Chapter II ("Il Miglior Fabbro") of *The Spirit of Romance* (1910) begins: "The Twelfth Century, or, more exactly, that century whose center is the year 1200, has left us two perfect gifts: the church of San Zeno in Verona, and the canzoni of Arnaut Daniel; by which I would implicate all that is most excellent in the Italian-Romanesque architecture and in Provençal minstrelsy."

cold & grey and full of tears] A play on Yeats's "When you are old and grey and full of sleep."

your altar] See Letters **34** and **144n.**

un vento . . . del norte] "A wind, a wind from the North," mixing Italian and Spanish.

"quidquid est domi cachinnorum"]   The last line of Catullus 31 is *ridete quidquid est domi cachinnorum,* "ripple forth all the laughter in the house."

Maecenas]   Gaius Maecenas, the wealthy Roman diplomat who was a friend and patron of Horace and Virgil.

met three spirits . . . the carnage]   This phantasy was the source of "April" (P), first published in *Poetry* (Chicago), 3 (November 1913); the epigraph to the poem, adapted from Ovid, is *Nympharum membra disjecta* ("the scattered limbs of the nymphs").

> Three spirits came to me
> And drew me apart
> To where the olive boughs
> Lay stripped upon the ground:
>
> Pale carnage beneath bright mist.

Sturge Moore's "Amazons"]   T. Sturge Moore, *The Rout of the Amazons* (1903), a long mythological poem in which one of the speakers is "Faun."

no posta . . . tempo]   "No post today because of the wicked weather."

144   Dorothy to Ezra

St. Antonio
Tivoli
Rome
13 April 1913
Sunday

My dear.

I wonder whether you are yet at Sirmione. The weather here continues very wet & cold: and the Pope is going to die, so that Rome will be filled with people & excitements when we wish to go in. We have been in once: saw the Forum Romanum & of Trajan, also a museo of the "Terme"; where there were some most exquisite little terracottas and one or two pleasant statues. I loved the Forum: parts are still being excavated; some great pink-y pillars—and mosaic pavements.

We still haven't been [on] any expeditions owing to rain. This morning we have been for a long exploration walk among the hills: We got extraordinarily muddy, & brought back lovely flowers. We saw a wonderful old Roman viaduct-remains in the distance, had to walk a quarry-bridge over the river, a ploughed field, the railway-line, & then the road home! Mad

Inglese! Yesterday we shopped in Tivoli in perfect desperation at the weather. I bought stripy stuff for two blouses, and postcards to finish off all my friends. I can't be bothered to write letters here. One can't do anything here indoors—and as we only have one sitting-room, we are very desultory when all together. It will never be hot again, & I shall never be able to sketch while we are here.

Yes: I liked Rome–not the Tram via part of it!–I feel comfortable with fluted pillars and "moseggs" [mosaics]. From my window here I can see the upper part of a lovely little round temple of Vesta, with stone-pines beside it (in Tivoli).

Actually a little blue sky & sun–my word! Whatever next!

Tuesday

The other two gals [Georgie Hyde-Lees & Edie M. Wood] have gone into Rome. Its a heavenly day, hot sun & mountain air. Last evening we had snow on the Alban mountains, and the air was more like the Lago [di Garda]. I have sketched vilely in giardino [in the garden] this morn: and have heard as soon as I get home on 17th May I am to go away for a week's lessons. I wish to goodness I had had them before, but it couldn't be arranged.

Yesterday I got *two* letters from you! One by first post, & the second because we went into Tivoli & asked for letters. Caroline (THEIR [CHARS'] new cousin Cawroline) is to stay on with us for the first of our two weeks in Rome. Which is a great relief to us all as we need not go in & out from here now. I am sunning myself in my own window: its too good to be True, & can't possibly last. Georgie & I found an exquisite new mauvy/ pink flower last evening–about 6 blossoms of it - - - alas! it was a garlic of some sort! As she & I went out along the road, a porter-man carrying a jug passed the letter to us: & asked if we were happy at S. Antonio–etc: then by way of explanation–told us that "io tengo" as wife the sorella of the wife of Agostino (our cook is Ag:). The expression "io tengo per moglie" amused us a deal.

The Lago [di Garda] must have been looking lovely in its blue & green, and white feathers. I am glad you had such an interesting time in Paris. Did you have to talk french to all of them? Yes, dear W. [Walter Rummel] is getting stout–it seems to be the inevitable result of enough to eat–except on me - - - I am eating hugely here: macaronis & vegetables done in all sorts of heavenly ways, cheese, & a small portion of meat in the evenings. Old Agostino is a jolly good cook. We wear our dressing-gowns for breakfast & dinner–& all our coats to go to the dining room, which has been icy cold.

Tivoli & the p. card sellers, also the cars who say "Villa d'Este, villa d'Este" are getting used to us. The Cats are quite friendly, and Orazio's [Horace's] nymphaeum colder & queerer than ever. Old Searle (original owner of house) says in his work it was a nymphaeum - - - I believe he says that Suetonius says so also. I thought it was a kind of conservatory with a large bath?

Oh! G. [Georgie] & I were very troubled by Caroline in Rome, who mixed a lovely statue of "L'Ermafrodite" with Aphrodite! Oh! the sun is good. I must do up my hair, & then go down & try to go on with an "interior" of above conservatory. I have taken to a little plait over each ear, in the hopes that it may be Primavera & the Spring.

Love my dear & thanks for the letters & yellow flower. Is it a sign of luck that the Altar is still standing?

A toi.

D.

the Pope is going to die]   Pius X died on 20 August 1914.

Caroline]   Caroline Bernard, the daughter of Canon Edward Russell Bernard. She married Romeo Spani on 27 January 1923 and settled in Italy. Her correspondence with Dorothy and EP continued until her death in July 1961.

"io tengo per moglie"]   "I have a wife."

Old Searle . . . his work]   F.A. Searle, *Sketches of Tivoli, The Ancient Tibur and Its Neighbourhood* (1906).

the Altar]   See Letter **34,** where DS asked EP to "build a little altar of stones" at Sirmione. "The Altar" (P) was first published in *Canzoni* as Part X of "Und Drang."

> Let us build here an exquisite friendship,
> The flame, the autumn, and the green rose of love
> Fought out their strife here, 'tis a place of wonder;
> Where these have been, meet 'tis, the ground is holy.

145   Dorothy to Ezra

Tivoli
[Rome]
[18] April 1913
Friday

Dearest.

Thanks for yours. Yesterday we had another great excitement in the form of lunch & oranges in a "barkie" [small boat] at Hadrian's Villa. ("Villa Adriana"–which sounds quite a different place). I was thoroughly over-excited, & dreamt of ruined passages & temples all night. I had no idea what huge buildings there are still standing–nor any idea of what lots there must have been. I had yr. letter with me unread all day–& when at home again find you saying that exteriors are reality or some such! Certainly they are to me at a place like that. Its all so very large & plain. The brick-work all in neat squares, point-upwards [sketch] and in some places remains of pink or green or blue marbles–Also a certain amount of moseggs (know what moseggs are, EP?).

☐ [Georgie Hyde-Lees] likes it all I fancy very much. I do too–its restful, even the size is restful after one's first gasp. I wonder what your objections to it all are? Or were you too young merely? I don't imagine that any of the Roman statuary is much go beside Greek,– –haven't seen any yet– –but great villas seem most satisfying! Finer weather too has been a relief–although the Campagna no longer looks blue & green & Lago-ish.

I am longing to get to the Vatican statuary–also there are fine Egyptian things there I gather (bagged from "Adriana") - - - one has to forget Chinese ideas entirely. One of the books I have been reading in, says that the Romans liked the country because they disliked the Town: which I think may be good?

Someday I suppose I shall get to Greece? Having waited for Venice about five years, & now for Rome for about six–perhaps ten years hence some chance will take me to Greece. I am not strong enough in my desires, I have come to the conclusion– –Is self-analysis always egotistical?

I see Edward Dowden is dead. Will WBY's [Yeats's] election come up again I wonder for that Dublin post?

We don't discuss the Universe much–I used to do so a good deal–lately I have an idea its no use, & that one can only be apathetic & shrug one's shoulders. It makes no odds whether one believes this or that or 'tother–one writes, or paints, or is bored just the same.

Certainly the outside things (Villas, etc!) are much the most pleasing on nine occasions out of ten–the tenth–I don't know–perhaps it never comes. I like Lucretius and his theory that one's soul-atoms–are intermingled with one's body-atoms all over one (perhaps I have gathered wrong: I have only read half "De Rerum Naturae"). Anyway CHARS had a fine time yesty. grubbing along underground passages, and having dust-baths where d'autan were water-baaves [water-baths]. Dust is much better–You *try* it.

The people here are much more phle[g]matic than in the North: they are quite resigned to the fact that we won't buy promiscuous p. cards & that kind of thing. I go to my sketching class on May 19–or if I get home in time on May 17th–for a week. Then I shall have my room to arrange, & hope to start Museum-ing again. I found it a good plan - - - if only I can go on–& do some copies for my room.

Any other suggestions for my welfare? Everything needs such a damned lot of application–& it never seems worth the trouble. I also am wearing all my winter clothes: & shiver every morning in my bath. Midday if the sun happens to 'fa' [be out] is boiling.

Sat. morn. early

This had better go. Its going to be hot & I shant want to write today!

A toi

D

Edward Dowden] Edward Dowden (1843–4 April 1913), a scholar and man of letters best known for his work on Shakespeare. He was Professor of English Literature at Trinity College, Dublin.

WBY's election . . . that Dublin post] As early as 1910 it had been suggested that Yeats might succeed Dowden to the Chair of English Literature at Trinity College, Dublin. Allen Upward remembered that when Yeats was proposed for the Chair, Dowden " 'rose from the grave,' as my friend Ezra Pound puts it, to prevent such a breach with academic tradition" [*Some Personalities* (London, 1921), p. 59].

146   Ezra to Dorothy

Hotel Eden
Sirmione am Gardasee
[21 April 1913]

Dearest:

No, I shouldn't say that self-analysis is egotistical–even if the epithet were opprobious. Anyhow "know thyself" is about the only way to find out about any thing or body else. Neither did I mean that the objective is "The real" except in comparison with inductions from the objective. i.e. notions, ideas (of a sort), opinions. As for the soul being "mixed up" I dare say we've the whole divina commedia going on inside of us. Yeats rather objects to cells being intelligent, but, I think the 'Paradiso' is a fair stab at presenting a developed "phantastikon". The real meditation is, however, the meditation on one's *identity*. Ah, voilà une chose!! You try it. You try finding out why you're you & not somebody else. And who in the blazes you are anyhow? Ah voilà une chose! I can give you "Mantua" if its any use to you, & perhaps "Perigord".

For the rest of your letter: I believe a mosseggg to be a small stone–one of a large number–so called from Mosegs [Moses] having got the dekalogg on a large stone CHARS think, and thats why the café tables have marble tops. Also there's a "g" in phlegmatic, if that was the word you intended.

Yesterday I rowed, bathed, fished up a large chunk of what I believe to be porphyry from one part of the lake and deposited it in another–as I didn't know what else to do with it. It's now in easy reach if one ever happens to want it - - - "The Bishop of St. Praxed's" etc.

I begin to think Catullus' Sapphics not much nearer the mark than my own–which is some comfort. I shall have to retire to a monastery & abide a year with nowt but an unabridged lexicon. Bar his laudable attempts at the impossible Aeolic perfection & one or two long poems he is a very charming person–At times "post-imp" [post-impressionist] in your sense of the word–very!

Propertius–except in spots–and Tibullus remind me of french poetry of 1878. Propertius has all the bad points of a troubadour & none of the Provençal's excuses. I perceive that I shall soon be reduced to learning greek.

There's one happy thought in C. [Catullus]–"to Calous on Quintilia"–where he says of Q.'s death, "It can't have been as much grief to *her* as it was to have enjoyed your affection". He, the good Valerius, has a nasty way of putting things now and again. Martial's was the lighter, more exuberant spirit. (I can't be absolutely certain of the above translation, still - - -).

I have an idea I shall go home via Munich, when I go–a. for the Pinacoteka [picture-gallery], b. to get out of the tiresome *andare* [trip] to Paris.

I think the combination of Richard [Aldington] & Venice will amuse me. I expect him to detest most of it. The Dryad [Hilda Doolittle] has some slight affiliation with Verona, but the pair of 'em, wholly Hellenized at Capri, are going to be very much [out] of place in bella Venezia.

Hi Wow! I *am* glad to have this balcony. There are such a *lot* of germans in the giardino [garden]. I begin to fear that April is *the* month for this corner of Italy. However, I shan't be pushed off the peninsula for a while yet. Dei agrestes [the rustic gods] look after you at your villula.

Yours

E.

"*phantastikon*"]   In "Psychology and Troubadours" (1912), later Chapter V of *The Spirit of Romance,* EP remarks that the consciousness of some men "seems to rest, or to have its center more properly, in what the Greek psychologists called the *phantastikon.*"

> Their minds are, that is, circumvolved about them like soap-bubbles reflecting sundry patches of the macrocosmos. And with certain others their consciousness is "germinal". Their thoughts are in them as the thought of the tree is in the seed, or in the grass, or the grain, or the blossom. And these minds are the more poetic, and they affect mind about them, and transmute it as the seed the earth. And this latter sort of mind is close on the vital universe; and the strength of the Greek beauty rests in this, that it is ever at the interpretation of this vital universe, by its signs of gods and godly attendants and oreads [mountain nymphs].
> [*The Spirit of Romance* (New Directions, 1952), pp. 92–93].

In "The Condolence" (P), first published in *Poetry* (Chicago), 1 (April 1913), EP uses the term in addressing his "fellow sufferers, songs of my youth":

> We went forth gathering delicate thoughts,
> Our '*fantastikon*' delighted to serve us.

"*Mantua*" . . . "*Perigord*"]   That is, the Virgilian or Provençal *phantastikons.*

"*The Bishop of St. Praxed's*"]   In Browning's dramatic monologue "The Bishop Orders His Tomb at Saint Praxed's Church," the Bishop is much concerned about the stone to be used in his splendid tomb.

"to Calous on Quintilia"]   Catullus 96. The poem is addressed to Catullus's friend Licinius Calvus, on the death of his young wife Quintilia.

the good Valerius]   Gaius Valerius Catullus.

Martial's . . . spirit]   Marcus Valerius Martial, the Roman epigrammatic poet of the 1st century A.D.

the Pinacoteka]   The Alte Pinakothek, or Old Picture Gallery, in Munich.

147   Dorothy to Ezra

> *Tivoli*
> *[Rome]*
> *20 [April] 1913*
> *Sunday*

Dearest.

Yours came this morning just after I had sent off one to you. What adventures on the blessed Lago [di Garda]. It is always rather apt to blow up very sudden & swift as far as I remember. You had a wild plan 'autrefois' of taking us for the night in a boat to that town opposite Catullus - - - We should probably have been drowned. I am glad you are not "pining"! What's the good of going to the Lago to pine? I am not either. I was horribly bored during the wet here, & still can't paint–but I am really enjoying it all very much. We have a sudden wild plan to go right up into the mountains for two nights before descending to Rome & best hats & Baed [Baedeker]. We go up–if we go at all–to Subiaco: 23 miles up the Avviene, to 1400ft high—to see some frescoes & the mountains. I suppose the above-mentioned lack of "pining"! shows that we both really love the country & the sun? Also Italy–is it a good or a bad sign? I take it as meaning a delight in physical health and an outside joy of new sights - - - to which much might be added were we in the same, instead of different, parts of Italy.

I am reading about Emperor Hadrian, as I admire his manner of Villa so much. He must have been very energetic & very artistic–I speak from slight knowledge. It amuses me to start for Rome without the very vaguest information on any Emperor! I am at all events unbiassed–At least I am developing a liking for the profile of Augustus–and a certain curiosity about them all may show itself in Time. It is quite remarkable to know *nothing*–ma mérite–about Rome. I feel positively proud–but I may take to Gibbon on my return. I am not sure.

I am sure I am naturally half Roman & equally sure I am half Greek–
Which am I to be? Can one be both without any worry? Yes. Why not.
Dear Hadrian was both after all–Hush! speaking rubbish now! I am "vastly
entertained" to find that Hadrian rebuilt Jerusalem - - - put a temple to
Aphrodite on Calvary: & one to Adonis at Bethlehem–& that it was over
Hadrian's J. [Jerusalem] that the Crusaders did all their fighting & fuss.
Apropos of something else–O.S. [Olivia Shakespear] has just said that I
am more pagan than she is–What ho! Is it true? Again I am amused.

Don't die of the cold bathing or get cramp.

Wednesday

Yesterday we went again to Hadrian's Villa. We had scratchy conversa-
tion in Italian with a native who was headman of some excavations going
on–a temple–of Neptune or of Diana–They don't yet know which. The
dear man gave us each a lovely bit of marble pavement–I had green ser-
pentine–O.S. red porphyry–So today we girls did a little "scavi'ing" [exca-
vating] of our own with a candle in underground passages, near here. It
is a villa of one Quintilius Varus, a governor of Syria, who was murdered
by Commodus. We found heaps of bits of white marble and □ [Georgie
Hyde-Lees] found 3 square inches of mosaic flooring - - - which makes me
long for more. Bats & wierd things are an objection–but with a scarf over
one's head & plenty of matches - - -

It never occurred to me that perhaps you might find bits of Catullus?
We all mean to go to Q.V. again this evening and continue–A penknife,
a razor (□'s) & a trowel are our instruments.

I did two memory-impressions of Hadrian yesty: on my return: one is
quite nice. I have hardly painted at all.

We hope to go up to Subiaco for two nights on Monday next–Then our
address will be

> Hotel Flora
> Via Veneto
> **Roma**

You had hardly better write here again as any letters arriving after we
leave will never get forwarded.

Wouldn't it be dreadful if I got excavation mania! But I have not the
persistance.

> Blow! It is raining again.
> 'ow begusting.
> Love. Yours.

148   Dorothy to Ezra

[*Tivoli*]
[*Rome*]
[*24 April 1913*]

Thursday morning early!
8 ocl!

Yours came yesterday, as the other two went into the Town, & to the post office. The lump of porphyry of course *might* be useful some day–I am trying to get a nice bit of marble from our "excavations"–Heaven knows what for - - -

(I don't think I can have used "phlegmatic" about anything–unless it was the Roman temperament?). We have altogether lost the Dryad [Hilda Doolittle]–Is she already in the North?

Yes, I am afraid if they (she & R) are feeling very Greek, the barbaric Venezia will be somewhat a shock. I have never felt Venice yet myself–except St. Marc's–There of course is everything one can want–Marbles, mosaics, and gold shining in the dark. (Yr. poem with the pattern of gold woven in the stuff is like that).

"Poetry" [*Poetry,* Chicago] came for ☐ [Georgie Hyde-Lees]. I haven't heard a syllable about yours from any of the Company! Oh, yes! one fierce bit about conventions appealed to Carolina–à propos of some family horror she was telling me about.

I must dress.
Your loving.

Yr. poem with the pattern of gold]   "The House of Splendour" (P), first published as Part VII of "Und Drang" in *Canzoni* (1911).

149   Ezra to Dorothy

Hotel Eden
Sirmione am Gardasee
[*25 April 1913*]

Yes, of course you can be Graeco-Roman–all the decent Romani were doped with Hellas–vid. Propertius, Catullo translated Sappho–Orazio [Horace] boasts about being the "primus" to bring in the Aeolic fashions.

As for O.S. [Olivia Shakespear] she has a nasty 3rd-century-christian streak in her nature. That's why she hates Christ like the devil. You are, I suppose, a decadent empress when alls over & done with, perhaps the member of the family whose carelessness got poor Ovid exiled to Pontus. It seems more'n likely. Charlotte, when I first met her in New York, had a vision of all of us in some late empire romanorum villa–and a frightful row going on–I don't know that she identified any of you when she was in London, but I knew right enough at the time. She knew me, all right.

As to O.S. [Olivia's] conversion by Origen, or what ever it was, I can give you no enlightenment. The Dryad [Hilda Doolittle] in a fit of rage once called her "an assiduous vestal"–but not to her face.

The Theocritan Idyll is, I think still at Anacapri. They've stopped going to Capri for their mail–but restez tranquille, they won't get into your nunnery.

O.S. was probably Byzantine, Greek–late, and married into by some roman or other–that will docket you nicely.

Saturday

Quest'oggi [Today] is decently hot. I have splashed in the lake all the morning & have managed to change my colour. Have been (yesterday) reading Omero [Homer], with an Italian crib. It is curiously naive balderdash mixed up with glorious lines. As to Hadrian & Jerusalem. What but a temple of Venus would have taken the Provençals & the Plantagenets to that part of the world. I believe it was the good Leo X who had a crystal nude Venus set in the apostolic crucifix, so that he might kiss the same at the elevation of the host. There's Renaissance for you, THEY [CHARS] think.

The Quattro cento has points, despite your affecting the ancients.

I am rejoicing in the "resa di Scutari". THEY [CHARS] have any number of explanations–all foolish.

Kipling has written a play. Bryan has given a boozeless dinner to the foreign ambassadors. The "Corriere" does bring one choice bits of Anglo-American news. I believe the last mail this week is collected at 4.

The poppies are coming out. I don't quite know why I am going to Venice. I'm going to Verona for a pair of breeches–There's no mystery about that and I suppose I'm going to Venice because I *had* intended to go there.

I have written some more minute poems–a few of them proper.

The Gods attend you.

E.

Charlotte]   Probably Charlotte Herman, the older sister of William Carlos Williams's wife Florence. Both William and his brother Edgar had been in love with Charlotte, and for a time she was engaged to Edgar. In 1914 she married Ferdinand Earle, editor of *The Lyric Year* (see Letter **127n**). EP must have met her during his visit to America in 1910–11. For further information on Charlotte Herman see Paul Mariani, *William Carlos Williams: A New World Naked* (New York, 1981).

The Theocritan Idyll]   Richard Aldington and Hilda Doolittle.

Anacapri . . . Capri]   Towns on the west and east ends of the Isle of Capri.

"resa di Scutari"]   "Surrender of Scutari." The Turkish garrison at Scutari (in northwestern Albania) surrendered on 22 April 1913, ending the first Balkan War.

Kipling . . . a play]   *Harbour Watch,* a one-act play first produced in May 1913.

Bryan . . . foreign ambassadors]   William Jennings Bryan, the U.S. Secretary of State, had given a dinner for forty members of the Washington diplomatic corps at which only grape juice was served. The *New York Times* of 25 April 1913 carried this front-page headline: "MR. BRYAN DEFENDS GRAPE JUICE FEAST. Explains That He Solaced Ambassadors with Words Instead of Wine." Bryan's courage was praised by many temperance groups in the U.S., but the London *Pall Mall Gazette* of 24 April took a different view: "We fear that the capital of the great Republic is destined to be known as 'Wishywashington.' "

The "Corriere"]   The Milan newspaper *Corriere della Sera.*

more minute poems]   Probably some of the crisp, imagistic poems published later that year in *Poetry* (Chicago), 3 (November 1913) and the *Smart Set,* 41 (December 1913).

150   Ezra to Dorothy

[*Lago di Garda*]
[*29 April 1913*]

Dearest:

Can you make head or tail of this dam'd thing. I *thought* I'd done a pome, and *now* I'm hanged if I can tell whether anything gets over the footlights.

The Faun

I.

Soul of a dog, un-hound, capriped,
I have seen you sniffing and snoozling about
                    among my flowers,
So, ho! and at last they have tamed you.

Ut flosculus hyacinthus - - -
                    What do you know of these things?
What *do* you know of horticulture?
But take it, I leave you the garden.

II.

Come Auster, Come, Apeliota,
    And see the faun in our garden.
And if you but move or speak,
    this thing will run at you
        and scare itself to spasms.

The Faun]   "The Faun" (P), much revised, was first published in *Poetry and Drama*, 2 (March 1914). In recasting the poem EP was guided by DS's criticism (see Letter **151**).

> Ha! Sir, I have seen you sniffing and snoozling
>   about among my flowers.
> And what, pray, do you know about horticulture,
>   you capriped?

> "Come, Auster; come, Apeliota,
> And see the faun in our garden;
> But if you move or speak
> This thing will run at you
> And scare itself to spasms."

The "Faun" was the nickname EP and DS gave to Richard Aldington. It was derived in part from Aldington's youth and his interest in Greek literature; in part from the recurrence of fauns in his poetry (two of his early poems are "The Faun Sees Snow for the First Time" and "The Faun Captive"); and in part from the Mallarmé/Debussy/Nijinsky "L'après-midi d'un faune" (see Letter **137n**). In *Poetry and Drama* "The Faun" is placed next to "Tempora" (P), a similarly ironic poem about "The Dryad" (Hilda Doolittle).

capriped]   A combination of *capripes,* the Latin for "goat-footed," and Capri, where Aldington and Hilda Doolittle had recently been staying (see Letter **149**).

Ut flosculus hyacinthus]   "Like a little hyacinth flower." EP may have had
in mind Sappho's epithalamium (fragment 105c), "Like the hyacinth which the
shepherd tramples underfoot on the mountain, and it still blooms purple on the
ground"; he is certainly playing on the "flos hyacinthinus" in line 89 of Catullus
61, a marriage hymn with a Greek framework. The phrase also recalls a poem
by the Renaissance Latinist Marcus Antonius Flaminius, "Ut flos tenellos,"
which EP quotes and translates in Chapter XI ("Poeti Latini") of *The Spirit
of Romance:*

> As a fragile and lovely flower unfolds its gleaming foliage on the breast-fold of
> the fostering earth, if the dew and rain draw it forth; thus doth my tender mind
> flourish if it be fed with the sweet dew of the Fostering Spirit.
> Lacking this, it straightway beginneth to languish even as a flower born upon
> dry earth, if the dew and the rain tend it not.

Like Catullus, Flaminius was linked in EP's mind with Sirmio and Lago di
Garda.

Auster . . . Apeliota]   The south and east winds. Both names occur in
Catullus 26.

151   Dorothy to Ezra

29 April [1913]
Tuesday

Convent of French Nuns
at Subiaco
by The Shadow of Lizabef.

Cher–Its an over-cultivated locality & horribly mediaeval-built on a
rock, with a castle on top–Only a cardinal's summer-residence Castle–
Once Nero had a palace here–but there are only a few pillars in churches
to tell the tale. The town is too Dantescan I think: like Purgatory:
[sketch of the Mount of Purgatory]
[This] kind of shape & when one has reached [the top] after many 100s
of stone steps one just has to come down again, & the castel on top is
nothing akin to Paradise. However this morning we have done the "Giro"
[tour] we came to do. One goes up the mountains to two monasteries (the
place swarms with monasteries & convents–half a dozen of each it seems
like). There are wonderful frescoes in the topmost one: Giotto-esque
things, and two rock-caves round which the churches have been built–
S. Benedetto lived as an Eremita [hermit] in them for a long time. He grew

roses for their Thorns, (in which according to a frescoe he used to roll naked) and then a long while after S. Francis came along & put Benedetto's nose out of joint by turning all the Thorns into Roses! and now they have a lovely rose-garden from S. Francis' roses.

In the lower monastery there were Nero remains, pillars & a marble well-head–heaps of old manuscripts & the first Italian printed books–and there are such lovely cloisters, with a double row of pillars reminding one of those at the Cath: [cathedral] in Verona.

There is a terrific thunder-storm coming up.

Continued in Rome & very muddled & dull!

[1 May]
Thursday

Heavens! What a pen.

My dear. "Yours to hand". I have not yet had time to read the poems properly–anon - - - We arrived yesterday–We drove from Subiaco about 16 miles to catch a train here. To-day being 1 May & "Festa" we find no trams, no carriages–& have wandered long & far round the top of some hill–Pulciano I think: but I can't disentangle them.

And now two humans are singing to the drawing-room piano, Italian opera duets I suppose. *She* sings flat mostly. I hope it won't go on long. We have rencontré a couple unexpectedly who are friends of Nelly's [Georgie Hyde-Lees's mother]–not in our hotel mercifully.

I am dreadfully sorry at leaving S. Antonio. It was the nicest place in the world. You don't think that can have been the place "Charlotte" saw us squabbling in?! I hope you & I were not at loggerheads–but only our adherents. We might go there some day - - - for you to learn Greek.

I thought you were learning Rabindra's [Tagore's] lingo? It might have some connections perhaps?

So you are in Venezia–Have you left the Lago [di Garda] for ever? or do you return presently? We are getting awfully tired of Carolina Nuova–She has lost the personality she used to have & we none of us ever remember she is there, except by a sense of restraint. I hope she goes home next week. She is still very pretty. Francese [French], people think.

Friday

Dear, to continue! Your faun has come–I saw some pleasant ones in the Vatican Museum–to-day.

Yes. Having read yours five times or so! I like it–very much–I am always doubtful of anything underlined–("What *do* you know" etc.). It presupposes so much intonation–or is that only a fad? of mine? The gist of it all lies I gather in the last lines–"scare itself to spasms" sounds somehow ungrammatical–But I think it comes over - - - about as much as the Faun would think fit. What I really mean is that I like the beginning & end best, & the middle seems a trifle out of drawing perhaps–the latin is hard or something.

Beastly place, St Peters–shocking–We go back to Old Rome this evening after tea.

A toi.

Charlotte]   See Letter **149n.**
Your faun]   The poem of Letter **150.**

152   Ezra to Dorothy

Venice
3 May 1913

Dearest:

Here after divers troubles by land & sea, behold us. It is now about 9.30 A.M. I spent last night in a picturesque lodging sul Canal Grande, with a vista of nearly everything, but arose with a firm conviction that I would not spend another night in the same locality. This I have accomplished at a net loss of 3 lire which is fairly good considering I'd paid a week in advance. The signora had mai visto una persona tanto dispiaciuta, and to my certain knowledge *no* other Venetian has ever restored cash once rec'd.– on any ground whatever. I've now a tile roof & sun and a small canal, so even the picturesque has not been wholly sacrificed.

At 3 A.M. I thoroughly detested travel. I couldn't tell which I hated worse, travel or the stupid & defenceless condition that one gets into when one stays in the same place & is served hand & foot, videlicit Ch.W. [Church Walk] & Sirmione. The last is too cushioned, tho' the food is not what it might be. They say 'stia sempre nella memoria', so I must have paid them too much–No, I won't say that the whole staff was/were *gentile* & even Cracco [the proprietor] whom I detest redeemed himself by telling *Come si fece la donna.*

Jesu Christo stando nel paradiso terrestre
pensando come fare compagna d'Adamo—

it needs gestures but you shall have it later.

This place has a cuisine as THEY [CHARS] happen to know, for we
dined here yesterday (& lunched before that). The first orzzo in 5 years,
and this A.M. positively the 1st cup of coffee that I have ever had in Italy.

The country is looking up—what with Marinetti & the war with Tripoli
etc. Venice seemed yesterday like one large Carlton Hotel. I have ordered
delicate trousers, & bought gloves that are I fear more ornate than dura-
ble. In fact I may say that yesterday was unsullied by any sort of economy.

R & H. [Richard Aldington & Hilda Doolittle] appear to be falling in
love with each other somewhere en route from Napoli. I suppose I'll have
to be ready with a pontifical sanction & then try to soothe their respective
progenitors— at least their communications are *very* vague.

My last wooing of the sun & the lago was so violent that I've very nearly
got a whole new hide, which is worse than getting new raiment - - - it is
more economical in one way, but it devours one's time. Anyhow I arise on
this the 3rd day of Maggio [May]—or rather arose some hours since & was
brought hither by swift oarsmen—but am now soothed & at peace & feel
ages wiser and more mature than I did 24 hours ago. Yesterday, also, I
saw one gondola crawl about six feet over another gondola's middle. I've
never seen anything of the sort before—New Italy! cosa di Sport! etc.—still
it produced the same antique mode of eloquence so I suppose there is a
conservative principle somewhere.

That 'Faun' thing is no good—don't worry about criticizing it—or rather
do—go ahead & see if you can diagnose it.

On the whole mi piace Venezia. I felt that way when I arrived & despite
the uneven fortunes I am restored to the belief, even in the absence of the
two people who in all decency ought to regard it as their sole duty to stand
present & keep me amused. If not, why have I reared them with such per-
sistent solicitude—You had much better do your sketching here—& Horatio
Brown might be persuaded to "instruct" you. God!! hast ever seen an opus
Brownensis!?!!?!

Ebbène its a charming morning, aura dolce, just enough to flutter my
papers without being a d——d nuisance. I go forth seeking mail, c/o Tho.
Cook, as I scribbled on the back of my last envelope.

Dieu te garde et le bon soleil.
E.

The signora . . . dispiaciuta]   "The lady had never seen a person so displeased."

'stia sempre nella memoria']   Correctly *sarà sempre nella memoria,* "we will always remember you."

Come si fece . . . compagna d'Adamo]   "How woman was created: Jesus Christ, while standing in the earthly paradise, thinking how to create a companion for Adam . . ." EP recalls this moment in Canto 22.

first orzzo in 5 years]   When EP was living in Venice in 1908 and short of funds, his usual dinner was *orzo,* barley soup.

Marinetti]   See Letter **70n.**

war with Tripoli]   The Italo-Turkish war of 1911–12 began with the occupation of Tripoli.

That 'Faun' thing]   The poem of Letter **150.**

Horatio Brown]   Horatio Robert Forbes Brown (1854–1926), who spent much of his life in Venice, was the author of several books and articles on Venetian history, printing, and architecture.

Ebbène]   *Ebbene,* "Well."

aura dolce]   See Letter **130n.**

153   Ezra to Dorothy

ALBERGO RESTAURANT
"BELLA VENEZIA"
Propr. PIERO P. DIODÀ fu ETTORE
S. MARCO, CALLE DEI FABBRI, N. 4710
PONTE DELLE BALLOTTE, N. 4701
VENEZIA

[*3 May 1913*]

Yes, Dearest Heart:

I consider underlining *very* bad. What I want on the "do" is a greek accent, to show that its the first note in the *bar,* not that anyone reading the poem would know that there was any intention of bars but then - - -

I was very bucked on analyzing 'The Return'–which I did straight away–that it is in almost uniform feet (systema graeca, – – ᵕ –) as to quantity–if one counts certain pauses after the unit is determined, etc. *They* (CHARS) *think* I'm getting a little too *much* ear.

As near as I can make out Bengali has some of the faults of Italian, quant à phonetique. It n'has pas les reins du Grec. All this from a few moments with Omero [Homer] παρὰ δινα θαλασσα πολυφλὸιςβοιο. etc. Naturally I dislike to come to this conclusion for everyone else says that greek is *the* language. (In the above quotation *lago* will have to be substituted for θἀλασσα, which sounds like "molasses" & means sea). To think that I should come to be explaining a thing of that sort–needlessly perhaps–to a niece or something of the 1.1.L. [late lamented Lionel Johnson].

And so poor dear it [Dorothy] has had a secret desire to have a row with me & my accursed placidity does not offer etc.–I was going to say I would look to the matter at once, only that sounds a little too docile. Let me say, "I contradict you flatly". And I think I've given you a number of very choice chances which you have been either too indolent or too obstinate to accept. Or did you, light of my ροδοδακτἰλος aurora, only mean that you hoped all seeds of discord had been buried in the archaic past. The accursed & irritating thing about you that I shall probably *never* find out–even supposing–which–is unlikely–that you ever had the slightest intention of meaning either.

I am very glad you mailed your letter when you did, for that state of my mind which is not ennui, but which is distinguished therefrom only by the present felicity of my digestion, was getting beyond all decency. I am very glad I don't have to do nothing–pure & unadulterated nothing, all my life.

How do you like the "propr.'s" [proprietor's] variation of your praenomen? THEY [CHARS] prefer–no! NO! it is not fitting to state what they prefer, but between ourselves its the familiar "Spurco 'iu". They think the proper variation with a greek accent on its coda is positively silly.

Poor R. [Richard Aldington] will find himself so forestalled with the Venetian public, his head–back view, & his back view–when seated–have already arrived. I chortled for eight minutes observing it in S. Marco this P.M. The front of it is a skimpy musician (at least I should think it hardly looks intelligent enough to be more than that).

Venice is full of beautiful clothes, and the italian people deplorable as they doubtless are in many respects–are often in their immature stages of development very cheering to look upon. Also the swank of the Piazza is diverting–especially when one pauses long enough to consider that positively nobody who *is* anybody *ever* comes to Venice to be it. And even the last extravagance in molasses-taffy canes is being imitated or even sold @ 5 lire. I wonder if I shall give way to the pressure and purchase a "wesket", such a wesket as I haven't flown to, since I was a sophomore–So nearly have I attained to the last and final vacuity.

As for S. Benedetto living in a cave, THEY [CHARS] don't think it fitting in a saint and it reminds 'EM anyhow of that old wheeze about Newman's apology for living in a sewer–De contemptu mundi etc., and as for S.B.'s rolling in anything but rolled oats, it was Belshazzar–who started the craze for breakfast cereals.

And there ain't no such place as New Carolina. There are only North & South–which seems to be what you've discovered.

About the 'Faun'–you are quite right. The middle simply isn't imagiste & the beginning plus the end aren't enough. Sometime one *might* do a poem about a faun.

Sunday

I think the stuff on the piazza gets better each year, however I've found nothing I really want except a plum coloured pearl–even so the setting is a little too middle aged for you (no! not mediaeval). I have explained to one aged Venetian gentleman that we stare at each other in mutual & puzzled recognition NOT because we have been decently introduced & know each other, but because we have seen each other upon the piazza 41111111 times. I was afraid his mental struggles to place me would injure what brain he's got–which is venetian.

Sandy preached this morning without damning the pope–either out of respect for Pio's health–or because the Scarlet Woman of Babylon is to be furiously castigated this P.M.

Monday

Confound it they always steal my inchiostro [ink]–Rien.

I found the dryad's [Hilda Doolittle's] family disconsolate on the piazza yesterday afternoon & spent the evening consoling them for the absence of their offspring. "Charles" is placidly considering his end. We discussed the heresy of planetary influences & the possible inoculation of life from one planet to another, etc.

Dieu te garde.

E.

underlining . . . the "do"]   See Letter **151**.

'The Return']   "The Return" (P), first published in the *English Review*, 11 (June 1912), is not—like "Apparuit" (P)—a direct imitation of the Sapphic form, but it suggests Sapphics in its falling rhythms, and especially in the Adonic

meter of the last four lines. EP claimed to have written the poem in a quarter of an hour.

παρὰ δινα θαλασσα πολυφλὸισβοιο] παρὰ θῖνα πολυφλοίσβοιο θαλάσσης, "along the shore of the loud resounding sea." Homer used all or part of this phrase many times: see *Iliad*, 1.34, 9.182, 23.59, and the *Odyssey* 13.220. The phrase was EP's favorite example of Homer's onomatopoeia:

> Of Homer two qualities remain untranslated: the magnificent onomatopoeia, as of the rush of the waves on the sea-beach and their recession in: παρὰ θῖνα πολυφλοίσβοιο θαλάσσης untranslated and untranslatable; and, secondly, the authentic cadence of speech; the absolute conviction that the words used, let us say by Achilles to the 'dog-faced' chicken-hearted Agamemnon, are in the actual swing of words spoken.
>
> ["Translators of Greek: Early Translators of Homer" (1920), *Literary Essays*, p. 250]

a niece or something] Lionel Johnson (1867–1902), Olivia Shakespear's first cousin on her mother's side, was an accomplished classicist. See Letter **67n.**

ροδοδακτὶλος *aurora*] ῥοδοδάκτυλος, the Homeric epithet for "rosy-fingered" dawn.

"propr.'s" variation of your praenomen] See the letterhead for the "Albergo Restaurant 'Bella Venezia,' " reproduced at the beginning of this letter. EP is playing on the proprietor's name (Diodà) and Dorothy ("Dorotea" in Italian), both of which mean "gift of God."

THEY prefer . . . "Spurco 'iu" . . . accent on its coda] In their perverse way CHARS prefer the familiar curse *Sporco Dio* ("Dirty God") rather than the proprietor's variation, Diodà. "Spurco 'iu" is EP's phonetic rendering of the Venetian pronunciation of *Sporco Dio.*

S. Benedetto] See Letter **151.**

Newman's apology . . . De contemptu mundi] EP is playing on two titles: John Henry Newman's *Apologia pro Vita Sua* (1864), and the 12th-century work of Lotario di Segni (later Pope Innocent III), *De contemptu mundi, sive de miseria humanae conditionis* ("On contempt for the world, or on the miserable condition of man").

the 'Faun'] The poem of Letter **150.**

Sandy] Rev. Cavaliere Alexander Robertson (1846–1933), the Church of Scotland pastor in Venice, who wrote several books on Venice, Italian politics, and the Roman Catholic Church. In a letter sent from Venice to Mary Moore of Trenton, 12 May 1913, EP reported that "the Reverend Cavaliere Dottore Alexander Robertson" had given him a pamphlet on the evils of the Roman Catholic Church. That pamphlet was almost certainly *The Great Harlot on the Seven Hills*, an abridgement of *"Babylon"; or the Divine Foreview of the Rise, Reign and Destiny of the Church of Rome* (1910), a book written by Albert W. Close with an introduction by the Rev. Alexander Robertson. Robertson's anti-Papal sermons are recalled in Canto 76:

"Dawnt let 'em git you" burred the bearded Dottore
when was the Scottch Kirrrk in Venice
to warn one against Babylonian intrigue
and there have been since then
very high episcopal vagaries

"Charles"] Hilda Doolittle's father Charles Leander Doolittle (1843–1919), Professor of Astronomy at the University of Pennsylvania and first director of the nearby Flower Observatory.

154   Dorothy to Ezra

[*Hotel*] *Flora*
[*Rome*]
[*6 May 1913*]
Tuesday

Mon cher.

Today again sun. Yours came yesterday–or the day before–I expect you suffered yr. first night in Venezia the same way that we did at the Sanctissimo Sacramento Convent [at Subiaco]! Only yours was probably worse.

I have seen a lovely Carlo Crivelli this morning–a Madonna & Child–and yesterday the Sistine [Chapel], which is fine–but of course the opposite of anything archaic. I am collecting some postcards & photos - - - which will *not* contain any Raphael.

The Colosseum also I have seen since I wrote. I don't grasp its size at all: some huge remains in the Forum seem much larger in proportion - - - in fact they really gave me an impression of megalomania that nothing else has done.

I have got a photo for dear-Walter [Rummel] of an exquisite little Greek-Egyptian - - - & have run to earth the plaque of a chariot that I have in my own room.

You will have had my so-called criticism of yr. Faun. What *is* the matter with it??

Oh! yes: we have also been to the Zoo! Some nice tigers, & two charming plump Zebras–and we fed the elephants.

You might go to the Accademia while you are in Venice & give my respects to the Bellini Madonna, and another one or two of his: also (I *think*) a Mantegna Madonna with a background of cherubim. Then there is the

Tiziano [Titian] of the Presentation in the Temple–at the Palazzo Ducale–
(free on Sundays!) and a blue & gold ceiling, somewhere in the Palazzo.

As to Rome–New Rome simply doesn't seem to matter at all. Its shops
& trams, & noisy: but Nothing - - - ugly or beautiful.

I have bought a very pet hat, with cherry things round it & a blue-green
brim, & O.S. [Olivia Shakespear] has got a very pretty smart frock. Caro-
line can't find anybody to travel home with, & we all feel very unsettled &
vague as to whether she goes or stays - - - She will probably get into a row
anyway at home: perhaps I shan't ever be asked there again to stay!

I wonder whether yr. Hilda & R.A. [Hilda Doolittle & Richard Alding-
ton] are falling in love with each other. My Hilda [Strutt] has produced a
daughter, I hear from Frank [Deverell, her husband].

I must rest a little after taking Caroline out all the morning. She is very
vague, & follows in & out of trams very obediently–but she is, I believe,
absolutely inartistic, & I am certain Roman remains overwhelm her.

A toi

D

In case you haven't been told by anyone:–Tagore lectures at 8.30 at Cax-
ton Hall.

Monday	May	19	The Relation of the Individual & the Universe.
"	"	26	Soul Consciousness.
"	June	2	The Problem of Evil.
"	"	9	The Problem of Self.
"	"	16	Realisation in Love.

10/6 the set.
2/6 each.

yr. Faun]   The poem of Letter **150**.

155   Ezra to Dorothy

Albergo Bella Venezia
Venice
[8 May 1913]
Thursday

Dearest:

Madame Brass gave me a ticket to the concert at the Fenice last night–music surprisingly good–and "all Venice" there & diverting, & the whole effect pleasingly 18th century–Goya, Rossini, Goldoni sort of effect, delighting my sense of history–*not* my "historical sense"–a difference to be explained at length later if you ever ask me what it is. I mean I shouldn't have been in the least surprised to see Browning or Verdi looking down,

"to where Rossini sits
Silent in his stall".

I should think *that* poem was of the Fenice–any how it seems to be all the napoleonic & Austrian periods.

The Dryad [Hilda Doolittle] has arrived with its faun [Richard Aldington]. She doesn't seem much more in love with it than when she left london, but her family distresses her & seems to drive her more fawn-wards. I glared at Mrs Horatio on the piazza yesterday–I hope I escaped recognition.

I think the Eagle's "Grey Rock" is very fine–but his syntax is getting obscurer than Browning's. I'm fed up with Tagore. I wish he'd get thru' lecturing before I get back. I don't want to be any more evangelized than I am already–which is too dam' much. And I much prefer the eagle's gods to any oriental beetle with 46 arms.

I've been reading Petronius in 18th century french. It is almost too indecent to be amusing but it has the occasional light of a phrase, and one easily sees where Voltaire created himself. For the rest we hope we can be almost as improper without being so monotonous.

Chicago seems to have produced parodies of us, at the rate of one a day for at least a week–evidently we are creating a vulgar stir & will have to retire to Sapphics.

The sky is lovely Venetian (4.15 p.m.) but pale after our *lago* [Lago di Garda].

I wonder which is worse, to die in the aromatic subtlety of a disappearing cadence (*à la* ME) or to stodge ones nobility into an incomprehensible narrative, *à la* The eagle [Yeats]. I've got his poem down the Dryad but R. [Richard] simply sulked and read his Baedecker. He has made a good trans. of Moscus on 'The death of Bion' & done some things of his own which are of no use.

If I am going out to tea I may as well go now. I send along a little of the furore. Please keep the same. - - - Ti Baccio gli occhi [I kiss your eyes] - - - I can't remember any picture in Rome save the Aurora–which may be in Florence–so I can't send you any instructions anent them.

'dio.

E.

Madame Brass]   The wife of Italico Brass (1879–1943), the Venetian painter and sculptor whom EP met during his 1908 stay in Venice. Brass received an inscribed copy of *A Lume Spento*. A poem "For Italico Brass" is in the San Trovaso notebook that EP compiled in 1908 (CEP, p. 253).

the Fenice]   A rococo opera-house built in the late 18th century. As its name implies, "The Phoenix" survived several fires.

"to where Rossini . . . in his stall"]   From Browning's "Bishop Blougram's Apology," lines 381–86.

> Like Verdi when, at his worst opera's end
> (The thing they gave at Florence,—what's its name?)
> While the mad houseful's plaudits near out-bang
> His orchestra of salt-box, tongs and bones,
> He looks through all the roaring and the wreaths
> Where sits Rossini patient in his stall.

Mrs Horatio]   The fussy bachelor Horatio Brown (see Letter **152**).

the Eagle's "Grey Rock"]   Yeats's "The Grey Rock" appeared in *Poetry* (Chicago), 2 (April 1913).

Petronius in 18th century french]   Perhaps *Satyre de Pétrone,* trans. by M. Boispréaux (1742).

parodies of us]   After the publication of EP's "Contemporania" series in *Poetry* (April 1913), several parodies appeared in the Chicago newspapers. Harriet Monroe printed two of them in *A Poet's Life* (New York, 1938), p. 311. The first is a parody of "Tenzone" called "Spring in State Street," the second a spoof of "Salutation"; both are from the Chicago *Tribune*.

> Will people accept them?
>   (i.e. these bargains).
> O dainty colorings and range of prices!
> Gowns of charmeuse in all
>   the colors of the season;
> Blouse skirts of Russian cloth,
>   tucked belt of softest satin,
> and only $37.50.

> O degenerates in the art of writing,
>   and fallen ones,
> I have seen Cubists splattering their paints. . . .
> You are far worse than they are,
> And they are much worse than nothing;
> And the nude descends the staircase,
>   and does not even own clothing.

trans. of Moscus on 'The death of Bion']   Richard Aldington's "The Mourning for Bion (From the Greek of Moschus)" and four of his poems—"Amalfi," "Oneirodotes," "Beauty, Thou Hast Hurt Me Overmuch," and "In the Via Sistina"—were published in the *New Freewoman*, 1 (15 September 1913).

156   Ezra to Dorothy

Albergo Bella Venezia
Venice
[9 May 1913]
Friday

Dearest:

I enclose a portrait sketch of you and a reminder of the precise meaning of the term "Quattro cento" (all on one P.C.). I've got the bases of the columns in larger reproduction.

H. & R. [Hilda Doolittle & Richard Aldington] are submerged in a hellenism so polubendius and so stupid that I stop in the street about once in every 15 minutes to laugh at them—convulsed & deprived of the powers of motion. R. retired at about 11.30 this morning to write to the N. Age [*New Age*]—impotent to find any other form of expression. I don't know—Hellenism? True, they have attained a dullness almost equal to the expression (*facial*) of gk. statuary—but I wonder—I think they *must* be in love.

I can't get interested in yr. Hilda [Strutt] even if it progenerates. Your Nancy [Maude] I rather like. The Dryad [Hilda Doolittle] has a new niece but I learned the fact from its mother (I mean the Dryad's mother).

Eheu! [Alas!] would that I had the pencil of Giotto that I might depict les jeunes Hellenistes doing Venice with their eyes firmly fixed to the pavement [sketch]. No. It don't come off.

Verily the more people I meet the more respect I have for F.M.H. [Ford Madox Hueffer]—When I think of how he struggled with me in germany!!

It being highly improbable that there is any mail at the Piazza, I shall go thither in quest of it. It is very stupid of you to be at the other end of the peninsula.

Yrs.

E.

portrait sketch . . . "Quattro cento"] EP enclosed a postcard showing the interior of the church of Santa Maria dei Miracoli, known in Venice as "The Jewel Box." EP refers to "Santa Maria dei Miracoli/where Pietro Romano has fashioned the bases" in Canto 74, and again in Canto 76:

> and Tullio Romano carved the sirenes
> as the old custode says: so that since
> then no one has been able to carve them
> for the jewel box, Santa Maria Dei Miracoli

Hilda Doolittle remembered that during this stay in Venice EP led her through a labyrinth of streets and bridges to a church he insisted she "must" see. "The church was cool, with a balcony of icy mermaids, Santa Maria dei Miracoli" [*End to Torment* (New Directions, 1979), pp. 5–6].

polubendius] From the *Odyssey*, 4. 406: ἁλὸς πολυβενθέος, "the depths of the sea."

F.M.H. . . . . struggled with me in germany] EP is remembering his visit to Giessen in August 1911, and Ford Madox Hueffer's response to the archaisms in *Canzoni*.

> . . . he felt the errors of contemporary style to the point of rolling (physically, and if you look at it as mere superficial snob, ridiculously) on the floor of his temporary quarters in Giessen when my third volume displayed me trapped, fly-papered, gummed and strapped down in a jejune provincial effort to learn, *mehercule,* the stilted language that then passed for 'good English' in the arthritic milieu that held control of the respected British critical circles, Newbolt, the backwash of Lionel Johnson, Fred Manning, the Quarterlies and the rest of 'em.
> And that roll saved me at least two years, perhaps more. It sent me back to my own proper effort, namely, toward using the living tongue (with younger men after me), though none of us has found a more natural language than Ford did. [*Selected Prose, 1909–1965,* ed. William Cookson (New Directions, 1973), pp. 431–32; from "Ford Madox (Hueffer) Ford; Obit" (1939)]

157   Dorothy to Ezra

Hotel Flora
Rome
10 May 1913

My dear Ezry.

Thanks for yr. letter–which as usual crossed one of mine–and for the enclosures, which I am keeping for you. You had certainly better take to Sapphics. How very vilely the American press writes.

I want you to do something for me in Venice. There is a certain shaped purse O.S. [Olivia Shakespear] wants a new one of–and here non c'è. It holds notes & money, & should cost in tooled leather 5 or 7 lire. [Sketch of purse, open and shut.] (I only want it when you come back–not sent by post). Will you try to get me one for her? Up to 10 lire & a nice colour with gold pattern on it.

We went yesterday to the Baths of Carcalla. □ [Georgie Hyde-Lees] & I nearly quarrelled/ quarreled/ quarelled because I felt something slightly sinister about them!–& they were so large! She loved & adored them & their size.

Oh! yes. Did I tell you Nuova C. [Caroline] had been taken with German measles & been shipped to a Nursing Home? Very awkward–& queer co-incidence–as she left the hotel the very day she was to have gone home to England.

We saw some queer, queer, Mexican & South-Sea-Island 'things' in a museum–All rather gruesome–& a whole row of mummies sitting with their knees up to their chins in various attitudes of horror. Also a strange Mexican black stone–a fetish I imagine–with symbols all over it that gave □ [Georgie] the horrors! The only one that I remember was a part of one side & went thus [sketch] with more squiggles in the thing underneath.

At Caracalla we were taken privately over the latest "scavi" [excavations] & saw a terrible temple of Mithraic worship: with a grille for the blood of the sacrificed bull to drip down onto the person-to-be-baptised, who was alone below in a dark hole of a place. The worship was in the dark always, except for four lights in little niches on the level of the floor.

It is really hot today.

Did I also tell you that I have procured my tortoiseshell brushes?

I don't think you can remember *any* picture in Rome–except perhaps a lovely Carlo Crivelli. Yr. Aurora must be Florence. Oh! Here also is Tiziano's [Titian's] (What Baed: [Baedeker] calls) "Earthly & Heavenly Love".

It is a nude & a very much clothed couple of females–And C. Nuova [Caroline] didn't get the hang of it–because a short time after, she said something about not seeing "that the" (rather ugly) "clothed one" was a good symbol of "Heavenly Love". ("Amor Sacro e Profano" is the *real* title!). So she ratted that up quite well!

> I must sleep
> A toi
> **D.**

Sunday morning early

I just got yr. letter & p. card before sending mine off. I remember S.M. [Santa Maria] dei Miracoli as the most exquisite little place that ever was built–with lovely marble patterns? I am glad you have loved it. Did we go there together or not?

As to the Hellenised couple [Richard Aldington & Hilda Doolittle]– Venezia would be barbaric after Greek temples, I daresay. But there is nowhere so wonderful as S. Marc's, I'll be bound, temples or no. I am now longing to see those Greek things myself!

I wish I were all of a piece like the Miracoli: and so composed & lovely!

> **Yrs.**
> **D.**

the enclosures . . . American press] Probably the parodies from the Chicago *Tribune* (see Letter **155n**).

p. card] The postcard showing the interior of Santa Maria dei Miracoli (see Letter **156n**).

158   Dorothy to Ezra

> [*Rome*]
> [*13 May 1913*]
> *Tuesday*

Dearest.

Just done packing, & its begun to pour with rain–so I can't go out. We go home tomorrow and O.S. [Olivia Shakespear] goes to the Rummels; G. [Georgie Hyde-Lees] & I continue to London by ourselves. We rush through from 9 ocl. A.M. Wednesday, until 10.45 P.M. Thursday–which

is pretty good! Its really much less trouble than spending the night any-
where. My clothes are an awfully tight pack, owing to the new hat. I have
nothing to say except, write home now.

I do not know yet whether I shall be able to go to my sketching class,
or whether I shall be infectious! It is a nuisance. I suppose I must try to
"Career" on my return!

My newly papered room will need some Jap prints perhaps. Or you
might like one? Then I *might* read up Roman Emperors: but I fancy they
are stodgy, when not epileptic.

> Yrs.
> D.

159   Dorothy to Ezra

> [*Kensington*]
> [*London*]
> [*24 May 1913*]

My dear.

I wonder if your congé is what *you* want? I wish I knew. If I gave it you,
it would certainly be directement–or You can take it if you wish. As to my
room, it is you who can give me an answer, as to whether there is any
prospect of my being able to leave it within, say, the next six months? I
feel you might have got a job if you had really wanted to, by now, - - - and
yet, and yet - - - Have you or haven't you wanted? I think I have waited
very quietly all this Spring for you to have time.

I am afraid I cannot change Thursday as I have arranged a lot of
stupid things. I shall be going to Tagore on Monday evening–So please
come on Thursday–I shall expect you unless I hear to the contrary.

> My love
> à toi.

Wed. I hope to get to Mrs. Barker's, to hear Walter [Rummel] play his
new Debussys.

Mrs. Barker's]   Probably the residence of Elsa Barker (1869–1954), the
American writer and magazine editor who lived in Paris and London, 1910–14.

She had published two volumes of verse, *The Frozen Grail and Other Poems* (1910) and *The Book of Love* (1912). Writing to Harriet Monroe in March 1913, EP added a postscript which indicates he had just met Mrs. Barker: "Who the deuce is Elsa Barker? Says she has 5000 lines in her last vol., which sounds suspicious. Otherwise, personally agreeable with a Christian Science voice" [*Letters*, No. 15]. In 1913 Mrs. Barker began experimenting with automatic writing, and produced three volumes of "spiritualistic messages": *Letters from a Living Dead Man* (1914), *War Letters from the Living Dead Man* (1915), and *Last Letters from the Living Dead Man* (1919). She believed these "messages" came from Judge David Patterson Hatch of Los Angeles (1846–1912), who was the author of *Straight Goods in Philosophy* and several books on the occult.

160   Dorothy to Ezra

[London]
[24 May 1913]

The boredom was of four square walls–not you. I am feeling better since I decided to have an Archaic Greek frock in sea-green.

A toi
D.

I have just been making love to Jim [Fairfax] in my dreams–Also a few nights ago I dreamt of a really beautiful Mother & Child–statuesque, but warm & alive–nude & grouped Rodinesquely.

161   Dorothy to Ezra

[*Kensington*]
9 June 1913

Venez mercredi si vous pouvez. J'ai déjà lu la première histoire de Flaubert. Cela me plaît beaucoup.
D.
lundi.

162   Dorothy to Ezra

[*Kensington*]
[*10 June 1913*]

Don't you know by this time that one of the things it is *pas permis* to do, is to interfere with other peoples' drawing rooms? *You'd* be mighty pleased, wouldn't you, if anybody said you have four, or six or eight or ten people on such & such a day?? Four people is enough in our room, but unfortunately things are never anywhere near perfection–It is better that W. [Walter Rummel] should play to Tagore, being 8. people, than not at all. It is a most unkind thing to be so rude as to let Eva [Fowler] or Thérèse [Rummel] think they would not be wanted.

I think you fortify yourself too much against other people, & so do not realize how you hurt them by doing that kind of thing. I think it is a great interference on your part. On this occasion W. & Tagore would be the important people–not yourself. Also W. wants his wife & Eva.

So please recover your temper & sense.

D.

You affect not to care about other people - - - but you try to interfere a good deal with their doings when they affect yourself.

interfere with other peoples' drawing rooms]   Walter Rummel gave a piano recital at the Aeolian Hall in New Bond Street on Thursday, 12 June 1913. The program included Schumann, Brahms, and the first performance in England of all of Debussy's Preludes (2nd Book, 1912–13). On the Friday before the concert he gave a private recital at Mrs. Fowler's home (*Letters*, No. 20). DS is apparently referring to a similar evening at the Shakespears' home when EP tried to dictate the guest-list.

163   Ezra to Dorothy

[*Kensington*]
[*14 June 1913*]

["The Choice"]

It is true that you said the gods are more use
                    to you than fairies
But for all that I have seen you
                    on a high, white noble horse
'Like some strange queen in a story'.
It is odd that you should be covered with long robes
                    and trailing with tendrils and flowers;
It is odd that you should be changing your face
                    and resembling some other woman, to plague me,
It is odd that you would be hiding yourself
                    in the cloud of beautiful women who do not
                                        concern me.

And I, who follow every seed-leaf upon the wind!
                    They will say that I deserve this.

"The Choice"]   This poem, untitled in the letter, was published three times under the title "The Choice" and appears in *Lustra* as "Preference." It was not included in *Personae* (1926). All the printed texts differ from the letter in small matters of wording, lineation, and punctuation. See *Poetry* (Chicago), 3 (November 1913); *New Freewoman*, 1 (1 December 1913); *The New Poetry*, ed. Harriet Monroe and Alice Corbin Henderson (New York, 1917); and *Lustra*

(London, 1916). The major difference between "The Choice" and "Preference" is that the latter (printed below) alters the last line from "They will say that I deserve this" to "You will say that I deserve this."

> It is true that you say the gods are more use to
>   you than fairies,
> But for all that I have seen you
>   on a high, white, noble horse,
> Like some strange queen in a story.
>
> It is odd that you should be covered with long robes
>   and trailing tendrils and flowers;
> It is odd that you should be changing your face
>   and resembling some other woman to
>   plague me;
> It is odd that you should be hiding yourself
> In the cloud of beautiful women who do not
>   concern me.
>
> And I, who follow every seed-leaf upon the wind?
> You will say that I deserve this.

164   Dorothy to Ezra

12 Brunswick Gardens
Kensington
[14 June 1913]
Saturday

Dearest.

I am afraid that I am troubling you. Will you come in nevertheless to see me on Thursday 19th?–It is an ungodly world. Cernikoff [the pianist] plays here on Wed: aft. His is not for the likes of you.

Yours with love.

(My own writing-paper is run out, but more is ordered: bluey gray with a peacock blue stamp.)

Sunday

O.S. [Olivia Shakespear] says if you will come in on Wed: morning about 11 ocl. you would be useful to help arrange chairs etc. You may come in in the afternoon if you care to–But I think tennis will be better for you!

Love.

165   Dorothy to Ezra

12 Brunswick Gardens
Kensington
[25 June 1913]

My very dear.

I cannot marry you. (I can but hope it's not mere cowardice, but a true instinct.)

I am sorry, sorry, sorry
and send my

Love.

166   Ezra to Dorothy

[Kensington]
[June 1913]

you can not.
    you can not.
you can not.

167   Dorothy to Ezra

12 Brunswick Gardens
Kensington
[30 June 1913]
[2.15 P.M.]

You might come in at teatime on Friday–if you care to–I *must* go out in the aft. to get paints.

As you will
Love   D.

168   Ezra to Dorothy

[*Kensington*]
[*30 June 1913*]
[*7.30 P.M.*]

Bien. At what hour preciso? alle quattro? or are you going to buy paint after tea?

Je t'aime

169   Dorothy to Ezra

Goathland's Hotel
Goathland
[*Yorkshire*]
[*1 August 1913*]
Friday

My dear,

The cold is bitter up here today–I can't possibly go out painting–I have been out once only: One has to walk long ways before getting anywhere. The moors are all round, & the heather should be out if there is any more sun ever–The walks are beautiful: I wish I could walk ten miles every day. One could then get out away from everybody. I wish to goodness I had Georgie [Hyde-Lees] up here. I am started reading "Madame Bovary", Flaubert, but haven't had much opportunity yet–We have been various longish walks and yesterday spent a tripperish day in Whitby, buying fruit, seeing ruins and sitting on the sands. The sea looked lovely and a fine sky.

Nelly & ☐ [Georgie & her mother] are on the Norfolk Broads at a Farm where they have had to have the cocks shut up 'cos they crow so early in the morning.

Very, very dull day. There is a poor old hen with three ducklings–& they found their way to a muddy ditch yesterday which altogether beat her–She watched, & clucked helplessly–while they found Life really pleasant for once.

Saturday

Terrific hot sun–I spent a morning on the moor among the Turf cuttings. Such lovely dragonflies: but the ordinary flies nearly drove me distracted: my water-can leaked–my chocolate melted–& I messed instead of painting. But the sun was hot & the moor lovely. There is a very picturesque old man who walks about the Village Road–in whitish trousers to match his beard & a fawn-coloured coat. He is most majestic. This *is* a dull letter. But shall go to show I haven't forgotten you!

D.

What more of Breszcha [Gaudier-Brzeska]??? and yr. Daisy Meadow [Eva Fowler's] news?

Sunday

You may care to hear that I am very happy at this moment! I am sitting grilling in the middle of a huge moor with no body in sight. I had an idea to get up early as it was so very hot–and, thinking of your dictum–I did it. I was out before seven & sketched until 8.30.–Then I came here directly after breakfast. The moors are getting a more lovely colour every minute– and the heat is wavering in long transparent flames along each ridge.

There's a solitary horseman on the top of the hill–I haven't even heard a grouse. I put up two yesterday from under my feet, & was much more scared than they were! I also saw some lovely great dragonflies.

Breszcha]   Henri Gaudier-Brzeska, the Vorticist sculptor who died in combat in 1915. See Biographical Appendix.

170   Ezra to Dorothy

[Kensington]
[3 August 1913]
Sunday

Dearest Coz:

You are probably a beast not to have sent me an address. I have played tennis & typed my "Lustra" & been to Daisy Meadow (peaceably) & I aren't going to take The Eagle [Yeats] *there* but to something more convenient where there'll be a landlady to blame for everything that gets out of order. Also I've had fat dinners with Miss [Amy] Lowell & launched her on Ford [Madox Hueffer] & the Eagle. The Eagle is burning tapers to some new scion or scioness of the house of [Maud] Gonne on Monday. I have read "Mr. Apollo". It has decent spots in it.

By the end of the week I may have gotten the editorial decks clear enough to return to my greek.

The Dryad [Hilda Doolittle]—with no sense of modernity has writ a poem to Tycho the god of little things. That in an age of "Tatcho" & "Little Tich" and with all the decent names in the classical dictionary to choose from.

[Gordon] Craig has sent an orange coloured pamphlet from Florence proclaiming his greatness.

I suppose "Mr. Diomedes' his horses" will start in the N.F. [*New Freewoman*] on the 15th.

Nothing else new & strange save the offspring of the new Roumanian ambassador who play really good tennis & thus enliven the heights of Campden Hill.

[John] Cournos' book on american painters (Trial chapters in private) is starting in a fairly interesting manner. My other consolation is a new box of apricots—gone a bit dry—malheureusement.

The gods of the moor attend you.

ever

E.

Monday

Dearest: Thank you for two letters all to onc't. I am glad you sit on the heather & have *joie de vivre*.

Had tea with J.G.F. (no. *not* James Gwyffwyth) John—anyhow he gave me some £s wherewith to feed [F.S.] Flint & [Skipwith] Cannell & R.A. [Richard Aldington] & such others as I may want to print in The Freewoman, which was, I think, fairly decent of him. I'm waiting for [John] Cournos to have Bzrskz [Gaudier-Brzeska] to dinner.

"Frances" has returned to the island & presents me with a pleasing youth full of deferential admirations. One Rogers who's had two plays at home. I'm taking him to tennis this P.M.

Enclosed from Little Bill [William Carlos Williams] this morning.

No. Its "bynk ollerday" [Bank Holiday]. I won't be able to get a postage stamp until *demain*.

I'm trying to do an article on "The Tradition", hoping it will take *all* the bristles off all the dead pigs in Chicago, etc. The sun is flopping over all the court & over all the trees in the grave yard.

Yrs.

E.

my *"Lustra"*] A gathering of the new poems written since *Ripostes* (1912). On 30 March 1913 EP wrote to Harriet Monroe: "I shall send you two or three pages of very short poems later, if you survive the April number [which contained EP's "Contemporania" sequence]. I'm aiming the new volume for about the Autumn" (*Letters*, No. 16). Another letter to Miss Monroe of August 13 makes it clear that the "Lustra" sequence was first sent to *Poetry*: "Of course my *Lustra* lose by being chopped into sections . . . Anyhow, do hack out ten or a dozen pages in some way that will establish the tone and in some way present the personality, the force behind this new and amazing state of affairs" (*Letters*, No. 22). The selection from "Lustra" appeared in the November issue of *Poetry*.

Miss Lowell] Amy Lowell (1874–1925), the American poet and critic who played a dominant role in the later history of Imagism. EP included one of her poems in the anthology called *Des Imagistes* (1914). When Miss Lowell edited the subsequent anthologies called *Some Imagist Poets* (1915, 1916, 1917) EP felt she had diluted the movement, and he dissociated himself from "Amygism." Writing to Margaret Anderson in August 1917 he said: "Is there any life into which the personal Amy would not bring rays of sunshine? Alas! and alas only, that the price, i.e., equal suffrage in a republic of poesy, a recognition of artistic equality, should come between us" (*Letters*, No. 133).

scioness of the house of Gonne] Iseult Gonne (1895–1954), the daughter of Maud Gonne and the French political journalist Lucien Millevoye. Yeats transferred to her some of his long-standing devotion for her mother.

"Mr. Apollo"] Ford Madox Hueffer's *Mr. Apollo: A Just Possible Story* (1908).

poem to Tycho] In Hellenistic and Roman times the goddess Tyche was identified with Fortune. It seems more likely, however, that the poem was addressed to the Danish astronomer Tycho Brahe, since Hilda Doolittle's father was an astronomer. The poem was apparently never published.

Tatcho] A commercial hair-restorer that was aggressively advertised in the early years of the century. Harry Champion, the music-hall artist, is reported to have had a popular song about "Tatcho" in his repertoire.

"Little Tich"] Harry Relph (1868–1928), the English music-hall performer known as "Little Tich."

Craig . . . pamphlet] *A Living Theatre: The Gordon Craig School, The Arena Goldoni, The Mask. Setting Forth the Aims and Objects of the Move-*

ment and Showing by Many Illustrations the City of Florence, the Arena (Florence, 1913).

"Mr. Diomedes' his horses"] *The Horses of Diomedes,* a translation of Remy de Gourmont's novel *Les Chevaux de Diomède* (1897), was published serially in the *New Freewoman* (later the *Egoist*) from 15 August 1913 to 2 March 1914.

Cournos' book on american painters] The book was never published, but four articles by John Cournos on recent American painting appeared in 1914–15: "Arthur B. Davies," *Forum* (New York), 51 (May 1914); "John H. Twachtman," *Forum,* 52 (August 1914); "John S. Sargent," *Forum,* 54 (August 1915); and "Three Painters of the New York School," *International Studio,* 56 (October 1915).

J.G.F. (no. not James Gwyffwyth)] The American poet John Gould Fletcher (see Biographical Appendix), not the Australian poet and journalist James Griffyth Fairfax.

"Frances"] Frances Gregg. See Letter **113n.**

One Rogers] Probably Robert Emmons Rogers (1888–1941), who spent the year 1909–1910 as an assistant to the American actress Maude Adams, and who published two one-act plays: *Behind a Watteau Picture* (1918) and *The Boy Will* (1921). From 1913 until his death Rogers taught literature at the Massachusetts Institute of Technology. He was most famous for advising the 1929 graduating class at M.I.T. "to be snobs and to marry the boss's daughter."

Enclosed from Little Bill] A letter from William Carlos Williams (see Letter **171**).

article on "The Tradition"] "The Tradition," *Poetry* (Chicago), 3 (January 1914).

171   Dorothy to Ezra

> *Goathland*
> *[Yorkshire]*
> *[8 August 1913]*
> *Friday*

Dearest E.

I shan't be home until next Thursday–Will you come in on Friday afternoon to see me? I found a little piece of white heather this morning–supposed to be Lucky!

I have just come upon Kipling's "Sestina of the Tramp Royal". You probably know it?

Why don't you & W.B.Y. [Yeats] go to (Stylo pen given out) Mrs. Wheeler, [as paying guests] on Farnham Common? She *may* be v. expensive—but not likely—& cooks quite nicely—& there's a motor bus to Slough trains.

What a hand little Bill writes! He is married isn't he? therefore, the house?

Re "Frances"—Whose were the Twins? [sketch] She married that kind of Time[?] ago didn't she? was it anybody I know of?

I must go out to pick some bog myrtle to send to Granny—dutiful Child—& she won't care for it much—my birthday next month!

Love
D.

Kipling's "Sestina of the Tramp Royal"]   "Sestina of the Tramp-Royal" was first published in Rudyard Kipling's collection of verse *The Seven Seas* (1896).

little Bill . . . the house]   A reference to the letter from William Carlos Williams mentioned in Letter **170.** Williams married Florence Herman on 12 December 1912. In his letter to EP he may have mentioned negotiations for the purchase of the house at 9 Ridge Road, Rutherford, N.J., where he and his wife lived for the remainder of their lives.

"Frances"]   Frances Gregg. See Letter **113n.**

172   Ezra to Dorothy

10 Church Walk
[*Kensington*]
[*9 August 1913*]

Dearest:

You are, to use your own impassioned phrase, 'a good little thing—sometimes'.

Me great aunt-in-law is dead. I am rather sorry. She was a picturesque old monument—associated with cracker boxes & such other delights of childhood.

The S. Set [*Smart Set*] has cashed in £12.4. for poems out of Ripostes. The Freewoman [*New Freewoman*] is printing [Remy] De Gourmont vigorously, & it is a very lovely book, to supercede Mlle de Maupin as the "golden page"–much more readable & more sensuous & more healthy, a gracious wisdom of the senses–while Gautier always leaves the impression of nerves over-strained. De Gourmont is just green & the colour of petals. "Pink sensuality"!!! the outraged eagle [Yeats] calls him–ma!! I think the paper ought to be quite decent, with 2 chaps of Gourmont, 1pp. me.

F.M.H. [Ford Madox Hueffer] to write if we tell him what & various quotations from the French periodicals. [John Gould] Fletcher improves on acquaintance. R. [Richard Aldington] is perhaps coming back in a fortnight. Dont know whether its family or emotions.

I've got some proofs of the 'Chevaux' to run over & some tennis thereafter.

I've 2/3 forgotten the tramp royal [Kipling's poem]. The "rich come they, rich with wonders seen" is in a different poem, I think.

'Lustra' has gone off to shock publishers readers. F.M.H. is doing a book on Henry James. M. [May] Sinclair is desolated by the new Brontë letters.

Venerdi [Friday]–bien, only you needn't stop writing on that account, unless you want to.

yrs ever
E.

Me great aunt-in-law is dead]   Frances Beyea (1832?–1913), a relative of Isabel Pound, and the Aunt Frank of EP's *Indiscretions* (1923).

S. Set]   Seven poems from *Ripostes* (1912) were reprinted in the *Smart Set*, 41 (September and October 1913). Although Henry Mencken and George Jean Nathan did not become editors of the *Smart Set* until late 1914, their taste was evident in 1913, when the journal published Yeats, D.H. Lawrence, Hueffer, Dreiser, and EP. Over the next decade the *Smart Set* steered a successful course between popular writing and the avant-garde.

The Freewoman]   *The Freewoman,* founded and edited by Dora Marsden, appeared in the winter of 1911 with the subtitle "A Weekly Feminist Review," which was changed in May 1912 to "A Weekly Humanist Review." The magazine ceased publication after eleven months, but was revived in June 1913 as the *New Freewoman,* with Harriet Shaw Weaver (later the editor) as one of the shareholders. On the recommendation of Violet Hunt and Ford Madox Hueffer, EP became literary editor, and soon Richard Aldington replaced Rebecca West as subeditor. As the nature of the review changed there was agitation from EP and others for a new name, and the *New Freewoman* became the *Egoist* on 1 January 1914. For the history of the review and EP's connection with it, see Jane Lidderdale and Mary Nicholson, *Dear Miss Weaver: Harriet Shaw Weaver, 1876–1961* (New York, 1970), Chapters 3–5.

Mlle de Maupin]   *Mademoiselle de Maupin* (1835), a novel by Théophile Gautier.

2 chaps of Gourmont, 1pp. me]   In addition to the first two chapters of Remy de Gourmont's *The Horses of Diomedes* (see Letter **170n**), the *New Freewoman* of 15 August 1913 printed "The Contemporania of Ezra Pound," a group of seven poems selected from the longer "Contemporania" sequence in the April 1913 issue of *Poetry* (Chicago).

proofs of the 'Chevaux']   Proofs for the first two chapters of De Gourmont's *The Horses of Diomedes.*

"rich come they . . . wonders seen"]   From Kipling's "The Sea-Wife" (1893): "Rich are they, rich in wonders seen, / But poor in the goods of men . . ."

'Lustra' . . . publishers readers]   The collapse of Stephen Swift and Co. in late 1912 (see Letter **69n**) had forced EP to look for new publishers. It was not until September 1916 that Mathews published *Lustra of Ezra Pound,* containing most of EP's poetry written since *Ripostes.* Even then several of the more "indecorous" poems were deleted from page proof at the request of the printer and publisher (see Gallup, *Ezra Pound: A Bibliography,* All a.-b.).

F.M.H. . . . on Henry James]   Ford Madox Hueffer, *Henry James: A Critical Study* (1913).

M. Sinclair . . . new Brontë letters]   May Sinclair (1863–1946), the novelist and feminist writer whom EP had known since his arrival in London, published a study of *The Three Brontës* in 1912. A new edition of the book appeared in 1914, "With an Introductory Note on the Recently Discovered Letters of Charlotte Brontë." The "new Brontë letters" were four letters from Charlotte Brontë to Professor Constantin Heger given to the British Museum by Professor Heger's son in 1913. Published in full in the London *Times* of 29 July 1913, they created a journalistic sensation. The *Times* accompanied their publication with a leader on "The Lost Letters of Charlotte Brontë" that May Sinclair could have taken as an attack on her work.

> . . . we should like to insist upon the nature of the interest which these letters must have for every intelligent reader, since the interest shown in the life of Charlotte Brontë has not always been intelligent. She is a writer whose books arouse curiosity about herself because all of them more or less, and 'Villette' most of all, read as if they were autobiography. And now these letters read as if they were part of 'Villette' or of some sadder, unpublished, sequel to it. They prove, what we were sure of before, that Charlotte Brontë lived her life over again in her books and revealed herself in them with the audacity of her own innocence. And as she wrote in 'Villette' so she wrote in her letters to Professor Heger. Indeed, one might suppose from the letters that she wrote the book, too, for the Professor, and with that same desire to reveal herself to him. She gave 'Villette' to the public as a work of art; but she wrote it for one man, although she might not even wish him to read it.

The following day (30 July 1913) Sir William Robertson Nicoll wrote a letter to the *Times* that contained a specific reference to May Sinclair's 1912 study, in which she had dismissed all theories of a passionate attachment between Charlotte Brontë and M. Heger as "pitiful and silly."

> It has been very seriously and ably argued that Miss Brontë's regard for M. Heger was nothing more than an ordinary friendship. To suppose it went further is 'pitiful and silly.' It will now be seen that those were right who took another view.

In the Introduction to the new edition of her study, dated 1 September 1913, May Sinclair admits that she must "unsay much that I have said," and allows "that some passionate element, innocent and unconscious, was, for all its innocence and unconsciousness, present unmistakably in Charlotte Brontë's feeling for her 'master.' " But in the rest of the rather tortuous Introduction she argues (1) that the letters "ought never to have been given to the world," (2) that they only show Charlotte had a last-minute feeling for M. Heger at the time of her final departure from Brussels, and (3) that they do not really matter. "What greatly matters is the genius that appeased her; and the publication of these letters does not affect in the least my main contention that that genius owed nothing to her 'master,' that (in spite of her brief obsession) it was independent of all that he could do to her or make her feel."

173   Dorothy to Ezra

> *Leweston Manor*
> *Sherborne*
> *Dorset*
> *[24 August 1913]*
> *Sunday*

Dearest.

Sun & cloud today, & lovely blues on the hills. Also midges & harvest-bugs. There was a garden-party yesterday here, so this morning I refused to go to church, & walked in the fields–I heard aspens making a nice noise in the wind, and some huge great thistles–? called Teazles.

I am just finishing a translation from the Spanish of [Blanco] Ibanez– "Blood & Sand"–all about bull fighting. Its interesting to one who knows nothing whatever of Spain.

Yesterday I had to arrange flowers for the Chapel Altar–*me*–my word! They were such stupid ones.

I can't find anything to sketch here–but I am hoping & praying to be taken tomorrow to sketch at a lovely old house in Somerset. We went there to a garden party & saw the little church–with a beautiful old font– I probably *shall* be taken (or sent) and then given half an hour to do it in.

Love

Yours.

Ibanez–"Blood & Sand"]   *Sangre y arena* (1908), a novel of the bullring by the Spanish writer Vicente Blasco Ibáñez (1867–1928), was published in English in 1913 as *Blood and Sand.*

174   Ezra to Dorothy

[Kensington]
[25 August 1913]
Monday

Stella Lucente Diana or if you prefer–"Selvaggia Mia" [My Wild One].

Miss [Amy] Lowell motored me about 200 miles yesterday, to the White Horse, & to Burford & Oxford, and I am still wind scorched. I have been plagued with the De Gourmont article as I thought I'd done it & then found it was only ½ long enough. The Dryad [Hilda Doolittle] is coming over this week–ostensibly to meet its family which doesn't. Have done the "Romains" & begun the 'Vildrac' about one page.

The Eagle [Yeats] sends me a signed photograph of the winter quarters [Stone Cottage]. Tagore has a farewell dinner in a bad restaurant on Tuesday. Davray has done him in the "Mercure".

Oh for an end of song. Also I've found one lovely thing in a collection of Minnesingers, which I've got to revive myself after I get through approaching Paris [in the *New Age*]. My mind is maintenant merely a sort of provisory daze–of the Vildrac article, & the remains of yesterdays sun.

à toi

E.

Selvaggia]   The most famous poems by Dante's friend Cino da Pistoia (c. 1270–1336) celebrate his beloved "lady," Selvaggia.

De Gourmont article]   Part II of "The Approach to Paris," *New Age,* 13 (11 September 1913).

the "Romains" . . . *the 'Vildrac'*]   Part III of "The Approach to Paris" [*New Age,* 13 (18 September 1913)] was devoted to Jules Romains (1885–1972), the founder of the *Unanimisme* movement; and Part IV [*New Age,* 13 (25 September 1913)] to Charles Vildrac (see Letter **128n**).

Davray . . . *"Mercure"*]   Henry D. Davray (1873–1944), the French translator of Yeats, Wilde, Meredith, Kipling, Wells, and other English writers. He was a regular contributor on English literature to the *Mercure de France*.

175   Dorothy to Ezra

Leweston Manor
Sherborne
Dorset
[*27 August 1913*]
Wednesday

Dearest "Emira"!

The Prelude
   Coleman's Hatch
      Sussex

& the station is *Forest Row.* O.S. [Olivia Shakespear] is writing to Nelly [Georgie Hyde-Lees' mother] to say you hope she has got yr. telegram. Can you come in on Friday aft. 3.30? We go up tomorrow. I am glad you motored: it is exhilarating.

We have been doing nothing here–Yesterday the heat was terrific, accompanied by clouds of wasps! We have been to see one beautiful old house, where I painted–I am reading Montaigne–vaguely. He is very full of common sense & scepticism. Also he understands, what you always talk about, the joy of living–& that it is the most difficult & the most necessary thing.

Au revoir if you can. If you don't turn up–I shall know this letter hasn't reached you in time.

Yours
D.

176   Dorothy to Ezra

[*Kensington*]
[*31 August 1913*]
Sunday

Dearest.

I have been re-reading [Kipling's] "Kim", & I greatly prefer it to Oscar Wilde. It is full of open air and the snows, and intelligence.

Dorian Gray last night I hated. It is all wrong in a play–the picture was so dreadfully bad!–and I come ultimately to loathe O. Wilde. I am–perhaps you have helped me to know it, too–of another generation - - - The psychic part is so crude–& the rest so evil. I cannot tell you how stuffy the theatre was, and the atmosphere of the play was the same. I felt I had to *do* something after it–so I slept the wrong end of my bed under a dressing gown & pretended I was Kim.

Lou-Tellegen has a good deal of personality, I think; I should like to see him again in something quite different. He might rant of course.

Le Sacre du Printemps seems quite a useful reaction after '90s A.D.

I am doing some new early Vict. [Victorian] wool work–which is half Italian & quite pretty.

Pray for me.
Much Love –
D.

"Kim"]   *Kim* (1901), the adventure romance by Rudyard Kipling.
Dorian Gray last night . . . Lou-Tellegen]   A dramatic adaptation of Oscar Wilde's *The Picture of Dorian Gray* was presented at the Vaudeville Theatre on August 30 as part of "Lou-Tellegen's Season." Lou-Tellegen (1881–1934), the Dutch actor, had gained prominence as Sarah Bernhardt's leading man.
Le Sacre du Printemps]   This revolutionary ballet, with music by Igor Stravinsky and choreography by Nijinsky, created a scandal when first performed in Paris on 29 May 1913. The British audience was more restrained when the ballet was first performed in London on 11 July 1913. The next day the *Times* commented: "London takes both its pleasures and its pains more quietly than Paris."

177   Ezra to Dorothy

[*Kensington*]
[*1 September 1913*]

Dearest

I am not in the least sure that you ought to embroider. It kills time but it also draws off a lot of little particles of energy, that ought to be dammed up until they bust out into painting. I don't suppose you can "paint" every day, but you could experiment in colour–notably in green– simply trying to get the most beautiful shades & those that wont go black– brownish. I used to try with oils, & would again if I could ever get the names of the paints on my brushes etc. all at once. I couldn't draw a pig but it was entertaining just the trying to prepare a palette. I can't remem- ber which book on Whistler jaws so about the palette. It may be 'Mempes', anyhow that would do you better than silks & sewing–ca. ½ hr. per diem, at least, and let the colour make itself into designs when it will.

Have just been reading Corbière & think him fine. He calls Hugo "Garde-national épique" & Lamartine "Lacrymatoire d'abonnès" & is on the whole rather trenchant. I shall bring you the book. The Villon & Heine sort of thing in a french that you can lire. I've got him in the article with Tailhade & De Regnier–rather hard on De Regnier.

Yes, je prie, naturally, and the Kim is very proper for you, c'est ça. Et maintenant je m'en vais diner.

Amor
E.

book on Whistler . . . 'Mempes']   Mortimer Menpes, *Whistler As I Knew Him* (1904).

Corbière . . . the book]   Tristan Corbière (1845–1875), the Breton poet who was almost unknown until Paul Verlaine praised him in *Les Poètes maudits* (1884). EP is quoting from "Un jeune qui s'en va," one of the poems in Corbière's *Les Amours jaunes* (1873).

> —Décès: Rolla:—l'Académie—
> Murger, Baudelaire:—hôpital,—
> Lamartine:—en perdant la vie
> De sa fille, en strophes pas mal . . .
>
> Doux bedeau, pleureuse en lévite,
> *Harmonieux* tronc des *moissonnés*,
> Inventeur de la larme *écrite*,
> Lacrymatoire d'abonnés! . . .

—Hugo: l'Homme apocalyptique,
l'Homme-Ceci-tûra-cela,
Meurt, garde national épique;
Il n'en reste qu'un—celui-là!—

article with Tailhade & De Regnier] EP discusses Corbière, Laurent Tail-
hade (1854–1919), and Henri de Régnier (1864–1936) in Part V of "The Ap-
proach to Paris," *New Age,* 13 (2 October 1913). Both phrases from Corbière
quoted in this letter are used in the article.

178   Dorothy to Ezra

The Prelude
Coleman's Hatch
Sussex
[*4 September 1913*]
Thursday

My dear.

It is a pretty place–common, heather, & woods–Georgie [Hyde-Lees]
says the latter are haunted. I have only been in them once as yet–they
are gloomy–& were v. wet after heavy rain. The two kittens are charming,
we spend much time watching & helping them to play. One is Henry
André James–"Jimmy" mostly. The other 'Brahms' frequently pronounced
'Bramms'. They are Greuze-like - - - and rather over-fluffy after my dear
jungley Siameses!

My poor Georgie has been in bed with a quinsy in her throat–She gets
up today. We mystified her awfully all yesterday, by means of a photo of
Lou-Tellegen from our [theatre] programme sent in writing she did not
know saying "Do you ever have tea in Kens: Gardens on Wednesdays
between 4 & 5?" However, CHARS told her last night that THEY had
seen their Aunt [Olivia] & Coz concocting it with Hilda's husband [Frank
Deverell] after Sunday lunch!

I am painting greens every afternoon in the privacy of my–large–bed-
room. I haven't been sketching owing to greyness–of a dull kind–& damp.
I found a fine tuft of white heather over the moor.

I think one wastes more energy doing nothing & feeling miserable about
it, than in embroidery. Doesn't energy to some extent generate itself, the
more its used?

Your cottage is next door nearly to us. Its plain grey stone & right on the moor. There is a queer lake in the forest–with wonderful-coloured trees reflecting in it–It is a weird place–and possibly faerie.

I am recovering from Wilde–I hope your Shaw was entertaining? Are you doing any poems, or only french poètes d'aujourd'hui et demain? I am slowly re-reading the Venusberg. It is kept safe between times!

> Much Love
> Yours   D.

Lou-Tellegen]   See Letter **176.**

Your cottage]   Stone Cottage: see Letter **195n.**

recovering from Wilde]   See Letter **176.**

your Shaw]   *Androcles and the Lion* was playing at the St. James's Theatre, with Lillah McCarthy and Granville Barker.

the Venusberg]   *Venusberg, The Syren City, With It's Sequel—Ten Years After,* by Chilosà, was published in London in July 1913; the original *Venusberg* had appeared in November 1900. "Chilosà" was the pseudonym of an English lady who also published *Waif and Stray: The Adventures of Two Tricycles* (1896), an account of a four-month cycling trip to the north of Scotland, and *How's That, Umpire? A Story of an Unconventional Life* (1905), a novel which tells of the adventures of a late Victorian heroine in India, Rome, Monte Carlo, Paris, and London. *Venusberg* is an account of life at Monte Carlo, "The Mount of Folly," and its *Sequel* revises the scene in the light of changes in Edwardian society. Facing the title page of the 1913 edition is a note which begins: "My first Sketches of Life at Venusberg interested so many—among the number our beloved King Edward—that they may like to know how it has fared, since they were written, with her and her inhabitants."

"Chilosà" emerges from the book as a lively and stylish woman of independent views, attracted to the more leisurely ways of Victorian society but with a realistic appreciation of the present: at the end of the *Sequel* she describes herself as neither a "Suffragist" nor a "Doormat." She has a fine interest in motive and character: "If you wish to know anyone's real character, entice them to Venusberg, watch until they let themselves go there, then, if you have patience, you will have a very fair idea of their subconscious self, as the Psychical Researchers call it."

179   Ezra to Dorothy

10 Church Walk
[Kensington]
[5 September 1913]

No! that is *preciso* the point. It is not as if embroidery *exercised* any faculty or required any specialized concentration. Its not much better than smoking. Games (which you detest) do develop coordination–They are a rest because one is not–as in art–matching oneself against an absolute standard but only against an opponents skill.

Also that "feeling miserable" because one isn't doing anything is one of the strongest *drives* toward creation. One feels miserabler & misaberabler until one does the "young monk of Siberia" & busts into the creative act. Not, ma chère, that I *forbid* you embroidery, or hashish or *quidquid vis* [anything else]. Energy depends on ones ability to make a vortex–genius *même*. Chess, Tennis, fencing all help. They demand complete attention, in each case–the finest sort of their particular attention–in chess, reason; in tennis, physics; in fencing, to a great extent psychology, i.e. in thinking the other mans thought & muscular coordination. The foils are perhaps the most concentrative–you probably need to be "more awake", more versatile in shifting from one apprehension to another, [than] in boxing or with broad sword. Anything that demands only partial attention is useless, for developing a vortex. It draws from the circumference, in time it would incapacitate one for serious creation of any sort. If one is "exercising" or "generating" energy one must rest by concentrating attention on some different sort of thing–that won't weaken all the muscles of the mind.

Attention gained by one sense, or if you like, the quality of attention attained by one sense transfers itself to all the others. I mean just that– "a natural gift" don't. It is very likely to stick merely in its own department–it is sure to limit itself to one dept. until its possessor begins to think. (So few do).

No. I'm still doing "Approach to Paris"–am part through "Jammes" & shall only do one more after that. Sometimes I think I am learning to write prose–ah vain desire!!!!–anyhow, after I do the Approach to Paris I shall do a burst "On Style" for Poesy [*Poetry,* Chicago], and also a summary of "The Approach" for the same organ.

Little Bill's "revised" proof awaits m'attention.

"Lustra" so saith the pub's asst. "may be out in Oct."–so I suppose they are going to print it. Shall I send you 'Bill' [*The Tempers*] or will you await its proper publication.

The gods attend you
E.

a vortex]   EP's use of this term anticipates the Vorticist pronouncements of 1914. In a letter to William Carlos Williams of 19 December 1913 he refers to the London artistic world as "The Vortex" [*Letters*, No. 31]. *Blast*, No. 1., "A Review of the Great English Vortex," did not appear until June 1914.

"Jammes"]   Part VI of "The Approach to Paris" [*New Age*, 13 (9 October 1913)] is on the work of the poet and novelist Francis Jammes (1868–1938).

"On Style"]   Probably "The Tradition" [*Poetry* (Chicago), 3 (January 1914)], although some of EP's developing ideas about "style" were incorporated in "The Serious Artist" [*New Freewoman*, 1 (15 October–15 November 1913)].

summary of "The Approach"]   *Poetry* (Chicago), 3 (October 1913). "I have finished a series of critical articles on French verse ["The Approach to Paris" in the *New Age*, September–October 1913]. I propose to give here merely a summary of my conclusions."

Little Bill's "revised" proof]   William Carlos Williams's *The Tempers* was published by Elkin Mathews on 13 September 1913. EP arranged for publication and handled the proofs.

"Lustra"]   See Letter **172n.**

180   Ezra to Dorothy

[*Kensington*]
[*6 September 1913*]

Dearest:

I have got you up on the wall & like you there. You go very well in black rims–under glass. I think you might do that silk room full of copper rose leaves with your glorified self modestly concealed beneath 'em.

Vide. Venusberg line 441111111 or somewhere along there–It is quite lovely and all more or less of a tone pongee & orange-copper with a streak of pale gold & rose.

I have gone on with [Francis] Jammes, & done a brief note for Poetry [*Poetry*, Chicago]. H.J. [Henry James] writes suavely to say that he wont write for the Freewoman [*New Freewoman*]–one hardly expected he

would. [R.B.] Cunninghame-Grahame is going to send in something for
the S.S. [*Smart Set*] so we are not engulphed in gloom. The Dryads
family [Hilda Doolittle's] have descended on it, but she seems to have
survived. The family is trying to understand "Contemporania". WHY!!!
etc.

It is much better to concern yourself exclusively with orangish roses.

à toi.

E.

Vide. Venusberg]   See Letter **178n.** In the opening chapter of Part III of
Venusberg, "A Flat in Venusberg," the author tells of how her heroine-narrator
was persuaded to rent a "horrid" flat in Venusberg: "The walls were covered with
the most appalling papers imaginable; on one ramped gigantic monsters, sup-
posed to be heraldic lions." In the next chapter the flat is redecorated: "A clever
Italian painted flowers and birds on the dreary walls. The rooms were hung with
bright papers; the floors covered with pretty carpets."

Jammes]   See Letter **179n.**

brief note for Poetry]   The summary of "The Approach to Paris." See
Letter **179n.**

Cunninghame-Grahame]   R.B. Cunninghame Graham (1852–1936), Brit-
ish travel and fiction writer. One of the great Victorian eccentrics and adven-
turers, Cunninghame Graham was known to his friends as "Don Roberto" be-
cause of his Spanish blood and his extensive travels in South America. He was
the descendant of an old Scots family, but his grandmother was Spanish and he
spoke Spanish before he knew English. An aristocrat in appearance and character,
he was a Labour Member of Parliament from 1886 to 1892, and in 1887 he spent
six weeks in jail for leading the workers against the police in the Trafalgar Square
riots. He was also an early admirer of EP's work, and in a letter to the *Saturday
Review,* 27 November 1909 [Vol. 108, p. 662] he observed "with pleasure that
our best writers—as Conrad, Hudson, Galsworthy, George Moore, Henry James
and Ezra Pound—are devoting themselves more and more to short pieces, and
in them are doing some of their finest work."

something for the S.S.]   EP was acting as a London "finder" for the *Smart
Set* (see Letter **172n**). The contribution from Cunninghame Graham apparently
never materialized.

"Contemporania"]   Probably the shortened version of the "Contemporania"
sequence that was published in the *New Freewoman,* 1 (15 August 1913) as
"The Contemporania of Ezra Pound." The longer sequence appeared in *Poetry*
(Chicago), 2 (April 1913).

181   Dorothy to Ezra

[*The*] *Prelude*
[*Coleman's Hatch*]
[*Sussex*]
[*9 September 1913*]
Tuesday

My dear.

I found a translation of the Koran here: & its mighty dull. I daresay its the translation that is in fault. It seems to me unpleasantly Christian & very lacking in mysticism–which I have no business to say. I enclose the bits I liked–a little–and a thing on Poets which means something quite else with the context!

Everybody here is reading plays by one Paul Claudel. I am in the midst of one. But I don't think it has any vitality about it. Its in queer lines and phrases - - - and the language is dull. Perhaps that plainness is all to the good.

We sketched beech trees this morning & G. [Georgie Hyde-Lees] saw a family of 4 squirrels. I only heard their conversation–which was most cheerful!

My bed has been changed round–it was N. & South–and now it is E. & West (that the earth currents may not be interrupted–as Kim says). I really ought not to take to superstitions of that sort. They are too amusing–& too tiresome.

☐ & I [Georgie & I] plan to go mushrooming tomorrow morning at cockcrow. It is so lovely early, & so dull late & mushrooms are a good excuse. I can't yet 'see' the copper-rose-room–I will try to find it–(I have it in the poem).

Yours with love
D.

(Koran)

The *folded up.*

When the sun shall be *Folded Up,* (or thrown down)
And when the stars shall fall,
    "   "   " mountains shall be set in motion,
    "   "   " she-camels shall be abandoned,

"   "   "   wild beasts shall be gathered together,
"   "   "   seas shall boil
"   "   "   souls shall be praised with their bodies
"   "   "   female child that had been buried alive shall
        be asked
        For what crime she was put to death,
"   "   "   leaves of the Book shall be unrolled
"   "   "   Heaven shall be stripped away - - -

It is the *Poets* whom the erring follow:
Seest thou not how they rove
      distraught in every valley?
& that they say that which they do not?

Clots of Blood.
The Enwrapped.
The Enfolded.
The Brightness.
The Opening.
The Daybreak.
        Men.

Paul Claudel]   Paul Claudel (1868–1955), the French diplomat, poet, and dramatist who was converted to Roman Catholicism in 1886. The two plays that gave him fame were *L'Otage* (1911) and *L'Annonce faite à Marie* (1912).

Koran]   These passages come from a translation of the Qur'an by the Rev. J.M. Rodwell, first published in the Everyman's Library in March 1909. "The Folded Up" is the beginning of Sura XXXII; the passage on the poets is from the end of Sura LVI ("The Poets"). The final list gives the titles of the first seven Suras in this edition. Rodwell's sequence and numbering of the Suras, designed for non-Muslim readers, is not the traditional Qur'anic one.

According to Rodwell's footnote to the Sura "The Poets," the Prophet Muhammad "found it necessary to employ the pens of certain poets to defend himself and his religion from the ridicule and satire of other poets . . ." [*The Koran: Translated from the Arabic,* by the Rev. J.M. Rodwell, Everyman's Library (1909), p. 111].

182   Ezra to Dorothy

10 Church Walk
[Kensington]
[17 September 1913]
Wednesday

Dearest Coz:

I have writ all my french articles, & one foot of the first line of a Sapphic, & two articles on the nature of poesy for the Freewoman, and Ford [Madox Hueffer] has been in town for 24 hours, en route to Germany, and we rearranged his poems, & mucked about the preface of his "Henry James".

And I can't be bothered to read [Paul] Claudel or any more french for some time. I've pawed over two books of Minnesingers & found one or two nice things.

> Schönheit dieser Welt vergeht
> wie ein Wind, der niemals steht,
> wie die Blume, so kaum blüht
> und auch schon zur Erde sieht,
>
> wie die Welle, die erst kömmt
> und den Weg bald weiter nimmt.
> Was für Urteil soll ich fällen?
> Welt is wind, ist Blum und Wellen.

which is a very old burden indeed.

2 of R's [Richard Aldington's] things, & the last strophe of the Moschus were rather nice. The chinese things in "Poetry" are worth the price of admission. The Print Room B.M. [British Museum] is closed for ever so I can't look you out anything. Is there anything at the S. Kensington [Museum]?

The Koran is I suppose a fake & a compromise. I have nevei been able to get on with it. The Bible is, I think, a deal more human, far more indecent, and much more moral.

Be a good Kim & you will eventually find your river.

Everything else that I know is getting tucked into articles.

Venus dux tuo.

E.

french articles] "The Approach to Paris" in the *New Age*.

two articles . . . for the Freewoman] "The Serious Artist," Parts I and II, published in the *New Freewoman*, 1 (15 October 1913).

Ford . . . his "Henry James"] Ford Madox Hueffer, *Henry James: A Critical Study* (December 1913) and *Collected Poems* (November 1913).

Minnesingers] Here, as in some of his prose essays, EP is stretching the term to include lyric poetry of the Renaissance. The poem is by Martin Opitz (1597–1639); for EP's own translation, see Letter **184**.

> Schönheit dieser Welt vergeht
> wie ein Wind, der niemals steht,
> wie die Blume, so kaum blüht
> und auch schon zur Erde sieht,
> wie die Welle, die erst kömmt
> und den Weg bald weiter nimmt.
> Was für Urteil soll ich fällen?
> Welt ist Wind, ist Blum und Wellen.

EP found the poem in *Das erste Buch der Ernte* (1906), an anthology compiled by Will Vesper (1882–1962), the well-known popularizer of mediaeval poetry. In his essay "The Renaissance" [*Poetry* (Chicago), 5 (February 1915)] EP lists "German songs out of Will Vesper's song book" as components of "the palette" needed by the modern poet.

2 of R's things . . . the Moschus] See Letter **155n.**

chinese things in "Poetry"] "Scented Leaves—From a Chinese Jar," free translations by Allen Upward, appeared in *Poetry* (Chicago), 2 (September 1913), with the following note: "Mr. Allen Upward, born in Worcester in 1863, has had a varied life. A scholar, a barrister, a volunteer soldier who ran the blockade of Crete and invaded Turkey with the Greek army, he is also the author of plays, romances, poems, and of *The New Word*, that powerful plea for idealism which aroused England six years ago, and for which Mr. Gerald Stanley Lee, in *Crowds*, demands the Nobel prize. The *Scented Leaves* are not direct translations, but paraphrases from the Chinese."

Allen Upward, who committed suicide in 1926, was a writer for the *New Age*. EP reviewed his "general history of religion," *The Divine Mystery* (1913), in the *New Freewoman*, 1 (15 November 1913). For the impact of Upward's work on EP, see Bryant Knox, "Allen Upward and Ezra Pound," *Paideuma*, 3 (Spring 1974), 71–83.

a good Kim] See Letter **176.**

183   Dorothy to Ezra

> [*The Prelude*]
> [*Coleman's Hatch*]
> [*21 September 1913*]
> *Sunday*

My dear.

I am sorry not to have written before–I have been very unsettled, as poor Georgie [Hyde-Lees] was so ill again & they thought they might have to have a Nurse for her–in which case I should have had to go–heavens knows where. However for the moment I am in possession of a room. She has had tonsilitis & another quinsey. Yesterday however she began to get a little better–It has been very melancholy–with no G. to go a-painting and exploring with–& Nelly [Georgie's mother] looking worried to death. Of course at a place with such a name as the Prelude - - - one must expect things to happen.

I have been much amused in the woods here by Fungi–their names are Greek & Latin & impossible–but their colours are lovely–& I have painted a few. There are hardly any real mushrooms.

You & W.B.Y. [Yeats] will certainly get lost in the woods here. Bunk [Dorothy's uncle] frightens the poor little CHARS by telling them awful tales of vampires as we all come home late through the pines–I shall have to lend you my compass I think. We found our way home grandly one evening from an unknown spot by steering N.E.!! But I want my Georgie to do things of that sort with, really.

Your nice German poem is no use to me–I can't understand it. Ignorance is a great bore–but trying to learn is worse. I am battling with Pater's Plato. It's a terrible stodge–& none so easy to keep up with. His (Pater's) mind works so very rapidly & curiously.

Two more friends of mine engaged to be married–one male, one female (not engaged to each other). I tried to paint your brown silk Venus room. It turned into a very evil room, with blue & green Chinese tapestries, & isn't finished with regards to the rose petal drift. I will try another quite different some time.

I must now play some Brahms & Schumann for G. [Georgie] on the pianola–Spirit of Dear Walter [Rummel]! But I do my best. I am sending to have my Print Room licence endorsed–I hope they will: & shall try to go up there sometimes.

Much love
Yours D.

nice German poem]   See Letter **182.**
Pater's Plato]   See Letter **39n.**

184   Ezra to Dorothy

10 Church Walk
[Kensington]
23 September 1913

Dearest Love,

That print-room is closed INDEFINITELY–while they move into the new wing of the museo–which means, I should think, six months–There's small use of your imagining you'll be let into *that* plaisance, and unless there are prints at the S. Kens [Museum] I don't know what will become of you. You'll have to read the Mahabarata or something else extensive.

I hope G. [Georgie Hyde-Lees] has risen by now–you are having an —il stagione [Hell of a time].

[Allen] Upward of the chinese poemae is quite an addition. He is off for greece possibly in a months time. I may go down to the I. of Wight with him for a visit before then. *Il pense* that IS an addition. He seems to [know] things that ain't in Frazer, at least he talked sense about sun-worship & the siege of Troy, and he has been "resident" in Nigeria & divers other joyous adventures so far as I can make out. Also he has nice practical ideas, about acquiring Mt. Olympus, etc.

I week-ended with the N.Age [*New Age*] and caught a drenching gold-n-me-'ead. As to fungi, Upward also talked about fungi–(and Francis Bacon). The german poem means more or less

> "Beauty goes from the world
> Like a wind without rest
> Like a flower that scarce is spread,
> And boweth its crest,
> As a wave that scarce is cast

On the beach, retreateth fast.
What is there in it all,
World is wind & flower & wave."

You can find a nice rhyme for the last lines sometime when you've nowt better to do. The sound of the original is rather nice.

Plater's "Pato" is about his worst job. You might try the wholly illogical original, except that your mind's probably by now too mature to bother with it. I'm chalking up a Stendhal that may amuse you. "All the disciples of Pater came to a bad end". gee!!! You ought [to] meet McKail–a man composed entirely of cold cream.

I can't remember whether I've already distressed you with Spinoza & Swedenborg. The S.S. [*Smart Set*] goes on reprinting poems out of "Ripostes". [Kali Mohan] Ghose has vanquished a missionary on the S.S. City of Lahore, somewhere this side of Port Said.

Brigit Patmore has given delight to many by saying that "Masterman looked like a bandaged weasel". That pillar of your government together with their respective wives or concubines are now enjoying (or otherwise, probably otherwise in the case of V. [Violet Hunt]) the Rhine.

The N.F. [*New Freewoman*] is having spasms over my first article on art. N.A. [*New Age*] ditto over my french revelation.

[John Gould] Fletcher is back, improved by his walk. The dismal Hyde [Harold Hyde-Lees, Georgie's brother] descends for tea, presumably in 68 minutes–or, Oh Lord, less.

Bacci d'amore

ever

E.

the *Mahabarata*]   The Mahābhārata, or "Great Epic of the Bharata Dynasty," a poem of almost 100,000 couplets that contains the Bhagavadgītā, the most important Hindu religious text.

Upward of the chinese poemae]   See Letter **182n.**

Frazer]   Sir James Frazer (1854–1941), author of *The Golden Bough* (1890; reissued in 12 vols., 1907–1915), the great comparative study of magic and religion.

N. Age]   A.R. Orage, editor of the *New Age.*

The german poem]   See Letter **182.**

Plater's "Pato"]   Pater's "Plato." See Letters **183** and **39n.**

McKail]   John William Mackail (1859–1945), Professor of Poetry at Oxford, 1906–1911. Mackail published works on Latin and Greek literature, and a *Life of William Morris* (1899).

The S.S. . . . "Ripostes"] "Phasellus ille" (P) and "Portrait d'une Femme" (P) were reprinted in the *Smart Set,* 41 (October and November 1913).

Ghose] See Letter **129n.**

Brigit Patmore] See Letter **114n.**

Masterman . . . the Rhine] Ford Madox Hueffer and Violet Hunt were traveling in Germany with C.F.G. Masterman and his wife. Charles Frederick Gurney Masterman (1874–1927), politician and journalist, was the author of *The Condition of England* (1909). In 1912 he became financial secretary to the Treasury, and in 1914 he was a member of the Cabinet that declared war on Germany.

first article on art . . . french revelation] "The Serious Artist," *New Free-woman,* 1 (15 October 1913) and "The Approach to Paris," *New Age,* 13 (4 September–16 October 1913).

185   Dorothy to Ezra

> *Broadwalk Hotel*
> *De Vere Gardens*
> *Kensington*
> [*25 September 1913*]

My dear.

! What an address! But we had to leave The Prelude suddenly because Georgie [Hyde-Lees] is to have her throat operated on today–& there wasn't room for us and a nurse. My poor □. However–I am here for two nights: expected to be able to get a bed at the Club, but it was quite full. So had to come here–where I am under the very inquisitive eye of my Aunt [Florence] Tucker–(who goes shortly to Californy). I am off tomorrow to stay at the houses of the great–with the artistic Jews. A sudden invitation from them to their country house came in most opportunely. CHARS think that rich, stockbroking, Jews are *not* nice company for their Coz.

I searched Church Piazza [Church Walk] for H-d-d [Hamadryad, Hilda Doolittle] this morning & left a note for her at No. 8, which seemed a good deal more sympathetic than No 6. I have been to No. 12 BG.[Brunswick Gardens] to rescue some evening clo' for the Jews. My address there will be

at Balcombe House
Balcombe
Sussex

& if you don't write before Monday, wait until you hear from me–as heaven alone knows where I shall be. Wimborne, possibly.

I am sorry for your gold-in-the-head–I suppose you take measures of some sort to deal with it? Quinine–or Cinnamon? For future use I have ordered you 6 large handkies–which you shall have later on when I am home. They are being marked E.P.

I have got my 'Poetry' [*Poetry*, Chicago]–but have not read the Chineses yet.

If I had been at the Club, I should have hoped to see you–but under the circumstances–*no*! 'Ad my 'ead washed yesterday evening–and this morning found the housemaid an Italian - - - no connection.

I do wonder whether any more of the Sapphic has come?

I began another brown silk room for you. It is autumnal and a little closed-in so I have given it a green floor–which I suppose is wrong. I long to get some new, *quite* new, cool green place–mentally & for sketching.

> Much love
> Yours D.

the Club]   New Century Club.
'Poetry' . . . *the Chineses*]   See Letter **182n.**

186   Dorothy to Ezra

High Hall
Wimborne
[Dorset]
[1 October 1913]
Wednesday

My dear.

I begged a home here until Sat. when I go to London for Sunday– Then I have to go down to Georgie [Hyde-Lees] again, as she will be bored to tears all alone. I spent an interesting time at Balcombe. The house is all beautiful things, and very satisfactory–as they are not too crammed up. I met a certain Mr. Heron Allan who interested me–and Anstey was there–& a young Fitzgerald–?grandson of Omar. I was so glad to see the Hamadryad [Hilda Doolittle] last week. She is very incomprehensible.

I have read nothing & done no painting for a week. London by oneself was delightful–and the Aunt [Florence Tucker] has sailed today for 'Murrika. The colours are lovely–yellow & brown, and all the grass such a tremendous green. I lived quite a lot at Balcombe. Write & tell me you are pleased!

With much love
D.

Mr. Heron Allan] Edward Heron-Allen. See Letter **129n.**

Anstey] The pseudonym of Thomas Anstey Guthrie (1856–1934). A writer for *Punch* from 1887 to 1930, he was the author of many novels, including *Vice Versa* (1882).

Fitzgerald–?grandson of Omar] Probably Desmond FitzGerald (1889–1947), the Irish revolutionary and statesman who was only distantly related to Edward FitzGerald, the translator of the *Rubá'iyát of Omar Khayyám*. Born and brought up in London, he was a member of the 1909 "School of Images" that included T.E. Hulme, F.S. Flint, and EP. He is the "Fitzgerald" of EP's poem "To Hulme (T. E.) and Fitzgerald (a Certain)" [CEP], which was intended for *Canzoni* (1911) but canceled by EP on the page proof. The poem was later published in the anthology *Des Imagistes* (1914) with this note: "Written for the cenacle of 1909 vide Introduction to 'The Complete Poetical Works of T.E. Hulme,' published at the end of *Ripostes*." FitzGerald lived in France from around 1911 until 1913, when he moved to Ireland. He was deeply involved in the revolutionary activities that led to the Easter Rising of 1916 and was sentenced to life imprisonment for his part in it, a sentence later commuted to twenty years. In 1918 he was released from prison, and soon after visited his old friends in London. EP recalls this visit in Canto 7:

> The live man, out of lands and prisons,
> shakes the dry pods,
> Probes for old wills and friendships . . .

Before his retirement from politics in 1943 FitzGerald held a number of important positions in the Irish Free State, including Minister for External Affairs and Minister of Defence.

187   Ezra to Dorothy

10 Church Walk
[Kensington]
[2 October 1913]

Dearest:

Yes, of course I rejoice, besides Eva [Fowler] disapproves strongly of Flavian (Heron-Allen). Of course if you had the least talent for gallantry you'd have thrown a glove thru' my window while you were calling about the court yard–But, no, you have no vulgar instincts–C.B. Stevens & co. were also lodged in the piazza.

I would have writ before but I went to Ryde to visit [Allen] Upward. *Il pense.* It is a rare phenomenon. He has just finished "The Divine Mystery", digested golden bough with a lot more of his own intelligence stuck into it.

Have done shows chinesesques [Exhibitions], borrowed the Mahabarata, been taken to a new curious & excellent restaurant chinois.

'Dicky' Green has called (americanus). Met prof [Felix E.] Schelling in the museum, mine ancient professorial enemy. [John Gould] Fletcher turned up at the Italano [Restaurant] & dragged me to his lair wherein he displayed the glories of Georges Fourest. "La Negresse blonde" is the title of G.F.'s most glorious parody of the aesthetes.

Dined on monday with Sarojini Niadu and Mrs Fenolosa [Mrs. Ernest Fenellosa], relict of the writer on chinese art, selector of a lot of Freer's stuff, etc. I seem to be getting orient from all quarters. Also I got real japanese prints–I don't mean on paper–at Cedar Lawn ('Ampstead of all places), but I believe the Weavers are leaving it and as I've just met 'em I dont see how you can be set there to paint it. I'm stocked up with K'ung fu Tsze [Confucius], and Men Tsze [Mencius], etc. I suppose they'll keep me calm for a week or so.

Squakalaams aux CHARS
Ever
E.

Flavian (Heron-Allen)]   See Letters **186** and **129n.**

C.B. Stevens & co.]   Probably the family of Charles Bridges Stevens, friends of the Shakespears, who lived nearby at 8 Essex Villas. The son of a Dominie (master of a boardinghouse for boys) at Eton College, Bridges studied at Eton (1857–64). Later he read law and became a solicitor. He died in 1911.

Upward . . . *"The Divine Mystery"* . . . *golden bough*]   Allen Upward's
The Divine Mystery (1913), which EP thought more penetrating than Sir James
Frazer's *The Golden Bough* (see Letters **182n** and **184n**). In his review of the
book [*New Freewoman*, 1 (15 November 1913)] EP calls it "the most fascinat-
ing book on folk-lore that I have ever opened . . . It is a history of the develop-
ment of human intelligence."

the Mahabarata]   See Letter **184n**.

'Dicky' Green]   Richard Arnold Greene (1856–1931), pastor of the Grace
Presbyterian Church in Jenkintown, Pa., from 1886 to 1894. EP's mother and
father joined the Church in 1891. In the same year Homer L. Pound was elected
President of the Jenkintown Lyceum Association, and the Rev. R.A. Greene
Vice-President. [See Noel Stock, *Ezra Pound's Pennsylvania* (Toledo, 1976),
pp. 6, 13]. Greene published three volumes of religious verse: *Songs from the
Psalter* (1899), *Saint Peter* (1909), and *Songs of the Royal Way* (1925).

prof Schelling]   Felix Emanuel Schelling (1858–1945), a well-known
scholar of Elizabethan literature and Professor of English at the University of
Pennsylvania. For EP's running quarrel with Schelling about the role of the
artist in the University, see *Letters*, Nos. 71, 113, 207, 278.

Georges Fourest]   Georges Fourest (1867–1945), a master of pastiche and
parody, whose *La Négresse blonde* first appeared in 1909.

Sarojini Niadu and Mrs Fenolosa]   EP met Mary McNeill Fenollosa
(1865?–1954), the widow of Ernest F. Fenollosa (1853–1908), at the home of
Sarojini Naidu (1879–1949), the poet and social reformer known as "The
Nightingale of India." Ernest Fenollosa, a graduate of Harvard, first went to
Japan in 1878, and for the next twelve years was intensely involved in the study
and preservation of traditional Japanese art. At the same time he worked on a
study of the Japanese Noh drama. From 1890 to 1895 he was head of the Oriental
department of the Boston Museum of Fine Arts. After another stay in Japan, he
returned to the U.S. in 1900 to lecture on Oriental subjects.

When Fenollosa died in 1908 he left an unfinished study, *Epochs of Chi-
nese and Japanese Art,* which was edited by Mary Fenollosa and published in two
volumes in 1912. He also left behind the manuscript of an essay on "The Chinese
Written Character as a Medium for Poetry," translations of a number of Noh
plays, and notes from his study of Chinese poetry. After meeting EP and reading
some of his recent poetry, Mary Fenollosa decided to entrust her husband's liter-
ary manuscripts to him. On 19 December 1913 EP wrote to William Carlos
Williams that "I've all old Fenollosa's treasures in mss." (*Letters*, No. 31). For
EP's use of the Fenollosa material, see Hugh Kenner's *The Pound Era* (1971)
and Nobuko Tsukui's *Ezra Pound and the Japanese Noh Plays* (1983).

Freer's stuff]   See Letter **130n**.

Cedar Lawn]   The Hampstead home of Harriet Shaw Weaver, supporter of
the *New Freewoman* and future editor of the *Egoist*. See Letter **172n**.

188   Dorothy to Ezra

12 Brunswick Gardens
Kensington
[6 October 1913]
Monday

My dear,

I am going down to Georgie [Hyde-Lees] again tomorrow for about a week. I am longing to be back in London–but pity the poor child so!

I am sending you the six handkies–with much love & hopes for their being of use. I went one afternoon (at Wimborne) onto a British Camp, and enjoyed it very much. It is circular, with deep trenches and a huge clump of trees on the top–a most peaceful spot.

I heard a nice remark the other day–" 'double entente'–a thing that can only be taken one way"!

- - - Here were many interruptions and I only had time to pack this up today–Tuesday. I bought my winter frock (dark blue–with Chinese embroideries) yesterday, & one of two wedding presents.

Much love
Yours
D.

British Camp]   Badbury Rings, a large earthwork thought to have been an early British stronghold.

189   Ezra to Dorothy

[Kensington]
[7 October 1913]
Tuesday

Dearest:

Yes. I think it *is* about time you did come back & collect my disjecta membra. Thanks for les mouchoires (? plural). My cold is about over but I'm expecting some more later in the season. In the meantime the hanquer-chieves are very large & decorative. My head approaches a meal pudding as a variable approaches a limit. I dined last night with Heineman [William Heinemann, the publisher], Sarojini [Naidu] & Mrs Fenollosa–good food–cafè Royal–mild memories of Whistler.

Have read divers books, placidly - - - You know how I love the placid. I keep on writing prose which is a hell of a way to spend ones time–the deceitful appearance of activity. [John Gould] Fletcher raked up a new pote Georges Fourest, chef-d'oeuvre "La negresse blonde", much more exuberant than [Laurent] Tailhade but not quite so acidulated an edge.

I have a huge hunk of the Mahabarata on the "secretoire". I wonder if I'll ever read it. I find the chinese stuff far more consoling. There is *no* long poem in chinese. They hold if a man can't say what he wants to in 12 lines, he'd better leave it unsaid. THE period was 4th cent. B.C.–Chu Yüan, Imagiste - - - did I tell you all that before???

There's a lovely picture on the back of the N.A. [*New Age*] this week? Ruschieschwski *has* caught my Italian pants with such exquisite inflection. I was twice in Punch in Sept.–did I tell you or forget to–silly season. Oh, Lord. I suspect I should turn my thought to higher things?? *fugaces*.

God rest you, maitresse.

Ever

E.

Georges Fourest]   See Letter **187n.**
Tailhade]   See Letters **129n** and **177n.**
the Mahabarata]   See Letter **184.**
lovely picture . . . Ruschieschwski]   A caricature of "Mr. Ezra Pound" by "Tom Titt" (Jan de Junosza Rosciszewski) appeared on the back page of the *New Age*, 13 (9 October 1913). See p. 268.
twice in Punch]   In *Punch,* 145 (10 September 1913), 219, there is a mock account of a mass meeting of poets held "over the Poetry Bookshop in Devonshire Street, W.C.," to protest a pamphlet by Edmund Gosse, C.B., on "The Future of English Poetry." EP makes his appearance near the end of the piece.

> A slight hitch now occurred, brought about by a little misunderstanding as to whether MR. EZRA POUND or MR. LASCELLES ABERCROMBIE should speak first, which was settled by MR. POUND, who comes from Arkansas, in the ready manner of his country. MR. ABERCROMBIE's body having been removed, MR. POUND remarked that obviously MR. GOSSE was right, since he, the speaker, had already begun to employ a jargon of his own and to avoid the obvious. No one should ever be able to lay a 'Psalm of Life' to *his* conscience. (Applause).

Late in the month there was a report of a mass meeting held in Trafalgar Square as a result of "The Authors' Strike" [*Punch,* 145 (24 September 1913), 266].

It was stated that **MR. STEPHEN PHILLIPS, MR. LASCELLES ABER-CROMBIE** and **MR. EZRA POUND** had intended to be present, but a sudden attack of *afflatus,* a most distressing illness to which they are occasionally liable, had confined them to their homes. All three, however, sent a message expressing warm sympathy with the movement and pledging themselves to abstain from the publication of verse until the demands of the men were conceded. 'We may not,' they wrote, 'be able to control the poetic impulse so far as to prevent ourselves from *thinking* in metre, but we shall certainly write nothing down.' This declaration, when read to the meeting, was received with loud cries of 'The battle's won' and 'That finishes it.'

fugaces]   *Eheu fugaces,* "Alas, the years pass swiftly by." See Letter **131n.**

712   *THE NEW AGE*   OCTOBER 9, 1913

MR. EZRA POUND.

Caricature by "Tom Titt" (Jan de Junosza Rosciszewski), *New Age,* 9 October 1913.

190   Dorothy to Ezra

[*The Prelude*]
[*Coleman's Hatch*]
[*9 October 1913*]
Thursday

Dearest EP.

There is 6ft. odd of water in the tank–so you & W.B.Y. [Yeats] may be drowned yet during your sojourn in the country, during the coming months. You really must have a pair of very thick boots, or shoes, and warm socks. Its a drippy kind of place.

Georgie [Hyde-Lees] had an amusing dream about you two nights ago. You were hanging to the top of a very straight pine tree–all-stem-&-a–burst-of-branches-at-the-top-kind, and you had not climbed it–but got there "by translation" as she says. You seemed very happy–but hanged–(which latter I feel is due to her own throat trouble). You had on a yellow tie–(a few other clothes too) and your hair was standing bolt upright, and was *very* long. She won't tell me more–more there was, I feel sure. Don't you rather wish you could arrive at the top by translation–instead of climbing & tearing your clothes?

I see there is a new book of Tagore poems just out. That beastly Print Room *is* shut, with a vengeance. What will yr. poor coz do? - - - She won't have the strength of mind to tell the truth about EP.'s new poems–that they amuse her a good deal–but she doesn't think them necessary records. I suppose the Martian E.P. is raryfying his acquaintance again?

Please tell me about the 4th Cent. B.C. Chinese. I expect they're right about having no long poem.

Much love
D.

new book of Tagore poems]   Rabindranath Tagore's *The Gardener,* lyrics translated by the author from the original Bengali, was published in England in October 1913. EP reviewed it in the *New Freewoman,* 1 (1 November 1913).

Chinese . . . no long poem]   See Letter **188**. EP took up the question of a modern "long poem" in the endnote to his essay on "Vorticism" [*Fortnightly Review,* 96 N.S. (1 September 1914)].

> I am often asked whether there can be a long imagiste or vorticist poem. The Japanese, who evolved the hokku, evolved also the Noh plays. In the best 'Noh' the whole play may consist of one image. I mean it is gathered about one image. Its unity consists in one image, enforced by movement and music. I see nothing against a long vorticist poem.

191   Ezra to Dorothy

> 10 Church Walk
> [Kensington]
> [11 October 1913]

Dearest Love,

When the devil *are* you coming home. If □ [Georgie Hyde-Lees] has any more such dreams we shall end as a *ménage à trois*. Cosmophalique, she takes me for a corn-god. In lieu of the print-room you can have [Herbert] Giles' "Hist. of Chinese Lit", & a book of Japanese ditto, & the new Tagore, & [Allen] Upward's "Divine Mystery".

Yes, that upright hair was doubtless the spring crop. I don't get quite what "isn't a necessary record". As for rarifying my acquaintance the idea is a sound one. I've been only *meeting* people of late.

Tried the Cabaret on Tuesday with the F.M.H's—Konody & Czernikoff on the premises etc. till 3.20 A.M. Czernikoff says he is asking Evah [Fowler] for a chunk of opera there on the 19th.

There are some lovely things at the Spanish Old Masters–a Goya, etc. P.G.K. [P.G. Konody] says six of the 27 Velasquez's are real.

Madame Fenollosa has had me to two bad plays & to dinner with [William] Heinemann. She seems determined that he shall support me. Met an amusing Mrs Benson at the Hueffers.

The Dryad [Hilda Doolittle] & its mother & R. [Richard Aldington] are at this moment penned up, across the wet piazza. There are divers fat wads of proof etc. lying about. Also there are 8 sparrows on the board fence & many crumbs on the window ledge of the catholic refugees.

The gods attend you & drive you home shortly.

> à toi
>
> E.

Giles' "Hist. of Chinese Lit"]   H.A. Giles, *A History of Chinese Literature* (1901).

Japanese ditto]   W.G. Aston, *A History of Japanese Literature* (1899).

the new Tagore]   See Letter **190n.**

Upward's "Divine Mystery"]   See Letters **182n** and **187n.**

the Cabaret . . . Czernikoff]   EP had visited the Cabaret Theatre Club, also known as the Cave of the Golden Calf, a nightclub operated by Frida Strindberg, the second wife of August Strindberg. This fashionable club in a basement off Regent Street was decorated by Wyndham Lewis and Jacob Epstein. EP went with Ford Madox Hueffer and Violet Hunt; the art critic Paul George Konody and the pianist Vladimir Cernikoff were also there. Richard Cork gives some details of the decorations in the Club in his *Vorticism and Abstract Art in the First Machine Age,* 2 vols. (London, 1975–76), pp. 34–36.

> Nothing now survives of the paintings and sculpture which once helped to create the Cabaret's unforgettable atmosphere, but descriptions of Lewis's share have been recorded. [Edith] Sitwell considered the walls to be 'hideously but relevantly frescoed'. . . . Violet Hunt was reminded of 'raw meat' when she gazed at the 'Bismarckian images, severings, disembowellings, mixed pell-mell with the iron shards that did it, splashed with the pale blood of exhausted heroes'. . . . Madame Strindberg [considered the decorations] the product, 'not of talent, but of genius!' . . . . Epstein's part in the decorative scheme . . . may well have been as spectacular as Lewis's. His ambitious plan was to surround the 'two massive iron pillars' which 'supported the ceiling' with sculptured reliefs . . . . Violet Hunt, who remembered them as 'white wooden pillars like caryatids', was also able to testify that 'all had scarlet details, the heads of hawks, cats, camels'. . .

Spanish Old Masters] An exhibition of Spanish Old Masters opened at the Grafton Galleries on 4 October 1913; EP called it "the best loan exhibit I have yet seen" (*Letters,* No. 28).

P.G.K.] Paul George Konody (1872–1933), journalist and art historian. Born in Budapest and educated in Vienna, Konody settled in London in 1889. He published a number of books on both traditional and contemporary artists, and was art critic for the *Observer* and the *Daily Mail*. EP recalls a remark by Konody in Canto 86.

Madame Fenollosa] See Letter **187n.**

Heinemann] William Heinemann (1863–1920), who published a number of important authors, including Beerbohm, Masefield, Pinero, and H.G. Wells.

Mrs Benson] The actress Constance Benson (1863–1946), wife of the actor-manager Frank Robert Benson who founded a touring Shakespeare company. In her early career she took the stage name "Constance Featherstonhaugh," but was later known on the stage as "Mrs. F.R. Benson."

192   Dorothy to Ezra

12 Brunswick Gardens
[Kensington]
[22 October 1913]
Wednesday

Dearest.

When do you go to the Woods? Before you go–I want various books–including a A. [Anatole] France of O.S.'s [Olivia Shakespear's].

I visited the H-d-d.[Hamadryad, Hilda Doolittle] & her Faun [Richard Aldington] at some length yesterday: they were exceedingly cheerful!

With love
Yours D.

to the Woods]   A reference to EP's forthcoming stay with Yeats at Stone Cottage in rural Sussex. See Letter **195n.**

193   Ezra to Dorothy

[Kensington]
[22 October 1913]

Dearest

I have not heard from the eagle [Yeats], but I suppose I go away on the 1st. of Nov. When shall I bring you what books? I am quite idle on Friday, Oct. 24th.

yours
E.

194   Dorothy to Ezra

12 Brunswick Gardens
Kensington
[5 November 1913]
Wednesday 1 ocl.

Dearest–

I hope to see you tomorrow–but think it more probable that you will be on your way to Coleman's Hatch–If you do come in, come about 3.15 & I won't wait for you after 3.30 in case I want to go out. Hope your throat is better. O.S. [Olivia Shakespear] & I will probably go down [to] Arch 45 shortly. G. [Georgie Hyde-Lees] says Harold's [her brother's] dealer is

> Brown & Philips
> Leicester Galleries
>   ″   Square

(The Mr. Brown ½)

Yrs
D

Arch 45]   The correct address was Arch 25. Gaudier-Brzeska's "new studio was a railway arch [in Putney] over which the electric trains rumbled all day. He occupied only half of the arch, which had been divided lengthways by a wooden partition. It was a good workman-like place with a concrete floor, well-lit by windows at each of its quadrant-shaped ends. . . . On the inside of the double doors the Gaudier-Brzeska phallic monogram was painted, six foot high, in heavy black lines." [Horace Brodsky, *Henri Gaudier-Brzeska: 1891–1915* (London, 1933), pp. 127, 130].

195   Ezra to Dorothy

Stone Cottage
Coleman's Hatch
[Sussex]
[14 November 1913]

Dear Heliad:

It rains. I have not yet got lost in the wild, tho' the eagle [Yeats] tried to go the wrong way once, with amazing persistance. I read Kung-fu-tsu [Confucius], & a barbarous Indian thing and I read ghosts to the eagle.

I am coming up on Monday, I suppose you are going to a button-hole-makers, or a hair-dressers or something equally grave? If you don't want me you can send a note to Church Walk.

Homages.
E.

Stone Cottage]   Stone Cottage is near The Prelude, the house in Ashdown Forest where DS stayed. EP and Yeats spent part of the winters of 1913–14, 1914–15, and 1915–16 at Stone Cottage, with EP serving occasionally as Yeats's secretary. In Canto 83 he recalls those days "at Stone Cottage in Sussex by the waste moor," and the sound of Yeats's voice:

> as it were the wind in the chimney
>> but was in reality Uncle William
> downstairs composing
> that had made a great Peeeeacock
>> in the proide ov his oiye
>> had made a great peeeeeeecock in the...
> made a great peacock
>> in the proide of his oyyee

barbarous Indian thing]   Perhaps the *Mahābhārata* mentioned in Letters **184** and **187**.

196   Dorothy to Ezra

[*Kensington*]
[*20 November 1913*]
Thursday

Beloved 'Mao'.

–I thought I had things to say–apparently not. Everybody is Xmas shopping already, & the shops terribly stuffy. I try to read Plato–but find him much too "correlated"! I like [G.R.S.] Mead's version of him very much. It is full of pictures–

That beast Harold [Georgie's brother] hasn't answered me anything yet. He *may* be going to see [Gaudier] Brzeska, he *is* very busy, & is very 'particular' about recommendations, I believe - - - And now the piano-tuner is here–I am keeping Monday 24th free in case you come up–But find that Friday 28th I go to the Literary Society–for something–So if you come up on the Friday–we had better meet on Monday Dec 1st. Also we go to the Sauters on Sunday 30th, I believe.

I have got to write an Italian letter of congratulation to our friend Cecilia, engaged to be married. She was the parlourmaid & intelligence at S. Antonio.

Can *I* have any of the Chinese poems to read–some time? Do read James Stephens–"Here are Ladies"–It's excellent.

With much love – Yours D.

P.S.
I've just finished the Italian congratulatory epistle – Its queer–a' fu' [a bit] queer.

However!

Love D.

Please glean any thing you can for the suppression of ghosts, or else of the fear of them.

Plato . . . Mead's version]   DS is referring to G.R.S. Mead's special kind of neo-Platonism. Mead never published a book on Plato, but in 1895 he edited a new edition of *Select Works of Plotinus,* translated by Thomas Taylor.

   the Literary Society]   See Letter **199**.

   the Sauters]   See Biographical Appendix.

James Stephens]   James Stephens (1882–1950), Irish poet and story writer, author of *The Crock of Gold* (see Letter **199n**). His collection of tales, *Here Are Ladies,* was published in 1913.

197   Ezra to Dorothy

[*Stone Cottage*]
[*Coleman's Hatch*]
[*21 November 1913*]

Dearest D

I suppose I'll be up to Town on Wednesday, not Monday–Wednesday the 26th. I may come up Tuesday but that ain't certain and anyhow you go to [G.R.S.] Mead.

"Intellectual vision" is, acc. Wm. Blake & others, the surest cure for ghosts. You'd better begin by seeing fire, or else by doing that visualization of points that I recommended. Fix a point, colour it, or light it as you like, start it moving, multiply it, etc. Make patterns, colours, pictures, whatever you like. You will end as a great magician & prize exorcist.

I will copy those [poems]–no I won't I'll bring 'em on Wednesday. Them Chineze (Chinese poems). They are only very small 3½ poems.

I have started Kirk's "Secret Commonwealth" which is diverting. Have found a black panther and have also read some new plays to the eagle [Yeats]–some amusing. We conversed all last evening–a pastime preferable to labour. He (W.B.Y.) improves on acquaintance.

R's [Richard Aldington's] collected verse are to appear in a wad in the Cerry Brelist [*The Cerebralist*]. I have done small reviews of little Bill [William Carlos Williams], and of [Paul] Castiaux. There's nothing left to do but "The Collected Poems" of F. Madox Hueffer–or something useful.

I can't make up my mind whether to do a book on Contemporary France & England, or to rewrite the "Approach to Paris". The first might be easier. I may do both, worse luck.

I enclose the KATS. It has been duly copied for the N.F. [*New Freewoman*]. You must see Richard & make sure that it goes in. Has yr. "Poetry" [*Poetry,* Chicago] for Nov. come yet? R. will give you one if it hasn't.

E.

P.S.
Have I got to go to the Sauters?

Chinese poems]   "After Ch'u Yuan," "Liu Ch'e," "Fan-Piece for Her Imperial Lord," and "Ts'ai Chi'h" (all in P) were published in the anthology *Des Imagistes* in February–March 1914. Since the last two poems are each three lines long, EP might well have thought of the group as "3 1/2 poems."

Kirk's "Secret Commonwealth"]   *Secret Commonwealth; or, a treatise displaying the chiefe Curiosities as they are in use among diverse of the People of Scotland to this day,* by Robert Kirk, Minister of Aberfoyle (1691). EP was probably reading a later edition: *The Secret Commonwealth of Elves, Fauns, and Fairies. A Study in Folk-lore and Psychical Research* [with] comment by Andrew Lang (1893).

black panther]   The cat appears as a 'black panther" in the poem "Heather" (P), first published in *Poetry and Drama,* 2 (March 1914): "The black panther treads at my side . . ."

R's collected verse . . . the Cerry Brelist]   Eleven poems by Richard Aldington were published in the *Cerebralist,* No. 1 (December 1913). This was the only issue of the journal: on 8 January 1914 EP wrote to Amy Lowell that "The cerebralist hasn't come off, so don't bother with it" (*Letters,* No. 33). Founded by E. C. Grey and edited by Edward Hayter Preston, the *Cerebralist* was designed to spread the "philosophy" of Cerebralism, which is "harmony, balance, perfection—the Complete . . . . Cerebralism will thus give a mighty impetus to the *creative* energy of the race . . . . Cerebralism lifts man from the morass of the physical (which leads to retrogression) to a perfect realisation of the spiritual; and this is the only way to Progress." It was a "uni-sex" philosophy, as E.C. Grey described it in his article on "Modern Womb-man."

> Let womb-man become conscious of her cerebrality; let her realise that she is the physical and cerebral equal of man, that she is just as necessary to the attainment of the Complete as he. Let her realise that man is not essentially Masculine nor womb-man essentially Feminine, but both man and womb-man are of uni-sex undetermined, until sexual attraction brings about the oppositeness of Masculine and Feminine.

The Cerebralist Movement, which found expression in E.C. Grey's *The Mysticism of Sex and Happiness* (1914), had international ambitions. In his article on "The Cerebralist Movement in France," Lloyd Hartshorne observed that "London has already embraced Cerebralism, and many of the foremost English thinkers and artists can be numbered with its followers. And Mr. E. C. Grey, the philosopher and theorist of the Cerebralist movement, is rapidly converting Paris."

Half of the first and only issue of the *Cerebralist* was devoted to this propaganda; the other half, organized by EP, was given over to the "new poetry." In addition to Aldington's poems, it contained two poems by Frances Gregg, a piece on "Our Novelists and Poetry" by F.S. Flint, an essay on "Imagistes" by "R.S." [perhaps Richard Aldington, with the help of EP], and "Ikon" by EP.

IKON

It is in art the highest business to create the beautiful image; to create order and

profusion of images that we may furnish the life of our minds with a noble sur-
rounding.

And if—as some say, the soul survives the body; if our consciousness is not an
intermittent melody of strings that relapse between whiles into silence, then more
than ever should we put forth the images of beauty, that going out into tenantless
spaces we have with us all that is needful—an abundance of sounds and patterns
to entertain us in that long dreaming; to strew our path to Valhalla; to give rich
gifts by the way.

E.P.

reviews of little Bill, and of Castiaux]   A review of William Carlos Williams's
The Tempers and one of *"Lumières du monde" poèmes,* by Paul Castiaux, *New
Freewoman,* 1 (1 December 1913). Paul Castiaux (1881–1963), who studied
medicine at Lille, had published two earlier volumes of verse: *Au long des ter-
rasses* (1905) and *La joie vagabonde* (1909). He met Pierre-Jean Jouve (see
Letter **127n**) in 1906, and was closely associated with him in launching the liter-
ary review *Les Bandeaux d'or,* which published avant-garde writers such as Ro-
mains, Duhamel, Jammes, and Marinetti. By 1909 Castiaux had settled in Paris,
where he continued as director and principal supporter of the review. In the
January 1913 issue of *Les Bandeaux d'or* Jouve gave an account of the special
number of the *Poetry Review* (August 1912) devoted to F.S. Flint's long essay
on contemporary French poetry. During the First World War Castiaux was
classed with Georges Duhamel as one of the "médecins-poètes." He apparently
withdrew completely from literary life after the war.

"The Collected Poems" . . . Hueffer]   A review of Ford Madox Hueffer's
Collected Poems appeared in the *New Freewoman,* 1 (15 December 1913).

the "Approach to Paris"]   The series of essays on contemporary French
poets that appeared in the *New Age,* 13 (4 September–16 October 1913).

the KATS]   This could be "Heather" (see above), or a pun on the "Cas-
tiaux" review.

198   Dorothy to Ezra

12 Brunswick Gardens
[Kensington]
[22 November 1913]

Dearest.

I can't see you on Wed. aft. 26th because I am going to a concert.
Could you come in in the morning of Wed. 26? Or–if you will still be up,
on the morning of Friday, 28th (about 11 ocl.): in the aft. we go [to] the

'Academy' of Letters, or whatever they call it, to hear somebody about somebody. I am rather glad you aren't coming on this Monday, as I, as usual, have to go to the dentist–& he tires me. No, don't worry about the Sauters!

Thursday 27 I have to go to Burnham & spend a day with my uncle [Alexander Muirson Wake Shakespear] & the Siameses–the Cat Show is pending–(Dec 9th). And for the following week I shall keep Monday 1st free if you should be about, (until I hear from you) & go to that damned dentist on Wed. 3rd. I see an unending view of dentist once a week–for ever and ever and.

No. "Poetry" [*Poetry,* Chicago] hasn't come–Thanks for returning the Kats. I will speak to Richard [Aldington] about both when I see him next.

I shall be away for ages at Xmas–for Xmas itself, & then I shall stay on for the dance in the house on the 6th–& possibly get another dance or so thrown in. And after that I am going to stay, for a week possibly, with Edie [Edie M. Wood]–I have found a nice portrait of you in one of my Japanese picture books! I will try the 'point' again–I remember your telling me before–but I don't think I can have had any success–as I had quite forgotten it. I have been dreaming dreams - - - I mean to try & keep a record for a while & see [if] it will help to make them clearer–I mean to make future dreams less inconsecutive.

Love, D.

Byngdy [Dorothy's cat] is becoming literary–he has taken as toy my quill pen.

'*Academy*' *of Letters*]   See Letter **199.**

my uncle . . . Cat Show]   Alexander Muirson Wake Shakespear (1855–1927), Hope Shakespear's brother, retired from the Bengal Civil Service in 1907 and lived at Holly Lodge, Burnham Beeches. He bred Siamese cats that won frequent prizes. (For more details on A.M.W. Shakespear and other members of the family, see John Shakespear's *John Shakespear of Shadwell and his descendants (1619–1931)*, Northumberland Press, Newcastle Upon Tyne [1931].)

"*Poetry*" . . . *the Kats*]   See Letter **197.**

199   Dorothy to Ezra

[*Kensington*]
[*29 November 1913*]
Saturday

Dearest.

I ⟨conclude⟩ (nonsense) wonder whether you'll be coming up on Monday 8th? I am keeping it free at present–but as soon as you know, write–

The Academic Committee yesterday afternoon was entertaining beyond description!

WBY	Hewlett	W. Raleigh	A.C. Benson	Binyon
1	2	3	4	5

so – on the platform. Raleigh was quite good–Hewlett was mediaeval–or rather trying to be–in terrible commonplaces, called Mrs. Woods – "Madam" with a flourish. A.C. Benson is the finished product of self satisfaction–he inaugurated Dean Inge to Membership. Bin bin (speaking for Max) surpassed himself–he began solemnly & without humour, his mouth minute, about The Comic Muse–Then gave us a really exquisite appreciation of Max–Max & not Bin bin, he gave us–and the Eagle [Yeats] was awfully pleased! (wasn't he?). Then said bird awarded £100 to James Stephens. Poor Eagle–the committee must be a terrible & solid phalanx of A.C. Bensonism to battle against.

In [the] evening we went to the puppet show of Maeterlinck (O.S., you & I & WBY could manage one beautifully. You two to read & us to pull, [Gordon] Craig cardboard scenery, W.B.Y. plays, dresses by DS etc etc).

You were horrid yesterday. You walked down Church W. with H-d-d & Faun [The Hamadryad (Hilda Doolittle) & Richard Aldington], & refused to listen to me hawoshing behind–Then as I started after you, you turned to No. 10 & I was left running after the other two! (all on our way to Academic Com:).

O.S. has bad toothache today–& I have wasted money on a new evening frock.

I spent Thursday at Burnham with the Siamese cats. They are most lovely. Not pantherish quite–but sporting & untameable & most pleasant companions.

Much love–

I have tried to make pictures–I got one beautiful thing to start from–half a dozen duck rising from a pond, half-hidden by the splash from their own wings. It ended me beside a river with an old man swimming across to speak to me–I must try to get on to him again.

Love   D.

Stroke the panther from me.

The Academic Committee]   DS's description of the meeting of the Academic Committee can best be glossed from the account in the London *Times* (29 November 1913, p. 11).

> Sir Walter Raleigh presided at a meeting of the Academic Committee of the Royal Society of Literature, which was held yesterday afternoon at the Caxton Hall.
>
> The principal object of the meeting was the making of the third award of the Edmond de Polignac prize (£ 100). The conditions of the bequest require, amongst other things, that the Academic Committee should take into consideration the promise of the writer, that is to say, that they should give it rather to a young writer than to an old one. Mr. W.B. Yeats announced that the prize had been awarded to Mr. James Stephens, of Dublin, for his book "The Crock of Gold" . . . .
>
> Four new members were added to the Academic Committee. The addresses of reception were delivered to Mrs. Margaret L. Woods by Mr. Maurice Hewlett, to Mr. John Masefield by the Chairman, to the Very Rev. William Ralph Inge (Dean of St. Paul's), by Mr. A.C. Benson, and to Mr. Max Beerbohm by Mr. Laurence Binyon.
>
> Mr. Benson, in the course of his address to Dr. Inge, said those who knew nothing of the intimate working of such an institution as St. Paul's thought of a deanery as a fortress of refined and scholarly leisure, and were surprised at any sound, save the voice of mild and reasonable exhortation, issuing from so calm a retreat. But this was not Dr. Inge's way, and the world was pleasantly stirred and surprised to find him speaking with a frank directness and a bold originality words both wise and trenchant, finely edged and delicately barbed, upon the current thought and conventional opinion of the time. . . .
>
> Mr. Binyon said the Comic Muse had no more loyal, no more serious votary, than Max Beerbohm. He had sought and found expression in more than one art. His pen and his pencil were busy rivals. As 'Max,' the artist, he had made serene fun of the most august reputation; not even Emperors, not even editors, had escaped his vivacities. (Laughter.) The ambitious aspired to be his victims. (Laughter.) As a writer he masked a delicate effrontery with an imperturbable decorum. His sentences were like the gestures of a very finished actor. Even in the brief legends fastidiously inscribed beneath his daintily-coloured caricatures, the exquisite placing of a comma would discover the man of letters. (Laughter.)
>
> Mr. Yeats, announcing the award of the Polignac prize, said:—"The Crock of Gold" had given him more pleasure, he thought, than it could give to another man, wise and beautiful though it was, because it was a proof that his own native city of Dublin had vigour and lived with a deeper life . . . .

The reporter for the *New Freewoman* gave a somewhat different account (15 December 1913):

> The British Academy held a meeting or a séance or a gathering, or whatever they call it, on November the 28th. . . .
>
> Sir Walter [Raleigh] made what would be called a tempered speech. He praised Mr. Masefield just a little doubtfully. . .
>
> Mr. Hewlett welcomed Mrs. Margaret Woods to the Academy [and spoke of her] sensitive pen which has gained force among the ramparts of something or other. He said that its throb was the more intense for being sheathed in marble. He mentioned Milton and Gray. . . . He sat down unexpectedly and everyone clapped.
>
> [Mr. Benson] spoke of the glorious, the staunch, the noble, the flashing cavalier, the fearless and trenchant philosopher, etcetera, etcetera. He meant the Right Reverend Dr. Inge [who] is now a member of the British Academy. God save the King.
>
> Mr. Binyon soared above the heads of his predecessors [in speaking for Mr. Max Beerbohm. He] began by praising the Muse of Comedy—I think he said the Comic Muse—in a tone of dull melancholy, with a lugubrious countenance. But Mr. Binyon was shamming. He came out; he made a joke; it was a good one. Mr. Yeats, who, up till that time had been writing his speech for the press or fanning his forehead in an agitated way as he muttered Irish folk-lore to himself—Mr. Yeats turned round and smiled, and waved a delicate hand. Mr. Binyon went on; he made three witty sayings which I have forgotten. He was twice banal when I thought he was going to make a joke. He parodied the parodying Mr. Beerbohm. He was an admirable fellow.
>
> Mr. Yeats? Ah, Mr. Yeats. Mr. Yeats explained with Dublin Theatre gestures and parsonic elocution that he had no manuscript to read from. He had given his to the press. He smiled benignly, and recited his memorised speech perfectly. He spoke in his beautiful voice; he expressed Celtic lore with his more beautiful face; he elevated and waved his yet more beautiful hands. He blessed us with his presence. He spoke of spirits and phantasmagoria. He spoke of finding two boots in the middle of a field and the owner of the boots listening for the earth-spirits under a bush. He said that in Ireland the hedge-rows were rushing upon the towns. He praised Mr. Stevens' Crock of Gold. He read one of Mr. Stevens' poems, which was admirable as he read it.
>
> Mr. Yeats concluded the performance by giving Mr. Stevens a hundred pounds. We could not hear Mr. Stevens promising to be a good boy and not spend it all in toffee and fairy-books.

R.S. [Probably Richard Aldington]

For information about Margaret L. Woods, see Letter **127n.** *The Collected Poems of Margaret L. Woods,* FRSL, Member of the Academic Committee, was published in 1914. A.C. Benson (1862–1925), who specialised in graceful biographies and appreciations, was for EP the type of the "man of letters."

puppet show of Maeterlinck] On 1 December 1913 the London *Times* reported (p. 66) that Maeterlinck's *Ardiane et Barbe Bleue* had been presented the previous week at Crosby Hall by the Ilkley Puppets, in aid of the Working

Women's Legal Advice Bureau and the Industrial Law Committee. Maurice
Maeterlinck (1862–1949) wrote several plays for marionettes: one of them,
The Death of Tintagiles, was playing at the St. James's Theatre in December
1913.

   Craig cardboard scenery]   See Letter **95n.** Craig was fascinated by the use
of marionettes on the stage.

200   Ezra to Dorothy

> *Stone Cottage*
> *[Coleman's Hatch]*
> *[Sussex]*
> *[30 November 1913]*
> *Sunday*

Dearest:

   No! I shall be coming up on Friday the 5th and we aren't sure of stay-
ing till Monday. Ergo: you are requested to annihilate anything that tends
to blot out said Friday from the list of the candidly lapidated.

   As for Church St. you should holler louder–one can not be expected to
preserve *all* the sensitiveness of the jungle in this age of iron and contrap-
tions.

   As for the ⌒ (no, it don't look like an eagle), he [Yeats]
talks of the academic committee's "passion for the absolutely harmless".
Also the panther says "brrrr". O.S. [Olivia Shakespear] is to desist from
her toothache & also tell me what day the Eagle is to be reminded to
come up & lecture. Said Eagle is quite keen on puppets but I think you
may as well go on with Chinese.

   It looks & sounds unpleasingly cold without.

   I think the Eagle will probably propose W.W.Jacobs for the a.c. [Aca-
demic Committee] in a fit of desperation. The "Prelude" [where Dorothy
stayed] is quite empty–you'd better take it for Xmas.

> Love
> E.

   the panther]   See Letter **197.**
   W.W. Jacobs]   William Wymark Jacobs (1863–1943), a popular comic
writer who specialized in cockney dialect. He is most famous for his horror story
"The Monkey's Paw" (1902).

201   Dorothy to Ezra

12 Brunswick Gardens
Kensington
[3 December 1913]
Wednesday

Dearest Mao.

I am keeping Friday for you. I haven't found out what O.S.'s [Olivia Shakespear's] plans for that day may be so I may have to meet you at the Club, possibly. But come here 3 ocl: unless I write to you at 10 C. Walk. I went to the last [G.R.S.] Mead yesterday. He had a bad cold–and told us about the "Round People".

I shall be worn out on Friday–I am doing a heap of things this week– all totally unnecessary. I have been reading you as a Serious Artist in the New F. [*New Freewoman*] and have been much interested. Also [John] Cournos' criticism on the Cubists.

Yours
with love
D.

the Club]   New Century Club.

Serious Artist]   EP's essay "The Serious Artist" appeared in three instalments in the *New Freewoman*, 1 (15 October–15 November 1913).

Cournos' criticism on the Cubists]   John Cournos (see Biographical Appendix) published an article on "The Battle of the Cubes" in the *New Freewoman*, 1 (15 November 1913).

202   Dorothy to Ezra

[Kensington]
[6 December 1913]
Saturday

Beloved of the Black Panther.

What a beautiful day it has been–I lingered about this afternoon near the Round Pond [in Kensington Gardens] for ages, watching the seagulls– They have come in for the winter. It was cold though. I felt very happy–

"To my mind he [Gaudier] is at his best in the work he did before he became a Vorticist, such work as the delightful torso of a woman, which was in Mrs. Shakespeare's [*sic*] drawingroom, as beautiful a torso as was ever carved, hardly excepting that of Aphrodite of Cyrene."

—Edgar Jepson, *Memories of an Edwardian and Neo-Georgian.*

& wondered how sunny it was on your common. The Chinese Rosary is a great joy–Some very good Saint must have had it once-upon-a-time.

Thy Nov: No: of "Poetry" [*Poetry,* Chicago] has just come. I like yours, particularly Xenia, iii & iv. What does Xenia mean? I once knew a Russian girl of that name - - - ? Isn't the Millwins ["Les Millwin"] & the R. [Russian] Ballet too topical? No, CHARS! not tropical.

Are there any old Chinese M.S.S. at that blooming museum [British Museum] that you will want copied? (Brilliant idea! How can he want them copied until he knows what they're about?). I think the Rosary is of good augury.

The family talk of nothing at this moment but a beautiful portrait of a lovely Miss Shakespear, by Romney–being shown for the first time. Haven't seen it myself yet.

I had my *Mao* washed yesterday–and bought two *ming* /bright hair combs (paste, not China!). There is said to be a marvellous collection of Jap. prints at S. Kensington Museum [Victoria & Albert] now–a Loan Exh: & worth seeing.

Perhaps the Panther was away to me for a minute this afternoon? Tell me more about the snow leopard. I suppose its too babyish to want to know, have they either of them names?

Best love
D.

Sunday

Their Montpel-Bunk is wanting to know the price of [Gaudier] Brzeska's torse, of which he has heard so much from us–so you had better keep your eye on it if you really mean to get it! Brzeska comes on 18th & his sister!

Love
D.

Xenia, iii & iv]   The poems published by EP in *Poetry* (Chicago), 3 (November 1913), included the "Xenia" sequence. III and IV were the first two poems in "A Song of the Degrees" (P). For EP's explanation of "Xenia" see Letter **203.**

the Millwins . . . R. Ballet]   "Les Millwin" (P), published in the November 1913 issue of *Poetry* as the second poem in the "Lustra" sequence, begins with the line: "The little Millwins attend the Russian Ballet."

Miss Shakespear, by Romney]   George Romney (1734–1802), the fashionable portrait painter of late 18th-century English society, did a portrait of Mrs. Laver Oliver (formerly Miss Mary Shakespear) and her infant daughter.

Montpel-Bunk]   Dorothy's uncle, Henry Tudor Tucker, "The Bunk," married Edith Ellen Hyde-Lees. They lived at 16 Montpelier Square. See Letter **101n.**

Brzeska's torse]   In 1913–14 Gaudier-Brzeska carved two torsos in white marble of Nina Hamnett, a painter, and prepared at least one other of her, possibly in clay: all were classical in style. One is now in the Victoria and Albert Museum; the other, white marble on a veined marble base, was purchased by Olivia Shakespear for £10. See Roger Cole, *Burning to Speak: The Life and Art of Henri Gaudier-Brzeska* (1978).

Brzeska . . . & his sister!]   Henri Gaudier met Sophie Brzeska in Paris in
1910, and from 1911 onward (when he moved to London) joined her name with
his.

203   Ezra to Dorothy

> *Stone Cottage*
> [*Coleman's Hatch*]
> [*Sussex*]
> [*16 December 1913*]

Dearest

No, They have not names. From careful perusal of my works you might
learn that the snow leopard sits on his tail and observes one's departure.
The panther has been awa'. I dare say you had him.

I have cribbed part of a Nōh (dramatic eclogue) out of Fenollosa's
notes. The Eagle [Yeats] calls it charming & says *vers libre* is prose. He
has his nose kept down to his demon's, for the sake of L. [Lady] Gregory's
folk-lore. I have writ to Korshune [John Cournos] about Brzeska's torse,
so I suppose it's as good as asked for–provided he don't want argosies in
return. The Bunk [Dorothy's uncle] can buy something else. I don't think
we've either of us space for the post-post embracers. The Bunk can have
the flat-bellied torse if he needs it.

Xenia means a trifle, or a tag. THEY [CHARS] think they're a
trifle - - -

> Yr.
>
> E.

a Nōh . . . out of Fenollosa's notes]   "Kinuta," first published as part of
"The Classical Drama of Japan," *Quarterly Review,* 201 (October 1914).

Korshune]   The original surname of John Cournos. See Biographical Ap-
pendix.

Xenia]   See Letter **202n.**

204   Dorothy to Ezra

Leweston Manor
Sherborne
Dorset
[*26 December 1913*]
Friday

My dear–

I am busy learning the Tango: its amusing–and the [Fletcher] Boys are good dancers. This morning we went to the Meet, and then the hounds came across the Park–& I hared over a field or so after them–to return exhausted to late lunch.

I am trying "to get a holt" on a book of Gareth's [Gareth Fletcher's]– on elementary Logic–It all seems sense, and as though any writer of decent style must know it all, (and a great deal more besides?).

We had a family dinner party last night here–of 16, all sporting, & dull. I must sleep or die this afternoon!

Later (*Saturday*)

I saw the Bl. Panther lying on my hearth rug one night when I was wakeful with most alarming distinctness. He was stretched out on his side with his long tail round his hind ankles. I was quite alarmed! And another night I felt him sitting stiff up by the fire. Fortunately I am not in the room I usually have (which is undoubtedly haunted) or else I should have had to ask if I might borrow Him every night.

Much love
Yours D.

205   Dorothy to Ezra

[*Kensington*]
[*30 December 1913*]

Dearest EP.

I am home for a day or two, before going down to □ [Georgie Hyde-Lees] coz at Margate. Just imagine the cold at Margate! Is the snow leopard buried in snow yet? All the way up the line from Sherborne yesterday there was snow lying.

I have bought a little new treasure–in an old curiosity shop down there–it is a snuff box, I suppose–in tortoiseshell, beautifully carved. I hope you will like it as much as I do. It looks chinese. Do tortoises grow in the Yangtse Kiang?

I have also a new Toy–It is a film of oil & summat spread over a circle & then one sees wonderful colours & patterns forming.

Coz must go out & get warm.

Much love
Yours D.

[Gaudier] Brzeska's torse doesn't seem to feel the cold particularly!

Brzeska's torse]   See Letter **202n.**

206   Ezra to Dorothy

[*10*] *Church Walk*
[*Kensington*]
[*30 December 1913*]

Dearest.

I don't suppose you're "up" or if you are you're probably dumping one "box" into another & standing on your head in the midst. Anyhow, if you are neither "hollar out" & let me come in on Wednesday.

Yr.
E.

1914

1914

Stone Cottage
[*Coleman's Hatch*]
[*Sussex*]
[*6 January 1914*]
[*Tuesday*]

Dearest:

I suppose you have gone to Margate, quae cum ita sint. I won't come up with the Eagle [Yeats] on Wednesday. If you have stayed you'd better telegraph as this will hardly reach you till Wed. *a.m.*

I have done the 1st part & a bit more, of a longer Japanese play. [G.W.] Prothero has accepted "Kinuta" & Fenollosa's essay for the Quarterly [*Quarterly Review*]–I hope to get The Feather-Mantle in, also. We've been reading The Comte de Gabalis–a charming and spritely book about Sylphes & Salamanders, you must read it when the Eagle [Yeats] lends it to O.S. [Olivia Shakespear] as I suppose he will sooner or later– tho' he borrowed it from somebody else.

I am half a mind to translate only it seems too delicate to give to a prophane english vulgo. R. [Richard Aldington] says I've used the word delicate 947 times in "Lustra" so I suppose I've got to investigate–which means "re-read" the dam book to find out.

Later

I have much improved one passage by changing it to "sensuous". The other places are more difficult. The order in which the poems ought to be printed (or omitted) is a laborious question. I have just thought of the eagle's [Yeats's] *own* word "elaborate". I wonder if I can lift it for the 942nd passage–Enough of this nonsense!! I dare say I would be better employed doing Nishiki-gi.

Mr. Sung has told father that he thinks I would be interested in his country–it seems a sufficiently safe statement.

Yes, Someone is now at The Prelude–a respectable elderish female gazed from the road into our study at about 2.45 this P.M. with undis- guised awe & curiosity.

Ti baccio gli occhi.

E.

quae cum ita sint]   Catullus 68, line 37: *quod cum ita sit*, "And since this is so."

longer Japanese play]   "Nishikigi," translated from the Japanese of Moto-kiyo by Ernest Fenollosa and edited by Ezra Pound, *Poetry* (Chicago), 4 (May 1914).

Prothero . . . "Kinuta" . . . The Feather-Mantle]   G.W. Prothero was the editor of the *Quarterly Review*. In the issue for October 1914 he published "The Classical Drama of Japan," edited from the Fenollosa manuscripts by EP, which includes "Kinuta" (see Letter **206**) and "Hagoromo," the "Feather-mantle."

Comte de Gabalis]   *Le Comte de Gabalis, ou entretiens sur les sciences secrètes,* by the Abbé de Montfaucon de Villars (Paris, 1670), was frequently reprinted and augmented during the 17th and 18th centuries. Consisting of five discourses on the "Rosicrucian Philosophy," it provided Alexander Pope with the system of Sylphs and Gnomes for his enlarged (1714) edition of *The Rape of the Lock*. Pope describes it in his dedication "To Mrs. Arabella Fermor" as a book "which both in its Title and Size is so like a *Novel,* that many of the Fair Sex have read it for one by Mistake. According to these *Gentlemen,* the four Elements are inhabited by Spirits, which they call *Sylphs, Gnomes, Nymphs,* and *Salamanders.*"

delicate . . . "Lustra"]   The word occurs nine times in *Lustra* (1916).

Mr. Sung]   F.T. Sung, an official of the new Chinese Republic, visited Philadelphia in late 1913 and offered to find Homer Pound a position in China. On 4 January 1914 EP wrote to his father: "China is interesting, VERY. Make sure which Chinese government is giving you the job and then blaze away." By 19 January 1914 Mr. Sung had arrived in London and had made the same offer to EP, who wrote to his father: "We may yet be a united family." Sung returned to Peking, where he continued to search for suitable positions; but EP's marriage in April 1914 changed the situation. On 3 July 1914 Sung wrote to EP, congratu-lating him on his marriage and expressing regrets that the move to China was no longer possible.

During 1914 EP arranged to have two essays by Sung (signed "F.T.S.") published in the *Egoist*. The first, on "The Causes and Remedy of the Poverty of China," appeared in three installments, 16 March–1 April–15 May; the second essay, on Chinese manners, customs, language, and religions, was also published in three installments, 15 September–15 October–16 November. The first essay was introduced by this note from EP:

> The following MSS. was left with me by a Chinese official. I might have treated it in various ways. He suggested that I should rewrite it. I might excerpt the passages whereof I disapprove but I prefer to let it alone. At a time when China has replaced Greece in the intellectual life of so many occidentals, it is interesting to see in what way the occidental ideas are percolating into the orient. We have here the notes of a practical and technical Chinaman. There are also some corrections, I do not know by whom, but I leave them as they are.

Far-san T. Sung (b. 1883) was educated in the United States. He studied at Ohio Wesleyan University (1900–05), graduating with the degree of B.Sc., and at the University of Chicago (1905–07), where he also received a B.Sc. From 1908 until 1912 he was professor of chemistry at the Peking Government University. At the time of this letter he was Technical Expert of the Ministry of Finance and co-director of the Assaying Office. He later became Inspector General of Mints and held a number of high offices in government and business. Presumably he met Homer Pound during a visit to the U.S. Mint in Philadelphia.

208   Dorothy to Ezra

> [*Kensington*]
> [*6 January 1914*]
> *Tuesday*

Dearest.

I am joining Georgie [Hyde-Lees] on Friday, 9th,
    at 36 Fort Crescent,
        Margate.
How long I shall be there–I do not yet know. I am hoping to see Nancy [Maude] this morning or tomorrow–& I suppose her son–who will probably interrupt us! I have not read the Jap. play. I have been making myself curtains for my bedroom–and doing divers things–also reading a rather interesting novel by two folk called Brett Young.

I don't think you are in any hurry for the play back? By the way. Shall I send you a cheque for £5 for Mlle Brzeska? That would be easiest for me, if its any good to you!

Our chinese lunch was certainly v. good. On our way home–up Regent St.–O.S. [Olivia Shakespear] bought a fine magenta silk frock (sounds Early Vict. beyond recall!). Yesterday I got a fawnish coat & skirt for spring–wh. is being a little altered for me–Faun & H-d-d [Richard Aldington & Hamadryad, Hilda Doolittle] come to tea today & Fred M. [Manning].

I am in communication about an entrance ticket for British M. [Museum] reading room–where I *say* I am studying Symbolisme–but where I mean *privately,* to study Ching Chang Chinese!

There is more snow coming–

> Much love.
> Yours D.

I was glad to see you three days running.

Tuesday 7 PM

Yours has just come. But it's no use yr coming up for me, as I am busy tomorrow & all Thursday. R, H-d-d & F.M. all just been to tea. Heaven alone has any inkling of what they all thought of each other! I assured O.S. [Olivia] it was excellent for both parties to meet the other!

FM. has been aeroplaning–& I believe it has stirred up his brain nicely. R. [Richard] evidently doesn't consider himself in the light of a "householder". The H-d-d rather likes [Gaudier] Brzeska I take it–and I find consolation only in Mao [EP].

Yours
D.

I will take the "Feather Mantle" to Margate & send it to you from there, if I don't read it tomorrow. I shouldn't think you could change "delicate" to "elaborate"? The latter is rococco & heavy surely? Might do–can't tell minus context. What about "discontinued"!!!

two folk called Brett Young]   Francis and Eric Brett Young published a novel, *Undergrowth,* in 1913. Francis Brett Young (1884–1954) wrote a number of popular novels.

the "Feather Mantle"]   The Noh play "Hagoromo." See Letter **207.**

"delicate" . . . *"discontinued"*]   See Letter **207** for Richard Aldington's objection to EP's repeated use of "delicate." "Liu Ch'e" (P), which first appeared in *Des Imagistes* (1914), opens: "The rustling of the silk is discontinued . . ."

209   Ezra to Dorothy

Stone Cottage
[*Coleman's Hatch*]
[*Sussex*]
[*7 January 1914*]

Dearest:

Your 1st. letter has just come with "The Times". As you aren't going till Friday, I shall come up with 'is nibs [Yeats] today, and come tomorrow (Thursday *alle tre* [at 3]) unless I hear to the contrary–or I could come in the morning if the afternoon is taboo, or we could go out (?) to lunch & some prints or something afterward.

Will send this from Victoria [Station] when I get there.

à demain

love

E.

2 P.M. Your second note has just come. However, I've got all ready to come up–if anything else falls through you can let me know at Ch. Wk. [Church Walk] but dont bother.

210   Ezra to Dorothy

Stone Cottage
[Coleman's Hatch]
[Sussex]
[12 January 1914]

Dearest:

No there's nothing to be studied about symbolism–and as nobody pays the slightest attention to what you do or what books you read you may as well go to work on Chinese direct.

You brute, you gave me a very miserable half Wednesday & all Thursday. On Friday I found some consolation in Brinkley's book about listening to incense, vol. III, oriental series, re/ Nōh & japanese diversions.

There's no hurry about Mlle. Brzeska–any old time will do. I've written to M.F. [Mary Fenollosa] again for that simple introduction to Chang– besides, the oriental room is a much pleasanter place to work than the "reading-room"–I don't know how long it is before one really uses the oriental room.

It is very dam cold & we did 21 letters on the holy sabbath so I've got to go to the post about at once. The Eagle [Yeats] says he is going to hire a motor to take us to [Wilfred Scawen] Blunt–if it is as dammmmM cold sunday next as it is now we'll arrive like a box of marrons glacés. F.M. [Fred Manning] thinks he may come to Blunt's with us.

I hope you don't die of frost at Margate. Yours for eternity–I hope not a uniformly cold eternity–& with the Eagle beginning to fuss about that mail.

Yrs.

E.

Brinkley's book]   Frank Brinkley's twelve-volume study of *Japan and China: Their History, Arts and Literature* was published in 1901 in the "Oriental Series" and reprinted in 1903. Volume Three opens with a chapter on "Refinements and Pastimes of the Military Epoch" which contains a description of the ceremony "listening to incense" and a section on the Noh drama. Unfortunately, the lovely synaesthetic phrase "listening to incense" results from a misreading of the ideogram for "smelling."

introduction to Chang]   That is, an introduction to the Chinese language. DS owned a copy of the pamphlet by Sir Walter Caine Hillier, *The Chinese Language and How to Learn It: A Manual for Beginners* (1907–09; 2nd edition, 1910).

take us to Blunt]   On 18 January 1914 a "committee" of eight poets—Yeats, Sturge Moore, Victor Plarr, John Masefield, Frederic Manning, F.S. Flint, Richard Aldington, and EP—journeyed to Newbuildings Place, Sussex, to pay tribute to Wilfred Scawen Blunt (1840–1922). Blunt had spent some time in the Foreign Service, had traveled widely in Europe, Asia Minor, and North Africa, and was a famous breeder of Arabian horses. He was also a fine poet and a master of traditional forms, but the younger generation admired him most for his opposition to British Colonialism and his support of Irish Home Rule, for which he had been imprisoned by the British Government for two months in 1888.

On this occasion the committee presented Blunt with a "reliquary" carved in marble by Gaudier-Brzeska and bearing the inscription "Homage to Wilfred Blunt." The reliquary contained manuscripts of poems by the eight poets, including "verses of homage" by EP:

> Because you have gone your individual gait,
> Written fine verses, made mock of the world,
> Swung the grand style, not made a trade of art,
> Upheld Mazzini and detested institutions;
>
> We, who are little given to respect,
> Respect you, and having no better way to show it,
> Bring you this stone to be some record of it.

Blunt had declined, because of his age, to attend a more formal ceremony; but he entertained the poets over a dinner of roasted peacock.

Richard Aldington wrote a detailed account of the visit, including the speeches by Blunt and Yeats [*The Egoist*, 1 (2 February 1914)], and EP published an abridged account in *Poetry* (Chicago), 3 (March 1914). In the great passage on "Vanity" at the end of Canto 81 EP recalls this event:

But to have done instead of not doing
                    this is not vanity
To have, with decency, knocked
That a Blunt should open
            To have gathered from the air a live tradition
or from a fine old eye the unconquered flame
This is not vanity.
            Here error is all in the not done,
all in the diffidence that faltered . . .

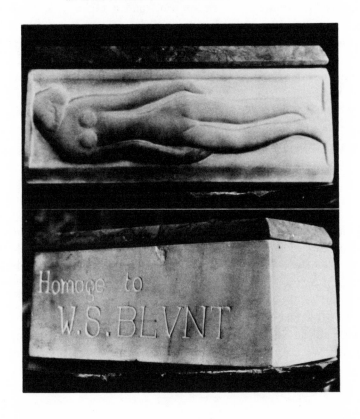

211   Dorothy to Ezra

36 Fort Crescent
Margate
[Kent]
[13 January 1914]

As cold as the Antarctic–a gale of wind–and a raging sea. Thanks for yours. I am sorry you had a bad 1/2 Wed & Thurs–I understood from your note that you were *not* expecting to hear from me - - - Its over now! You got the Jap. MSS. all right? + my remarks. Poetry [*Poetry*, Chicago] came this morning–I am amused by W.B.Y.'s [Yeats's] two letters about the £ 50! I haven't read Richard's [Richard Aldington's] yet. I am deep in [Flaubert's] "Salammbô". That is to say–I have made up my mind that I *will* get through it: it is an unholy Stodge, I do think–but I suppose quite fairly Imagiste?

I do think George Moore ought to be disdainfully kicked for the filth he writes about W.B.Y. & Lady G [Lady Gregory], I wonder whether, when it comes to [J.M.] Synge, rather than himself, W.B.Y. won't rise up in fury?

My only reason for wishing to pursue Symbolisme is that I shall have to tell my parents what I am doing–at first anyway–and I would much rather keep the Chinese secret–as it amuses me much more, & I am likely to go on longer if amused! Comprends-tu? I see a book about Japanese some-things is out by "Mary Fenollosa"–your friend, I conclude.

Has [Wilfred Scawen] Blunt's trough been accomplished? For goodness' sake wear all the clothes you possess, both of you, if you do motor up to the dinner. We are nearly frozen here. Our sitting-room faces North–has three nice large windows, and only muslin curtains–the wind is N.E.

Later

We battled out in all our clothes & went to see "The Grotto"–W.B.Y. & Bunk [my uncle] went to see it–It is very queer. I tried to make it into an underground Mithraic place–unsuccessfully. 'They say' it is Masonic in origin. What did the Eagle [Yeats] think of it? The patterns on the walls are all in different shells, and very strange. But the whole place has no "atmosphere". There is a passage, serpent-shaped, [sketch] leading to a badly-squared room, with two altars & an alcove–There are 4-pointed stars, & 8-ptd. ones and queer eastern-looking kind of thing!! [sketch]

Best love. I may go home on Friday– I may not. I will write again.

Yours D.

Poetry . . . W.B.Y.'s two letters] In *Poetry* (Chicago), 3 (November 1913), it was announced that Yeats had won the prize of $250 [£50] offered "for the best poem published during the magazine's first year." In the next issue (January 1914) the editors printed two letters from Yeats, the first suggesting that he keep £10 for a book-plate to be made by Sturge Moore, with the remaining £40 reserved for "some young American writer . . . some unknown needy young man in a garret"; and the second suggesting that the £40 be given to Ezra Pound. "His experiments are perhaps errors, I am not certain; but I would always sooner give the laurel to vigorous errors than to any orthodoxy not inspired."

Richard's] Richard Aldington published a suite of five poems in the January 1914 issue of *Poetry*.

"Salammbô"] *Salammbô* (1862), Flaubert's novel about ancient Carthage. See Letter **212.**

George Moore . . . about W.B.Y. & Lady G] George Moore (1852–1933), the Irish novelist and man of letters, had attacked Yeats in the earlier two volumes of his trilogy *Hail and Farewell*, making fun of the excursions into theosophy; but in a chapter of the third volume, *Vale*, first published in *The English Review*, 16 (January 1914), he launched a more vicious attack on "Yeats, Lady Gregory, and Synge." Moore was especially caustic in his comments on Yeats's hatred for the "middle classes" and pretensions to an aristocratic ancestry.

a book . . . by "Mary Fenollosa"] See Letter **212n.**

Blunt's trough] See Letter **210n.**

"The Grotto"] A network of underground passages in a chalk hill near Margate, decorated with patterns of sea shells. The "Grotto" has been attributed in local folklore to pre-Roman Phoenician traders or to Roman centurions, but it is clearly an 18th-century "folly."

212   Ezra to Dorothy

Stone Cold Cottage
[Coleman's Hatch]
[Sussex]
[14 January 1914]

Dearest:

Yes I know I wasn't supposed to be expecting to hear from you, but I don't see how that could (or can or whatever) have been supposed to add to my pleasure. However–I thought you'd gone to Margate for 3 weeks or some much hideous and unnatural period. I'm glad you're coming back before you are wholly congealed, cloaked with marine ice & masonic caves. I don't know that Friday is much use, save that it would get you settled in London by the first of the week.

Yes, "Salambo" is stodge. Flaubert at his worst & not imagisme as *I* understand it. What *do* you mean by symbolism? Do you mean real symbolism, Cabala, genesis of symbols, rise of picture language, etc. or the aesthetic ⟨symbology⟩ symbolism of Villiers de l'Isle Adam, & that Arthur Symons wrote a book about–the literwary movement? At any rate begin on the *"Comte de Gabalis"*, anonymous & should be in catalogue under "Comte de Gabalis". Then you might try the Grimoire of Pope Honorius (IIIrd I think).

There's a dictionary of symbols, but I think it immoral. I mean that I think a superficial acquaintance with the sort of shallow, conventional, or attributed meaning of a lot of symbols *weakens*–damnably, the power of receiving an energized symbol. I mean a symbol appearing in a vision has a certain richness & power of energizing joy–whereas if the supposed meaning of a symbol is familiar it has no more force, or interest of power of suggestion than any other word, or than a synonym in some other language.

Then there are those Egyptian language books, but O.S. [Olivia Shakespear] has 'em so they're no use. De Gabalis (first part only) is amusing. Ennemoser's History of Magic may have something in it–Then there are "Les Symbolistes"–french from Mallarmé, de l'Isle Adam, etc. to [Remy] De Gourmont, which is another story.

As for G. Moore, the Eagle [Yeats] does nowt but write lofty poems to his ancestors, thinking that the haughtiest reply. I've suggested that he get himself proclaimed Duke of Ormond–as that should be the final extinction of g.m. [George Moore].

Mary Fenollosa's Japan book is either her book of child verses or else is Fenollosa's "Hist. of Ch. & Jap art" with introduction and notes by *M.F.*

Brzx. [Gaudier-Brzeska] *says* the sarcophagus [for W.S. Blunt] will be done in time.

If your "grotto" was masonic I don't see as how it could be expected to have atmosphere–was it dug in the XVIIIth century? The wiggles [Dorothy's sketch] look like the serpent of knowledge & the tree of life *ma che?!*

Yes the *mss* arrived O.K. *gradeci* [?*gradirci:* accepted with pleasure]– I've written to M.F. again to send on the beginning book for Chang. I have about finished my stuff for the Quarterly [*Quarterly Review*] all except a few corrections in *'Hagoromo'–la!*

> Be good & you'll be happy–h-m-m.
> Love   E.

"*Salambo*"]   The title in English of Flaubert's *Salammbô*. See Letter **211**.

Villiers de l'Isle Adam]   Villiers de l'Isle-Adam (1838–1889), the Symbolist novelist and dramatist whose bizarre poetic drama *Axël* (first performed in 1884) made a strong impression on the English "decadents." To the Yeats of the 1890s, *Axël* was a "sacred book of the arts" with deep spiritual implications. He chose as epigraph for *The Secret Rose* Villiers' famous epigram: "As for living, our servants will do that for us."

Arthur Symons . . . the literwary movement]   In his *Symbolist Movement in Literature* (1899), Arthur Symons (1865–1945) gave the English public a coherent view of recent French literature. His study was crucial to the poetic development of both Yeats and T.S. Eliot.

"*Comte de Gabalis*"]   See Letter **207n.**

Grimoire of Pope Honorius]   *Le Grimoire* ["Black Book"] *du Pape Honorius,* also called *Le Livre des Conjurations du Pape Honorius,* first published in 1629 and frequently reprinted. Falsely attributed to Pope Honorius III, the book contains spells and charms for mastering diabolical powers.

dictionary of symbols]   Probably the *Dictionnaire des symboles, emblèmes et attributs,* by Maurice Pillard Verneuil, first published in Paris in the 1890s and often reprinted.

Ennemoser's History of Magic]   Joseph Ennemoser, *The History of Magic,* translated from the German by William Howitt (Bohn's Scientific Library, 1854). "To Which is Added an Appendix of the Most Remarkable and Best Authenticated Stories of Apparitions, Dreams, Second Sight, Somnambulism, Predictions, Divination, Witchcraft, Vampires, Fairies, Table-Turning, and Spirit-Rapping." In Canto 83 "Ennemoser on Witches" is part of EP's recollection of those winters with Yeats "at Stone Cottage in Sussex by the waste moor."

well those days are gone forever
  and the travelling rug with the coon-skin tabs
and his hearing nearly all Wordsworth
  for the sake of his conscience but
preferring Ennemoser on Witches.

G. Moore, the Eagle . . . lofty poems to his ancestors]   Yeats responded
to George Moore's attack on him (see Letter **211n**) by writing the two poems
that frame his volume *Responsibilities* (1914): "Pardon, old fathers . . ." and
"While I, from that reed-throated whisperer." The first poem, which rehearses
Yeats's distinguished ancestry, is dated "January 1914." It ends on an elegiac
note:

Pardon that for a barren passion's sake,
Although I have come close on forty-nine,
I have no child, I have nothing but a book,
Nothing but that to prove your blood and mine.

The closing poem, which was published in the *New Statesman* of 7 February
1914 under the title "Notoriety," is more aggressive in its response to

Those undreamt accidents that have made me
—Seeing that Fame has perished this long while,
Being but a part of ancient ceremony—
Notorious, till all my priceless things
Are but a post the passing dogs defile.

Mary Fenollosa's Japan book]   The book by Mary Fenollosa that DS in-
quired about in Letter **211**. It was probably *Blossoms from a Japanese Garden:
A Book of Child-Verses,* published in October 1913, not the *Epochs of Chinese
and Japanese Art* (1912) that she edited after her husband's death.
   the Quarterly . . . 'Hagoromo']   See Letter **207n.**

213   Ezra to Dorothy

[*Kensington*]
[*21 January 1914*]

Dearest

I perceive that this week will be unduly elongated. I think you'd better
perhaps marry me and live in one room more than the dryad [Hilda Doo-
little].

E.

214   Dorothy to Ezra

[Kensington]
[22 January 1914]

Dearest.

I cannot yet say which day you had better come in next week: I am waiting to hear from Nancy [Maude]–Anyway I am engaged on Wed: I was up at the [British] Museum yesterday morning. It is a most bewildering place at first! I read a book on Chinese literature, & found one or two nice sayings. I have also read the Incubi book, wh. made me giggle to myself–I liked the tale of the woman whose gray robes were torn from off her at the Church door by her Incubis.

Much love, dear
Yours
D.

the Incubi book] *De Daemonialitate, et Incubis et Succubis,* by the seventeenth-century Franciscan theologian Lodovico Maria Sinistrari. The manuscript was discovered in 1872 by the French bibliophile Isidore Liseux, who published it in 1875 with a French translation. DS probably read the English translation Liseux published four years later: *Demoniality; or, Incubi and Succubi* (Paris, 1879). Sinistrari tells of a married woman who was persecuted by an incubus. She made a vow to the Blessed Bernardine of Feltre that she would wear the gray habit of his order for twelve months if he would intercede for her.

> The next morning, which was Michaelmas Day, the afflicted woman repaired to the church of S. Michael . . . It was now about ten o'clock, a time when crowds of people were going to mass. She had no sooner set foot on the threshold of the church, than her clothes and ornaments fell to the ground, and disappeared in a gust of wind, leaving her mother naked. There happened, fortunately, to be among the crowd two cavaliers of mature age, who, seeing what had taken place, very decently hastened to divest themselves of their cloaks with which they concealed, as well as they could, the woman's nudity, and having put her into a close coach, accompanied her home. The clothes and trinkets carried off by the Incubus were not restored by him before six months had elapsed.

> [*Demoniality*, trans. Montague Summers (London, 1927), pp. 20–21]

EP owned a copy of the 1879 edition, which he cites in a footnote to "Note Precedent to 'La Fraisne' " in *A Lume Spento* (CEP, p. 8). While at Stone Cottage in 1913–14 he wrote to his father: "Yeats is doing various books. He wants my *Daemonalitas.* Will you try to find it along with the other thing I asked for. 'Daemonalitas' by the Rev. Father Sinistrari of Ameno. Paper cover, not very large."

215   Dorothy to Ezra

[*Kensington*]
[*23 January 1914*]

Dear,

I don't think I shall get the translation to you today–O.S. [Olivia Shakespear] is suffering agonies of toothache–& I can't worry her as to its whereabouts–I am taking her to the dentist some time today. Will you come up on Tuesday aft.? *unless* you hear to the contrary–which you may.

Love.
D.

216   Dorothy to Ezra

[*Kensington*]
[*13 February 1914*]
Friday even: 8.30

Dearest.

O.S. [Olivia Shakespear] said, that she thought it would be more diplomatic if she were to talk to H.H.S. [H.H. Shakespear, Dorothy's father] herself first. So she is doing so now–this minute–& I am feeling glad it isn't me–and very jumpy.

I had tea at No. 8 [The Aldingtons] today–I was dying to go over the next door flat! They never mentioned it–which rather relieved me–as I am sure I shouldn't have kept properly disinterested & calm! I told Georgie [Hyde-Lees] all about it yesterday afternoon–but she is secret as the grave abt. it until I say she may know. She was pleased, I think. I am sure she was–She didn't say much–I particularly don't want her to feel "deserted" by my marrying - - - I know how it is when one's girl-friends marry–Of course it can't be helped in a way–but you can help, if you like her–which I believe you do?

Later

Consent appears to be given–with some reluctance. Anyway please come in tomorrow morning to see me.

Yrs.
D.

217   Ezra to Henry Hope Shakespear

[*Typed*]   *10 Church Walk*
                                             [*London*] *W.*
                                             16 February 1914
                                             Monday evening

Dear Mr. Shakespear:

Dorothy says that you have suggested our being married in a church, unless you feel very strongly on this point I should much rather go through the simple and dignified service at the Registry.

I have some religion. What you say about a priest's benediction is sound enough but I count myself much more a priest than I do some sceptic who is merely being paid for public pretense of something he has probably never considered. It would be intolerable for instance to be put through a religious ceremony by an atheist like Galton [Rev. Arthur Galton], or by a cad like the bishop of London, who are fair examples of the upper sort of clergy.

I think, seriously, that the spiritual powers are affronted when a person who takes his religion seriously complies with a ceremony which has fallen into decay. I can not find any trace of Christ's having spoken against the greek gods. He objected, accepting the given documents, to Judaism which is the core of modern "Christianity". I should find myself much more in the presence of the aerial and divine powers in taking a formal legal oath with a spirit of reverence than in complying with rites of that religion "which the Nazarine has been accused of having founded".

I should no more give up my faith in Christ than I should give up my faith in Helios or my respect for the teachings of Confucius, but I think this superficial conformity, an act which would amount, practically, to an outrageous lie at what should be one of [the] most serious moments of a man's life, interferes.

On the other hand I shouldn't mind any ceremony if it were performed by someone who was really a priest, I mean some man who did actually and fervently believe in some sort of divinity. The whole sanity of classic religion was in their recognition that different men have different gods and that there are many sorts of orthodox piety.

                              Yours very sincerely
                              Ezra

I've typed this because [it is] rather intricate and it will be much easier to read than if I did it in my "egyptian".

E.P.

218   Henry Hope Shakespear to Ezra

[Draft letter, including substantial deleted section]

> *[Shakespear & Parkyn]*
> *[8 John Street]*
> *[London]*
> *19 February 1914*

My dear Ezra

I recd yr letter ⟨about your wedding⟩ which required my anxious consideration before I replied.

[Following section deleted]

I must first enter a protest agst. the phrase that I had "suggested" a marriage in church. It implies that it was I who was introduced some thing unusual & unexpected. When my consent was asked to Dorothy being married nothing was said as to her wishing to be married otherwise than in the manner in which people in her station of life are usually married & it came as a shock to me much later to learn that she contemplated being married other than in Church.

As to a part of your letter I don't really know whether you write seriously for I thought it a matter of common agreemt. that the validity of any ceremony perpetuated by a duly constituted official person was not affected by any personal disqualification of the official–Do you mean that you propose to satisfy yourself that the Registrar who is to officiate at the "simple & dignified service" is a man of irreproachable character.

But let that pass.

[Deleted section ends here]

What I tried to put before Dorothy was

1. That as an English Woman she is entitled to be married in the National Church.

2. That as she does not profess to belong to any other defined Religion there is no procedure other than a marriage in Church by which she can show that she enters into the solemn obligations of marriage with the conviction that she does so in the sight of & seeking the assistance of the Divine Powers.

3. That the one thing definitely indicated by a merely Civil marriage is the precise negation of this.

4. That in my opinion with which I venture to believe the vast majority of her countrymen agree is that the Church of England is vastly wider than some of its members try to make out, and that in conforming to the usual custom she is not thereby hypocritically pretending to believe what she does not.

However I shall in no way try to force my views upon her, & if she conscientiously believes it is not right for her to take her vows in a Church I shall say no more of it tho' it will be more distressing to me than perhaps you can understand.

I am a man of few words & keep my views on religious matters between myself & God and it pains me to have to write on such matters.

Yours sincerely
H.H.S.

P.S.
Since writing the above I hear from D. that you have both decided to defer to my wishes & I heartily thank you. But I think you may still like to have my letter.

219   Ezra to Dorothy

10 Church Walk
[Kensington]
[28 February 1914]

[To Hotel Elysée, Rome]

Dearest;

Eva [Fowler] exhilarated, filled with benevolence, forgot to feed "Chukka", wroth because she didn't know before she disposed of old sofa that was too large for Chukka-room. (We couldn't have got it into no. 5

with a derrick). Says we can have Daisy Meadow right up to the end of May, so I have not written to Miss Wellfare. We can go to Stone Cottage later. Says she will send you a cheque–I thought that better than trying to get her to present anything in particular. She was raging at the telephone–"Nini" is moving. I dare say we shall get ALL the pink chairs. "Anita" instructed to purchase cutlery.

Eva can understand how you might fall in love with me but - - - marry me - - - well sh*e might* have done it herself, but she wouldn't have let anybody belonging to her attempt it. I suggested that we'd end in the workhouse. She flatly contradicted me & dwelt upon my virility. She was very nice really embraced me *mit vollem glut* [with gusto], etc.

James G.F. [Fairfax] came in after luncheon & congratulated me with some warmth (if that is not a contradiction in terms). He congratulated me & addressed to me several other remarks.

[Robert] Bridges is quite disarming–called his job "This Professorship", was very quaint about [Henry] James, invited me down to Oxford, showed a flattering familiarity with my works, went on to dine with the King (damndd anticlimax THEY [CHARS] think).

I retired to a Turkish Bath, emerged & met [John Gould] Fletcher, jawed at Italano & Café Royal till midnight with J.G. *Fletcher* & Wyndham Lewis, who is bringing out a paper [*Blast*] & decorating dining rooms for the lower knighthood & gentry. On the whole it was a quiet day–counting the two hours repose in Jermyn St. Bridges was really charming.

The gas is mostly in & *R.* [Richard Aldington] has observed a man carrying the chimney to the geyser. I expect to go in [to the flat] on monday. Eva has sent a telegram originally "Bombshell–every happiness". We suggest that it will get through the Italian p.o. "Bombs-hell every happiness." Là-là.

I have started another jap. play–so much for my margin of intelligence. I have also written letters & addressed envelopes. De profundis, domina, etc. CHARS have written an epithalamium.

a toi.

E.

Greetings to O.S. [Olivia Shakespear] & G. [Georgie Hyde-Lees].

Eva exhilarated] When, on 27 February 1914, Eva Fowler heard of the forthcoming marriage, she sent a telegram to DS in Rome which arrived with this wording: "BOMBSHELL BUTT EVER HAPPINESS–EVA."
"Chukka"] Mrs. Fowler's pet lemur.

Miss Wellfare]   One of two sisters who looked after EP and Yeats at Stone Cottage.

"Nini"]   Ynez Neumann, one of Eva Fowler's sisters.

"Anita"]   Anita Neumann, one of Mrs. Fowler's sisters.

Bridges . . . "This Professorship"]   Robert Bridges (1844–1930) was named Poet Laureate in 1913.

Lewis . . . a paper]   *Blast No. 1.* Although dated 20 June 1914 on the cover, the first issue probably did not appear until after June 25. John Lane the publisher wanted to see the proofs before publication, and then insisted that the printers black out three lines in EP's poem "Fratres Minores" (P). This was so inefficiently done that the original lines were still legible through the inking-over.

another jap. play]   Probably "Luya." See Letter **221n.**

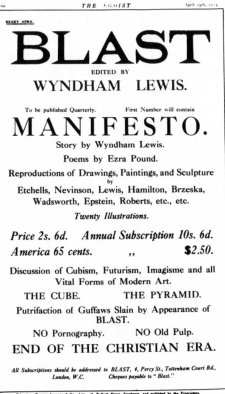

220   Dorothy to Ezra

Hotel Elysée
[Rome]
[Selections from letters of
1–3–5–6 March 1914]
Sunday

Dearest.

I sent you a p.c. yesterday before I had time to write to you. We arrived at 7 oclock A.M. exhausted–but rather excited by a very exquisite sunrise. G. [Georgie Hyde-Lees] & I spent a loitering morning in the Borghese gardens & at the Zoo, because the sun was hot & we felt in need of it after the train. The weather coming was awful–rain; snowstorm on the Mt. Cenis, & rain again below. We thought of Eva [Fowler], the Laureate [Robert Bridges] & you while we were having our own lunch on Friday– which was about TWO hours before yours. I am dying to know what happened! I wish you were out here: the sun is really hot–wh. surprizes me, the sky quite a summer blue, & there are heaps of bird-noises in the Borghese.

Two leopard-cubs yesterday at the Zoo found the sun most invigorating. They played delightful games, in a kind of rabbit-hutch place–which was quite unsafe I should imagine. We fed three elephants, & gave the seals a meal–& enjoyed ourselves thoroughly! [- - -]

I do want to try to paint in the Gardens–ma–it needs a good deal of energy. It is very lovely colouring–as the trees are still brownish from the winter & then with the sun on that colour - - - I cannot think of Chinese of any kind out here! You can understand–it would not suit!

G. [Georgie] found a stone (coffin?) this morning, covered with Romans, all exactly like T. E. Hulme. [- - -]

Oh! yes! "Erb" [Herbert Leaf] suggested to G. that we should [have] a *canvas* bath at No. 5 which folds up–(when you are in it probably). [- - -]

The flowers at the Spagna Steps are the most wonderful sight. Such colours, & so sunny & smelling. I shall have to buy a lot one day. This afternoon we potter about the Forum. I enclose a Borghese violet. [- - -]

Tuesday afternoon

We will certainly go to Daisy Meadow–not until the end of May though? I conclude somebody can char [i.e. do the housework] there for us? Have you heard when Walter [Rummel] goes to London? We ought to be back for his concert, I think.

I am glad [Robert] Bridges takes his blooming laurels in such a manner. [- - -]

I wonder–will James G.F. [Fairfax] turn up in Rome!

CHARS says they have *not* written an epithalamium–(CHARS coz. hasn't any idea how long a job it would be? Is it an ode?) [- - -]

I have found out that " 'Erb" [Herbert Leaf] also suggested that I should change my Christian name to 'Jane'–to suit Pound better. *No thank* you–no more ceremonies. I won't be baptized as well as married. [- - -]

Thursday

About Daisy M. [Meadow], Eva says we should have to take a servant– unless we could do with Fanny someone who can't cook & is deaf & dumb. Seems to me she wouldn't be much good? I can try to get our own char [charwoman], who is very nice & cooks well–& might like a fortnight in the country. Or I can try for our cook's sister, who is also a nice person & cooks v. well–I suppose either would want about 10/– a week? It would work out much [the] same as Stone Cottage? And I should like it better, as the air suits me at D.M. so well–& the rooms would be more cheerful? What do you think? Will you answer in yr. next? I shall write to Louisa [the Shakespears' housemaid] to ask her whether either of the two above-mentioned could manage it–but you don't want to have to cook entirely all that time, do you?

Good night–best purry one.

Friday morn:

[- - -] Are you very, very uncomfy at No. 5? If you are in despair about anything, perhaps Louisa [the housemaid] would help you! I bought two white blouses & a petticoat the other day. But its a dull shop place.

No. 5]   EP had just moved from 10 Church Walk to 5 Holland Place Chambers.

221   Ezra to Dorothy

5 Holland Place etc.
[Kensington]
[Selections from letters
of 3–4–6–7 March 1914]
Tuesday

Dearest:

Thanks for your [post card of the] Tempio di Vesta, you can go down there & be properly married to me if you like. [- - -]

Brzx. [Gaudier-Brzeska] came in & watched me grill a chop last evening & R. [Richard Aldington] came in to try a *mss* & they mutually disapprove of each other to *such* an extent. Dryad [Hilda Doolittle] says Faun [Richard] waters your flowers with tears every morning & that nothing else will get him out of bed. I tried to borrow enough sugar for my morning

coffee at 10.30 this A.M. but with no success. Your coffer is a fine object (with Hulme's initials on it). [- - -]

[Wyndham] Lewis says he is coming in sometime or other to get some poems for "BLAST", the revue cubiste. I've done a sketch of an epithalamium–which I shan't give him.

the Friday scrap, or Wednesday's

Rejoice in your sunshine & leopards. *Nec me respicit Apollo*. I have a cold in the head. I am dissolved as Niobe, I pour down, yea veritably pour down in showers. Neither has anything happened since I wrote this morning. I had tea in the faun-pen [with the Aldingtons] & grilled a fine steak for my supper. I am trying to translate a jap play "Luya". [- - -]

Saturday

Fat Ford [Madox Hueffer] has come back & the days are mercifully shorter. Also I have evicted Niobe. The London Group privately viewed yesterday & I have just done it for The Egoist. Epstein has done a new bird, gracious & aerial. Brzx [Gaudier-Brzeska] has a lot of stuff there. Ford wants to buy something of his. Of course G.B. isn't Epstein–not yet. Epsteins stuff throws him into the shadow, but then Epstein is 20 years older.

Bx's [Brzeska's] bust of me begins to look like father Tiber. It will be less outrageous than I thought, & eternally calm–which I ain't. He says it is for my Kā.

I find [Edward] Wadsworth, cubist, very pleasant, am going on to his place after supper. He is just up the rd. in Gloucester Walk.

[G.W.] Prothero is fussing over that jap article, but was placid when I met him at the private view yesterday. Sat for G.B. [Gaudier] this A.M. & have been scribble-scrabbling ever since. The table has come, it *is* enormous but it furnishes the big room. Wadsworth has laid his cubistic approbation upon it.

I shall be lord of that room & you shall govern the other two. I can keep all my much there, & work there.

I thought I'd go melancholy mad night before last but I've been too busy since. Thank heaven.

I don't see why we can't come up for the week of W.R.'s [Walter Rummel's] concert & then return to D.M. [Daisy Meadow]. I shall get so much more done in the country if I'm allowed to settle in for 5 or 6 weeks, & there's endless japanese notes to contend with.

Fred [Manning] has written me two nice letters. Ford gave me a large dinner last evening. He has done a really fine long poem that will be in Poetry [*Poetry*, Chicago] for June (bar messes). His new novel is–as far as it has gone–above his others. [- - -]

I don't know whether we'll need another rug or not. I must bind the ends of the carpet. There've got to be enough dishes & implements to last the day & they'll only get washed once per diem. However we're not a large family & can't be expected to have more than 2 visitors except to tea. Là-là.

The Faun [Aldington] told Ford *all* about Elizabethan drama last night–just like [Edmund] Gosse, & he has just been in with the Dryad [Hilda Doolittle] to tell me *all* about it again–*electric*. And now it's 9.30 and I'm to go to Wadsworth. [- - -]

Saturday late

Here's the beginning of a letter that I evidently mislaid–rushing off to Brzx. [Brzeska] on Friday–so the letter after will have two or three unintelligible allusions in it.

Wyndham Lewis & [Edward] Wadsworth have just been in. Lewis is starting a quarterly "BLAST". He has gone off with eleven nice blasty poems of mine. At last there's to be a magazine one can appear in without a feeling of degradation–without feeling that one is slumming among mentalities of a loathsomely lower order. Also he has taken a "school"–a nice floor in London, W.C. We're to have an Imagiste evening there. Probably we'll have the little Theatre or The Savoy [Theatre] to hold forth in, about May 26th–Imagisme & Cubism.

Poor fat Ford, all his reviews are beginning to allude to Mr. Hueffer a member of the Imagiste school of which E.P. is the leader. I've writ to three papers this A.M. to say that I didn't lead him.

The Poetry bookshop sends me an invitation to an afternoon when Hewlett, Basil Watt, Gosse, Monro, Newbolt, & Abercrombie will ALL speak = clean sweep.

Professions of admiration from the Laureate [Robert Bridges] this A.M. I shall go up to Oxford for half day sometime probably next week–it appeals to my spirit of mischief. I wonder can I get him to issue a manifesto abolishing Gosse. [- - -]

If we get that theatre [Wyndham] Lewis will do a drop scene & Brzx. [Brzeska] some large plaster figures. I wonder will dear Walter [Rummel] be here (his concert is June 3rd). And if he'd have a vocalist within call–we'll get £10.10 (to be lugubriously divided). Still it would be worth his while as adv. if he is going to have a concert later–only he *is* so unmodern (in the sense of that afternoon)–we lean towards Strobinski–did I tell you about the duck & The Sacre du Printemps? [- - -]

"BLAST"]   See Letter **219n.**

Nec me respicit Apollo]   "And Apollo has no regard for me."

jap play "Luya"]   EP translated "Luya," by Zeami Motokiyo, but it was never published.

The London Group . . . Epstein . . . Brzx]   An exhibition by the London Group (an amalgamation of the Camden Town Group and the English "Cubists") at the Goupil Gallery in Regent Street. EP went to the private viewing on Friday, March 6, but it was first advertised in the London *Times* on 12 March 1914. Among the artists exhibiting were Lewis, Wadsworth, Epstein, and Gaudier-Brzeska. T.E. Hulme did a thorough review for the *New Age,* 14 (26 March 1914), and EP a somewhat briefer comment for the *Egoist,* 1 (16 March 1914). Both Hulme and EP took special note of Epstein's "Bird Pluming Itself," EP describing it as "a cloud bent back upon itself—not a woolly cloud, but one of those clouds that are blown smooth by the wind. It is gracious and aerial."

Bx's bust of me]   EP purchased a large block of marble, the largest Gaudier had ever had to work with. "The cutting of the marble was considerably slowed down because Gaudier had poor tools, and anyone who happened to be near the studio would be called upon to help him operate Fabrucci's portable forge while he tempered his chisels" [Roger Cole, *Burning to Speak: The Life and Art of Henri Gaudier-Brzeska* (London, 1978), p. 37]. By early April 1914 it was finished; 36" high, "phallic," as both EP and Gaudier called it. After Gaudier's death it remained in Violet Hunt's garden for many years, and in January 1932 arrangements were made to ship it to Rapallo. The sculpture remained in Italy until, in November 1982, it was publicly exhibited at the D'Offay Gallery in London.

Prothero . . . jap article]   See Letter **207n.**

Wadsworth, cubist]   Edward Wadsworth (1889–1949), English artist who was closely associated with Wyndham Lewis in the Vorticist group. He was particularly original in the making of woodblocks, which he colored individually. After being invalided home during the First World War he applied his Vorticist skills to painting "dazzle-camouflage" on British naval vessels.

Ford . . . fine long poem]   Ford Madox Hueffer's long poem "On Heaven," dedicated "To V. [Violet Hunt], who asked for a plan for a working Heaven," was published in *Poetry* (Chicago), 4 (June 1914). Writing to Harriet Monroe on 23 May 1914, EP called it "the most important poem in the modern manner. The most important single poem that is" (*Letters,* No. 45).

His new novel]   Hueffer's *The Young Lovell: A Romance,* published in October 1913.

eleven nice blasty poems]   Twelve poems by EP were published in the first issue of *Blast.*

Mr. Hueffer a member of the Imagiste school . . . writ to three papers]   In the "Books of the Day" section of the *Daily News and Leader,* 6 March 1914, p. 4, J.C. Squire reviewed Ford Madox Hueffer's *Collected Poems* and four other volumes, including *Poems* by James Whitcomb Riley. In his comments on the *Collected Poems* he labeled Hueffer an "Imagiste."

> Sincerity of approach and exactitude of expression are blazoned on the banners of the self-denominated 'Imagiste' school, of which Mr. Ezra Pound is the Lord High Image, and of which Mr. Hueffer is a member. Mr. Hueffer, whose early work in verse was pretty, derivative, and dull, now holds that the realities (such as anaemic shop-girls, streets, and the White City) of our own day should be written down in the vernacular of our own day: he wants vivid metrical impressions of the diurnal things we see. His own eyes are certainly open, and there are passages in such later poems as 'To All the Dead' and 'The Starling' which have all the vividness of depiction and the imaginative power of the best of Mr. Hueffer's historical novels. Unfortunately—possibly because of his habit of writing things down 'quite powerlessly, and without much interest,' to tunes that run in his head—he is in verse loose and diffuse, and far from avoiding the superfluous word theoretically so obnoxious to the imagiste, he pads continually with meaningless repetitions and remarks obviously dictated by the need for rhymes. Curiously, his best poems are uncannily like Browning—whom he says he has never read.

EP's reply to this review appeared in the *Daily News and Leader,* 10 March 1914, p. 4.

> Sir,—In your 'Books of the Day' for March 6th you refer to Mr. Ford Madox Hueffer as a member of the 'Imagiste' school, and refer to me as if I were in some magisterial masonic manner the archimandrite of this order.
> Mr. Hueffer is not an Imagiste but an Impressionist. His poem 'The Market Place' happens to be included in a forthcoming anthology of Imagistes [*Des Imagistes*], but that is because we happen to admire his work, and not because he is a member of anything that I am in command of.

> EZRA POUND

Holland Place-chambers, Kensington, W. March 7.

Poetry bookshop . . . clean sweep]   Harold Monro's Poetry Bookshop, at 35 Devonshire St. near the British Museum, was a meeting place for poets of all persuasions. Monro believed that modern poetry should be read aloud, and public readings were held at the Bookshop on a regular basis, sometimes as often as twice a week. To EP, caught up in the avant-garde movements of 1914, the group assembled on this particular afternoon represented the conservative taste and "safe" attitudes of two generations of English poetry. The average age of those reading was well over forty, and all the poets except Watt had been represented in Quiller-Couch's *Oxford Book of Victorian Verse* (see Letter **114n**). Basil H. Watt is an obscure figure among these well-known men of letters. A friend of Harold Monro, he published an essay arguing that poetry must be declaimed or recited if it is to be appreciated ["The Poet Articulate," *Poetry Review,* 1 (November 1912)]. Watt, who was killed in World War I, is the subject of Monro's "Lament in 1915 (B.H.W.)," published in *Strange Meetings* (1921).

Strobinsky]   Stravinsky. See Letter **176n.**

222   Dorothy to Ezra

[*Hotel Elysée*]
[*Rome*]
[*7 March 1914*]
Saturday

Dearest.

I am taking a morning 'off' in the sun, in the Borghese Gardens–I have just been amused—Truly this is Italy—Three companies of soldiers have just marched past my bench. Being the only female about, they were looking at me as they passed, and the officer called to them something about 'Occhi diretti'–'Eyes front!' I gathered–& a melodramatic sigh went up - - - I was sure then that I was in Italy!

Also–Fond ma ma in black, descended just now from her car, with three pale children. For ½ hr. these three have been doing a serious Hyde Park Church Parade step between the car & mama's bench–and they are of course in the shade–not the sun–Poor little devils: its too young to be trained for society & bored with the shady side of the path.

'Step' [Georgie Hyde-Lees] has rushed off to baths of Caracalla–CHARS & their Aunt [Olivia Shakespear] are elsewhere–I am gathering in sun for you.

Later

I have had a charming letter from Mr. Eden, Venezia–and an enormous cheque from them. I see visions of all sorts of things possible with £20. We seem to be getting a good start–"unberufen"!

I want to hear from your parents. Do you think they will write (or yr. Mother)? I can't possibly write to them until they say something to me, can I?

I believe that wretched Father of mine is getting influenza–He writes that he has an awful cold & left the office early one afternoon–wh. was what happened last year.

We have been here a week–It seems ages & years since I last saw you. Oh! Yes! My cousin Harty [Harriet Childe-Pemberton] writing to O.S. [Olivia] says that after all "it is only human" that she should chiefly remember your hair!! (never having been introduced to you).

Will you shove enclosed under the opposite door for me?

Goodnight.
D.

I do hope yr. new bed will come soon–& have plenty of springs.

Sunday

Love.

Must write to H.H.S. [Dorothy's father]. O.S. [Olivia] has heard from W.B.Y. [Yeats] who seems to quite approve of us.

Yours D.

Mr. Eden, Venezia]   Rev. Frederick Eden, an old friend of Olivia Shakespear, to whom she dedicated her novel *Uncle Hilary* (1910).

"unberufen"]   "Touch wood," "knock on wood."

cousin Harty]   Harriet Louisa Childe-Pemberton, a novelist and one of Hope Shakespear's first cousins. See Letter **101n.**

223   Dorothy to Ezra

[Hotel] Elysée
[Rome]
9 March [1914]

Mon cher.

A letter from you by 2nd post. [- - -] Fred [Manning] hasn't written to me–and what is much worse, A.G. [Rev. Arthur Galton] hasn't written to O.S. [Olivia Shakespear]! Do you think its fury?? Mr. & Mrs. Fletcher [of Leweston Manor, Sherborne] have both written–the latter a little pathetically–says she knows she'll "lose" me.

I shall be delighted to spend May at D.M. [Daisy Meadow]. (W.M.R.'s

[Rummel's] concert is fixed I understand for beginning of June) but *what about the cooking?* I don't suppose either of my people could come for so long–and would you undertake to do it for so long yourself? Remember, I can't do a thing myself. If we couldn't bear it, we cld. always go back to No. 5.

What kind of fuss is [G.W.] Prothero in about the Jap article? Isn't it long enough, or lucid enough, comprehensible enough?

Is the geyser really successful?

There is a young chestnut tree outside my window, just close under, & I can positively see its leaves busting in the sun. I believe Mars & something culminate over Rome in March–so perhaps that accounts for strikes. I hope it won't be prolonged, anyway.

Tuesday evening

Strike continued this morning; no trams etc: So we have been bored: also the weather has been disgusting–all thundery & edgy. Last evening we spent at the Zoo, and Their Cousin Georgie [Hyde-Lees] made love to a keeper, & was taken into a hencoop to play with two leopard cubs–most enchanting people, and having the chief joys of the CAT. Your Coz was not quite brave enough–but spoke to them later, when they were being led on a string to their bed place–They were soft & lovely, & extremely cheerful. Their tails wave magnificently, & are very long [sketch]. I expect we shall go to speak to them again!

This afternoon G. [Georgie] has bought a very fine green enamel chain. Found a letter from F.M. [Fred Manning] at Cook's. He said you & he had quarrelled (did you know it?) but have now forgotten it. Mat Mat [Arthur Galton] says he is waiting to write to me, until he hears what O.S. [Olivia] thinks about it - - - I *do* think! - - - I supposed he always had an opinion of his own about everything.

I wrote a pile of those blessed [wedding] invitations this morning, & O.S. did some last night. Are your American ones gone yet?

I don't fancy (on rereading yr. last) that we shall have many visitors except for tea time? Tea time, we can do them quite nicely–only they'll have to have bread, butter & jam–*not* ready cut for them–because its much less trouble, and also much more in keeping with a colossal table and an oak chest! Shall we have to keep a tinned tongue for stray hungries? I think we had better go provided to D.M. [Daisy Meadow] with a small ham–as food there is rather complicated, I expect.

By the way, what *do* you mean by "I have evicted Niobe"??

Wednesday

Yours has come, & I now understand "Niobe"! Silly little thing to get a bad cold. Was it getting very wet?

I don't yet grasp W. [Wyndham] Lewis's theatre–is it to be for a season, or a day? And will Jap plays be done there by any chance?

Who & what is Strobinsky? Or do you mean Stravinsky? No; tell me about the duck & the "Sacre". [- - -]

Love

Yours

D.

Prothero . . . Jap article]   See Letters **221** and **207n.**
Cook's]   The Rome office of Thos. Cook & Son, travel agents.
Strobinsky . . . the "Sacre"]   See Letter **221.**

224   Ezra to Dorothy

5 Holland Place Chambers
[*Kensington*]
[*10 March 1914*]
Tuesday

Dearest.

I can't find anything the matter with the flat. It fits like an old glove, & seems about as convenient as my new typewriter. Its very comfortable since I got a mattress.

Fat Ford [Madox Hueffer] is going to give us six High Wycombe chairs, if thats the proper sort of small chair. He says it gives tone. I dare say he'll let you choose 'em. He says V. [Violet Hunt] has got to give us something else & she says they are both going to give us something together– Unanimism again!

Eva's cheque [Mrs. Fowler's] is for both of us so that may account for the size. My family mumbles indistinctly about table-silver, if that comes off. [- - -]

5.50 P.M.

The Daily News has been interviewing me for 2 hrs & one half. I trust they are enlightened. Anyhow they've departed & I have got on with my tea, & [Allen] Upward is going to lecture about the magical siege of Troy. I ought to have invited H.H. [Dorothy's father, Henry Hope Shakespear]– but shall take Richard [Aldington] instead.

Brzx's [Brzeska's] column gets more gravely beautiful & more phallic each week. I think it will have a deal of energy as a composition of masses. [Wyndham] Lewis & [John Gould] Fletcher & I jawed for hours last evening.

Wednesday

A very nice letter last evening. £20 is much too much to spend on anything but a magnificent work of art. At least I want you to see Epstein's new "Bird pluming itself". He has been so shocked by the Egoist that he has given up–or at least desisted from doing horrors. Besides its the proper quattro-cento thing to patronize living artists & it [is] the sort of thing to do with old [Fred] Eden's munificio anyhow. *And* in a few years no one but millionaires will be able to afford Epstein.

I don't suppose you'll hear from my family for another fortnight at least. It is only about a week or two since I wrote them to write you. I don't see how you've heard from W.B.Y. [Yeats] unless O.S. [Olivia Shakespear] wrote him before I did. He appears to be puffing me in the Abyssinian [U.S.A.] backwaters.

Upward was amusing last night. I took him on to [T.E.] Hulme's where he told scandalous facts about the deity & the Jerusalem council, etc. with great solemnity in the midst of uproarious laughter.

I have corrected proofs for that blame Egoist & scribbled until it is 2.30. I must get what sun there is going.

a toi

E.

The Daily News . . . interviewing] The interview appeared in the *Daily News and Leader,* 18 March 1914, p. 14, under the title " 'The Imagistes,' A Talk With Mr. Ezra Pound, Their Editor."

"By far the newest poet going," is how "Punch" once described Mr. Ezra Pound, one of the leaders of the "Imagiste" School of Poetry, and Editor of the Anthology of Imagiste Verse which the Poetry Bookshop will publish soon [*Des Imagistes*]. Mr. Pound, who is an American, and perhaps the most erudite of the younger poets, has spent thirteen years studying poetry in various languages, including French, German, Italian, Japanese, Portuguese, Chinese (he is now preparing for press the late Professor Fenollosa's big work on Chinese and Japanese art), Latin, and Greek. The troubadour poems of Provence, as well as the works of the Italian

poets, Arnaut Daniel and Guido Cavalcanti particularly attract him, and he has
published curiously individual and beautiful translations from each. It is interesting
to recall that it was to Mr. Ezra Pound that Mr. W.B. Yeats transferred the money
prize awarded to him by "Poetry," the well-known American magazine, not very
long ago. Mr. Pound will be one of the contributors to "Blast," Mr. Wyndham
Lewis's new Cubist art quarterly.

Steindhal [sic], when he said that clear and precise prose was better than
superfluously ornamental poetry; Goethe, when he declared that modern poets put
too much water in their ink; and Keats, when he said he hated poetry that had a
palpable design on him, were all, albeit unconsciously, talking in the language of
the "Imagiste." That was the impression gathered when I asked Mr. Pound to
explain "Imagism" in terms comprehensible to "the man in the street."

Imagiste Don'ts.

"Here," said Mr. Pound, "is a list of 'Don'ts' I tabulated for those beginning to
write verse. They embody a good many of the Imagiste ideas [adapted from "A
Few Don'ts by an Imagiste," *Poetry* (Chicago), 1 (March 1913)]:

"Pay no attention to the criticisms of men who have never themselves written a
notable work.

"Use no superfluous word and no adjective which does not reveal something.

"Go in fear of abstractions. Don't retail in mediocre verse what has already been
done in good prose.

"Don't imagine that the art of poetry is any simpler than the art of music or that
you can please the expert before you have spent at least as much effort on the art
of verse as the average piano teacher spends on the art of music.

"Be influenced by as many great artists as you can, but have the decency either
to acknowledge the debt outright or try to conceal it.

"Consider the definiteness of Dante's presentation as compared with Milton's
rhetoric. Read as much of Wordsworth as does not seem to be unutterably dull.

"If you want the gist of the matter go to Sappho, Catullus, Villon, Heine when
he is in the vein, Gautier when he is not too frigid, or if you have not the tongues
seek out the leisurely Chaucer.

"Good prose will do you no harm. There is good discipline to be had by trying
to write it. Translation is also good training."

The Crime of Mediocrity.

"But there are great poets," I suggested, "who have not undergone such a vigorous
discipline as this—Burns, for instance!"

"Ah, but Burns was a great genius, and his natural gifts were not corrupted by a
smattering of education wrongly directed. The training he received at home may
have been narrow, but it was deep. It is better for a poet not to be educated at all
than to be half-educated.

"Poetry," continued Mr. Pound, "is the one art in which mediocrity is unpar-
donable. Literature is the poor man's bridge to the beautiful. A shepherd, a plough-
man or a miner may never be able to see the best art or the best sculpture, but he
need never be shut out from the best poetry. To my mind, the object of poetry is
to focus the light on something, and I do not care what the reader sees in a poem
so long as he sees beauty. There are two ways of presenting beauty—by satire,

which clears away the rubbish and allows the central loveliness to reveal itself; and by the direct presentation of beauty itself."

The Unemotional Poet.

"I heard a famous poet say not long ago that the great poet was never emotional. Do you agree with that?"

"Yes, absolutely; if by emotion is meant that he is at the mercy of every passing mood, and that he sits down and writes a dirge about the hollowness of life because he happens to have indigestion, or because he cannot pay his baker's bill. The only kind of emotion worthy of a poet is the inspirational emotion which energises and strengthens, and which is very remote from the everyday emotion of sloppiness and sentiment. So many young poets today, both here and in America, are swayed chiefly by the latter feeling. They write stuff which rhymes, it is true, but which is far inferior to good prose, and infinitely easier to do."

"What do you find is the most noticeable difference between the young poets of England and America?"

"What I have noticed chiefly is that the Americans are more alive and quicker, but they do not appear to rely so much on their own judgment. They refer to authorities, and are too fond of quoting. In England they are less alive, but they quote less."

Humour and the Poet.

"Do you think a sense of humour helps a poet? Shelley did not."

"No, but Heine did, and I agree with Heine. A sense of humour prevents a poet from mistaking sentiment [for] emotion, and also keeps him better balanced. Even a poet can take himself too seriously."

In connection with the forthcoming Anthology of Imagiste poetry, which will include works by Mr. Ford Madox Hueffer and Mr. Allen Upward, it has been stated that these well-known writers are Mr. Pound's followers, a suggestion that he strongly repudiates. "Next to Mr. Yeats," said Mr. Pound, "I regard Mr. Hueffer as one of our strongest forces to-day. Besides, it was Mr. Hueffer who first introduced me to the English public when he was editor of the 'English Review,' so it is foolishness to call him one of my followers. The Anthology does not represent the personalities of those included, nor does it represent their differences, but the line where they come together, their agreement that the cake-icing on the top of poetry—the useless adjectives and the unnecessary similes which burden verse like cumbrous ornaments—should be avoided."

[The interviewer ("M.M.B.") then adds the following samples of "Imagiste" poems: "In a Station of the Metro" and "The Return" by Ezra Pound; "A Chinese Queen on a Lacquered Throne . . ." by Ford Madox Hueffer; "The Milky Way" and "The Bitter Purple Willows" by Allen Upward.]

Upward . . . siege of Troy]   At the Ordinary Meeting of the Royal Anthropological Institute on 10 March 1914 Allen Upward read a paper on "The Magical Siege of Troy." See Letters **182n** and **184**.

Brzx's column]   See Letter **221n**.

Epstein's new "Bird pluming itself"]   See Letter **221n**.

shocked by the Egoist]   Either a reference to the general avant-garde content of the magazine, or a specific allusion to EP's article on "The New Sculpture" [*Egoist*, 1 (16 February 1914)].

225   Henry Hope Shakespear to Ezra

[*Fair copy of original, from H.H.S.'s office files*]

[*Shakespear & Parkyn*]
[*8 John Street*]
[*London*]
12 March 1914

Dear Ezra,

As you are not a British Subject it is important to ascertain definitely whether a marriage carried out with the formalities required by the Laws of England is all that is necessary.

This is a matter on which I have no means of forming any professional opinion. It may for instance be necessary to give some notice to the U.S.A. consul.

I want you to write to the U.S.A. Consul a letter somewhat in the form enclosed. He will no doubt take more notice of a request addressed to him by a compatriot than if I were to write to him.

I do not know what facts determine the particular State to which you belong and it is notorious that the marriage laws vary with different States in the U.S.A. It is possible that the Consul may refuse to advise you and refer you to some Lawyer conversant with the American Laws. If so you can leave me to communicate with such lawyer as I don't want to put you to any expense.

Please don't delay & let me hear the result.

yr. sincerely
H. Hope Shakespear

P.S.
The address is: The Consul General U.S.A,
                    42–45 New Broad Street, E.C.

[Enclosure]

Suggested letter

Sir,

I am a Citizen of the U.S.A. & am about to marry an English lady. I am asked to produce an authoritative Statement as to whether any, & if so what, formalities beyond those required for a marriage between two English persons, are necessary to make such marriage valid according to the Laws of the U.S.A.

To enable you to reply it may be necessary that I should inform you that I was born on the .... at .... & that my Parents who are both still living reside in Philadelphia.

Although I have for the ...... years last past resided in England I have not changed my allegiance & remain a citizen of the U.S.A.

226   Ezra to Henry Hope Shakespear

[*Typed*]

> 5 *Holland Place Chambers*
> [*London*] *W.*
> [*12 March 1914*]

Dear Mr Shakespear

I have written at once to the consul general. Of course divorce is a much more difficult job in America than you seem to think, and as for Pennsylvania, originally a quaker colony, the original inhabitants were so on guard against illegitimacy that it [was] practically impossible even to cohabit without being legally married. At least I believe if you live there with a woman and call her your wife you are ipso facto united in the eyes of the law. At least a friend of mine in the law told me a number of curious facts of this sort. It's from the old quaker ceremony of standing up before witnesses in meeting–gradually extended, I believe, to those who don't attend meeting.

Also it is impossible to get into the United States with a woman who isn't your wife. As you may remember Maxim Gorky was shut out. And Marie Lloyd and a certain Dillon were recently let in only for a few weeks on agreement to leave at the end of 'em, and have since been married almost by force. Gorky went over with a mistress or two wives or something or other.

Even the Nevada divorces which were a luxury for the rich have been, I believe, more or less shut down on.

Anyhow I've written off to the consul and if there is any machinery for registration, I will see that it is complied with.

yours sincerely
Ezra

Maxim Gorky . . . Marie Lloyd . . . Dillon]   When the Russian author Maksim Gorky (1868–1936) toured the United States in 1906 with his mistress, there was a public outcry. When Marie Lloyd (1870–1922), the English music-hall performer, sailed for the United States in 1913, she was accompanied by the jockey Bernard Dillon, who had been disqualified from racing. Although still married to Alec Hurley, she traveled as "Mrs. Dillon." When she and Dillon arrived in New York they were arrested, sent to Ellis Island, and threatened with deportation. But a last-minute reprieve allowed her to stay in the United States.

227   Ezra to Henry Hope Shakespear

5 Holland Place Chambers
[London] W.
[14 March 1914]
Saturday

Dear Mr. Shakespear

I sent your draft of letter on to the consulate with a note of my own & have received the enclosed, which seems to cover the matter.

yours sincerely
Ezra

228   American Consular Service to Ezra Pound

[*Typed*]

American Consular Service
45 New Broad Street
London E.C.
14 March 1914

Dear Sir:–

In reply to your letter of the 12th. instant, I have to say that to the best of my knowledge and belief a marriage legally solemnized in the United Kingdom is duly recognized in every state of the United States.

In order to have immediate proof of marriage it frequently happens that a certificate of marriage issued by the Registrar is presented to this office for authentication which certificate is acceptable in all parts of the United States as proof of marriage.

The letter of Mr. Shakespear is returned herewith.

Yours faithfully,
[sgnd.] Carl R. Loop
Deputy Consul General.

229   Dorothy to Ezra

[*Hotel*] *Elysée*
[*Rome*]
begun 16 [*March 1914*]
Monday

Mao!

We have just taken our tickets for the "auto" to *Ostia* for tomorrow. We pray for fine weather. There are all sorts of things to see there, we believe. This morning we saw one of the most lovely idols in the world. We managed a special permit–as the Creature is not yet on view. It is a little bronze image, gilded, surrounded by a snake. We have no information about it yet, except that it was lately found on the Janiculum in a tempio [sketch]. Slightly Egyptian, & with the most wonderful little Greek face–The whole

figure is shrouded–the garment covers its head making large sort of ears &
then forms the body [sketch]. The arms are bound close to the sides by the
snake–whose tail begins at the feet, & whose head makes a helmet-shaped
crest on the figure's head. The whole is some 18 inches high. I really do
wish you could see it–I'll bring a photo back.

Yesterday, Sunday, we went in to a Futurist Exh: of paintings. One man,
Balla, seems to be able to paint; his were quite fine, & full of life & move-
ment–But most distractingly restless. I think one would go mad quickly
with them in a room. There were two other enlightening ones by Severini
(I think). One was centripetal force and the other c. fugal. The former,
yellows and white, outside, and blues & greens inside [sketch]. Centrifugal
was a [sketch] of yellows & white in centre & blues & greens solidly sur-
rounding it. Georgie [Hyde-Lees] & me–we decided! My receptive yellow
outside–her ferment inside, being calmed by the ring of blue & green! I
don't make out how to apply it to you! [- - -]

Have you ever heard from my Uncle Herbert Leaf?

Tuesday?
17th anyhow.

We have been to Ostia–a little disappointing as we are not archaeological.
A queer Mithraic temple, and a lovely "Victory". Also the finest storm–
We had to flee before it, to a lunch Trattoria–I got yr. typed letter when I
got home.

Personally I don't care for prints–except Japs! I am sure cushions would
be more satisfactory–and one gets very tired of many things on the walls–
& there are already several to go on to them.

I wrote plainly to A.G. [Arthur Galton] that I was afraid "my news was
unpalatable" & then about Roman remains. We have taken our return
berths, you may like to hear–so that I am coming back, unless the Gods
waft me away–G. [Georgie] & I spend a night in Paris on the way, as we
really cannot stand that journey through. We ought to arrive in London some
time on March 30th–a Monday, and from that day is three little weeks to
our 'ceremony'–I have just been told by O.S. [Olivia Shakespear] that the
Church of Eng. does not consider marriage as a sacrament - - - A quoi bon
alors - - - ? You are now with The Laureate [Robert Bridges]–I am really
very amused to hear that he seems a decent kind of person: so unexpected.
Also I felt convinced you did not know you had quarrelled with F.M.
[Fred Manning]! I suppose because of "the effect of constantly talking
with inferior people", the ultimate wisdom becomes contemplative &
mountain-top-py?

The Romans must have been a vile & practical people–but their large remains are exciting. Ostia, I believe, was suburban–therefore small.

Au revoir–
A toi.

Futurist . . . Balla . . . Severini]   The Italian painters Giacomo Balla (1874–1958) and Gino Severini (1883–1966) were among the signers of the 1910 "Manifesto of the Futurist Painters." DS probably saw their works at the Galleria Futurista, which had been recently opened by the painter and critic Giuseppe Sprovieri. In April–May 1914 the gallery mounted a Free International Futurist Exhibition which contained paintings and sculptures by twenty-four artists.

230   Henry Hope Shakespear to Ezra

[*Fair copy of original, from H.H.S.'s office files*]

[*Shakespear & Parkyn*]
[*8 John Street*]
[*London*]
17 March 1914

Dear Ezra,

I thank you for your letter enclosing reply from the American Consul which appears quite satisfactory. I must give notice in the next few days for the Banns.

Will you please let me have a line to say whether you have any Christian name other than Ezra as we must get that right.

Yr. sincerely
H. Hope Shakespear

P.S.
I shall be in this evening if you care to come in & smoke a cigarette.   H.S.

231   Dorothy to Ezra

[*Hotel*] *Elysée*
[*Rome*]
[*20 March 1914*]
begun Friday

Cher.

[- - -] Thank you for a letter with a telegram & W.B.Y.'s [Yeats's letter]. Rather a poor, little depressed thing? Have you been? I wish you had some of this sun–Though we have had two or three awful storms.

A copy of The Egoist came yesterday, but I have not read any of it yet.

O.S. [Olivia Shakespear] has had a long letter from her sister Florence [Tucker] from Los Angeles. She (F.) heard some people talking about you only a day or two before, & they said that of course E.P. was only your nom de plume, & that *really* you were - - - mentioning a name which she had forgotten. So shall I be Mrs E.P. or something quite different?! Just think how we might worry H.H.S. [Dorothy's father] about it! My Aunt F. wonders whether I shall be getting my clothes in Paris–wild idea!

I have received a cheque from Isabella Johnson [Lionel Johnson's sister]. It strikes me we shall have to have a safe next! [- - -]

Have you written to your consul to find out abt. the marriage being valid?

We found "scavi" [excavations] yesterday of a Mithraic Temple (where the gold & bronze idol was found).–& it was built in a queer (mystical?) shape–& □ Coz. [Georgie Hyde-Lees] played at making triangles fit into it all the afternoon, instead of sleeping: then she had bad indigestion–wh. I daresay was triangular–I had to use circles before I rested - - - I don't much like triangles–They are so cornery.

Love
D.

W.B.Y.'s] On 8 March 1914 Yeats, then touring the United States, wrote to EP from Pittsburgh congratulating him on the forthcoming marriage. "You will have a beautiful & clever wife & that is what few men get."

232   Dorothy to Ezra

[Hotel] Elysée
[Rome]
21 March [1914]
Saturday

Dearest.

I am starting home, with any luck, today week–Sat. 28. *and* J.G.F. [James G. Fairfax] arrives here on 29th!! We have taken a room for him– I have had two priceless letters from him–which I am keeping for you. G. [Georgie Hyde-Lees] & I spend Sunday night in Paris, and start home on Monday 30th by a 9.50 A.M. train, which gets in to Charing X some time about 5 ocl. (I am uncertain of 5 ocl.). So you might come to meet me, if you care for the hurly-burly at Ch. X.

G. & I have been for an old-book-shop prowl: She found one work on astrology–for 10c. [centesimi]. It is in Latin, & has nice looking diagrams. [- - -]

What on earth were you & W.B.Y. [Yeats] to have done, if you had had the Cottage last winter?

I have been reading the Egoist. I wonder why you are "off" the Epstein bird? It doesn't last, I suppose.

I have written to F.M. [Fred Manning]. I wrote last Sunday, and to Mat Mat [Arthur Galton]–*not* in the same envelope. Any forrader about F.M.'s magazine idea? Surely there are enough magazines going, mostly useless? And I am sure BLAST will be horrible. I WON'T have a W. [Wyndham] Lewis Lobster picture, anyway. I think they are filthy.

I knew A.M.W. Sh's kat had taken a prize at Madison Sq. Kat Show– I expect it was that–& not another prize? It was abt. Xmas-time. Who told you about it? [- - -]

I am glad you & H.H.S. [Dorothy's father] spent an evening together. I wonder what you talked of, & what he makes of you.

Sunday

A letter from your Mother came today which I am answering at once. She wants me to persuade you to take me over to them–but I shan't– You don't want to, do you? I am sure it would be much better for them to do the journey! I probably shan't have said a thing in my letter that she will want–but how are either of us to know about each other. Her letter is most kind. I wonder what her hand-writing means! I am afraid I must ask you to stamp my answer (no Eng. stamps with me) & address it–because–I thought 'The Mint' was Philadelphia–and yet I thought you said "Wyncote Pa." meant Pennsylvania–ROT. It's gone to the Mint??? Sorry to be so silly.

I shan't write her a longer letter until I have seen you–& know more what you have, and have not told her–about the flat etc: etc: or what might interest her.

Là là là

O.S. [Olivia Shakespear] has done another Gabalis entretien which I shall bring back with me for you.

A toi cher

D.

W. Lewis Lobster picture]   For a period in 1912–13 Lewis did drawings of troglodytic figures cavorting in forms that look remarkably like up-ended lobsters. See Walter Michel, *Wyndham Lewis: Paintings and Drawings* (London, 1971), particularly illustrations 43, 45, and 54.

A.M.W. Sh's kat]   Alexander Muirson Wake Shakespear. A show "of rare Siamese cats" was held at the Astor Hotel in New York beginning on 17 December 1913. See Letter **198.**

'The Mint' . . . *"Wyncote Pa."*]   EP's father was an assayer at the Philadelphia Mint; the Pound home was in Wyncote, a suburb of Philadelphia.

another Gabalis]   See Letter **207n.** Olivia's translation, "Memoirs of a Charming Person," appeared anonymously in the *Egoist* in five "Conversations" (16 March–1 June, 1914).

233   Dorothy to Ezra

[Hotel] Elysée
[<i>Rome</i>]
24 [March 1914]
Tuesday

Dearest.

I had a long epistle from Eva [Fowler], saying Fanny DeafMute *can* cook, a little, plain - - - I shall not do anything until I am home again. Mat Mat [Arthur Galton] sent O.S. [Olivia Shakespear] the Times Lit.

Sup. with Henry James on the modern novel. It is hopelessly involved but I think he means that there is Much Ado: It is to be continued.

Angela, our housemaid here, is very glad that I am to be married. She says she likes 'ragazze' [lasses] to get married if it's going to be a success—otherwise 'migliore' [better] that they remain unmarried. She wanted to know from O.S. [Olivia] if I wasn't rather young? Was I 20? She is a nice soul—and knows only Italian.

Yesterday I bought a delightful Square of worked brownish linen—do for a tea table-cloth, or a cushion—or various - - - 30 inches square. Did I say I had also bought a green silk 'En tout cas'? It has an amberish handle, and is a little flashy, but charming.

We were taken into a courtyard this morning to visit "the-nicest-of-all-cats"—an enormous two year old—tabby & white: Its belongings *are* so proud of it! and wouldn't take £1,000 for it, or some such equivalent.

I shall post this tomorrow (Wed:) & not write again—as with any luck, we ought to meet on Monday.

Wednesday

Horrid Little Thing—no letter from you today—! It has been pouring all the morning—& I have been trying to read, in Italian, some of the wisdom of Hermes Trismagistus. I believe it to be *very* much diluted for the use of the R. Catholics. It feels like the shell with nothing inside: not even a rattle.

CHARS have enclosed some folly—about Aunt Lou, the Min Min etc. *etc.*

The train is
>   5.12 P.M.
>   Charing X
>   on Monday.

You will probably meet Bunk [Dorothy's uncle] waiting for G. [Georgie Hyde-Lees].

I can't make much out of "Little Bill's" poem in the Egoist. I can't grasp the intrinsic value of the old woman at all.

>   Au Revoir
>   à bientot
>   A Toi D.

[*Enclosure in Olivia Shakespear's hand*]

E.P. from CHARS.

CHARS beg to observe that they've had niente to do with that silly business about the old Min Min. They knew it would end in disaster, & now Their Aunt is quite upset at such a scandal in a hitherto abjectly respectable famiglia—in fact Their Aunt can hardly believe it, after a career of solid virtue for 94 years. They think Binny must have been napping. CHARS are inclined to think, if there is any truth in what the Gnome says, that it will be a case of a Concepzione Immaculata—but even if there *is* no truth in it, the Gnome must be kept an eye on, because the Old Min Min will be back with her Coz on the 30th. Dio Loro! What a world. They are saturated like Henry James' Novelists in the Times Litt. Supp. because its raining so hard.

CHARS

Times Lit. Sup. . . . James]   Henry James's article on "The Younger Generation" was published in the *Times Literary Supplement* in two parts, 19 March and 2 April 1914. It was reprinted with revisions as "The New Novel" in *Notes on Novelists* (1914).

Aunt Lou]   Harriet Louisa Childe-Pemberton, "Aunt Lou" to Olivia Shakespear but "Cousin Harty" to Dorothy. See Letters **101n** and **222n**.

the Min Min]   See Letter **39n**.

"Little Bill's" poem]   William Carlos Williams's "The Wanderer: A Rococo Study" was published in the *Egoist,* 1 (16 March 1914). In the poem Williams reflects on his own poetic development, and presents the Muse of "modernity" as a powerful old woman/goddess.

E.P. from CHARS]   Communications from CHARS are essentially unparaphrasable, but this seems to be the gist: "CHARS want EP to know that they had nothing to do with the fuss between Dorothy (the Min Min) and Aunt Lou (probably Harriet Louisa Childe-Pemberton, the Gnome) concerning the coming marriage. Olivia (CHARS' aunt) is upset over the family squabble. CHARS think Binny (a cat named after Laurence Binyon) must have been napping. If there is any truth in what Aunt Lou says, some of the family may not be at the wedding reception; but even if this is untrue, she must be watched carefully, since Dorothy will return to London on the 30th with her Coz (Georgie) and may be subjected to family pressure. What a world! The pouring rain in Rome has left CHARS saturated like the novelists in Henry James's review."

234   Ezra to Dorothy

> *5 Holland Place Chambers*
> *[Kensington]*
> *[25 March 1914]*

Dearest:

Right. I will hang round Charing X. in the vague hope that the channel boat wont sink. The Brzx. [Gaudier-Brzeska's head of EP] looks better. [John] Cournos returned from U.S.A. tremulously joyous at his escape.

NO, I am not going to America. I dare say my family would be glad to see you, but if you want to go, you can make the perrilllllous voyage alone. Mother's handwriting??? New York, born 14th St. & second ave. when it was the thing to be born there, porched house, 23rd. st. also at proper time. Uncle's estate on Hudson, reckless rider. Married wild H.L.P. [Homer Loomis Pound] & went to a mining town, returned east to domesticity–traditions, irony, no knowledge of french literature in the original, admiration for the brothers De Goncourt. Early painting lessons, penchant for the pretty–horror of all realism in art. Belief in the pleasant. Would like, or would have liked–to see me in the Diplomatic Corps– "Ambassadour to the Ct. of St. James." Believes that I should be well clothed. Prude if god ever permitted one to exist.

"Anthologie des Imagistes" arrives from U.S.A. so *that's* all right.

Man has just been in to adjust the springs of the box-couch, so *that's* all right.

Richard [Aldington] & I are going down to visit old [Wilfred Scawen] Blunt tomorrow (Thursday)–till Saturday. The Egoist has had £250 chucked at it so R. [Richard Aldington] has got a job for 6 months anyhow. I am doing articles on Hueffer (done) & W.B.Y's new book for "Poetry" [*Poetry,* Chicago] & trying another batch of Fenollosa. The Poetry Bookshop magazine [*Poetry and Drama*] has a perfectly appalling misprint in my crocus poem.

F.M. [Fred Manning] hasn't got much further with his review. It would be an excellent counter Blast.

I wonder will this get to you in Roma at all. là là. I will quit anyhow & get on with that critique of W.B.Y.

> à toi
> E.

"Anthologie des Imagistes"]   The book version of *Des Imagistes: An Anthology* was published in New York by Albert and Charles Boni on 2 March 1914. EP's use of the phrase "Anthologie des Imagistes" explains the title, in which "Anthologie" is to be understood.

The Egoist . . . £250]   When EP's negotiations to have Amy Lowell take over and finance the *Egoist* fell through, Harriet Shaw Weaver gave £250 anonymously to maintain publication. See Lidderdale and Nicholson, *Dear Miss Weaver,* pp. 86–91.

articles on Hueffer . . . & W.B.Y.'s new book]   "Mr Hueffer and the Prose Tradition in Verse," a review of his *Collected Poems* [*Poetry* (Chicago), 4 (June 1914)], and "The Later Yeats," a review of *Responsibilities* [*Poetry* (Chicago), 4 (May 1914)].

another batch of Fenollosa]   This could be the Noh material that led to *Certain Noble Plays of Japan* (1916) and *'Noh' Or Accomplishment* (1916/17), or the notes that formed the basis for the poems in *Cathay* (1915).

misprint in my crocus poem]   When "Coitus" (P) was published in *Poetry and Drama,* 2 (March 1914), the first line ("The gilded phaloi of the crocuses") was misprinted as "The glided phaloi of the crocusses."

235   Dorothy to Ezra

> *Hotel Elysée*
> *Rome*
> [*27 March 1914*]
> *Friday*

[*Postcard*]

Yes: I will come to see you & F.M.H. [Ford Madox Hueffer] choose chairs with pleasure (unless I am much more tired than I expect to be). So will you arrange–the morning would be best, I expect? Have just had a congrat: card from Miss Wessells - - - qui è? Have been packing - - - The [wedding] notice in the Morn: Post seems to have led to much work for our postman at No. 12 [Brunswick Gardens] - - - all about wedding-cakes etc: too!

Au revoir   D.

Miss Wessells]   A relative of Isabel Pound.

Mr & Mrs Hope Shakespear
At Home,
on the occasion of
the marriage of their daughter,
Dorothy,
to
Ezra Pound,
on Saturday, April 18th,
3·30 – 6·30.

12 Brunswick Gardens,
    Kensington, W.   R.S.V.P.

Appendix I
Biographical
Notes

ALDINGTON, RICHARD (1892–1962). Born in Hampshire, educated at Dover College and University College, London. He began writing poetry at an early age, and worked energetically with EP to promote the first phase of Imagism, although later he took a somewhat ironic view of the movement. For a time he was sub-editor of the *New Freewoman* and its successor, the *Egoist*. In October 1913 he married Hilda Doolittle; they were divorced in 1938 after a long estrangement. His first volume of poetry, *Images, 1910–1915* (1915), was followed by several other volumes, including *Images of War* (1919) and *Collected Poems* (1928). Aldington was shell-shocked in World War I and later wrote one of the best novels of the war, *Death of a Hero* (1929).

> They put him on Hill 70, in a trench
> dug through corpses
> With a lot of kids of sixteen,
> Howling and crying for their mamas,
> And he sent a chit back to his major:
> I can hold out for ten minutes
> With my sergeant and a machine-gun.
> And they rebuked him for levity.

(Canto 16)

Although the relationship between EP and Aldington cooled in the years after World War I the two poets kept in touch with each other, and Aldington wrote to Ezra and Dorothy in Washington throughout the 1950s.

Aldington met D.H. Lawrence in 1914 and became a devoted friend. After Lawrence's death he edited collections of his prose and poetry, and wrote a sympathetic study, *Portrait of a Genius, But . . .* (1950). Aldington's autobiography, *Life for Life's Sake,* was published in 1941.

BRZESKA, HENRI GAUDIER. *See* GAUDIER, HENRI.

CHARS. Central figures in the private mythology of the Shakespear family. The name may have originated in a child's mispronunciation of the French *chats*. It has several related meanings that vary with the context.

1. Cats; specifically, the cats in the Shakespear household.
2. The cat spirit; the quiddity of cat.
3. The spirit of mischief, sometimes with overtones of the grotesque. One member of the family sent a post card of the Ely Imps (a grotesque carving in the choir of Ely Cathedral) addressed to "Messrs. Chars, c/o Miss D. Shakespear." In May 1922 while Dorothy and EP were on a walking tour in Italy, DP sent Mrs. Shakespear a post card of a fat saucy angel from the Tempio Malatestiano in Rimini, commenting: "Good marble one, this, CHARS." And about 1929/30 EP sent Omar Pound a post card of more cherubs on a font in San Marco, Venice, to which DP added the note "from Ezra. Observe CHARS." After a visit to the cinema (Letter **115**) DS told EP that "in front were two CHAR-children: they were stout & active, with fair curly heads & gray eyes–aged anything between 3 & 300 years. Such loves, & full of wickedness."

COURNOS, JOHN (1881–1966). Poet, playwright, novelist, reviewer, and translator. Born in Russia (with the surname Korshoon), he came to the United States at age ten, where he first learned English. He held a number of jobs before turning to newspaper work. In 1912 he left his position as Sunday editor of the *Philadelphia Record* and moved to London, where he met EP and wrote an article on him for the *Record* ("Native Poet Stirs London," 5 January 1913; see Letter **132n**). EP included a poem by Cournos in the anthology *Des Imagistes* (1914). Cournos also knew the Aldingtons, D.H. Lawrence, and John Gould Fletcher. His first three novels—*The Mask* (1919), *The Wall* (1921), and *Babel* (1922)—form a trilogy based on his own experiences. His later works were mainly biographical and historical studies. In 1935 he published his *Autobiography*.

DOOLITTLE, HILDA (1886–1961). Born in Bethlehem, Pennsylvania, the daughter of a well-known astronomer, she was educated in Philadelphia and spent two years at Bryn Mawr College, where Marianne Moore was a classmate. In the spring of 1905 she met EP, who later gathered a number of his early poems into *Hilda's Book,* a hand-bound, vellum-covered volume that he presented to her (see Appendix II). EP named her "The Dryad," and one of the poems in *Hilda's Book* is "The Tree," which was first published in *A Lume Spento* (1908) and later became the opening poem in *Personae: The Collected Poems.* EP and Hilda were "engaged" for a time, but when the engagement was broken off—partly as a result of opposition from her parents—Frances Gregg "filled the gap" left in her life (see Letter **113n**). In the summer of 1911 Hilda traveled to Europe with Frances and Mrs. Gregg, and by October they were in London, where Hilda joined EP's circle and met Richard Aldington, whom she married in October 1913. Meanwhile EP had launched the Imagist movement, and a group of her poems published in the January 1913 issue of *Poetry* (Chicago) was signed—at EP's insistence—"H.D., *Imagiste*." *Sea Garden*

(1916), her first collection of poems, displays the classical, chiseled qualities of her early style. Twenty years after the publication of her first poems EP declared that "imagism was formulated almost in order to give emphasis to certain qualities that she possessed to the maximum degree: a mytho-poetic sense which was deep, true and of Nature" (*Il Mare,* 18 March 1933).

Hilda Doolittle's early relationship with EP is the subject of her novel *HERmione,* completed in 1927 but not published until 1981, where he appears as "George Lowndes." See also the autobiographical *End to Torment* (1979), which includes *Hilda's Book,* and Barbara Guest, *Herself Defined: The Poet H.D. and Her World* (New York, 1984).

EMERY, FLORENCE. *See* FARR, FLORENCE.

FAIRFAX, JAMES GRIFFYTH (1886–1976). Born in New South Wales, he was educated at Winchester and New College, Oxford. His first book of poems, *The Gates of Sleep* (1906), was followed by *Poems* (1908), *The Troubled Pool* (1911), and five later volumes of verse and translations. He was a member of Frederic Manning's circle, and first met EP in January 1909. Fairfax served with distinction in Mesopotamia during World War I, attaining the rank of captain. Later (1924–29) he was a Conservative member of the House of Commons. Although he visited Australia several times and was admitted to the New South Wales Bar in 1920, Fairfax spent most of his life in England before retiring to the south of France.

FARR, FLORENCE (1860–1917). An accomplished actress, she married the actor Edward Emery in 1884; they were divorced in 1894. She was a close friend of George Bernard Shaw and thought of herself as a "new" or "transitional" woman. One of her stage roles was Rebecca West in Ibsen's *Rosmersholm.* She produced *The Land of Heart's Desire* in 1894 (written by Yeats at her request); acted in *The Countess Cathleen* in 1899; and arranged a performance of *The Shadowy Waters* at a Theosophical convention in 1905. With Yeats she developed a method of speaking verse to music, and Arnold Dolmetsch made an instrument for them, "half-lyre, half-psaltery." Mabel Dolmetsch called her Yeats's "muse." Her semi-autobiographical novel *The Solemnization of Jacklin* (see Letter **100n**) was published in 1912, the year in which she left England for Ceylon to teach in a Buddhist college. In Yeats's poem "All Souls' Night," an epilogue to *A Vision,* he summons the spirit of Florence Farr

> Who finding the first wrinkles on a face
> Admired and beautiful,
> And knowing that the future would be vexed
> With 'minished beauty, multiplied commonplace,
> Preferred to teach a school
> Away from neighbour or friend,
> Among dark skins, and there
> Permit foul years to wear
> Hidden from eyesight to the unnoticed end.

FLETCHER, JOHN GOULD (1886–1950). Born in Little Rock, Arkansas, Fletcher was educated privately and at Harvard. He lived in London from 1909 to 1914, and published five slim volumes in 1913. Reviewing two of them—*The Dominant City* and *Fool's Gold*—in the *New Freewoman* (15 September 1913), EP praised Fletcher for his individuality and his knowledge of modern French poetry: "Mr. Fletcher is one of the very few men on this side of the channel who are in any sense in touch [with] the poetic activity on the other." But later, after Fletcher joined Amy Lowell in promoting "Amygism," EP delivered a harsher judgment. Writing to Harriet Monroe on 31 January 1915 he said that Fletcher "has a lawless and uncontrolled ability to catch certain effects, mostly of colour, but no finishing sense" (*Letters,* No. 61). After Fletcher returned to the United States in 1914 he published a number of volumes of poetry, including *Irradiations: Sand and Spray* (1915) and *Goblins and Pagodas* (1916). His *Selected Poems* (1938) won the Pulitzer Prize. Fletcher's years in London and his association with Imagism are recalled in his autobiography, *Life Is My Song* (1937).

FORD, FORD MADOX. *See* HUEFFER, FORD MADOX.

FOWLER, EVA (1871–1921). Eldest daughter of Paul Neumann (1839–1901), a naturalized American of Prussian origin who was Attorney-General in Hawaii and represented Queen Liliokulani when Hawaii was annexed to the U.S.A. She married Alfred ("Taffy") Fowler (1860–1933), a maker of steam ploughs referred to as "Hamish" in Canto 18.

Eva Fowler was deeply interested in psychic and occult matters, and some of Yeats's experiments in automatic writing took place in her cottage, Daisy Meadow, near Brasted in Kent. She was buried in St. Mary's Catholic cemetery at Kensal Green, London, near Frederic Manning.

GALTON, REV. ARTHUR (1852–1921). Went to Clare College, Cambridge, in 1873, but joined the Roman Catholic Church before completing his terms. He became a priest in 1880 and was sent to Windermere in 1884. There he met Matthew Arnold, who impressed him greatly: hence his nickname "Mat-Mat." He left the Roman Catholic Church in 1885 and completed his University career at New College, Oxford, where he met Lionel Johnson. Served as private secretary to the Governor of New South Wales (1893–98), where he first met Frederic Manning. On returning to England he was re-admitted into the Church of England in 1898, took Holy Orders, and in 1904 was appointed to the living at Edenham in Lincolnshire, where he eventually provided a home for Frederic Manning. He wrote literary essays on the Roman Church, on Thomas Cromwell, and on controversial religious and political subjects, and in 1897 published *Two Essays upon Matthew Arnold, with some of his letters to the author.* One of his pamphlets, *Acer in Hostem* (Windermere, 1913), is dedicated to "Dorothy Shakespear: In Memory Of DREAMING HOURS At OXFORD. With a Hope Of MORE GOLDEN REALITIES in ROME." He was a fine classical scholar and an ardent Francophile. He be-

queathed his 50-volume edition of Voltaire's works to Olivia Shakespear, and
it was later read and extensively used by both EP and DS.

GAUDIER, HENRI (1891–1915). French sculptor and artist, the son of a car-
penter. He moved to Bristol, England, in 1907 and later worked for a coal
exporting company in Cardiff, where he was partially supported by a French
Government scholarship. Visited Germany in 1909, where he soon learned
fairly fluent German. In 1910 in Paris he met Sophie Brzeska, a Polish woman
twenty years his senior, who encouraged him to become a full-time artist. He
attached her name to his, and is therefore generally known as Henri Gaudier-
Brzeska. Returned penniless to London with her in January 1911, where he
met Lovat Fraser, Jacob Epstein, Edward Marsh, John Cournos, and other
artists, gaining a few commissions for sculptures to supplement his meager
wages. In 1913 he exhibited at the Albert Hall, where EP first saw one of his
sculptures, *The Wrestler*. A review of this exhibition in the *Observer* (13 July
1913) coupled his name with Epstein's. Through Pound Gaudier met Wynd-
ham Lewis, T.E. Hulme, Edward Wadsworth, and other members of the Vor-
ticist group. He was killed in France in 1915.

> And Henri Gaudier went to it,
>   and they killed him,
> And killed a good deal of sculpture. . .
>
> (Canto 16)

HEWLETT, MAURICE HENRY (1861–1923). Born in Kent and educated in Lon-
don, Hewlett was called to the Bar but never practiced law. Remembered in
Canto 74 as "Maurie who wrote historical novels," he gained great success
with his first historical romance, *The Forest Lovers* (1898), which was fol-
lowed by other popular works in this genre. He was less successful in his
treatment of modern life, as in the trilogy *Halfway House, Open Country,*
and *Rest Harrow* (1908–10). In his later career he devoted much of his energy
to poetry, and his most famous poem—*The Song of the Plow* (1916)—cele-
brates his favorite theme, the enduring qualities of the English people and
their land. Hewlett was a prolific essayist and a power in professional societ-
ies—a quintessential Edwardian man of letters. EP spent the Christmas of
1911 at Hewlett's country house, the Old Rectory at Broad Chalke in Wilt-
shire, and recollected the visit many years later in Canto 80.

HUEFFER, FORD MADOX (1873–1939). Named at birth Ford Hermann Hueffer,
he adopted the additional Christian names Joseph Leopold Madox, and in
1919 legally changed his surname to Ford. His father, Francis Hueffer, was
a well-known German music critic who became a British citizen; his mother
was the younger daughter of the artist Ford Madox Brown. The family was
closely connected with the Pre-Raphaelite movement, and Hueffer grew up in
an artistic atmosphere. In the early years of his career he produced historical
novels and studies of the Pre-Raphaelites, and collaborated with Joseph Con-
rad in writing *The Inheritors* (1901) and *Romance* (1903). In 1908 he

founded the *English Review,* which had a brilliant year under his editorship before financial difficulties forced him to sell it. Many established writers such as Conrad, Hardy, and Henry James appeared in the *English Review,* but Hueffer took most pride in the discovery of young writers, publishing D.H. Lawrence, Wyndham Lewis, and EP.

Hueffer married in 1894 and had two children, but by 1908 the marriage existed in name only. In 1909 he began a liaison with Violet Hunt that lasted nearly ten years. They hoped to marry, but Mrs. Hueffer refused to grant a divorce and in 1910 obtained a court order for restitution of conjugal rights. In 1911 Hueffer unwisely gave the press the false story that he had married Violet Hunt in Germany after divorcing his wife on technical grounds. The next year, when the *Throne* referred to Violet Hunt as "now Mrs. Ford Madox Hueffer," Mrs. Hueffer sued the newspaper and won her case, effectively blocking any respectable relationship between her husband and Violet Hunt.

Hueffer held a commission during World War I, and served on the Western Front. In the 1920s he lived in Paris and edited the *Transatlantic Review* (1924), which published Joyce and Hemingway; later he divided his time between France and the United States. Although he published over seventy works, his literary reputation now rests primarily on *The Good Soldier* (1915) and the four novels of 1924–28 (later collected as *Parade's End*) which deal with the impact of the war on an idealized English gentleman, Christopher Tietjens. Hueffer was a stylist whose view of the "prose tradition" had a profound effect on EP's writing. In an obituary published in the *Nineteenth Century and After* (August 1939) EP said: "For the ten years before I got to England there would seem to have been no one but Ford who held that French clarity and simplicity in the writing of English verse and prose were of immense importance . . . for the expression of reality and emotion."

HULME, THOMAS ERNEST (1883–1917). T.E. Hulme was born in Staffordshire and received his early education there before entering Cambridge in 1902. In 1904 he was sent down for misbehavior. He enrolled at University College, London, for a degree in biology and physics, but spent most of the next two years in Cambridge attending lectures on philosophy. In 1906 he traveled in Canada, and in 1907 went to Brussels to study French and German. By 1908 he was back in London, where he helped to organize the Poets' Club. But he soon found the rules and atmosphere of the Club restrictive, and in 1909 formed a group of writers who met weekly to read and discuss poetry. EP joined the group in April 1909, and Hulme's call for a "visual concrete" language made a lasting impression on him. In 1912, when Pound printed "The Complete Poetical Works of T.E. Hulme" (five poems) as an appendix to *Ripostes,* he said in a prefatory note that *Les Imagistes* were "the descendants of the forgotten school of 1909."

Hulme first met Henri Bergson in 1907 and soon became a tireless expounder of his philosophy. In 1912 he published a translation of Bergson's *Introduction to Metaphysics.* In the same year he was reinstated at his old college, St. John's, partly on a recommendation from Bergson, but he soon moved back to London, where the weekly gatherings at his home in Frith Street attracted avant-garde writers and artists. Hulme enlisted in the army at the outbreak of World War I, and after being wounded in 1915 was invalided home for a time.

> And ole T.E.H. he went to it,
> With a lot of books from the library,
> London Library, and a shell buried 'em in a dug-out,
> And the Library expressed its annoyance.
>   And a bullet hit him on the elbow
> ... gone through the fellow in front of him,
> And he read Kant in the Hospital, in Wimbledon,
> in the original,
> And the hospital staff didn't like it.

(Canto 16)

Hulme returned to action in 1916 and was killed in September 1917.

Although Hulme was so little known at the time of his death that he received no obituaries, his writings and conversation had profoundly affected those around him, and his influence spread with the publication of *Speculations* (1924, ed. Herbert Read) and *Further Speculations* (1955, ed. Sam Hynes), which collected materials left in manuscript. Reviewing *Speculations* in the *Criterion* (7 April 1924) T.S. Eliot remarked that when Hulme died "he was known to a few people as a brilliant talker, a brilliant amateur of metaphysics, and the author of two or three of the most beautiful short poems in the language. In this volume he appears as the forerunner of a new attitude of mind, which should be the twentieth-century mind, if the twentieth century is to have a mind of its own."

HUNT, VIOLET (1866–1942). Daughter of the Pre-Raphaelite painter Alfred William Hunt and the writer Margaret (Raine) Hunt, she grew up in the "Rossetti circle" and studied painting until she was twenty-eight. Then began what she called her "years of usefulness" as a journalist and novelist. Her first novel, *The Maiden's Progress* (1894), marked the beginning of a prolific career, but she is now best remembered as a literary hostess and the friend of great writers such as James, Conrad, and D.H. Lawrence. From 1909 to 1919 she had a troubled love affair with Ford Madox Hueffer, whose wife refused to give him a divorce (see the biographical note on Hueffer). Life at her home in Campden Hill (where Gaudier's bust of EP was placed in the garden after the sculptor's death) has been vividly described by Douglas Goldring in *South Lodge: Reminiscences of Violet Hunt, Ford Madox Ford and the English Review* (1943). Her autobiography, *I Have This to Say: The Story of My Flurried Years,* was published in 1926.

HYDE-LEES, BERTHA GEORGIE (1892–1968). Born at Hartley Wintney near Odiham, Hampshire, she entered St. James's School in the Easter Term of

LIONEL JOHNSON - TUCKER - HYDE-LEES - W.B. YEATS

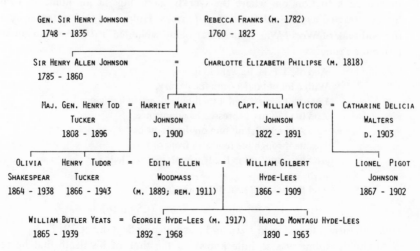

© Omar S. Pound

1907, and left in July 1908 to go to Miss Douglas's school at Queen's Gate in London. During the years 1910–14 she was Dorothy's best friend, and they remained close after DS's marriage to EP in 1914. After her marriage to W.B. Yeats in 1917 she adopted the name "George," but her earliest friends still called her "Georgie." She was deeply involved with Yeats in automatic writing and other psychic experiments.

HYDE-LEES, EDITH ELLEN (?1868–1941). Née Woodmass, in 1889 she married William Gilbert Hyde-Lees, who died in 1909. Her second marriage in 1911 was to Olivia Shakespear's brother, Henry Tudor Tucker, after which she was always known in the family as "Nellie." She was deeply interested in psychic matters. Her son, Harold Montagu Hyde-Lees (1890–1963), became an archdeacon in the Church of England, and Georgie, her daughter, married W.B. Yeats in 1917.

LEAF, HERBERT (1854–1936). Assistant Master at Marlborough College, Wiltshire (1877–1907; 1917–19). He served as Mayor of Marlborough and as a Justice of the Peace for Wiltshire and was on the Governing Body of Marlborough College (1916–35). At his death he left £20,000 to the school, £10,000 to Harrow, and "£15,000 and his freehold land and property not otherwise disposed of to the Mayor and Corporation of Marlborough for the benefit of the inhabitants." His wife, "Rosie" Leaf (1862–1922), was the sixth child of Alexander Shakespear, Dorothy's paternal grandfather.

LEWIS, PERCY WYNDHAM (1882–1957). Born on his father's yacht off the coast of Amherst, Nova Scotia. Moved to London with his mother in 1893. Went to Rugby and the Slade School of Art where he met Augustus John, William Rothenstein, Spencer Gore, and other artists. He met EP in 1909 through Laurence Binyon.

> So it is to Mr Binyon that I owe, initially,
> Mr Lewis, Mr P. Wyndham Lewis.

> (Canto 80)

His first stories were published in the *English Review* and *The Tramp*. He exhibited with the First and Second Camden Town Groups in 1911, and in 1912 met Roger Fry, Rebecca West, David Bomberg, and Edward Wadsworth. With Epstein he decorated the Cabaret Theatre Club. In 1912–13 he exhibited at Brighton (The Cubist Room), with Roger Fry's Second Post-Impressionist Exhibition, and with the Third Camden Town Group. Joined the Omega workshop, but left the group after a row. As one of the central figures in Vorticism he had considerable influence on Pound's writings, as is evident in the "eleven blasty poems" by EP published in *Blast* (see Letter **221**). Both Olivia Shakespear and Dorothy admired his paintings and drawings greatly, and he did several drawings of Olivia in the 1920s. In 1938 he did an oil portrait of EP, now in the Tate Gallery, and planned to do one of Dorothy in the summer of 1939, but World War II intervened. Lewis went to Canada, returning to England after the war to blindness and poverty.

> The scientists are in terror
> and the European mind stops
> Wyndham Lewis chose blindness
> rather than have his mind stop.

> (Canto 115)

LOW, ANNE PENELOPE HARRIET ANGELA (Lady Low), daughter of General Robert Percy Douglas, 4th baronet. In 1885 she married Sir Hugh Low, who died in 1905. She lived at 23 De Vere Gardens and was a close friend of Olivia Shakespear. Lady Low provided a distinguished drawing room for EP's earliest readings and social contacts in London.

MANNING, FREDERIC (1882–1935). The son of Sir William Patrick Manning, mayor of Sydney from 1891 to 1894, Manning was taken to England at age fifteen by Arthur Galton, a friend of the Shakespear family who had been private secretary to the governor of New South Wales (see biographical note on Galton). Manning spent only six months at school in England and did not attend University, so Galton must have been largely responsible for his classical education. His first volume of poetry, *The Vigil of Brunhild* (1907), appeared in the year that he became a literary reviewer for the London *Spectator*. In 1909 Manning published a collection of imaginary conversations, *Scenes and Portraits,* that was highly praised by Max Beerbohm and E.M. Forster.

EP met Manning in January 1909, and in April he published a favorable review of *The Vigil of Brunhild* in the *Book News Monthly*. In October he spent a "delightful" week at the vicarage in Edenham, Lincolnshire, where Manning lived with the Rev. Arthur Galton. In spite of occasional sharp disagreements, EP and Manning maintained a close relationship over the years, based partly on their mutual friendships with Olivia Shakespear and Eva Fowler (who saw Manning's war poems through the press in 1916–17). EP's poem "Canzon: The Yearly Slain," first published in the *English Review* (January 1910), was "written in reply to Manning's 'Korè.' "

Although he suffered from acute asthma, Manning enlisted in the Shropshire Light Infantry as a private in 1915. He was offered a commission, but declined because he felt he did not possess the qualities required of an officer. Some of his war experiences are reflected in the earlier poems of *Eidola* (1917), and in 1929 he published anonymously one of the great novels about World War I, *The Middle Parts of Fortune: Somme and Ancre,* by "Private 19022." When an abridged version was published in 1930 as *Her Privates We* Manning's authorship was recognized by T.E. Lawrence, who detected similarities with the style of *Scenes and Portraits.*

For an account of the relationship between Manning and EP see Jonathan Marwil, "Combative Companions," *Helix* (Australia), Nos. 13/14 (1983).

MARSH, EDWARD HOWARD (1872–1953). Educated at Westminster and Trinity College, Cambridge (where his father was Professor of Surgery and Master of Downing College), Marsh entered the Civil Service and was for some years private secretary to Winston Churchill. Early in 1912 his piece in the *Poetry Review* on Rupert Brooke led to a friendship with Harold Monro, and acting on a casual remark of Brooke's they decided to produce an anthology of contemporary poetry. *Georgian Poetry 1911–1912,* edited by Marsh, was published by Monro's Poetry Bookshop in December 1912, and its success led to a series of five volumes published over ten years. For EP's reactions to the first anthology of *Georgian Poetry* see Letter **127n.**

Marsh developed an interest in art while at Cambridge and became a leading connoisseur and collector of British painting. On his retirement from the Civil Service he was appointed a trustee of the Tate Gallery. He was knighted in 1937. His autobiography, *A Number of People* (1939), confirms the observation of his biographer Christopher Hassall that Marsh was "off stage even in his own life story."

MATHEWS, CHARLES ELKIN (1851–1921). Mathews began his career as a bookseller in Exeter. In 1887 he and John Lane opened a shop in Vigo Street, London, as booksellers and publishers. The firm was known as "Elkin Mathews" until 1891/2, when Lane quit his job at the Railway Clearing House and added his name to the business. *The Yellow Book* (1894) was published by "Elkin Mathews and John Lane." The partnership was dissolved in 1894, and many of the authors left with Lane, but Lionel Johnson stayed with Mathews. Among the authors of the 1890s published by Mathews and Lane or Mathews alone were John Addington Symonds, Oscar Wilde, Arthur Symons, and Yeats. Later Mathews published many volumes of verse, including Joyce's *Chamber Music* (1907) and EP's *Personae, Exultations, Canzoni, Cathay,* and *Lustra.* He was noted for his sympathetic support of young authors. In a letter to the Boston *Transcript* of August 1915 EP recollected a "touching little scene in Elkin Mathews' shop some years since" (*Letters*, No. 73).

> Mathews: 'Ah, eh, ah, would you, now, be prepared to assist in the publication?'
> E.P.: 'I've a shilling in my clothes, if that's any use to you.'
> Mathews: 'Oh well. I want to publish 'em. Anyhow.'

MAUDE, NANCY (?1886–1974). Went to St. James's School (1899–1902) with Dorothy. She was a daughter of Charles John Maude (b. 1847) and a granddaughter of Sir George Maude, Crown Equerry to Queen Victoria. She married Joseph Campbell (1879–1944), the Irish poet, and had four sons and one daughter, her eldest son being "le p'tit Jesu irlandais" of Letter **127**. In 1900 Dorothy played Lucy, Nancy Maude Sir Anthony Absolute, and Hilda Strutt Sir Lucius O'Trigger in Sheridan's *The Rivals*. In 1901 Dorothy and Nancy's sister Ruth wrote a play, "The Fortunes of Another Nigel," in which Hilda Strutt played a leading part. Nancy Maude published some poetry and wrote the prologue to *I Was There* (Worcester, 1956), a book of recollections of St. James's School.

MEAD, GEORGE ROBERT STOW (1863–1933). After completing his degree at St. John's, Cambridge, Mead worked for a time as a teacher and joined the Theosophical Society. In 1889 he gave up teaching to devote his full time to the Society and its founder, Madame Blavatsky. He served as her private secretary until her death in 1891 and helped edit her monthly magazine *Lucifer*, which he renamed *The Theosophical Review* when he became editor. In 1890 Mead was appointed General Secretary of the Theosophical Society, a position he held for eight years. In 1908 he resigned from the Society (along with some 700 other members) in protest against charlatanism, and the next year founded the Quest Society to "promote investigation and comparative study of religion, philosophy, and science, on the basis of experience" and to "encourage the expression of the ideal in beautiful forms." Mead edited a quarterly review, *The Quest*, from 1909 to 1930, publishing literary works by Yeats, Pound, Laurence Binyon, and others, as well as essays on the occult and religion. After the death of his wife in 1924 he became actively involved in psychic research. Mead was a prolific scholar who wrote on Gnosticism and early Christianity as well as Theosophical subjects. His publications range from *Simon Magus* (1892) to *The Sacred Dance in Christendom* (1926).

MONRO, HAROLD EDWARD (1879–1932). Born in Brussels of Scottish parents, he was brought to England at age seven and educated at Radley and Caius College, Cambridge. In 1903 he founded the Samurai Press. After a stay abroad he returned to London in 1911 and in 1912 founded the *Poetry Review*, which was published from his Poetry Bookshop in Bloomsbury, as were the famous anthologies of *Georgian Poetry*. The Poetry Bookshop became a rendezvous where poets could meet and read their verse. Financial difficulties forced Monro to give up the editorship of the *Poetry Review* after a year, but he immediately started another magazine, *Poetry and Drama* (1913–14) and later edited the *Chapbook* (1919–25). Although Monro is best remembered as a publisher, editor, and anthologist, he was a poet of some distinction. His first volume, *Poems* (1906), was followed by nine others, and *Collected Poems* appeared in the year after his death. Although some of his poems are, as he himself said, "almost too Georgian even for *Georgian Poetry*," others display those "honest and bitter" qualities that T.S. Eliot admired.

MONROE, HARRIET (1860–1936). Born in Chicago, where she spent most of her life, Harriet Monroe gained a local reputation early in life as a poet and was paid the astounding sum of $1,000 to write the "Columbian Ode" for the Chicago Exposition of 1893. Over the next few years she continued to write and publish rather conventional verse, and frequently lectured on poetry. In 1911 she conceived the idea of a magazine devoted to the cause of contemporary poetry. Raising the necessary funds from a hundred patrons, she published the first number of *Poetry: A Magazine of Verse* in October 1912 and for the rest of her life fought to keep the magazine alive. She asked EP to lend his support, and on 18 August 1912 he replied "I *am* interested," beginning a long and often heated correspondence in which he tried to convert Miss Monroe to his standards and his view of the modern movement. The November 1912 issue of *Poetry* announced that "Mr. Ezra Pound has consented to act as foreign correspondent of POETRY, keeping its readers informed of the present interests of the art in England, France and elsewhere." It was through EP that *Poetry* came to publish Yeats, Frost, Eliot, and many of the greatest modern writers. Twenty years later, in the Italian journal *Il Mare* (18 March 1933), EP made a final assessment of Miss Monroe's contribution:

> The talent of Monroe—conscientiousness and goodwill, we might even say a maternal instinct towards poetry—in whom critical sense was lacking, but who performed the miracle of extracting the money needed from the pockets of the biggest butchers in Chicago to carry on a review, one might say the bulletin of the union or the profession of American poetry, which has lasted for twenty years.

Harriet Monroe's autobiography, *A Poet's Life,* was published in 1938.

MOORE, MARY S. (1885–1976). In the early summer of 1907, after EP had decided to leave the graduate program at the University of Pennsylvania and look for a teaching job, he visited a friend who lived near Trenton, New Jersey. There he met Mary Moore. Her father was a prominent Trenton businessman, later president of the Broad Street Bank. Ezra and Mary were immediately attracted to each other and began to exchange letters. The correspondence continued after EP took up his teaching position at Wabash College, Crawfordsville, Indiana, in the autumn of 1907, and he considered himself engaged to her. But she soon wrote to tell him that she intended to marry another man, Oscar MacPherson (in the end she did not marry MacPherson, but in July 1912 she was married to James Frederick Cross, Jr.). In one of his last letters to her from Crawfordsville EP said: "I do not love you at all except as I love all beautiful things that run around in the sunlight and are happy."

When Mary Moore received a presentation copy of *Personae* she did not notice for some time that it was dedicated to her:

This Book Is For
MARY MOORE
Of Trenton, If She
Wants It

After 1907–08 EP and Mary Moore occasionally exchanged letters, and remained on friendly terms. She visited him in London in 1912, and in Rapallo during the winter of 1931–32, and wrote to him at St. Elizabeths in Washington. See Noel Stock, *Ezra Pound's Pennsylvania* (1976), Chapter III.

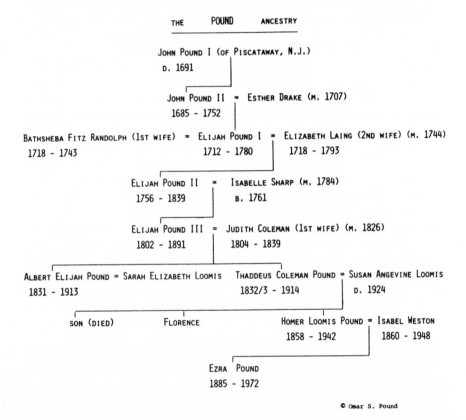

THE POUND ANCESTRY

JOHN POUND I (OF PISCATAWAY, N.J.)
D. 1691

JOHN POUND II = ESTHER DRAKE (M. 1707)
1685 - 1752

BATHSHEBA FITZ RANDOLPH (1ST WIFE) = ELIJAH POUND I = ELIZABETH LAING (2ND WIFE) (M. 1744)
1718 - 1743   1712 - 1780   1718 - 1793

ELIJAH POUND II = ISABELLE SHARP (M. 1784)
1756 - 1839   B. 1761

ELIJAH POUND III = JUDITH COLEMAN (1ST WIFE) (M. 1826)
1802 - 1891   1804 - 1839

ALBERT ELIJAH POUND = SARAH ELIZABETH LOOMIS   THADDEUS COLEMAN POUND = SUSAN ANGEVINE LOOMIS
1831 - 1913   1832/3 - 1914   D. 1924

SON (DIED)   FLORENCE   HOMER LOOMIS POUND = ISABEL WESTON
                                        1858 - 1942   1860 - 1948

EZRA POUND
1885 - 1972

© Omar S. Pound

POUND, HOMER LOOMIS (1858–1942). Born in Chippewa Falls, Wisconsin, where his father, Thaddeus Coleman Pound (1832/3–1914), later Lieutenant-Governor of Wisconsin (1870), was in the lumber business. Homer's mother, Susan Angevine Pound (d. 1924), married Thaddeus Pound in 1856, and her sister, Sarah Elizabeth Loomis, married Albert Elijah Pound, Thaddeus's brother. Both girls were daughters of Nathanial Loomis, a lawyer from Oneida

County in New York State. Both Albert and Thaddeus are buried in Chippewa
Falls along with their father, Elijah Pound III (1802–91).

Homer Pound went to military school in Minnesota and was accepted at
West Point Military Academy but decided not to enter it. On 14 July 1883
the United States Land Office was opened in Hailey, in the Territory of Idaho,
and Homer—who had recently married Isabel Weston—was appointed the
first Register. He became an expert assayer of silver and in 1889 received an
appointment to the U.S. Mint in Philadelphia, where he remained until he
retired in 1928. In 1929 he and his wife moved to Rapallo, where he died in
1942.

POUND, ISABEL (1860–1948). Born in New York and christened "Isabella." Her
father, Harding Weston, born in Barre, Massachusetts, in 1835, was a son in
the large family of John Wheeler Weston, who was born in Hardwick, Massa-
chusetts, in 1797 and married Asenath How in 1819. Harding Weston, a ne'er-
do-well, married Mary Parker but failed to support her and her daughter.
Isabel's mother, Mary Weston, ran a boardinghouse in New York City. Isabel
married Homer Loomis Pound and went with him to Hailey, Idaho, and
eventually to Philadelphia and Rapallo. She died in Italy in 1948.

RUMMEL, WALTER MORSE (?1887–1953). Composer and pianist, son of Franz
Rummel, of a distinguished German musical family, who married a daughter
of Samuel F.B. Morse. Morse arranged for Rummel's early musical educa-
tion in Washington, D.C., which was later continued in Germany and France.
A close friend of Debussy, Rummel gave first performances of some of his
piano works in Paris and London.

> Debussy preferred his playing
> that also was an era (Mr. W. Rummel)
>
> (Canto 80)

Rummel also worked extensively with Pound setting Troubadour poems to
music. In 1912 he married Thérèse Chaigneau, a French musician, whom he
later divorced; his second marriage was to an Englishwoman, Sarah Harring-
ton. Later he became involved with the dancer Isadora Duncan.

Of his piano playing a reviewer ("C.H.") wrote in the *Spectator* (1 July
1922):

> When Mr. Rummel plays Bach neither his technique nor his personality ob-
> trude, he so completely identifies himself with the spirit of the seventeenth century,
> and the spirit of the composer, that we are conscious of nothing but a dazzling
> clarity; it is no exaggeration to say that we are *en rapport* with the musical idea
> in Bach's mind before it took its final lifeless form in printer's ink. Composition
> is too often interment, for rare is the executant who is both a pianist and a
> Prometheus. It would be rash to say that Mr. Rummel is a greater technician
> than Mr. Rubinstein. It would be unwise to say that he is a greater pianist than
> Mr. Busoni. Yet in effect we have to choose between Mr. Rubinstein's dexterity,
> Mr. Busoni's interesting personality, and Bach himself!

Rummel wrote a travel book in German on Provence (1911); set to music
words and poems by Katherine Ruth Heyman, Pound, and others; and pub-
lished an edition of Vivaldi's cello sonatas (1916), which may have been one
of the sources of Pound's later enthusiasm for Vivaldi. In 1917 he wrote the
incidental music for Yeats's *The Dreaming of the Bones.*

Rummel's enduring interest in the Troubadours led him to Montségur, near
Toulouse, between the two wars. He and a German archaeologist wrote a study
claiming that Parsifal and Lohengrin had originally lived there in the ninth
century and that Montségur was the Temple of the Holy Grail. Rummel also
claimed to have tracked down various Albigensian manuscripts proving his
theories. Much of Rummel's musical theory and practice emanated from his
theosophical and occult enthusiasms.

In his *Ezra Pound and Music* (New Directions, 1977, p. 41), Murray
Schafer writes: "Three musical personalities have had cardinal influence on
Ezra Pound: Walter Morse Rummel, Arnold Dolmetsch, and George An-
theil." When Rummel died in Bordeaux in May 1953 he was—as one obituary
noted—"isolated and deserted by everyone."

SAUTER, GEORG (1866–?1937). Portrait painter and lithographer. Born in Ba-
varia, he was apprenticed to a church decorator and later studied art at the
Academy in Munich. First came to London in 1889. In 1894 he married Lilian
Galsworthy, the sister of John Galsworthy; their romance was the basis for
Galsworthy's story *Villa Rubein* (1900). During World War I Sauter was in-
terned as a German national and later repatriated to Germany, from which
he never returned. In the years before the war the Sauters lived near EP at
1 Holland Park Avenue.

SHAKESPEAR, HENRY HOPE (1849–1923). Born at Serampore, India, on 19
February 1849. His father, Alexander Shakespear (1821–1884) of the Bengal
Civil Service, was then a District Officer for the North West Provinces. In
1846 he had married Catherine Mary Tayler (d. 1918), second daughter of
Benjamin Tayler, also of the Bengal Civil Service; they had two children,
Helen Catharine Augusta (b. 1847) and Henry Hope. Hope was named after
his distinguished military godfather, Sir Hope Grant, who later took part in
the relief of Lucknow during the Indian Mutiny. Hope was sent back to
England in 1855 and in 1858 went to Leamington College. The headmaster,
the Rev. St. John Parry, suggested to his father that because of his mathe-
matical abilities he should go to the Royal Military College at Woolwich to
train for the Artillery or Engineers, but since Hope proved to be an excellent
Greek and Latin scholar he was sent to Harrow, and then to Cambridge,
where he read law in Sir William Blackstone's old college, Trinity Hall. On
8 December 1885 he married Olivia Tucker. They had one child, Dorothy,
born on 14 September 1886. Mr. Shakespear became a solicitor and had his
own legal practice, Shakespear and Parkyn, at 8 John Street in London, but
his greatest interest was in painting watercolors and playing the cello. His

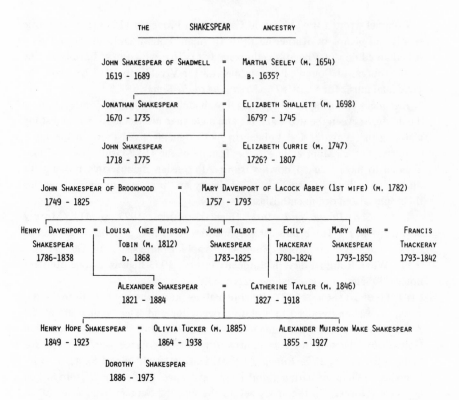

THE   SHAKESPEAR   ANCESTRY

watercolors, of which over two hundred fifty survive, are almost exclusively
of English and Scottish landscapes. In 1961 the Boston Museum of Fine Arts
arranged a small traveling exhibition of thirty-six of his watercolors to illus-
trate the English countryside in the nineteenth century and to give insight
into the workings of an excellent but amateur craftsman of the "Peinture de
Dimanche" sort.

Hope and Dorothy used to go out painting together, and his observations
of nature must have influenced her own painting considerably. At least one
painting by Mr. Shakespear, done about 1907, is very close in style to some
of Dorothy's early watercolors. Geological formations, cliffs, rocky beaches,
and water were favorite subjects with both.

During World War I Hope used his skill at carpentry to make wooden
limbs for returning amputees and received a Red Cross award for his work.
He died in London on 6 July 1923.

SHAKESPEAR, OLIVIA (1864–1938). Born in Niton, Isle of Wight, on 17 March
1864, second and youngest daughter of Major General Henry Tod Tucker,
C.B. (1808–1896), Adjutant General of the Army in India, and Harriet Maria
Johnson (d. 1900). On 8 December 1885 she married Henry Hope Shake-
spear. She was a first cousin of Lionel Johnson (1867–1902) through her

THE   THACKERAY - SHAKESPEAR   MARRIAGES

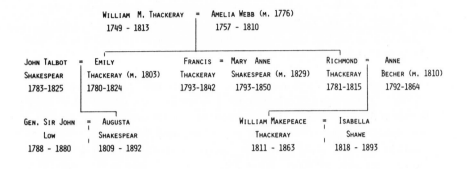

© Omar S. Pound

mother, and her brother, Henry Tudor Tucker, married Mrs. Edith Ellen Hyde-Lees, whose daughter Georgie Hyde-Lees married W.B. Yeats in 1917.

Olivia first met Yeats in 1894, and in 1895–96 they had a love affair which lasted less than a year. She is the "Diana Vernon" of Yeats's autobiographical writings. The "Two Love Poems" that Yeats published in the *Savoy* of January 1896 ("He Bids His Beloved Be at Peace" and "The Travail of Passion") were probably written for Olivia.

When EP first arrived in England Olivia introduced him to her literary friends in London, including Yeats. She also introduced him to the works of various late 19th-century French poets and to books in French on contemporary philosophy. In the early 1920s she read much of Spengler at his request, reporting back to him on it—all this in spite of her constant claim that she was a Buddhist.

She died in London on 3 October 1938, and on hearing of her death Yeats wrote to Dorothy Wellesley:

> Yesterday morning I had tragic news. Olivia Shakespear died suddenly. For more than forty years she has been the centre of my life in London and during all that time we have never had a quarrel, sadness sometimes but never a difference. When I first met her she was in her late twenties but in looks a lovely young girl. When she died she was a lovely old woman. . . . She was not more lovely than distinguished—no matter what happened she never lost her solitude. . . . For the moment I cannot bear the thought of London. I will find her memory everywhere.

Novels: *Love on a Mortal Lease* (Osgood, McIlvaine & Co., 1894), *The Journey of High Honour* (Osgood, McIlvaine & Co., 1895), *The False Laurel* (Osgood, McIlvaine & Co., 1896), *Rupert Armstrong* (Harper & Brothers, 1898), *The Devotees* (William Heinemann, 1904), *Uncle Hilary* (Methuen & Co., 1910).

Novella: *Beauty's Hour, A Phantasy* (In Two Parts), *The Savoy* (August–September 1896).

Plays: *The Beloved of Hathor & the Shrine of the Golden Hawk,* written jointly with Florence Farr (Croydon, [1902]), colophon by Gordon Craig.

Reviews: Reviewed for *The Kensington,* mostly in 1901; see also "The Poetry of D.H. Lawrence" (*The Egoist,* 1 May 1915).

STRUTT, HILDA (1886–1982). Born in Brisbane, Queensland, only child of the Hon. Hedley Vicars Strutt, who died in 1891 at the age of twenty-seven. Head girl at St. James's School when Dorothy was there, and one of DS's closest friends at that time. When Hilda married Francis Deverell in 1912 DS was a bridesmaid. Dorothy and Georgie Hyde-Lees used to stay with her at St. Catharine's Court, Bath, and after Georgie married Yeats in 1917 Hilda visited them both in Dublin. While EP was in St. Elizabeths Hospital, Hilda wrote to Dorothy and in 1964 visited her in Italy.

TAGORE, RABINDRANATH (1861–1941). Born in Calcutta, the son of a wealthy Brahmin, Tagore was educated at private schools and in 1878 went to live with a brother in England. He attended University College, London, before returning to India. In 1891 he began to manage his father's estates, where he lived in close contact with the villagers and came to know their poverty. From 1876 on he published prolifically in Bengali, writing poems, novels, and short stories. He was also a talented composer, setting hundreds of poems to music, and a gifted painter. The English version of his most famous collection of songs, *Gitanjali,* was published in 1912 with an introduction by W.B. Yeats. It won him the Nobel Prize in 1913, and in 1915 he was knighted; but four years later he surrendered the honor in protest against British suppression of the Punjab riots. In his later years he lectured widely in Europe and America. Tagore translated much of his own work and occasionally wrote in English, but it is said that the true musical quality of his work is lost in translation. The "Tagore Craze" that swept through England and the United States in 1912–15 was partly a response to his personality: his sincerity, his mysticism, and his anti-imperialism had a special appeal at that time. Writing in *Poetry* (Chicago), December 1912, EP declared that "world-fellowship is nearer for the visit of Rabindranath Tagore to London."

TUCKER, HENRY TUDOR (1866–1943). Youngest of the three children of Major General Henry Tod Tucker (1808–1896), he was educated at Charterhouse. In 1911 he married Mrs. Edith Ellen Hyde-Lees, becoming the stepfather of Georgie Hyde-Lees, who married W.B. Yeats in 1917. He had independent means and lived mostly in Suffolk and the west of England. He collected drawings and prints and in a modest way supported young avant-garde artists such as Gaudier-Brzeska, Wyndham Lewis, and Augustus John by buying works while they were still little known. He had an eclectic taste for the engravings of Dürer, Legros, Lalanne, McBey, Whistler, and others, and also collected Japanese prints. He read several languages fluently and was very

ST. GEORGE TUCKER, etc.

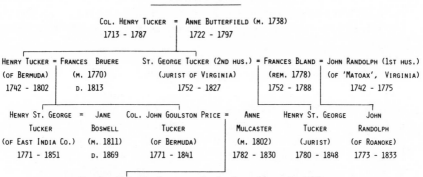

© Omar S. Pound

close to his sister, Olivia Shakespear, and to Dorothy throughout his life. In the late 1930s he became mentally ill and died in a nursing home in 1943.

WILLIAMS, WILLIAM CARLOS (1883–1963). Williams and Pound met in September 1902, when Williams had just entered the University of Pennsylvania and EP was a sophomore. They were together again in 1905–06, after EP returned to the university from Hamilton College, and these early associations became the foundation of an enduring—if often stormy—personal and artistic friendship. In early March 1910 Williams visited EP in London, where he met Yeats, Olivia Shakespear, and Dorothy, and had to suffer through EP's energetic attempts to "broaden his mind." In October of that year EP and Hilda Doolittle visited Williams at his home in Rutherford, New Jersey, and later EP spent Thanksgiving Day with the Williams family. In February 1911—just before his return to England—EP made a final visit to Rutherford. He would not see Williams again for thirteen years, but Williams was always in the forefront of his mind. *Ripostes* (1912) is dedicated to him, and over the next two years EP persuaded Elkin Mathews to publish Williams's *The Tempers,* promoted his work with Harriet Monroe, and arranged for his long poem "The Wanderer" to appear in the *Egoist.*

As the years passed Williams became more and more irritated with EP's literary, political, and economic ideas. He felt that the international style promoted by Pound—and embodied most powerfully in Eliot's *The Waste Land*— had stifled a native American modernism, and he was outraged by many of EP's actions during the 1930s and 1940s. But the friendship endured, as if each possessed something essential to the other's life. The day after Williams's death EP sent a cable to his widow Floss: "A magnificent fight he made of it. For you he bore with me sixty years. I shall never find another poet friend like him."

For further details on the relationship between Williams and EP, see Paul Mariani, *William Carlos Williams: A New World Naked* (1981).

YEATS, WILLIAM BUTLER (1865–1939). EP began to write under the shadow of Yeats, whom he considered the greatest living poet. *A Lume Spento* (1908) is filled with echoes of Yeats, and when EP arrived in London in 1908 his greatest ambition was to meet the Irish poet. The meeting finally took place in May 1909, when Yeats invited EP to attend one of his "Monday Evenings." A friendship soon developed, strengthened by their mutual interest in the Shakespear family, and as EP found his own modern voice the relationship shifted from that of apprentice and master to a somewhat uneasy companionship of equals. Yeats, who was struggling to purge his style of a nineties softness, was often unsure of himself, and EP began to find the advice of Ford Madox Hueffer more relevant than that of Yeats, who—as he told Harriet Monroe on 13 August 1913—"is already a sort of great dim figure with its associations set in the past" (*Letters*, No. 21). Yeats turned to EP for help and found him a useful critic. Writing to Lady Gregory on 3 January 1913, he said that Ezra "is full of the middle ages and helps me to get back to the definite and the concrete away from modern abstractions. To talk over a poem with him is like getting you to put a sentence into dialect. All becomes clear and natural."

During the three winters of 1913–16 Yeats and Pound spent much of their time at Stone Cottage in Sussex, EP acting as companion and "secretary." He entered into the arrangement with some misgivings, but the winters turned out to be of great benefit to both poets. They discussed symbolism, the occult, and the Japanese Noh drama, criticized each other's work, and wrote some of their finest poems.

The two poets met frequently after Yeats's marriage to Georgie Hyde-Lees in 1917, and although Yeats had difficulty appreciating the *Cantos* and EP was unsympathetic to much of Yeats's later poetry, the friendship was sustained by memories of the London years and by the strong ties between Georgie and Dorothy. When EP, who was then nearly 80, flew to London in 1965 to attend the memorial service for T.S. Eliot in Westminster Abbey, he traveled on to Dublin to see Georgie for the last time.

For a full assessment of the relationship between Yeats and EP, see the chapter "Ez and Old Billyum" in Richard Ellmann's *Eminent Domain* (1967).

Appendix II

The Dawn

On 29 December 1908, shortly after *A Quinzaine for This Yule* was published in London, EP wrote to Mary Moore of Trenton that his next book would be ready as soon as he received one more sonnet mailed from home. This "next book" was almost certainly *The Dawn,* a collection of early verse reaching back to 1905–06. On Thursday, 18 February 1909, EP read from *The Dawn* after a luncheon at the Shakespear home, and soon after that DS copied out these "Extracts" from the collection, following EP's phrasing and spelling as best she could. Throughout 1909 EP continued to plan on publication of *The Dawn,* which he described to his father (17 March 1909) as a "sequence of prose and verse. The poems being from the last lot I had you send over to me." On 11 October 1909 he told his mother that the book would be published by Dent, probably in the early spring; but this arrangement fell through, and on 29 April 1910 Elkin Mathews agreed to "take on 'The Dawn' together with the poems you have ready for a new Autumn volume on the same terms as 'Exultations.' " On 8 May 1910 EP assured his father that "Mathew's publishes 'The Dawn' together with a few Canzoni as his fall exposition of yrs. truly." This is the last mention of the title.

EP clung to *The Dawn* long after the poems ceased to meet his new artistic standards because it memorialized crucial passages in his early sentimental and poetic life. Some of the "Extracts" are also found in *Hilda's Book,* a gathering of poems from 1905–07 that EP presented to Hilda Doolittle in a handbound, vellum-covered volume [printed in *End to Torment: A Memoir of Ezra Pound by H.D.,* ed. Norman Holmes Pearson and Michael King (New Directions, 1979), pp. 67–84]. Others were inspired by Katherine Ruth Heyman (1877–1944), the American concert pianist whom EP first met in 1904, and to whom *A Quinzaine for This Yule* is dedicated: "To the Aube of the West Dawn." She visited Venice in June 1908 as part of a European concert tour, and for a while

EP thought of giving up poetry to act as her manager (Stock, pp. 47–48). The poem "Nel Biancheggiar" (CEP), included in *A Quinzaine for This Yule*, was first published in the London *Evening Standard and St. James's Gazette* (8 December 1908) under the title "For Katherine Ruth Heyman. (After One of Her Venetian Concerts)." *A Quinzaine* also contains "Aube of the West Dawn. Venetian June" (CEP). The idea of a "dawn song" obviously had a deep emotional appeal for EP. Among the first poems he published were "Belangal Alba"— later "Alba Belingalis" (CEP)—and "A Dawn Song" (CEP) [*Hamilton Literary Magazine*, 39 (May 1905); *Munsey's Magazine*, 36 (December 1906)].

Of the ten "Extracts" from *The Dawn*, six have been previously published:

"The Summons"   Found in a somewhat different form in typescripts at Yale (CEP, pp. 262–63, 323).

"Wings"   A different version appears in *Hilda's Book*, pp. 70–71.

"Rendez-vous"   *Hilda's Book*, p. 84.

"Shadow"   *Hilda's Book*, pp. 75–76.

"The Wind"   *Hilda's Book*, p. 83.

"Roundel"   In the "San Trovaso Notebook" (CEP, p. 234).

Extracts from a set of M.S.S. verses entitled
' "The Dawn", For it is a little book of her praises'

– – by Ezra Pound   Feb. 1909.

[*The Summons*]

I cannot bow to woo thee
With leaves of words & kisses of the flowers
Nor may I scatter dew upon the fragrant-grass
Of old sweet love tales of the days foredone
Nor in the murmurous twilight, on the Tower stair
May I bend down & kneel beside thee worshipping
With whispers that as far-heard bells ring tremulous.

All these have I known once, & passed
And they are now as shadows mid the curtains of the wind.

Pardon! hay! Star, no Pardon that tis not
                          mine to seek thee thus.

For, ever as am I swept upward to the centre
                                of all Truth,
Rapt, as in that great involving flame,
Thee must I bear ever with me,
Calling ever from the midst thereof:
    "Follow!",   "Follow!"

And in the glory of our meeting shall the
                                power be reborn.
And together in the midst of this power
Must we, each outstriving each, cry eternally:

"I come! Go thou yet further!"

And again:
        "Follow!"

For we may not tarry.

Wings.

                A wondrous holiness hath Touched me
And I have felt the whirring of its wings
Above my spirit from all Terren things.

Twas half light when her fingers silently
She lay upon my trouble-weary hands
Not as a mistress that would give commands
But one that saith "Vos Benedicite".
And tremulous the whirring of the winds
Dwelt round about us with its holiness.
Whereof I can nowise speak worthily
And the power passed. The murmurings
That wind makes in the pines, can tell not less
Of whence the wind is than of this can I.

Rendez-vous.

        She hath some tree-born spirit of the wood
About her, and the wind is in her hair

Meseems he whispereth & awaiteth there
As if somehow he also *understood*.
The moss grown kindly trees it seems she could
As kindred claim. For tho to some they wear
A harsh dumb semblance, yet for those that *care*
They guard a marvelous-sweet brotherhood.
Behold! she dreams into the soul of things
Forgetting me, and that she hath it not
Of dull man-wrought philosophies, I wot
She dreameth thus, so when the woodland sings
I challenge her to meet my dream at Astalot
And give him greeting for the song he brings.

[*Shadow*]

Darkness hath descended upon the earth
And there are no stars.
The sun from zenith to nadir is fallen
And the thick air stifleth me.
Sodden go the hours
Yea the minutes are molten lead
            Stinging & heavy.
I saw her yesterday
And lo, there is no time
Each second being eternity.
            Peace! Trouble me no more.
Yea, I know your eyes are clear pools
Holding the summer sky within their depth
But Trouble me not.
I saw *Her* yesterday.
Peace! your hair is spun gold fine wrought & wondrous
But Trouble me not I saw her yester e'en.
Darkness hath filled the earth at her going
And the wind is listless & heavy.
When will the day come: when will the sun
Be royal in bounty
From nadir to zenith upleaping
For lo, his steeds are a-weary not having beheld her
Since sunset.
Oh that the sun steeds were wise
Arising to seek her.

The sun sleepeth in Orcus
From zenith to nadir is fallen his Glory.
Is fallen, is fallen his wonder.
I saw her yesterday
Since when there is no sun.

As dull rain-beaten waves the days draw past
As dull grey waves of some rain-weary sea
That hath not seen the sun in majesty
Nor known the little winds that blowing fast
Upraise the gleaming spray wherever are cast
A thousand jewelled hues, by alchemy
More subtly magical & sweetly free
Than trixters spells that make men stand aghast.
So, without thee my heart is filled with rain,
Dull grey, monotonous with no Keen Gleam
Of sun upon the overshadowing cloud,
Nor may I feel thy fingers move again
Across my face, as little winds that dream
But dare ⟨not⟩ in no wise tell their dream aloud.

[untitled]

As dull rain-beaten waves the days draw past
As dull grey waves of some rain-weary sea
That hath not seen the sun in majesty
Nor known the little winds that blowing fast
Upraise the gleaming spray whereever are cast
A thousand jewelled hues, by alchemy
More subtly magical & sweetly free
Than trixters spells that make men stand aghast.
So, without thee my heart is filled with rain,
Dull grey, monotonous with no Keen Gleam
Of sun upon the overshadowing cloud,
Nor may I feel thy fingers move again
Across my face, as little winds that dream
But dare ⟨not⟩ in no wise tell their dream aloud.

[*The Wind*]

"I would go forth into the night" she saith.
"The night is very cold beneath the moon,
Twere meet, my Love, that thou wentst forth at noon
For now the sky is cold as very death."
And then she drew a little sobbing breath:
"Without a little lonely wind doth crune
And calleth me with a wandered elfin rune
That all True wind-born children summoneth.
Dear, hold me closer, so! Till it be passed.
Nay I am gone the while–Await!"
And I await her here for I have understood.
Yet held I not this very wind bound fast
Within the castle of my soul, I would,
For very faintness at her parting, die.

The Mist.

"I can not see your face at all" I said
Meseems a veil of memory is drawn
Between your eyes & mine, as at the dawn
Strange clouds do hold the eager sun & spread
Abroad rare harmonies of gold & red
While all the colors God doth hold in pawn
Upon the path of coming day are strawn
As flowers for her ivory feet to tred.
So round thy face is every dear remembrance
–of smiling, or of eyes that sought the sun,
or shew your soul gone forth upon the wind
Togathered in royal mist-fair semblance
That minds me of a song thy heart hath sung,
And shows thee kin of all the elfin kind.

Egarée.

     I can not seem to hold it here; your song
that seems a multitude of shadowings
I clasp the wind & to my lips it brings
A rare vague sweetness, but the whispering throng,
Your words, pass by. And tho for very long
I strove to follow where their whirring wings
Made way, I hear but what their memory sings
Invisible, the star-pierced clouds among.
"An angel, & a (wind-worn) cup of wonder-ment
And flowers that you dreamed & brought me, sweet
As dreams may find spring rain."
                   These things were blent
In child-sweet words as skill can not attain.
And thro it all I knew your heart did greet
Some wandered heart not then to thine made plain.

[*Untitled*]

When I behold the Dawn's reflection
Rise in the West & reach her arms toward me
Making herself one splendid gueredon
Witholding naught but giving utterly,
All that she is becomes my halidom
Behold I take her clear virginity
When I have clasped the Dawn's reflection
Unto my heart. I ask God's benison
That I remain her lover steadfastly
So naught can set aside this unity
That she & I have set our bond upon.
'Tis why I serve the Dawn's reflection.

[*Roundel*]

     I come unto thee thru the hidden ways
Soul of my soul whose beauty quivereth
Within Her eyes, to whom my former days

As wined libation poured I, while my breath
Strove to her homage in unskillful lays
And bade my heart make his high vaunt gainst death.
I come unto thee thru the hidden ways,
Who art the soul of beauty & whose praise
Or color, or song, or form championeth
And of whom Time as but an herald saith
"Trust tho thou sense not, spite of my delays
Her whom I bring thee thru the hidden ways".

———————————

end

Appendix III
The Letters: 1910-1972

Approximately 2200 letters between Ezra Pound and Dorothy Shakespear have survived, of which less than 10% are printed here. Over the entire period of their correspondence (62 years) about 1250 are from Ezra and 950 from Dorothy, but from January 1910 until April 1914 only 73 are from Ezra and 124 are from Dorothy.

Since no letters survive from 1909 we have used extensive entries from a black school notebook Dorothy kept after their first meeting, and one entry from her more formal commonplace book. We have also used entries from the notebook to augment the letters of 1910 and 1911.

We believe that between 25 and 30 of the earliest letters are missing, probably burned. Dorothy would have almost certainly destroyed the most personal ones. This would be quite in keeping with her practice in later life of cutting small sections from letters and destroying the rest.

Of the unpublished letters after April 1914 about 20 were written during World War I when one or the other was out of London. From 1920 to the end of 1929 (covering the time in Paris and the final move to Rapallo) there are about 230 letters. From 1930 to the beginning of World War II there are about 950 letters, mostly written during Dorothy's summer visits to England.

The wartime letters (September 1939 to the end of 1943, with none for 1944) number about 450, and about 140 letters are from the time between EP's arrest (May 1945) and July 1946, when Dorothy was able to renew her American passport and move to Washington to be with him. The remaining letters (approximately 200) are either undated or cover the period until Ezra's death in 1972.

That so many letters and the notebook should have survived two world wars and a peripatetic life is remarkable. It suggests that they were mutually treasured.

Acknowledgments

This edition could not have been completed in its present form without generous assistance from many individuals and institutions. Our first debt is to Donald Gallup, whose exemplary *Ezra Pound: A Bibliography* was our indispensable guide in annotating the letters, and who read and criticized the entire manuscript at a late stage. Others who read the manuscript and offered valuable suggestions were David Anderson, Wendy Stallard Flory, Giovanni Giovannini, the late F. S. L. Lyons, and the late Walter Pilkington. James Laughlin was as always a constant source of comfort and support. We are most grateful to the staff of New Directions, and especially to our editor Peter Glassgold, for expert help and advice. We owe special thanks to Richard M. Ludwig and the staff of the Department of Rare Books and Special Collections, Firestone Library, Princeton University, and to Mary W. George, Head of the General Reference Division of Firestone Library. From the beginning the Trustees of the Ezra Pound Literary Property Trust gave their full support to the project.

The edition profited greatly from the work of two Princeton University graduate students who served as research assistants. We take pleasure in thanking Julie Peters, who did preliminary work on the index, and James Longenbach, who was largely responsible for its final form.

We gratefully acknowledge assistance to A. Walton Litz through a John Simon Guggenheim Memorial Foundation Fellowship and a Princeton University research grant; and to Omar Pound through a Marguerite Eyer Wilbur Foundation grant initiated by its vice-president, William Walter Longstreth.

The Pound Archive in the Collection of American Literature, Beinecke Rare Book and Manuscript Library, Yale University, was an invaluable source of information, and we are especially grateful for permission to quote from D.D. Paige's typed transcriptions of Ezra Pound's letters to his parents, since the originals were not available for examination. Other libraries that provided information or research facilities were the Bodleian Library, Oxford; British Library, London and Colindale; Cambridge University Library; University of Chicago Library, whose Department of Special Collections allowed us to quote from the papers of *Poetry* magazine; Cornell University Library (Wyndham Lewis Collection); Eton College Archives; Lilly Library, Indiana University; Marlborough College Archives; Van Pelt Library, University of Pennsylvania (we are grateful for permission to quote from Ezra Pound's letters to Mary Moore of Trenton); Piscataway Township Libraries; Firestone and Mudd Libraries, Princeton University; St. James's School Archives, West Malvern; George Arents Research Library, Syracuse University.

Illustrations were provided through the courtesy of the Beinecke Rare Book and Manuscript Library, Yale University; Bishop Grosseteste College, Lincoln; Cumberland Galleries, Wellingore, Lincolnshire; D'Offay Galleries, London; Clem Fiori; Olin Library, Cornell University. We are grateful to Charles E. Greene of the Department of Rare Books and Special Collections, Firestone Library, for his help with the photography.

We are indebted to the following individuals for advice and information. F.L. Arnold, Conrad Balliet, Gavin Borden, Lady Boucher, Victor Brombert, Fran Burke, Ronald Bush, William Cagle, Flann Campbell, Phyllis S. Cohen, Roger Cole, Earle Coleman, Elizabeth Comstock-Smith, W. Robert Connor, Michael Curschmann, Caroline Cuthbert, Anthony D'Offay, Donald D. Eddy, John Eills, Theo Erik, Betsy Erkkila, Joyce Evans, Robert Fagles, Richard Fallis, Jane Farrington, Stephen Ferguson, Richard Finneran, Mary FitzGerald, Ian Fletcher, Emery George, Charles Gibson, Warwick Gould, Anthony T. Grafton, Nicolete Gray, Barbara Guest, J. Arthur Hanson, E. Parker Hayden, Jr., Walter Hinderer, Etienne-Alain Hubert, Samuel Hynes, Mary Ann Jensen, E.G.H. Kempson, Rosemary Kilbridge, J. Merrill Knapp, Arthur Knodel, Wilfred Lockwood, Edna Longley, Susan Lovenburg, Louis Martz, Jonathan Marwil, Timothy Materer, Stuart Y. McDougal, Juliet McMaster, Kathleen Moran, Frederick W. Mote, J.M. Nixon, Homer Norton, Louise M. Parkin, Gordon E. Parks, Alvise Perosa, Sergio Perosa, Peter and Dinah Plowden-Wardlaw, Elizabeth Pound, Oriana D. Pound, David Quint, Thomas P. Roche, Robert Rosenthal, Steven B. Schlosstein, Jim Schoff, David E. Schoonover, Ronald Schuchard, Sanford Schwartz, Muhammad Shahin, Jeremy Smith, Patrick Strong, Lola Szladits, Saundra Taylor, Carol Tobin, Elizabeth Twisdon-Davies, Emily M. Wallace, Eleanor Weld, Neda M. Westlake, Susan White, James J. Wilhelm, J. Howard Woolmer, Michael B. Yeats, James Zetzel, Rosella Mamoli Zorzi.

Copies of reviews and other research materials used only in part in the endnotes are on file and available to scholars, along with Dorothy Shakespear's manuscript transcription from *The Dawn,* in the Department of Rare Books and Special Collections, Firestone Library, Princeton University.

Elephant carved on a pebble for EP by Gaudier-Brzeska (*ca.* 1913).

Index

This index does not include the Appendixes.